UNIVERSITY OF WASHINGTON P!
IN
THE SOCIAL SCIENCES

Volume 10, pp 1-378   October, 1939

THREE OLD FRENCH CHRONICLES
OF THE CRUSADES

The History of the Holy War
The History of them that took Constantinople
The Chronicle of Reims

Translated into English

by

EDWARD NOBLE STONE

PUBLISHED BY THE UNIVERSITY OF WASHINGTON
SEATTLE, WASHINGTON
1939

CONTENTS

PREFACE

The title "Old French Chronicles of the Crusades" inevitably suggests the names of Villehardouin and Joinville But the lively memoirs of these two leaders in the Fourth and the Sixth Crusades have been so charmingly presented to Britons and Americans in the masterly translations of Sir Frank Marzials[1] that the offering of a new English version of them, for another generation at least, would seem almost an impertinence There are, however, several other very interesting chronicles belonging to the same period as these that have long awaited an introduction to English readers Among them are the three which I have attempted to reproduce in this volume—Ambrose' *Estoire de la guerre sainte*, Robert of Clari's *Estoires de chiaus qui conquisent Coustantinoble*[2], and the anonymous *Chronique de Rains*—known also as *Récits d'un ménestral de Reims*

Like Villehardouin and Joinville, the authors of the first and second of these chronicles participated in the events which they describe, while the third writer recorded chiefly what he had heard from others, but all three are speaking, not like Villehardouin and Joinville from the standpoint of the high nobles and directors of affairs, but from that of the "man in the crowd", and whatever their accounts may lose thereby in historical accuracy they more than make up in human interest Some readers may be inclined to criticise the classifying of the Tales of a Minstrel of Reims as a chronicle of the crusades True, this rambling narrative devotes more space to affairs in western Europe than to campaigns in the Holy Land, yet—more fully than any of the other chronicles here mentioned —it is permeated with the later spirit of the crusading age

By the rather literal translation of many quaint words and phrases, by a rather free use of archaisms in order to preserve the "illusion of antiquity," I have tried to present to the modern English reader a version that will give him, in some degree, the same set of impressions that an educated Frenchman of the present day receives from the perusal of the original To have rendered the rugged speech of the chroniclers into classical English would have been absurd, to have attempted to put their simple, honest thoughts and words into the language of twentieth-century journalism would have been sacrilege

E N S

---

[1] *Memoirs of the Crusades, Translated by Sir Frank Marzials, Everyman's Library,* No 333

[2] The copy for my own translation of Robert of Clari's work was ready for the printer before I learned of the publication of Edgar Holmes McNeal's *Conquest of Constantinople* (Columbia University Press, 1936)

THE HISTORY OF THE HOLY WAR
(L'Estoire de la Guerre Sainte)

Being an account of the Third Crusade

Composed, in Verse, by

AMBROSE

A jongleur in the service of Richard Lion-heart

about the year 1196

Rendered into English Prose

by

EDWARD NOBLE STONE

1937

FOREWORD

L'Estoire de la Guerre Sainte is (with the exception of one or two Anglo-Norman documents) the oldest historical work in the French language dealing with contemporaneous events The author, Ambrose (or Ambroise), a jongleur in the service of Richard Cœur de Lion, was an eyewitness of many of the incidents of the Third Crusade and completed his history of this "holy war" in the year 1195 or 1196

The prose chronicle had, as yet, hardly made its appearance in French literature, and our minstrel naturally employed for his narrative the form already established by Wace, Benoit de Sainte-More, and Chrétien de Troies—that of octosyllabic verse arranged in couplets Ambrose possessed no great amount of poetic genius, but he was master of the art of versification (how many, alas, of our present-day "poets" are unable to write even verse!), and as a rhymester he is still unsurpassed When Samuel Butler says of the French poets of his day "They infinitely affect rhyme, though it becomes their language the worst in the world, and spoils the little sense they have to make room for it, and make the same syllable rhyme to itself, which is worse than metal upon metal in heraldry," we could almost believe him to be writing of the age of Philip Augustus rather than that of Louis XIV Indeed, Ambrose himself might have suggested such couplets as these, of Butler's own composition

"And pulpit, drum ecclesiastick,
Was beat with fist, instead of a stick",

or

"Beside, he was a shrewd philosopher
And had read ev'ry text and gloss over "

But while the author of *Hudibras* uses such redundant rhymes and "syllables rhyming to themselves" merely to enhance the comical effect of his lines, Ambrose seems to regard the duplication of the greatest possible number of sounds in a couplet, even in his most serious passages, as a work of supreme merit Consequently, stripped of the glamour of homophony by translation into alien prose, many of his lines seem colourless and superfluous When we read "*Li Gualais ot nom Marcaduc,*" we are glad to learn that the Welshman's name was Marcaduc , but when the poet adds the gratuitous information "*Si n'iert filz n'a rei ni a duc,*" we wonder who ever could have entertained the slightest suspicion that the fellow might be the son of a king or of a duke

Nevertheless, I think that the reader who has the patience to read this chronicle to its end, even in the form of an inadequate English translation, will find himself cherishing a very friendly feeling for "that honest Ambrose, who has left us in his work, if not the evidence of his poetic talent, at least the proof of his sincerity, of his candour, of his devotion to the cause that he believed to be holy, of his loyalty to his king, and a valuable index to the sentiments of the humbler and better part of the crusaders who accompanied the King of England on that heroic and useless Third Crusade "[1]   E N S

[1]Gaston Paris, *L'Estoire de la Guerre Sainte* Paris, Imprimerie Nationale, 1897 The present translation has been made from Paris' text

(3)

CONTENTS

(5)

CONTENTS— (Continued)

CONTENTS— (Continued)

(7)

CONTENTS—(Continued)

THE HISTORY OF THE HOLY WAR

Book I, of

Three Old French Chronicles of the Crusades

I

HOW GOD PUNISHED CHRISTENDOM FOR ITS SINS, IN THAT HE SUFFERED THE HOLY CITY TO FALL AGAIN INTO THE HANDS OF THE INFIDELS

Whoso hath in mind to indite a long history, greatly doth it behoove him to watch straitly lest he begin by laying on himself a task so heavy that he cannot arrive at its fulfilment, rather, let him so go about and undertake it that he may bring to a good end the thing that he hath conceived And for this reason have I begun briefly, that the matter wax not too heavy Straight to this matter will I betake myself, the history whereof is worthy to be told—an history that relateth the evil fortune which befell us (and justly) but a few years agone, in the land of Syria, because of our own exceeding folly For God would no more consent thereto, that He should not make us to perceive our folly, nay, in sooth did He make us to perceive it, and in Normandy, in France, and throughout all Christendom, be that folly but little there or most abundant, He made men to perceive it right speedily through the Cross which the world worshipeth, which at that season was carried away of the heathen and borne afar from the land where it abode, the land wherein God Himself deigned to be born and to die   [2] of the Hospital and of the Holy Temple, because of which many a brow was smitten, of the sepulchre wherein God was laid and whereof sin had dispossessed us—nay not so should it be said, but it was through God, who would fain draw again unto Himself His people, whom He had redeemed, and who now were serving Him not at all

II

HOW ALL CHRISTENDOM TOOK THE CROSS

By such disaster were great folk and lowly throughout all Christendom sore disheartened, so that hardly could they be heartened again Forgotten were the dances, the singing of lays and of ballads, sweet converse, and every earthly joy, by all Christian folk, until the Pontiff of Rome, through whom God hath saved full many a man (this was the eighth Gregory, as is found in the histories), decreed a profitable pardon, to the glory of God and in the Devil's despite, to the intent that he should be shriven of all his sins who would go against the misbelieving folk that had disinherited the glorious King of Truth Therefore so many kings, so many counts, so many other folk that they cannot be numbered, took the cross for to seek God in Syria, that far country

Then took the cross together all the men of high repute The Count of Poitiers, the valiant Richard, would not be lacking there or fail God's need and His call, so he took the cross through love of Him [3] The first was he of all the

---

[2] Here follows a lacuna of several lines in the MS
[3] Richard Cœur de Lion took the cross in November, 1187

highborn men of the lands this side the sea, wherein we dwell Then the king[4] entered God's service, whereto he devoted great labour and great expense Nor did any hold back from taking the cross because he must needs sell his heritage, neither old men nor young bachelors were willing to hide their purpose or forbear to shew their wrath and to seek vengeance of the shame that had been put upon God without His desert, and for His land that had been laid waste, wherein His people were so hard pressed that they knew not what counsel to take Yet none should marvel that they were thus discomfited, goodly and chosen people though they were, but God willed that these should die, and that other folk should come to their help They died, after the flesh, but they live, in Heaven Even so do they that are dying there now, who remain in the service of God

III

HOW PHILIP AUGUSTUS AND HENRY OF ENGLAND TOOK THE CROSS

A war there was, of long standing, between France and Normandy, a war fierce and fell, arrogant, and full of bitterness and peril Twixt King Philip and Henry, King of England, was this war—Henry, who had that goodly household, valiant, wise, and prudent, father of the young king who jousted with such ardour—father of Richard the cunning, who was so wise and so shrewd, father of Geoffrey of Brittany, who likewise was a man of great deeds, and father of John Lackland, because of whom he suffered much strife and warfare A king that had such an household and that knew himself so mighty was well able to sustain a war, if any desired to make war upon him, and had he done what they desired, such folk as they were   [5]

The two kings lived in discord such that none could bring about any concord between them, until God brought them together in that parliament that proved so precious 'Twas twixt Gisors and Trie, in the fair wide meadow-land There was spoken many a word—many a wise one and many a foolish One was in quest of peace, another cared nought therefor Much people was there, and of many a sort, nor knew they how peace was to be sought, howbeit, God willed (so meseemeth) that they all should take the cross together Many a quarrel was there at this meeting, many an ancient one and many a new, and many were stubborn, bitter, and rank with pridefulness And many sought such quarrels without cease

Right fair was the weather that day[6] There was present an archbishop who was come as a messenger from Syria, a worthy man and sage, whom the Syrians sent thither because of his wisdom which they perceived and knew Him saw we greatly striving and interceding for to set the kings in the right way, and so greatly did God move them (and the worthy men and the wise) that the two

---

[4]Henry II of England
[5]Another lacuna in the MS
[6]21 January, 1188

kings kissed each the other, weeping and adoring God for the great joy that
they felt and for the need which God had that they should come to His aid Then
might ye see knights running, vying each with the others to take the cross, nor
did they seem a weary folk and spent, so that about the archbishops and about
the bishops and the abbots (so help me God and keep me!), I saw the press so
great, what with the heat that was so sore (nor could any one ask for aught more
grievous), that it lacked but little that they had choked

IV

OF THE DEATH OF KING HENRY

Because of the joy of that parley, of the peace, and of the preaching of the
cross, all men were coming to take the cross, for none might hold himself aloof
or refuse the great pardon But sorely to be chidden was the delay in setting
forth For the Devil bestirred himself to bring about again between the kings
a dissension that could not be laid until the one of them died, and death laid him
low This was the aged King of England, Henry, he who had thought to seek
the Holy Sepulchre and to follow God's steps, but death knew how to overtake
him [7] AMBROSE saith (who made this book) that wise is he who acquitteth himself of his vow so soon as he hath vowed it to God, his lord

V

HOW RICHARD LION-HEART WAS MADE KING IN HIS FATHER'S STEAD

After the death of the king their father, there remained only the two brothers the elder was named Richard, the illustrious Count of Poitiers, John Lackland was the younger called, who was a youth of tender years Richard, the
elder, had the crown (and by right was it given him), and the treasures, riches,
lands, and fiefs

Because he was the first who took the cross, even as we have told you, fain
would he suffer hardship in God's behalf Then made he ready for his journey
and passed over into England, and but little time was gone by ere he had himself crowned at London There did I see great gifts given, and I saw such abundance of meats set forth that none might keep account or tally thereof, nor ever
in my life have I seen a court served in courtlier fashion And I saw vessels of
great price in that hall that is so fair, and tables saw I so close pressed together
that they could in no wise be numbered But wherefore should I give you a
long account thereof? Every one of you knoweth well what it signifieth and
how great a court he is able to maintain who holdeth England in his sway

Bounteous was the feast, stately, and magnificent, and for three days did it

---

[7] 6 July, 1189

endure in full course There did the king bestow great gifts, and he restored to the barons both their fiefs and their inheritances and invested them in their seigniories [8]

VI

HOW KING RICHARD MADE READY FOR TO GO TO THE HOLY LAND

And when the court had broken up, they went every one to his own land Every one betook himself to his own manor, but not long could they abide there, for the king had summoned them all by name and commanded them to make ready for their journey, by borrowing and pledging, because he desired to send forth his fleet with all things needful, so that he might be in time for the passage and ready for his pilgrimage For night and day his heart was turned toward his valiant folk that were awaiting him—both them of Normandy and Anjou, of Gascony and of Poitou, of Berri and of Burgundy—of whom right many were in this undertaking Throughout his churches in England and those of his other lands, on his departure he established archbishops in those places where there had been none, and bishops also Then would he not await the winter, but hasted to make ready his passage and to put on board his rich treasure which he well knew how to employ But a little space had he tarried by the sea ere God prepared a fair and favouring wind which bare him back to Normandy [9]

VII

HOW KING RICHARD AND KING PHILIP MET AT DREUX

So soon as he was hither come, with great rejoicing was he received, this can ye well believe Then swiftly did he cause his company to press on, and he sent them ahead to Lion[10] for to celebrate the day of the Nativity, the day whereon God deigned to put on humanity At Lion did the king hold festival, but few were the lays sung there Rather, he had a letter written in all haste and gat him a speedy messenger, him he sent to the King of France, and he bade the messenger, so soon as the letter was delivered, say that he himself was fully prepared for his journey And because of this (an I mistake not) a parley was appointed betwixt the twain So did they meet before Dreux, which lieth some seven leagues distant from Evreux

But even as the two kings spake together of the pilgrimage that they were devising, lo, in all haste came a messenger to the King of France, with head bowed low, and told him that the queen was dead [11] And because of this great misfortune, and because of another cruel and dire, even the tidings of the death of Apulia's king[12] (whereof ensued great grief, which yet endureth), all the

---

[8]In theory, on the death of a sovereign all his feudal contracts were dissolved His successor took possession of all his fiefs and immediately restored them to their former holders

[9]11 December, 1189

[10]Lion-la-Forêt, Eure

[11]Isabel of Hainaut

[12]William II of Sicily (and Apulia), surnamed "the Good," husband of Richard's sister Joanna

people were sore distressed, and it lacked but little that the journey to Syria had been put off But, thanks be to God, the journey was not set aside, save only until the feast of Saint John, which every one observeth

VIII

OF THE GREAT ASSEMBLY THAT WAS HELD AT VÉZELAI HOW THE HOST DEPARTED THENCE AND TARRIED AT LYONS OF THE BRIDGE THAT BRAKE HOW THE PILGRIMS EMBARKED AT DIVERS HARBOURS

When the rose was sweetly blowing, then came the season whereat God willed that the pilgrims should set forth and that other folk should elect to follow, and that all should be ready with all the substance which God had committed unto them—ready to suffer hardship on God's behalf and to set forth at the feast of Saint John, so that on the eighth day, with no delay, was the great assembly held at Vézelai[18], and then departed the king from Paris and bade farewell to Saint Denis Many a chosen knight there was who had not yet set forth, albeit the more part of the French were already on their way Then did the Duke of Burgundy depart with the king on his pilgrimage, and the Count of Flanders quickly departed, nor tarried any great space Then might ye see so many folk moving, coming from every side thick as the drops of rain, and such a company attending them, and such sorrow at their parting, and such distress, that the hearts of them that accompanied the host were nigh to breaking

King Richard was at Tours with all his harness and his equipage The city was so full of people that scarce could they be contained therein Straightway he sent word to the seacoast, calling together his fleet with all speed To sea he bade the fleet put forth and besought them to proceed on their way with no dallying An hundred and seven ships were counted there, besides those that later followed, which all held their course hard after the others They all passed the straits, those narrow waters and difficult, the perilous Straits of Africa, where the sea beateth and breaketh ever, nor did one of them founder, or strand, or strike And by God's grace straight on they sailed until they came to land at Messina

King Richard with his baronry set forth from Tours with good cheer Many good knights were there and many crossbowmen of high repute Had ye but seen the host when forth it came! The earth trembled with their coming, but all the folk were sorrowful because of their lord so full of prowess There was weeping of ladies and of damozels, of young and old, of ugly and of fair Grief and pity oppressed their hearts because of their friends that were departing A more piteous convoy had ye never seen, nor folk more sorrowful when they turned back There many a tear was shed and many a good vow made in prayer They that had accompanied them returned, and the pilgrims went their way, so that on the term that the kings had set—neither sooner nor later than they

---

[18] 1 June, 1190

had appointed—there was gathered at Vézelai all that great assembly which God had stolen from the Devil Stolen? Nay, He took it openly, for 'twas on His behalf that they were come together

At Vézelai, in the mountain, there did God lodge His company, and much people was there also in the valley that had gone forth in His service There had He brought together the goodliest company of youth that ever was gathered in this world These had on God's behalf left behind their lands and their households and had impawned their inheritances or lost them for the residue of their days They had suffered themselves to be dispossessed of these that they might buy the love of God, for no better bargain can be made than to gain the love of the heavenly King

At Vézelai, where the kings were, an oath they sware together that, whatsoever fortune might befall, each might be assured of the other, and that whatsoever gain they gat together, this would they loyally divide Likewise it stood in their engagement that he of the twain who first came to Messina, at whatsoever moment or in whatsoever way this might be, should there await the other Thus pledged they each the other

From Vézelai they all set forth The two kings rode before, conversing of their great pilgrimage, and great honours did they pay each to the other whithersoever they came And there saw I a courtesy paid these folk that ought not to be passed over in silence All along the way that the host was going might ye behold (as God seeth me) lads and ladies and maids, with goodly cruses and pitchers and buckets and basins, bearing water to the pilgrims Straight to the road they came whereon the host was moving, holding the vessels in their hands and crying "God, heavenly King! Whence come so many folk? What may this mean? Where were born such youth as these? See ye their faces, how ruddy they are? Sad, in sooth, are now their mothers and the kinsmen, sons, brethren, friends, and acquaintance of these that I see coming in such number!" All the host did they commend to God, and wept at their passing Then prayed they fervently to God for them—and softly—that He would lead them to His service and bring them back again at His good pleasure So came they by God's good grace—which blessed them then and yet shall bless—with great joy and rejoicing, and without sadness, anger, bitterness, or mocking, straight on to Lyons on the Rhone

At Lyons the host halted, beside the Rhone with its crested waves There the two kings waited for the folk that were yet to come Never was seen such a marvel, nor ever so many folk a-moving At an hundred thousand were they reckoned, the more part whereof lay within the city But neither in the city nor in the orchards were the kings lodged, beyond the Rhone they bade their pavilions be pitched, there to await the host—and wait in sooth they must, for many a man was yet coming So there they waited on them until they saw that all were come and assembled And when they yet waited so long that they knew of a truth and were assured that all the host was come, then were they exceeding glad because of their coming So bade they their tents be struck, which stood, fair and of great price, far in the front by the sandy shore because of the great host that came behind them Philip, king of the French, had already afore this engaged passage of the Genoese, because they were skillful and wise in such matters But Richard, king of England, followed the seacoast from region to region and came straight on to Marseilles by the guiding of God, who inspireth every good thing

So soon as the host knew that the kings had set forth, some there were that arose long before the day, others, so early in the morning as they were able, for to make the passage of the Rhone They that had arisen ere daylight had no cause for plaint, for they passed over the bridge in all safety, nor ever had they any reason for halting But they that passed over in the morning and were close pressed together on the bridge, these were fated to fare ill, for one span of the bridge gave way because of the water, which was no longer safe, so was it risen out of bounds More than an hundred men were on that span, which was of firwood, this was too great a load Down fell the span, and they were all hurled headlong The folk cried and shouted, and every one of them, since he wist not the truth, thought that he had lost whatsoever companion he had, be it son, brother, or kinsman But God straightway so wrought in the matter that of all them that fell there were not more than two that perished—I mean, in so far as could be discovered, for none durst affirm this of a certainty, since so swift and strong is the stream that scarce aught falleth therein that ever escapeth again But if these perished to the world, yet are they now before God's face, pure and clean They were going about His business, so will they receive mercy, as is but just

The span of the bridge was broken and the people all turned from their course, neither knew they which way to go, whether up-stream or down, nor in the bridge was there any help, nor found they any workman there, neither on the Rhone were there any boats or barges great enough or wide enough so that in them they might follow those that had already crossed and overtake them So, since they knew not what else to do, they did the best that they could, in little skiffs, narrow and shallow, wherein folk suffered great unease, crossed they over with exceeding difficulty, but so fareth he who laboureth on God's behalf

For three full days did the crossing endure, and there was a great press of people, and then both the simple and the wise went on to seek their passage overseas To the nearest harbour, even to Marseilles, went a marvelous great multitude, likewise to the port of the Venetians went many most worthy Christians, to the Genoese, also, went so many that they may not now be numbered, and to Barletta and to Brindisi, so many that they were much talked of And to Messina did full many wend their way, against the coming thither of the two kings.

IX

OF THE CITY OF MESSINA, OF TANCRED, AND OF THE COMING OF THE TWO KINGS

Messina is a city whereof the writers of books have told us many things—a town fair and well situate, for it lieth at the extreme of Sicily, above the roadstead,[14] over against Reggio, which Agoland[15] took of yore in his emprise Messina was full of all manner of goodly wares, but the people thereof found we an evil folk Their king was called Tancred, who possessed fine gold in abundance, which his forefathers had gathered who reigned from the days of Robert Guiscard[16] And at that time there was in Palermo a lady who had sojourned there for a long season, queen had she been of the realm, the wedded wife of King William, but that honourable man and worthy had died without an heir, which was a great misfortune The queen was own sister to the King of England, who took it upon himself to cause her dowry to be restored to her, so that Tancred, who had seized himself both of the dowry and of the queen's person, durst not gainsay him

Ye who have understanding and memory, in sooth have ye heard how the fleet and the marvelous multitude of transport ships had already passed the coasts of Spain On to Messina did the navy come (nor ever saw I other such in all my life) which King Richard was awaiting, by whom England was held in fee There were folk of many sorts, and tents and pavilions and banners set up all along the shore, for the city was forbidden them Hard by the shore had they kept themselves until the kings should come, for the townspeople, the Grecian[17] rabble of the city and the baser rout—a tribe sprung from the Saracens—railed at our pilgrims, they thrust their fingers in their eyes, to mock us, and called us stinking dogs Every day did they evil entreat us and murdered our pilgrims and cast them into draught-houses, which deeds were proved against them

My lords, it is the custom and the use that whensoever a prince of lofty lineage—so lofty as that of the King of France, of whom the whole world speaketh, or of the King of England, who holdeth such high honour on earth—when such a prince entereth a town or a city or such a land as is Sicily, that he do this as befitteth an high lord, because of that which many folk will say For it is a good saying, after my thinking, which saith "As I see thee, so do I esteem thee" Therefore, I say, when the kings came much people gathered there The King of France came first to Messina, where many folk had assembled for to see him But never a sight of him did they get, for he had but one single ship and on the shore was a great throng and press, and to escape this press he went on and landed by the palace

And when King Richard landed there were likewise a many that strove to

---

[14]*Desus le Far* Cf Howell, *Letters*, I, 1, 26 (about 1650) "About the dawn of day we shot through Scylla and Charybdis, and so into the Phare of Messina"

[15]A Saracen king, hero of the *Chanson d'Aspremont*

[16]1015-1035, founder of the Sicilian dynasty

[17]Ambrose occasionally uses the word *Griu*, "Greeks," in speaking of the Hellenic subjects of the Byzantine Empire, but far oftener he employs the depreciatory diminutive *Grifon* of both these and other Greeks I have generally rendered the latter term by "Grecians"

see him on the strand, both wise folk and simple, who as yet had never beheld him but had great desire of beholding him because of his prowess And he came in such pomp that all the sea was covered with his galleys full of eager folk, warriors with faces bold, bearing pennons and banners Thus came the king to the shore, and to meet him came all his baronry His goodly steeds they brought that had hither come in his dromonds [18] So he mounted, and all his people after him And they that saw this company said that even thus ought a king to make his entry and such a king ought to possess much land But the Grecians were wroth and the Lombards murmured because he came with such a fleet to their city, and with such magnificence

X

OF THE EVIL DEEDS OF THE LOMBARDS, AND OF THE DISCORD THAT AROSE BETWIXT THE PILGRIMS AND THE PEOPLE OF MESSINA

When the two kings had landed, then the Grecians remained quiet, but the Lombards were ever stirring up strife and threatening our pilgrims that they would cut down their tents and carry off their goods, for they distrusted their women folk with whom the pilgrims conversed, though many a pilgrim spake with them but to vex their men nor had any thought to carry the matter further The Lombards and the commonalty of the town ever cherished bitterness against us, for that their fathers had told them how our ancestors had conquered theirs [19] Therefore could they not love us, but rather sought to starve us   [20]

This did they not for to advantage us, for they raised their towers higher and deepened their trenches This but made the affair the worse and increased the quarrels and the threats that were arising on every hand

And it chanced one day that a woman (whose name, they say, was Emma) was bearing bread to sell throughout the host, and a certain pilgrim, seeing that the bread was warm and fresh, bargained with her for it, but the woman so scorned the price which he offered that she lacked but little of striking him, so angered was she and beside herself And lo, the broil was begun! And the townsfolk mingled therein, and took the pilgrim then and beat him and tare out his hair and otherwise evil entreated him E'en to King Richard's ears the uproar came He demanded of them peace and amity, peace betwixt them he sought and obtained and his own folk drave he back But the Devil, who by nature hateth peace above every other thing, stirred up the strife anew upon the morrow, and only with great ado was it allayed The two kings were together at a parley with the justices of Sicily, I ween, and the notable men of the city, and there they spake of bringing about peace And lo, in the very midst of this meeting, even as the kings were speaking of the peace that they thought to bring about, came the rumour which had gone forth that our folk were attacked, and twice came tidings that they had suffered great loss But the third messenger that

---

[18]Large, swift galleys
[19]In the days of Robert Guiscard
[20]Another lacuna in MS

came cried to the king "Ill peace is here, when the men of this land are slaying England's folk within the city and without!" Then, in sooth, did the Lombards who were there withdraw themselves, and they said to the kings (but they lied!) that this did they for to put a stop to the brawling, for it was only to work mischief that they went Jourdain du Pin and Marguarit (may every ill befall them!) —these twain brewed the broth and were the source of all this evil The King of France was there and the King of England with him, and with him also was he that told this tale The King of England mounted his steed and went forth to separate the fray, but on his setting forth they of the city spake right churlish words to him and reviled him sore So the king made haste to arm himself and caused them to be assailed by sea and by land, on every side, for such another warrior was there not in all the world

XI

HOW THE KING OF FRANCE CONSPIRED WITH THE LOMBARDS, HOW KING RICHARD PUT THE LOMBARDS TO FLIGHT, AND HOW KING PHILIP KEPT KING RICHARD'S GALLEYS FROM THE HARBOUR

Great was the noise and the tumult, and the city was in a sorry pass The French came seeking their lord at the King of England's lodging, for the town was in such an uproar that they scarce hoped to find him So went he back with them and returned to the palace where he dwelt Then the Lombards came to him and held him fast by the left stirrup, and they made him promises and gave him gifts and yielded him the honour of the day, and they besought him to support them in the city and to keep them in his service and under his sway And such urging and such outlay did they use that anon the king armed himself, and one told us who was worthy of our belief, that the king helped the people of that land more than he helped the people of the King of England

And lo, the strife is begun anew and the noise waxeth greater throughout the host The French were within the city and at their ease, and the Lombards were trusting themselves to them, but they of our host cared nought for that And behold, the gates are shut, and the people of the city armed and gone up for to defend the walls, but presently it behooved them to get themselves down again And they who had sallied forth from the gates and attacked the lodging of my Lord Hugo le Brun were battling in a body, when the King of England came upon them, nor do I believe that he had a score of men with him at the first Then did the Lombards cease their threatening, so soon as they saw him, and turned and fled away, and the brave king charged after them And in that hour did AMBROSE perceive how, when they beheld the king coming, ye might well think of sheep fleeing before the wolf Even as oxen dragging at the plough, so did they drag themselves toward the postern gate that standeth over against Palermo, whither he drave them on amain, nor know I how many of them he laid low

The host rushed to arms and mounted all, assaulted as they were by the Lombards in their arrogance, and by the Grecians, false and full of madness But the folk that had taken up the task of their own defense were the same that had already taken many a city Normans were they, and men of Poitou, Gascons, folk from Maine, and Angevins, and from England were far more there than one could tell Boldly did they attack the foe when they saw them atop of the walls Round the whole city did they run, nor rested until they were within And their enemies, with bows and arbalests that they had hard at hand, were shooting at them from atop the walls, causing them great loss And rocks they cast upon them, and hurled stones, and smote our folk with grievous blows Bolts and darts were flying there, which wrought destruction amongst our pilgrims

If the Lombards had been more steadfast, then had it cost the king's men dear, but their own folly was their bane, kindling in us a fire to burn themselves They that defended the town were more than fifty thousand, upon the walls and towers, with shields and targes There might ye have seen an assault most fierce and fell Over toward the palace were the galleys gone to make their attack, but the King of France was there, who held fast the shore and kept the galleys from the harbour so that they were not able to seize it And his men shot until they slew two of the rowers, wherein they did sore wrong But on this side, from the landward, the King of England was leading the attack, and so vigorously did he assail the Lombards that he had great success there Then might ye have seen his people going up, scaling the embankments, and cutting the bars of the gates asunder, and there were many taken or slain Into the midst of the streets rushed certain ones, but soon repented them thereof, for they that were in the upper storeys of the houses launched missiles and shot arrows against them But despite all their defense these were taken in the assault And whosoever may have been the last, the king himself was one of the first that durst enter the town Thereafter entered full ten thousand men Then might ye hear the shouting of our men   [21] the discomfiting, the storming, the wounding, maiming, and battering of heads In less time did they take Messina than a priest needeth to say matins And very great had been the slaughter there, had not the king been moved to pity of them But in sooth can ye well believe that there was lost great riches, when the great throng had entered in, for presently was all the city put to the sack Their galleys were burned, which were neither mean nor poor, and many fair women were won, both clever and wise

Now I know not all the truth of this matter, howbeit, rightly or wrongly, or ever the news was known throughout the host, the French had already seen our pennons and banners in divers places on the walls, whereof the King of France conceived such envy as shall last him his whole life long, and there was the war engendered whereby thereafter Normandy was laid waste

---

[21]One line is missing from the MS

XII

OF THE JEALOUSY OF KING PHILIP, HOW THE TWO KINGS SENT MESSENGERS TO KING TANCRED, AND OF THE RETURN OF THE MESSENGERS

When the king had taken Messina and set up his banners on the towers, then was word sent him from the King of France (he had great envy and bitterness because King Richard had raised these banners, and his people, too, were very wroth thereat) that his men would take down the King of England's banners and cause his own to be raised on the walls of the city And this word did he send him in sooth that in doing what he had done Richard was setting his suzerainty at nought and displeasing him grievously My lords, I ask your verdict whether of the twain had the better right to set up his banners there, he who would have no part in the assaulting and taking of the city, or he who dared to make this undertaking?

King Richard listened to this message but deigned not to enter on any long controversy over such a request with the other king, whose mind was tempest-tossed Natheless, many a foolish word was spoken, many a bitter, but not all follies should be written down or put into a book Howbeit, the highest clerks and notable men spake together in one wise or another until, at the last, this was the outcome whereby peace was made to wit, that each of the two kings kept his own banners on the towers and turrets

Then they took in hand straightway to send word to the King of Sicily concerning the commonalty of the city and the villainy and violence that these had wrought against them Moreover, King Richard's messengers were to tell him, on the king's own several behalf, that he demanded as his rightful due the dowry of his sister, and that his own share of the late king's treasure be fairly apportioned to him, together with whatsoever appertained to the lady, which were but just and right

The messengers were named—folk of high and gentle birth and great renown, lords of lofty lineage and of wide seigniory, men of great affairs—who went upon this errand The first of them that were charged with this business was the Duke of Burgundy, another was Robert of Sablé, an eminent man and a worthy, and most gracious And others of them might there also be, whose names I could not learn These rode and journeyed and so sped their course that within a brief space they delivered their message to the king at Palermo

King Tancred, who was a very prudent man, had listened to the messengers Many adventures had he known and a right good clerk was he, well skilled in writing Already was he well acquainted with the matter in hand, nor did he long delay to give his answer Answer he made, without any deferment, to the King of England's men, that to the statutes of his land, to the barons of his realm, and to the customs of King William would he refer the settling of this complaint, so that his decision might seem fair to every one, and that, if the townsfolk of Messina had offered wanton insults and so angered the kings, ample redress would they be forced to make

And when the messengers heard this (they that came from King Richard), some there were who said that never would the king consent to plead his cause, and many were the words exchanged over the matter But on the messengers of France were goodly goblets bestowed, the others possessed their souls in patience Now shall ye hear of the great dissension (remembered then and thereafter) which, they say, was brought about by the King of France For he is said to have sent word privily to King Tancred (I know not what he hoped to gain thereby) that he would do that which the king desired, and would guard well the king's rights, nor ever, for the King of England's sake, would he make war upon him, for that he was bound to Tancred by an oath If this was so, in sooth was it a base thing to do History affirmeth not of a surety that he meditated this villainy, but, be this as it may, the people declared with no uncertainty that such word he did send

They that had no cups returned so quickly as they were able, their message they remembered right well, and back they came to Messina King Richard was then a-building a strong hold which pleased him much, it was a castle, Mategrifon,[22] because of which the Grecians were sore troubled The messengers came to the king and told him what they had demanded of King Tancred and the word which King Tancred had sent back to him concerning this demand—what he had said regarding the statutes of his land and the judgment of his baronry And King Richard, scarce pausing. made answer that never would he plead his cause before Tancred, but none the less would he gain his end

XIII

OF THE FURTHER DISCORD THAT AROSE BETWIXT THE KING OF ENGLAND AND THE KING OF FRANCE, OF THE WORD THAT KING TANCRED SENT TO KING RICHARD, OF THE RECONCILIATION OF THE KINGS, AND OF THE GREAT FEAST HELD ON THE DAY OF THE NATIVITY

When the news was made known that neither a peace nor a truce was established, then in sooth was there great fear of war because of the aid and comfort which the King of France was giving to our enemies, for the crafty Lombards had made an alliance with him Then, lo, our supply of victual was cut off, so that not a pennyworth came into the host, and had it not been for God and our fleet, many a one of us had led a sorry life But within the ships was their lading—corn and wines and flesh and other provision The town was guarded by night and watchmen set about the host The two kings were at odds because of jealousy, which stirreth up all manner of trouble This was neither a good thing nor honourable, and greatly did the men of high estate strive to bring peace and accord betwixt them To the palace they rode, and to Mategrifon, but back they came over the same road, nor ever were they able to accomplish their purpose, howsoever much they sought to intercede   [23]

[22]"Subduer of the Grecians," "Greek's-bane"
[23]Lacuna of one or more lines

Even as the book beareth witness, the King of Sicily, who knew the offenses committed by the city, took the son of his chancellor and along with him another knight (his constable, an I mistake not), whom he held to be an upright man and loyal, and him he despatched to the King of England, sending him word that he desired not at all to have war with him, but that if King Richard were willing to accept moneys in satisfaction of the demands that he made, gladly would he make peace with him and would give him twenty thousand ounces of gold which he would draw from his treasury, and if he were willing, on the advice of his baronry, to hold speech with him concerning a marriage, then would he give one of his own daughters, a maiden fair and damsel virtuous and wise, to Arthur of Brittany to wife Moreover, to consummate this intent, he promised him without guile or deceit yet other twenty thousand ounces of gold, save only that Richard should give him back this gold if Arthur took not the maid to wife Richard's sister, also, would he restore to him withal

When the king heard this, then delayed he not at all to send back other men for to seek a firm and durable peace The Archbishop of Monreale[24], the Archbishop of Reggio, a loyal man, Bishop John of Évreux, who suffered so much labour and expense—these did the king bid bear his message, for well did they know their task and understand the matter, other folk, also, went with them Peace they sought and peace they brought, the moneys likewise did they fetch whereof ye have just now heard me tell And when they were come back, then all rejoiced over the peace Then were the charters read and copied and scanned, and the peace affirmed and sworn to whereby the people were made safe, and moneys counted and weighed, whereat the king was in no wise grieved, who was very fain to receive them that he might spend them in the service of God And then was his sister restored to him, who was well worth a dear ransom Then was it the king's will that there should be given back to the townspeople, without any delay, whatsoever his own folk had taken which was theirs, and this act redounded greatly to his praise On pain of excommunication, and after confession, did they restore these things in accord with the sage and excellent counsel of the Bishop of Rouen

And now was the city in good case and free from brawling and strife, for whoso ventured to begin these, he was hanged or otherwise put to death And in the host everywhere justice prevailed—blessed be the soul that brought it thither! Then were the highways trodden once more, and again did we get fodder for horses and victual for men Thus, in sooth, did the affair end The townsfolk made their peace with us and gave lodging to the pilgrims The two kings were reconciled (but many a time thereafter did they fall out again) and divided the moneys between them, and each had that which was justly his

But the knights who had been there throughout the whole summer lamented and complained because of the expense to which they were put, and high and low the plaint was spread abroad until it reached King Richard's ear, and he said that he would give them so much that every one of them could felicitate himself

---

[24]Near Palermo

And rare indeed and rich were the gifts that were given them by Richard (who is neither niggardly nor mean) goblets of silver, gilded cups, that were brought in armfuls to the knights according to the station of each one, so that for his bounteous gifts he was acclaimed of those of high, of middle, and of low degree Nay, with his wealth such honour did he shew them all that even they that were on foot received of him at least an hundred pence each one And to the ladies dispossessed of their heritage, who had been driven out of Syria—to dames and damozels alike—he gave rich gifts at Messina And the King of France, in his turn, gave generously to his own folk

Lo, all the host was blithe and of good cheer because of this honour and this largesse and because of the peace that was come So was the great feast celebrated, for on the day of the Nativity King Richard caused it to be cried about that all might come and celebrate the feast with him, and such pains did he take that he brought even the King of France to his table At Mategrifon the feast was held, in the hall which the English king by his might had raised despite the people of the land I, too, was at this feast, nor ever saw I there soiled napery or wooden bowl or porringer Rather, there saw I rich plate of work incrusted and inlaid, with molten images adorned and set with rich and precious stones, so that verily there was nothing paltry therein Likewise, such noble service saw I there that every one was served to his content A goodly feast it was and honourable, even as befitteth such a festal day, nor ever saw I (so meseemeth) so many rich gifts made at one time as did King Richard give that day and bestow upon the King of France and upon his people—gifts of golden plate and silver

XIV

HOW THE TWO KINGS DEPARTED FROM MESSINA FOR THE HOLY LAND

Now came the season of our departure, and wise and shrewd indeed was he who had made provision for his passage From the Nativity of the Blessed Virgin[25] (by my reckoning) even until the outgoing of Lent did the host sojourn at Messina, and greatly did they long for the day when they should go on to take Acre together with them that had already dared to make this undertaking, who suffered great hardships there, far greater than men knew, for grievous pain in sooth did these endure and sore distress during that half-year And when the pilgrims had sojourned there so long that God had suffered all things to be made ready for their voyage, then in sooth did the King of France put forth to sea— he and his company—a little before Palm Sunday But King Richard could not then set out, for he had not yet ready his fleet, his galleys, and his transport ships for carrying his swift coursers, his arms, and his victual, for to make war upon the infidel pack Therefore must he needs wait and make further preparation for his voyage The King of France did he convoy, on his setting out, with his own galleys, then went he on beyond the harbour and straight to Reggio,

---

[25] 8 September, 1190

whence word had been brought to him that his mother was come thither, bringing to the king his beloved

This was a prudent maid, a gentle lady, virtuous and fair, neither false nor double-tongued, and her name was Berengaria The King of Navarre[26] was her father, he had entrusted her to King Richard's mother, who did her diligence to bring her to him there Thereafter she bare the name of queen And the king had loved her much from the time that he was Count of Poitiers, and she had been his heart's desire

His mother he caused to be brought straight to Messina—her and her women and to his mother he spake openly his mind (and she to him), nor hid he aught from her The maid, whom he held so dear, he kept with him, but his mother he sent back to guard his land that he had left, so that his honour might not be brought down And the Archbishop of Rouen, Walter, who is an exceed-ing wise man, had from him the ward of England, and many an hazard of warfare had he there Thence, also, did Gilbert of Vascœuil then return, who afterward suffered Gisors to be taken

Thereafter the king rested not, straightway were his ships made ready, freighted, and fitted out, and his galleys likewise Then was there no more delay, he bade his baronry put forth to sea, and his beloved, the virtuous maid and wise, and his sister also with his love (and with them he caused a great body of knights to embark on a large dromond), that the one lady might cheer the other His dromonds bade he take the lead and sail toward the rising sun But the larger transport ships, swift-sailing craft, departed not until the king had eaten Then, in well-ordered ranks, forth moved the vessels of the marvelous fleet It was in Holy Week that from Messina the fleet put forth, to the service of God and to His glory On the Wednesday of that week wherein God suffered pain and anguish it behooved us also to undergo perils and watchings But well may Messina boast herself—where so many ships were seen together—that never on any day that yet hath dawned had so rich a fleet departed from her haven

XV

OF KING RICHARD'S VOYAGE, HOW HE TARRIED AT THE ISLE OF RHODES, AND HOW HE CAME THENCE UNTO CYPRUS

So the fleet went on, all in due order ranged, towards God's unhappy country, out through the harbour, and came forth upon the waters of the high sea, to-ward Acre bound On we went, and overtook the dromonds, then saw we the wind fall, so that the king was minded to put back But that night must we needs bide where we were, whether it irked or pleased us, between Calabria and Mongibello [27] But on Maundy Thursday He who took the wind from us, and who is able both to give and to take away, gave it back to us again and granted it to us through all that day But it was a feeble wind, and presently the fair and noble fleet was forced to halt On Good Friday we were met by a contrary

[26]Sancho VI
[27]Mount Etna

wind off Viaires,[28] which lay to the larboard The deep sea was troubled, the wind was violent and doubled the tumult of the sea, high were the billows tossing to and fro, and we were but driven out of our course Great fear had we and sore distress and much misease in mouth and heart and head But all things that we suffered we endured right gladly, and well ought we to endure them for the sake of Him who deigned on that day to undergo His passion for our redemption Fierce was the wind that buffeted us about until the evening, when night fell, then we had a settled wind, favourable and mild

Now a right laudable thing did King Richard do, whose mind was always vigilant and keen By night it was his custom to keep a great candle lit within a lanthorn on his ship, which sent out an exceeding bright and shining light All night long was it burning, to shew the other ships the way With him he had able seamen, brave folk that understood their business well, so after the king's light all held their course and saw it always near at hand But if the fleet began to go astray, then would he generously wait for them So led he that proud and noble fleet, even as a mother hen leadeth her chickens to their food This was both prudence on his part and natural kindliness So sailed we all that night without disquietude or hinderance, and on the morrow, Holy Saturday, God led us on without mishap, and that night also without any stay, and all through Easter Day Three days did the fleet move on apace with no sail lowered, and in the forefront sailed the king himself On Wednesday we sighted Crete Thither the King of England turned his course and coasted the island, keeping nigh to the land There he rested, and the fleet with him, but that night five and twenty of the transport ships lost sight of us, whereat the king was sore displeased and very wroth On the morrow, a Thursday morning, with sails hoisted the fleet went on toward Rhodes, another island hard by The wind was high, and lofty were the waves Swift as a swallow flieth, on sped the ship with bended mast Coasting the isle of Rhodes, God led us on prosperously and with marvelous speed, for it seemed that He was well pleased with the course that His folk were following So on we voyaged in sooth until black night came And in the morning we steered into a strait, strake sail, and so were free of travail, resting there until the Sunday, and in the morning we were at Rhodes, the city wherein Herod was born[29]

Rhodes was of yore a great city and is of great antiquity, whilom well-nigh so great as Rome herself Hardly could the truth of this matter be known, for so many ruined houses are there, so many crumbling walls and towers, and so many minsters that yet are standing—because of the multitude of people that have dwelt there through so many years and so many ages and under so many seigniories—that no man might reckon, without exceeding difficulty, either its greatness or its magnificence, that now is fallen through eld None the less there were yet dwelling there folk who sold us victuals, and because the king

---

[28]Possibly Cape Spartivento

[29]*E le matin fumes a Rodes,*
La cité u fud nez Herodes
As there is no other reference to Rhodes as Herod's birthplace, it looks as if Ambrose had invented this circumstance for the sake of the rhyme

was sick and suffering much misease, we must needs tarry a while at Rhodes The king caused search and enquiry to be made whither his lost ships were gone, and awaited his galleys which were following him from place to place along the coast   Likewise did he make much enquiry concerning the tyrant[30] who was governing Cyprus and holding captive certain of our pilgrims   Ten days tarried we at Rhodes, then we put forth again   The first day of May it was, forsooth, when the fleet with all sail spread set forth in order straight for the Gulf of Adalia, which is a most perilous passage—none more perilous is found in any course—for there four seas are ever battling, each striving to overcome the others   Into this gulf were we entering, when a wind assailed us which brought us back by evening to the very place where first the fleet had entered Then the wind, which changeth oft, did us a more courteous turn, for it took us right aft and drave us, so swiftly that all were afeared, back through the gulf where we had been, whereof we gat many a fright   The king's ship was foremost, as was ever the custom   The king looked out over the high sea and saw a dromond sailing, returning from the coasts of Syria, and he, being curious in the matter bade his own ship's course be turned toward the other vessel, for to seek tidings from the Holy Land   And they told him that the King of France was already there, awaiting him before Acre and busy every day a-building engines wherewith to take the town   But King Richard already had in mind another plan   Then, lo, the other ship passed on, and the king strove with the wind until, in the end, the Lord God brought him to Cyprus, near to the land that He caused to be conquered for him   There the king found his sister, his people, and his love

XVI

OF THE SUFFERINGS OF THE CHRISTIANS IN SYRIA, OF ISAAC COMNENUS, THE TRAITOR EMPEROR OF CYPRUS, OF THE SHIPWRECK OF CERTAIN PILGRIMS, AND OF THE DANGEROUS PASS TO WHICH KING RICHARD'S SISTER AND HIS BETROTHED WERE BROUGHT

Hearken, my lords! How many wrongs, how many troubles, how many great disasters, how many attacks, how many delays, how many long waitings, how many pains, how many longings, how many assaults, how many confusions, had this land of Syria to suffer or ever it could get any aid!   A great loss to the fulfilment of this task was that of the Emperor of Germany,[31] who moved with such pomp, yet died so suddenly   And great evil did this holy land suffer in the death of the King of England, the good Henry, who was so wise and had so great riches wherewith the land might have been sustained and the city of Tyre saved   And great ill befell the holy realm in the death of good King William,[32] who had succoured it full many a time, so was it a sore misfortune when he died   Verily, the kingdom had received many an evil heritage of mischievous

[30]Isaac Comnenus
[31]Frederick I. Barbarossa   drowned in 1190
[32]Of Sicily

mischances, but nought else worked it such mischief as did a certain island that lieth nigh to Syria to wit, the opulent Isle of Cyprus, which of yore was wont to support it, but now could nothing come thence to Syria For there dwelt a tyrant who was ever on evil bent—a worse traitor he and more false than Judas or than Ganelon! Saladin's privy friend was he, and the Christians had he deserted, and it was said in sooth that, to plight their alliance each had drunk of the other's blood, thereafter, this was known of a certainty Thus did he make himself emperor—nay, rather, *impairer*[33], for himself did he impair and worsen, nor ever, an he might, did he leave off to do and to work evil and to persecute God's Christian folk Off Cyprus had three of King Richard's ships been wrecked, carrying men of his own household, who had saved themselves from the wreck but were fallen into an evil case, for the emperor made them to give up their arms, then treacherously to be seized Yea, he had promised them their safety, which lasted but a little time For straightway he ordered them to be attacked, unworthy as he was of any trust But they defended themselves right well—making their foes pay dear for the outrage—with but three bows that they yet had, whereof the Grecians knew not a word There was Roger of Hardencourt, companion of the king and one of his court, who, mounted on a sorry jade, had lessened the number of their people And William of Bois-Normand, that good bowman, went on, shooting his arrows before and behind, so that they feared him worse than a petrary [34]

so that, in sight of the foe, they went back even to the galleys that lay in the harbour, wherein the queen had come There was fought a great fight, and bravely did the prisoners battle When the king, who had halted at the harbour, knew of the treachery whereby his men were put in jeopardy, when he saw the dromond of his sister, who was awaiting him in great fear, when he beheld the strand all covered with the base Grecian rabble—then, worse Saracens than these did he not care to seek So he had himself brought to land—the land which the tyrant had thought to hold against him, but now durst he not await the valiant king

XVII

HOW KING RICHARD CAME TO HOLD A PARLEY WITH THE EMPEROR ISAAC, HOW THE EMPEROR MADE MOCK OF HIS MESSENGER, HOW THE KING ATTACKED AND TOOK LIMASSOL, AND HOW THE EMPEROR FLED

'Twas for a Monday morn that God had appointed the task which He desired the king to perform—to save them that were shipwrecked, to set his sister free, and to carry his beloved to another place Each of these ladies rued the day that she had ever betaken herself thither, for the emperor would have seized them

---

[33]*Issi se fist' empereur,*
Nel fist pas, mais empereur

[34]A military engine for hurling huge stones
Here follows a lacuna of several lines The *Itinerarium Ricardi,* a Latin paraphrase of Ambrose's chronicle, says that these two and a third archer were rescued by their companions from the other ships

both an he had been able   But when the king would have seized the harbour,
there were folk a plenty there to hinder him, for the emperor himself was there,
who had taken his stand upon the shore with so many people as he could muster
for money or by command   And the king chose him a messenger and had him
rowed to the shore, and he sent a message to the emperor, courteously praying
him to restore their possessions to the prisoners and to make right the wrongs
that he had done to our pilgrims, whereby many an orphan was made to weep
But the emperor did but mock and rail at the messenger, until he himself well-
nigh went mad, nor could he temper his rage, but cried to the messenger,
"Tproupt,[35] sir!"   Nor ever would he thereafter speak him one fair word, but
began to growl at him disdainfully   Quickly the messenger returned to the king
and told him all   And when the king had heard this shameful word, he cried to
his people, "Arm yourselves!"   And that did they right speedily, nor wasted any
time   Into the boats of the transport ships must they needs get themselves, all
armed   In these embarked good knights and crossbowmen bold   The Grecians
also had crossbows and had their people drawn up on the shore, moreover,
they had five galleys which were armed   But when they saw our armoury, then
were their folk in no wise so confident

Within the city of Limassol, where began the assault and the fighting, was
there left neither door nor window nor aught that could be used for offense—
neither butt, nor tun, nor shield, nor targe, nor ancient galley or barge, nor
beam, nor plank, nor stair—all these were they bringing down to the strand for
to do mischief to the pilgrims withal   Waiting all armed upon the shore, more
arrogant than any other living folk, with pennons and with banners of rich tex-
ture coloured with precious dyestuffs, mounted on great horses strong and fleet,
on large mules goodly and stout—like dogs they howled at us, but speedily was
their pride abated   Sore were the odds against us then, who were coming in from
the sea, embarked in little tiny boats, worn by fierce storms, bruised by the
shock of waves, heavy laden with our armour, and all on foot, while they were
on their own ground   But we knew more of war than they

Our crossbowmen began the attack, and many a one of them missed not
his mark   First did they shoot at the enemy's rowers, who knew nought of
warfare, and so many of them did they hit and wound in their galleys where they
sat that into the sea they sprang, four by four, then might ye have seen them
thrusting one another down   Then were the galleys taken and were put with our
own transport ships   Thick and fast the archers shot, and the crossbowmen
likewise, and they forced the Grecians to give ground   And then might ye hear
our own men howl at them as they had howled at us ere we began to advance
On both sides was much shooting of arrows and hurling of missiles, but our
rowers moved ever onward, albeit whithersoever they came bolts and darts
rained down upon them

---

[35] I cannot find any translation of this ejaculation   Gaston Paris, in his paraphrase of
L'Estoire de la Guerre Sainte, says that this is an "exclamation d'injure et de mépris", but he
is equally unable to find a modern French equivalent for it, and leaves it unchanged in his
version

All the shore and the strand was filled with these savage folk, and there had ye seen a bold emprise and men well skilled in warfare For when the king saw his companions striving to make the land, forth of his boat into the sea he sprang and came on against the Grecians and attacked them And all the rest sprang after him The Greeks defended themselves, but our men came on along the shore, smiting and overcoming Into the town our people drave them back, so vigorously did they press and thrust them Like lions did they go after them, striking the bodies of men and of horses Before the valiant Latin folk fled Greeks and Armenians Even into the fields did our men pursue them so fiercely that they drave thence the emperor, who took to flight The king straightway pursued after him until he came up with a sumpter horse or mare (I know not which) that had a sack trussed behind the saddle, and stirrups of cord Straight from the ground into the saddle he leapt, and to the false and craven emperor he cried, "Come on, O Emperor, and joust with me!" But the emperor had no mind to joust

XVIII

OF THE BOOTY THAT KING RICHARD TOOK, AND HOW HE PURSUED THE EMPEROR

That night the king, with no more delay, caused all the horses that were in his transport ships to be discharged from the vessels, but the emperor had never an inkling that he had brought any with him The beasts were led about for a season, for they were all stiff and benumbed and dizzy, having been for a whole month on the sea, standing ever, without once lying down Then giving them no more rest than that they had had (though well did they deserve a further respite), on the morrow the king mounted his own horse, for yet was he pursuing the plan that he had in hand There, in an olive grove hard by and close beside the highway, were certain Greeks with their banners and pennons of divers sorts These he caused to be driven out, set his steel helmet on his head, and went after them full speed There had ye seen brave folk and undismayed! Our front rank drave the Greeks before them, the Greeks fled, and our men pursued until they saw the main body of the host, then they halted But whilst our men were pursuing, the Greeks howled so loudly and such a din and shouting did they raise (so said they that heard it) that the emperor heard them from his tent, which stood, I ween, more than half a league away Thither had he withdrawn himself because of the fighting, and there had he supped and slept, but rudely were he and his awakened Then he mounted, and his men also mounted, and they rode up to the hilltops for to see what their comrades would do, who understood nought but to shoot arrows These were ever circling round our men and howling, but our men moved not from their place Then came to the king an armed clerk, who was called Hugh of the Pool[36] who spake privily to the king, saying, "Get you hence, Sire, for they have a multitude of folk beyond all numbering!" "Sir Clerk," the king made answer, "attend thou to thy writing,

---

[36]*Huge de la Mare*

get thee out of the press, and leave to us the things of chivalry, in the name of
God and of Saint Mary!" This man and others spake thus to the king because
of the great multitude that they beheld, for with the king there were at that
hour not more than two score knights, or fifty at the most. None the less, the
brave king charged the foe (for he could wait no longer) more swiftly than the
falling thunderbolt, poised like the hawk that stoopeth at the lark, and they that
saw that charge lauded it exceedingly. So drave he full tilt right through the
midst of that press of savage Grecian folk, disordering them and putting them to
such a pass that not one of them could support another. In the mean time his
own men were coming, and so soon as they were arrived in sufficient number,
so many of the foe did they slay or take captive (to make no mention of them
that basely fled) that no man ever knew the number of the dead. For they that
had horses fled away up the hills and adown the dales, but they that were on
foot, the lesser folk, were all or slain or taken. Fierce was the fight and fell,
there had ye seen so many a steed brought down, and hauberks scattered, swords
and lances, pennons and ensigns, and other horses staggering with their loads.

The emperor saw how his men could not hold out against our own and how
our force was ever increasing, so fled he away to the mountain with his Armenian
and Grecian pack, leaving the whole field to us. When Richard, England's king,
perceived that they were fleeing thus, abandoning their own people, then did he
smite him who bare the emperor's banner, in such wise that he gat possession
of the banner itself, and he bade it be guarded right well. Then saw he their
people all routed, fleeing like a storm-cloud, with many a bleeding body and bloody
head, and he saw that it booted not to pursue them further, for he could in no
wise overtake them and already had two leagues been covered by our own bold
Franks in their pursuit. So came he riding slowly back. But the serjeants[37] left
not the matter there, rather, they gleaned great foison of rich and goodly golden
and silver plate that the emperor had left in his tent where it was pitched, his
harness, his own bed, and silken stuffs and stuff of purple dye, horses and mules
laden as for a market, hauberks and helms and swords which the Grecians had
thrown away, oxen and kine, nimble and stubborn goats, rams, ewes, and lambs,
mares with foals sleek and fat, capons and hens and cocks, plump mules with
embroidered cushions on their backs, raiment fine and curious, and goodly
steeds in better case than ours, which were a-weary. Likewise they took
the emperor's dragoman (whose name, I heard, was John), and so many Greeks
and Armenians that the roads were fair cumbered with them, and such quantity
of good wines and good victual that no man might keep count or tally thereof.
And the king caused a ban to be cried, that the people of the land might safely
come and go that is, those that desired not war, for they that did not desire
peace should have neither peace nor truce from him.

---

[37]Men-at-arms The term *serjanz* was used of any combatant who was not a knight

XIX

OF THE COMING OF THE KING OF JERUSALEM TO CYPRUS, OF KING RICHARD'S MARRIAGE, AND OF THE PARLEY BETWIXT HIM AND THE EMPEROR, AND THE PEACE THAT THEY MADE

On the Saturday of the week wherein the Grecians suffered such discomfort there came to Limassol three galleys which were returning from Cyprus, with which came also the King of Jerusalem, whom men hold in high esteem King Guy of Lusignan was he, who had endured such hardship and distress in the defense of God's land that he was constrained to depart thence For the King of France sought to do him a wrong (whereat his heart was sore grieved) in that he was seeking to make the marquis[38] king in his stead For this cause had he left his land and was coming to the King of England that he might help him to maintain his right The king rejoiced greatly at his coming and straightway went forth to meet him And well may ye know and believe that he was very fain to welcome him, for he was of lofty lineage and high affinity and his kinsmen who were present seemed in no wise folk of low estate The king had great joy of him and shewed him all manner of honour, and he gave him of his own moneys (which was a seemly courtesy) a sum reckoned at two thousand marks (no mean gift was this), also twenty drinking-cups out of his treasure, whereof two were of fine gold

And on the morrow morn was the damozel wed and crowned at Limassol —the fair maid with the bright countenance, the wisest lady in all truth that might anywhere be found Now was the king in his glory and in great joy over his victory and over his marriage with her to whom he had pledged his faith

And now were his galleys come that he had so long awaited, so well armed and provisioned that never in our lives saw we the like Joined to these were the five that had been seized there, and with these, together with the others that were in the several harbours, of which he now enjoyed the full use, had he full forty armed vessels that were so good as any fifty others Thus was it that he afterward took that marvelous ship[39] wherein were so many warlike folk, who were reckoned at eight hundred men—Turks and Persians unbaptized So was the king the more determined to go against the Greeks and the accursed Armenians Then had he his host made ready and bade his watchmen watch by night, for to go and seek the emperor in his own land

After the discomfiture wherein the Greeks suffered such shame, the emperor was at Nicosia—both he and his great company—wrathful, doleful, and desperate because of his men that he had lost and because he had been put to flight, nor could he get any comfort But greatly was he hated in his own land, and he feared the King of England, so he sought a parley of him for to make amends to him, and he sent word to the king that he would come to him and would keep fealty toward him and would bring five hundred men in his company to Syria,

---

[38]Conrad, Marquis of Montferrat Although Ambrose mentions him repeatedly in his chronicle, he almost never employs his full name or title, but refers to him simply as *li marchis,* "the marquis"

[39] See page 38

all mounted and ready for God's service, and that he would do the king's pleasure in all things And it stood in the covenant—that the king might have no doubt in the matter—that he would leave in gage his castles and all his rich inheritances, and for the losses that the king's people had suffered would he pay three thousand and five hundred silver marks, and if he should serve the king loyally, then should he have back his land in exchange The king agreed to the parley, and the emperor likewise A term was set for the parley by the two parties, nor did they seek any long delay It was held in a garden of fig trees, betwixt the harbour and the road that leadeth to Limassol, an I remember rightly There did they meet, and there were things said far better than the things that were done

The king called them of his household and the most able counselors amongst his people, then said he to those that stood before him, who were very desirous of peace "My Lords, ye are my right hand, see then whether this peace can be made, watch, that your honour be safe therein nor be put in any jeopardy, for if the peace please you, it will be made, if it mislike you, it will be deferred" "Sire," said they, "it suiteth us well, and such a peace seemeth to us honourable"

So straightway back they went, and the peace was agreed to, and the emperor sware an oath to the king in token of assurance and kissed him in sign of fealty The king returned unto his host that lay hard by, and soon was he there Then did he command them to load, without further delay, the three tents that he took at the discomfiting of the villainous Grecians (the emperor's own they were, and wrought of fustian), and of rich plate a plenty, and these things he sent most courteously unto the emperor, who kept the plate but had the tents sent back to that same place where was the parley held that we have told you of

XX

OF THE LYING COUNSEL THAT PAÏEN OF CAÏPHAS GAVE TO THE EMPEROR, OF THE SECOND FLIGHT AND PURSUIT OF THE EMPEROR, OF THE COMING OF DROON OF MELLO AND THE BISHOP OF BEAUVAIS

But on that selfsame evening on which the peace had been established, there was with the emperor a foul-spoken knight, Païen of Caïphas by name, false-tongued was he and more spiteful than a surly dog He gave the emperor to understand that the king wished to have him seized, and this lie did he cause him to believe And immediately the emperor mounted a swift steed, which was called Fauvel [40] On this Fauvel he departed in flight, yet as if he were but riding for his pleasure, and he left behind his harness and his tents (like to one that hath lost his head) and two chargers fleet and strong, then away he rode so fast as he might The king found out that he was fled, but suffered him not to be pursued, for he desired not to break the truce, neither had he any horse that could overtake him Howbeit, when he knew of his flight he was by no means ready to cry quits with him, but sought him by sea and by land and enquired diligently after him His galleys sped away by night and came betimes to Fama-

---

[40] I e, "Fawn-coloured," fallow

gusta Himself went he thither, for he was very fain to have an hand in the undertaking The King of Jerusalem he bade convoy him by land, along the coast, and follow the perjured traitor emperor until he gat sight of him So did King Guy set forth and came within three days, in sooth, to the city of Famagusta, whence the townsfolk had departed Thither came the king with his galleys, and with these galleys had he all the harbours watched and guarded, so that the emperor could not get himself thence to sea without meeting them And the galleys remained there for three days after they had left the transport ships

But during this season of waiting came thither two messengers from France, Droon of Mello (an I mind aright) and the Bishop of Beauvais, who came to press the king to make haste And press him they did, and right furiously, to go speedily on to Acre, for otherwise would the King of France never begin the assault before King Richard was come Greatly did they urge and press him— nay, in their pressing they were right discourteous—until the king waxed wroth and bent his brows Then were such words spoken as should by no means be written down But to no purpose did they urge him, and they wasted all their words in vain For the king was sore pressed on his own account and had begun his dealing with the Greeks in such fashion that not for half the wealth of Russia would he concern himself with Syria ere Cyprus were made subject to him—that isle that yielded so rich provision—nor would he deign to give over his emprise until he should have taken it For this reason were these men come to urge him, who pressed him so greatly in the matter [41] But he set out with his assembled host, going straight to Nicosia Thither did every one fetch his own victuals and his fighting-gear, and the emperor watched them, lying hidden hard by The king himself had the rear ward, that they might not suffer any loss from the rear On a sudden, the emperor made a sally from his ambushment with full seven hundred of his meinie, whom cowardice had rendered impotent On came they, shooting their arrows at the vanguard, and these suffered them to draw near So came the emperor, harrying the host on its flanks, like a Turcopole,[42] until he was come to the rear ward, which King Richard was guarding, at whom, in a trice, he let fly two poisoned arrows Forth pricked the king from out the ranks, and it lacked but little that he had taken his vengeance of the graceless emperor But the emperor was mounted on Fauvel, who bare him away with the swiftness of the stag that fleeth amain, straight to his castle of Kantara,[43] all filled with dolour and with bitterness The king, when he saw that he could not take him, turned his course toward Nicosia But our folk had gotten them good steeds, and of the Grecians had they maimed or taken captive a many— of them that had ventured themselves too near the host After the king they held their way, nor had they longer any care or fear To Nicosia came they in the morning, nor did the townsfolk hold themselves back, but came to the king from

[41]The reading of the MS is very uncertain in this passage
[42]This term originally meant the son of a Turkish father by a Christian mother During the time of the crusades the Turcopoles formed a species of light cavalry, employed chiefly in harassing the enemy
[43]Candaire

every side and acknowledged him their lord, yea, they came to him as to their father Then the king bade them shave their beards, and when the emperor heard of this, then had he such grief and anger that he well-nigh went raving mad and evil entreated both his own people and ours—his own, when they came to yield themselves, and ours, when he could catch any of them And when he was able to take them, he caused their hands or their feet to be cut off, their eyes put out, or their noses lopped off, since he could not revenge himself in any other way But the king received the homage of the most valiant and the wisest, who were very fain to forsake the emperor whom they hated The host did the king cause to be divided and ordered in three parts, and to besiege three several castles, whereof two were lightly taken And one division went against Cherines,[44] whereof, in due time it gat possession 'Twas the king from over the sea[45] that gave this place to King Richard For ably did he lead the host and direct it thither, and nigh to the castle he bade them arm, then did he lay siege to it by land and by sea, and his own men assaulted it fiercely And the enemy gat no succour, so were they not able to hold out, but must needs come to terms Then did they yield the castle to King Guy, the valiant warrior, the emperor's daughter also did they give up to him, whereat the emperor was in so great distress that never more had he his right mind or sense, for all the comfort that could be given him King Guy caused King Richard's banners to be set up on the tower round about and guards to be established in the castle, then led he the host to Didemus [46]

XXI

HOW CASTLE DIDEMUS WAS TAKEN AND THE EMPEROR'S DAUGHTER MADE PRISONER, AND HOW THE EMPEROR CAME AND PUT HIMSELF AT KING RICHARD'S MERCY

Didemus is a strong castle, nor ever would it have been taken by force But they that the emperor had sent thither were so dumfounded at the tidings which they had heard that scarcely did they make resistance Howbeit, more than once they hurled down great stones at our men The castle need have had no fear of being taken, but the craven pack therein were sore afeared None the less, King Guy sat some days before the place after he had laid siege to it, ere the emperor caused it to be yielded up and those that were within it to come down from thence When these had yielded to the king, as I have heard tell, then King Guy took possession of the castle And he gave command that the young maid be right well guarded in the tower so that she could not be taken away secretly Then did he lead back his host, but he found great dearth in the land

But King Richard had been lying sick at Nicosia So soon as he felt himself somewhat recovered he laid siege to Bufevent, an exceeding strong castle Now listen to the strange tale of the recreant emperor whom his own sin destroyed Within Kantara did he shut himself up, yielding himself to grief and

[44]Possibly the modern Ghyrna
[45]Gui de Lusignan
[46]The modern Audino

shame But when he heard of the siege of Bufevent, then was he caught in a snare, knowing also that his daughter had been taken and put in the tower of another castle—she whom he loved more than any other living thing And this drave him to bring about a peace, whatever be the loss he might incur And an accursed loss in sooth was his—of all those castles that he had and the great riches that he forfeited through his own recreance But that which was his bane and his undoing was that all his people had forsaken him Howbeit, this thing must perforce be done, nor did he tarry longer Down from Kantara he came, and went for to give himself up to King Richard But ere he came he sent word to the king, beseeching him to have pity upon him, and saying that he would lay all at the king's mercy nor keep aught for himself—or land, or castle, or house—and asking that in honour and in reason the king grant him this one grace, that he put him not in irons or cast him into chains Nor did the king so, but, lest the people should murmur, he put him in shackles of silver Humbling himself before the king, the emperor came to cry him mercy on his knees And the king perceived that he did this in all sincerity, and he considered his losses and misfortunes, and how it was God who was guiding this thing, and that the emperor could work them no more mischief, then would he bring this good work to its conclusion So he made the emperor to rise upon his feet and sit down beside him, and he suffered him to see his daughter And when he saw her he was more exceeding glad than an he were holding God by the feet An hundred times he kissed her, weeping But why should I longer delay you with this tale? Within a fortnight (an I misspeak not), since God had taken the matter in hand, the king had made Cyprus his own so that it was in the possession of the Franks

XXII

HOW KING RICHARD SET OUT FOR ACRE, AND OF HIS MEETING WITH THE TURKISH SHIP

When the king had brought Cyprus under his sway in so propitious wise for the service of God, and the castles and the strong holds whence he had driven out the Greeks, he found their towers all stored with treasure and with all manner of riches, with silver pots and kettles, with golden cups and bowls, with spurs and bridles and saddles, with rich and precious stones possessing virtue against diseases, with scarlet and with silken stuff (such have I never seen in any other place where I have been), and with all other wealth that becometh men of high station All this did the King of England gain for the service of God, to be employed in His land To Limassol he sent the host, and besought his companions to speed his vessel and their own without losing a moment of time The emperor he gave to the warlike King Guy to guard, and his daughter, who was very fair and a young and tender maid, he caused to be sent to the queen to teach and to train Then straightway the host returned to the fleet and made themselves ready and took on their lading with all the speed they could On board the transport ships they went, making sail so soon as they saw that the weather was favourable The queens they took with them, and the dromonds that were there And the king left in that land certain men who were skilled in warfare, who sent after him all manner of victual—barley, wheat, sheep, and cattle—wherewith that land was well supplied, but which were very precious in Syria

Now were tidings brought to the king by sea, and it was told him that the city of Acre was at the point to be taken, and that taken it would be or ever he could arrive there "Never may such thing befall," he cried, "as that any should be able to take it without me!" Then would he no longer wait for aught, save that his companions come for to bear him company   [47] but I know not how many took part therein

At Famagusta he put to sea There had he bidden his galleys be armed, and on one of these did he embark—a fair vessel, marvelous large, strong, and swift At galleys so marvelous and at so warlike folk is there no port or harbour under heaven that would not be affrighted Lo, now are the galleys under way, which were all chosen craft, the king in the forefront, as ever his custom was, hale and light as a feather So swiftly as a stag would run, on he went across the sea Then he sighted Margat[48] on the coast of God's own land, and after Margat sighted he Tortosa,[49] which overlooketh the ever troublous sea, and on past Tripoli and Infré[50] and Batrûn he swiftly sailed, and after these he sighted Gibelet[51] and the tower high up in its castle

Off Sayette,[52] hard by Beirut, there came in sight of the king's ship another craft filled with Saladin's people It had been equipped by Saphadin,[53] who had manned it with the best Turks that he could find in all Heathendom At Acre they could not get to land, so had they done naught else but cruise about until they should be come to some more favourable place But this plan was a vain one The king urged and pushed on his galleys for to overtake them, and when he had come up with the other ship he saw that she was large, broad in the beam, and very powerful With three tall masts was she furnished, nor did she seem an hasty piece of work With green felt had the boorish folk covered her over on the one side, and on the other the clowns had draped her all with yellow, so now our men beheld the ship decked out as if she were some work of faerie, and so filled was she with stores of every sort that thereof was no tale or reckoning And one who knew thereof (for he had been at Beirut when the ship was laden there, that was thereafter so shamefully unladen) declared that he saw carried on board an hundred camel-loads of goodly arms and keen—darts, bows, crossbows with winches, racks, or levers—also, eight hundred Turks, all picked men, whom the devils drave, and so great supply of victual that thereof

---

[47]Lacuna of one line
[48]Now Markab
[49]Now Tartûs
[50]Probably the modern Enfeh
[51]Now Jebeil
[52]Sidon
[53]Saladin's brother

was neither count nor tally, and Greek fire in vials, whereof much hath been told Moreover, there were put in that ship two hundred serpents hideous and grey (so saith the written history and the word of him that helped to put them there), which they should let loose amongst our host for to do mischief to our folk

The galley drew so nigh to them that it almost touched them Our rowers hailed them, not knowing who they were, and asked them whence they came and what lord's men were they Now they had a French interpreter, and through him they told us that they were Genoese and bound for Tyre Then came a wind blowing from Arsûf,[54] which drave them away from the galley But one of our rowers had recognized the ship and them that were within it and who were very fain to withdraw themselves And this man said to the king "Sire, hearken to me, and have me slain or hanged an this ship be not a ship of the Turks!" Quoth the king "Art certain thereof?" "Yea, Sire, in sooth am I! Now send quickly another galley after them, nor suffer it to hail their people, then shall ye see what they will do and how worthy of credence they are" The king so commanded, they of the other galley went toward them, but hailed them not Then they, who had no business with them that were in the galley, began to shoot at them with bows of Damascus and with arbalests But the king was near at hand and his people were ready, who fiercely assailed the Turks when they saw them shooting at our folk The Turks defended themselves right well and shot their shafts and launched their bolts thicker than hailstones fly On both sides began the melley The ship was moving with but a light wind, and often our men came up with her, but they durst not board her, nor were they able to overpower her Then straightway the king sware an oath that he would hang the rowers if they slacked or if the Turks escaped them Then forth these sprang, like the wind, and plunging head and body beneath the wave and passing underneath the ship, up came they again upon the further side And with cords they made fast the rudders of the ship of that base folk and vile, for to confound and undo them and to slow the ship Then they clomb and gat themselves up until they could cast themselves into the vessel But the Turks, who were no left-handed men, rushed on them for to cut them down, and our men, who were skilled in such business, by force gat themselves upon the deck The Turks hewed off hands and feet and did them much hurt every moment, but they in the galleys pursued them even to the harbour Then they, who greatly feared death, recovering themselves began to resist stubbornly There went up on the deck, with ranks already formed, new troops, excellently armed in armour most ornate On both sides were they combatting, so that within the ship itself they fought, but the Saracens so exerted themselves that they drave out the people from the galleys These rallied in their galleys and began the assault anew, and the king bade them ram the ship until they foundered her Forth they leapt and rammed her so that they sprang her timbers in divers places, and by the shock was she sunk So ended the fighting The Saracens

---

[54]I e, from the south Arsûf is about one hundred miles south of Sayette (Sidon)

lost heart and sprang by tens into the sea, and each man slew so many of them as he could There might ye see King Richard dealing deadly blows and slaying many an one But he spared, I ween, some five and thirty of them, whom he bade keep alive—admirals[55] and enginers who were skilled in the use of divers engines But all the rest were drowned—Turks, and Persians, and Renegadoes But had that ship reached Acre, then never had the city been taken, such means of defense would the ship have carried thither Howbeit, this was forestalled by God, who is mindful of His own, and by the good, brave King of England, who was ever venturous in war

The Saracens had beheld this combat from the hilltop Word thereof sent they to Saladin, for they were full of dolour and of bitterness When Saladin heard thereof, for very grief he thrice tare his beard, then like a man distraught he cried "God! Now have I lost Acre, and my people whereof I was so confident! Too much ill fortune hast thou dealt to me!" In the host of the heathen (so did they tell us who saw this thing) such moan did they make that the Turks cut off the locks of their hair and rent their raiment, because in that ship had perished both their friends and their high lords

XXIII

HOW KING RICHARD CAME TO ACRE

When the king had taken this strong ship and overcome its people, then unto Acre was all his desire, and thitherward he held his course right willingly, his galleys all in order ranged, which had taken their vengeance of the enemy's ship And as he and his fleet were going on, God sent them a wind out of the north, and with lightsome hearts he and his people lay that night before Tyre The next morning he sighted Candalion[56]—he the valiant king, the Lion-heart—and Casal Imbert,[57] then saw he clearly Acre and the flower of all the peoples of the world encamped around about it And he saw the hills, the mountains, the valleys, and the plains all covered with tents and with pavilions, and with folk who with all their might were seeking to do hurt to Christendom, and they were there in exceeding great number He saw the tents of Saladin and of his brother Saphadin so nigh to our Christian host that the heathen's camp fair crowded our own And on the other side, Kaheddin, seneschal of the paynim folk, guarded the seacoast and the land along it, waging fierce warfare on our host, oft making violent attacks, fain following them in swift pursuits The king looked forth, and considered, and ever forecast his devices But when he was come nigh to the strand, then had ye seen all the baronry of the host following the King of France and coming to meet him with great eagerness And many other folk were gathered there to meet him

Forth came he to the land from out his galley Then had ye heard the trumpets sound, honouring Richard, the knight without peer! All the people

[55]Emirs
[56]Iskanderuneh
[57]Ez-zib (?)

with one accord rejoiced at his coming, but the Turks that were within Acre were filled with dread at his arriving, for well they wist that gone now was all their chance of sallying from the city and entering in again, whereby many of our people had been destroyed The two kings accompanied each the other, keeping ever side by side Then did King Richard go to his own tents, meditating much and devising in his mind how Acre might be overcome and how it might most speedily be taken

Great was the joyance, and the night was clear Nor do I think that ever any mother's son hath seen or could describe so great a rejoicing as was made in the host over the king There was heard the sound of timbrels, of trumpets, of horns and pipes and flutes Then might ye see joy unrestrained, of folk of divers sort—the singing of goodly songs and lays, cupbearers bearing wine through the streets in goodly cups, both to the great folk and to the lowly For this thing had made glad the host—that the king had taken Cyprus, whence so great provision was coming to them that the whole host could subsist thereon, and all were filled with good hope 'Twas a Saturday, at eventide, nor do I think that ever have ye seen, in any place where ye have been, so many tapers or so great illumination, so that to the Turks of the opposing host it seemed that the whole valley was on fire and burning And when they knew of the coming of the king in whose honour the feast was held, then they seemed to pluck up heart, for in the morning they filled all the valley, shouting at us and harrying us by the trenches, causing us great annoy and pressing hard the host—that folk so false and fell!

XXIV

OF WHAT BEFELL IN THE HOLY LAND BEFORE THE COMING OF KING RICHARD, HOW GUY OF LUSIGNAN BECAME KING OF JERUSALEM, AND OF THE TREACHERY OF THE COUNT OF TRIPOLI

Now will we leave off to follow this matter—for he who tarrieth long enough with me will of a surety hear me take it up again so soon as the theme itself shall suffer it—the matter of the two kings and of their coming, whereof I have so long spoken that I have brought them clean to Acre Now hearken, and keep well in mind that I desire here to break off my thread and interrupt my matter, but it will be well knit together anon and joined again and put into its place For the kings were the last who came to the siege—not the first So doth AMBROSE wish to do them to wit, and to make them to understand, who desire to learn the truth, in what manner the city of Acre was first besieged, for himself saw he nought thereof or knoweth, save that which he hath read Now shall ye hear what folk laid siege to it and how bold an emprise they undertook

Ye have heard me relate and tell (and it were well to tell it yet again) at the beginning of this history, an any yet call it to mind, the great loss and great affliction that openly befell in Syria This was in the days of King Guy, who suffered so great persecution, but not every one hath known that he was betrayed through jealousy

Beyond the sea there lived a king who was reared there and was called King Amaury To him was born a son, King Baldwin the Leper Baldwin lived out his term of life and was given over to the worms But he had as sisters two damozels, ladies wise and virtuous and fair The one was wedded to a baron whose name was Hainfroi du Toron, the other had been taken to wife by Count William Long-sword,[58] Seignior of Jaffa, where the sea ever beateth, and brother to the Marquis of Montferrat The lady bare him a male heir, who was in sooth likewise named Baldwin The child lived, but the count died, for fortune so decreed Guy of Lusignan desired the countess and married her The child Baldwin was king, but not for long, for so doth God direct His affairs After the child had perished, behold, the kingdom escheated to the lady his mother, as was just, and in just and lawful fashion was Guy crowned king, for which cause thereafter many a blow was struck

Between the false Count Raimond and Saladin, of whom I have much to tell, was an alliance of long standing, whereof was much talk throughout all Syria This Raimond thought to gain the kingship through his wealth and because he was Count of Tripoli Howbeit, thanks be to God, it became not his When King Guy, to whom God gave that honour, was to be crowned, he bade all his barons of the realm be present at his crowning The Count of Tripoli was bidden thither, but needless were it to ask if he made mock of the bidding and sent back a railing answer The messengers returned, and the count set out to go and make plaint to Saladin that he was not able to remain in his own land because of King Guy, who hated him and to whom the kingdom had escheated So much did he tell him and such lies did he devise that all Christendom was filled with indigna- tion   [59] He asked him, if he held him dear, to help him to revenge himself My Lords, at this meeting was that treason agreed to whereby the Holy Cross was lost and Christendom confounded The count was yet again bidden to court, and greatly did they press him in the matter, but he would not go thither or of King Guy hold aught in fee The king sent for him yet the third time, saying that he would render him his lawful due, and the count went, to our woe, for he was already assured of putting the land in sore distress, and through him came its great misfortunes But thereafter, because of this, he died a shameful death, even as the history telleth

XXV

OF THE BATTLE OF TIBERIAS HOW KING GUY WAS TAKEN CAPTIVE AND RELEASED, AND OF HIS FURTHER ADVENTURES

Often enough—full many a time—have ye heard men tell, and tell again, that when this Guy was newly made king he rested not two full months, but sent a summons and a call to his people throughout the land of Syria that they come to his aid, for Saladin was causing his men to ride freely over the countryside, and his army had invaded the land and discomfited the king's folk—an hundred knights, all chosen men—and slain Jaquelin of Mailli,[60] to the great grief of them

---

[58]*Guillames Longe Espee, Sire de Jaffphe*
[59]Lacuna of two or more lines
[60]Marshal of the Temple, killed 1 May, 1187

of the Temple And with this discomfiture began those misfortunes through which holy Christendom was so long left in orphanhood Then the Count of Tripoli, who was ever hanging the lip, sent word to the king that he would come to him and would render him aid, but afterward the people affirmed that this was a false agreement, and that he suddenly betrayed the king in the great battle where they both were and where so many good men died And it may well be that he did this, and it may well be that he did it not, but the more part declare firmly that he did betray the king in that battle And if he did this, then did he well deserve to be destroyed Saladin had mustered his men from all his nine kingdoms, with bows, hauberks, and helms, and they came in great numbers, nor weak nor strong remained behind There were many admirals of high repute and noble men of great renown, ready to leave their own land for to lay Christendom low

King Guy and his own Christian folk (and with them certain Venetians), men of high station and of low, had gathered in force, and the one host came to Seffurieh,[61] the other to the port of Tabarieh[62] And our men who went down to Tabarieh went thither to a good end, for they that there lost their bodies gave back their souls to God The Count of Tripoli was leading them, who was going about to betray them Nor were our people wary of him, he spake, and they obeyed And so much did he say and do that he brought it to pass that the enemy's host drave ours clean to the Sea of Galilee, and they had no water Now the water of this sea is sweet and good to drink, and the traitor made them to drink of it, but when came the moment to set their lances in rest, when he ought to have acquitted himself most valiantly, he fled away, but they remained and laid down their lives and their bodies I know not who smote or who was smitten, who escaped or who perished, for I was not present at that battle But this do I tell you of a surety that God had so ordered this thing, for He had perceived that there were so many sins in the world, so many persons steeped in wickedness, that very few of them had come to Him had not this thing befallen

Now it was at Mareschaucie,[63] which is hard by Tabarieh, that King Guy gave battle and laid so many Saracens low But already were all our men lost— slain and beheaded—nor was there longer any hope of rescue Against the king the foe came rushing on, so that he was stricken to the ground and sore mishandled and grievously bruised The Holy Cross had he embraced, and had he not held it thus in his arms it would have suffered outrage when they took it, but it was very evident that God was guarding it [64]

When the battle was ended which God had ordained in this wise—when the king had been taken, and the Cross taken, and almost all the people slain (because of which things so many other folk themselves took the cross and left behind so great possessions)—then did it please Saladin to cause all the land to be seized

---

[61]In Galilee
[62]The ancient Tiberias
[63]4 July, 1187
[64]"On a hillock hard by was raised the relic of the true cross, and this hillock was many times a rallying point during that bloody day" G W Cox, *The Crusades,* 106

—all save Tyre and Ascalon (so doth God both give and take away His land) and Jerusalem alone This city also did he quickly gain, and he went on to lay siege to Ascalon, thinking to take it lightly But the men of that place defended themselves against him fiercely and vigorously and unceasingly And there died many of the Saracen folk or ever he could get possession of the town, until at last he caused the king to be shewn to them and to be led before their walls And he hoped to have the city in exchange for the king, but the king sent word to them within the city that they should hold out nor do aught in his behalf Howbeit, they could hold out no longer and must needs come to terms They yielded up Ascalon in exchange for the king and departed thence, taking their chattels with them Then was King Guy set at liberty, with this condition—so saith the book —that he forsake his kingdom and go away beyond the sea So in sooth he put out to sea, for to keep his word, and went to the island of Tortosa Then were his people exceedingly sorrowful, but Saladin, who was a very wise Saracen, and knew that Guy was unlucky but was neither violent nor cruel, and who de- sired not to change him for some other king who would be dangerous to him— Saladin sent him word that he released him of his promise So the king straight- way went back to Tripoli beside the sea, and there found he the queen, and the count who had so hated him that (men said) he had betrayed him But now the count shewed him a fair face, whatsoever he were thinking behind it But what booteth it to prolong the tale of this traitor—of the wicked count who brought such dolour upon Christendom and many an orphan into orphanhood? Dear did he pay for his treason and for the evil that he wrought, for he died shamefully, thanks be to God, and suddenly [65] Nor doth it profit aught to tell of the siege that was laid to Tyre—which Saladin found bitter to his taste—where William of the Chapel wrought many a fair deed of prowess—where the Brethren of Tabarieh, who had the ward of the city, shewed themselves so loyal to God and to His kingdom Nor need I hold long discourse of the marquis,[66] who at the first began well, for he came after the land had been taken, and for a little while was he in God's service, but after so good a beginning ensued a false and evil ending

'Tis with King Guy that this matter dealeth, nor will I fail him or forsake him—King Guy, who was come forth of his captivity, and to this matter let us hold fast For to Tripoli had he returned, to the joy of both great folk and small Now Guy, though King of Jerusalem, was so poor and wretched as any man that is just come out of prison He took nothing that was not his due, nor had he aught in the world to take, but spend he must, perforce And he knew that Acre, which was the key to his land, had been taken and its people driven out and scat- tered, nor knew he to whom he might have recourse To our Lord God he told his trouble, and God brought him again to great prosperity One morning, when the bells were ringing, thither came the Prince of Antioch,[67] seeking King Guy for to pray him to consent to return with him to Antioch, and to set himself up

---

[65]Ambrose does not relate the time or circumstances of Raimond's death According to some authorities, he died of despair only fifteen days after the battle of Tiberias
[66]Of Montferrat
[67]Bohemond III

there, and to sojourn there until he had sought out and gathered and ordered sufficient men and until he knew where he might attack the Turks and recover something from them, whatsoever it be So the king went away with the prince to his province of Antioch, and there he abode for a short season, shedding many a tear for the land that had been his, which was lost under his reign Then back to Tripoli he came, and there he made his preparations and provisions, and so many men as he could raise with the moneys that he had been able to borrow he caused to be summoned and made ready, for he would delay no longer But whilst he was thus waiting and busying himself with the assembling of his people, lo, thither came his brother, Geoffrey of Lusignan, reputed to be the most valiant knight in his land, for he had been brought up and nurtured in war First had he landed at Tyre, but there found he none of his friends, for the marquis and they that were with him forbade him the harbour So Geoffrey straightway departed thence and came on to Tripoli There found he King Guy his brother, who had great joy of his mother's son

And when the king had assembled all his people, then were they ordered, and he came along the coast to Tyre, having with him but few men of his baronry And he found the gates of the city shut, which were all forbidden him, for the marquis, through covetousness and foolhardiness, had caused them to be closed against him Evil inspired in sooth was he when he forbade the king his own demesne The king, seeing that he would not be permitted to enter there, said that he would not endure this outrage So he caused his tent to be pitched on the sand and abode there with all confidence

Over against Tyre was the host assembled And well can ye tell what it cost the king to see that the city was forbidden him, but this was a thing devised aforehand by the false Marquis of Montferrat, son of the true and valiant Conrad[68] who was taken in the great battle Never, of a surety, would he have forbidden him the city, for he was a true man and loyal, but the son was disloyal The men of Tyre that loved God and that held to Him gat themselves out of the city right speedily and came to the king in the midst of his host These were the brave Germans, who held high room there that year, and the Brethren of Tabarieh, the most loyal folk of all Syria There, too, were the brave people of Pisa, who, entering God's service, had left behind their homes and their many possessions and brought their wives and children unto Acre, wherein the Saracens were

The king made great rejoicing over his brother, and the history, which trippeth not nor stumbleth, telleth that full four months he tarried there ere he went back to encamp in the sand hills nigh to Tyre, the city that was lawfully his own But when he had brought thither his men that he had assembled throughout the land, together with them of high estate who had come with his brother, he had but four hundred knights and but seven thousand foot wherewith to undertake the siege of Acre This, of a truth, no other man had dared to do, and it was a

---

[68]The father of the marquis who plays such a prominent part in Ambrose's story was not named Conrad, but was William III of Montferrat He was taken prisoner at the battle of Tiberias

wonder (save that God was protecting him) that he thought to go on and to combat folk that were as four hundred to his four But God desired to bring about that which did come to pass—the gathering of that mighty host which came afterward against Acre, which Saladin was striving with all his might to strengthen, for well he wist that those would come who would seek to recover it from him The king entered upon this emprise for the sake of the Lord God, in whom was his trust He led what force he had by a path which he himself knew Between Acre and Tyre is a difficult passage, which the host passed over quickly This is the Pass of Candalion, through which the host went with King Guy; but Saladin knew nought thereof For, an he had known it, not all the gold which is in Russia had kept him from cutting them all in pieces But God willed that it should be otherwise, and this was the beginning of Christendom's deliverance, which waxed mightily thereafter And, lo, the king's host is before Acre, in the name of the Holy Body consecrate, which we Christians adore And the king is gone up into Toron [69]

XXVI

HOW KING GUY LAID SIEGE TO ACRE, HOW SALADIN CAME TO THE AID OF THE CITY, AND OF THE SUFFERINGS OF THE HOST

On Toron, before Acre, were the Christians who had marched from Tyre, and be it known to you that they clomb up thither in the darkness of the night For they durst not remain in the wood below, so they went up to encamp on the hilltop In the morning, when the Turks came forth from the city and saw them, lo, Acre was all in an uproar and all her chivalry a-stirring And they sent word to Saladin that an handful of Christians had madly risen against them, and that he should come quickly and cut off every one of their heads, for they would not dare to defend themselves When Saladin heard this, who was besieging Beaufort [70] and assailing it right vigorously, then may ye know that he rejoiced greatly He caused his arriere-ban [71] to be sent forth and proclamation to be made throughout his lands that every man of his seigniory should come to the spoiling of Syria And far too many of them came—may God, who made heaven and earth, confound them! For an our host had been hewn into little pieces, they had not gotten even a pinch apiece! On the third day after the coming of our men, who kept themselves upon the top of Toron and remained all night under arms because of the Saracens that were assailing them, behold, there appeared the men of Saladin—Turks and Persians and Bedouins—coming to seize the towns and to take possession of all the land And on the third day of the week came Saladin himself, thinking in sooth to have the heads of our folk right soon Nor is it any marvel if they were perforce worn with watching and with toil and sorely troubled, who thought to lose their heads For the hill of Toron, wherein they

---

[69] An eminence near Acre The name "Toron" was originally a generic term, signifying "hill," and was given by the Franks to several different heights in the Holy Land

[70] A castle to the north of Markab (?)

[71] A summons to all free men and their vassals, usually for three months' service

were, was assaulted by the Turks both night and day, and so continually did these press our men that they scarce found the time to eat There had Geoffrey of Lusignan great travail of defending the host Aforetime had he been held both bold and valiant, but now was he extolled indeed

So were they in great peril from the Monday even until the Friday But now shall ye hear how God keepeth watch over them whom he is willing to take under his ward Whoso will learn to serve God, him can nothing harm For whilst the king and all his company were in such fear, they were looking out afar upon the high sea and beseeching God most earnestly to send them some kind of succour And, lo, on came in a straight course a fair fleet of transport ships, and in them folk hitherward bound It was James, of Avesnes in Flanders; nor do I think that ever Alexander, or Hector, or Achilles was a more valiant or a better knight than he It was James—who had sold all that he had and pledged and expended the price of his heritage and given (and very wisely did he so) heart and body and soul to the aid of that King who died and rose again Fourteen thousand armed men had he with him, men of renown And it was the fleet from Denmark, and many a brave castellan from the March[72] and from Cornwall was therein And one that knew hath said that these had goodly steeds, both brown and pied, strong and swift And when they drew nigh to land, then had ye seen how the Turks raged! Adown the shore they ran, so that they even cast themselves into the sea, and they that were within Acre did likewise, shooting their arrows thick and fast But our men that were on Toron came down and pressed them hard on both flanks, until the Turks charged in their turn and drave them back, shooting their shafts continually Nevertheless, they of the fleet gat themselves to land And Saladin, when he saw this host, cried "Now is our spoil increased!"

When that high King whom men adore had so enlarged the host in so short time, so that it was something encouraged which had else lasted but little longer . [73] they all plucked up heart together and down from Toron they came They set up their tents and built them lodges and laid siege to the city of Acre, so that they were themselves besieged and hard pressed from both sides There the Pisans wrought valiantly, who made their camp along the strand and guarded the shore against the cruel Saracen folk, so that when the ships came to shore these might not seize them or attack them On a Friday, early in the morning, there was a fierce engagement over against Mount Musart, and men were slain on either side For they of the city sallied forth and seized by force and brought back into the city a great caravan of camels laden with victual, and they carried to Saladin the booty that they had gathered there And they continued to go freely in and out of Acre, as folk that have the power so to do

The men that were inside Acre (mark this well) were not folk that had been taken from the cart or from the plough, nay, afterward was it well known that amongst all those that believe not in God there were no better men than they for to guard and to defend a city or to take a castle by storm Not yet was a fortnight

[72]Of Wales
[73]Lacuna of two lines

gone by, when there came thither the Count of Brienne,[74] and with him Andrew his brother, son of a good lady and a good lord The Seneschal of Flanders likewise came, and with him barons more than a score, and the Landgrave[75] from Germany, who brought goodly steeds of Spain And thither came the Bishop of Beauvais, who was neither old nor feeble, and his brother the Count Robert, a nimble and a dexterous knight Thither came also the Count of Bar,[76] none more courteous than he was found twixt here and Messina And many another worthy man and wise came to the host in this passage But 'twas a wonder that, the more of them there came, the less did the Saracens fear them For they gave them many a skirmish and came even to their tents And they of the city continued to sally forth, and the others were ever increasing, whereby the land was so overrun that the men of our host looked on themselves as prisoners None the less, they clave to the high King for whose sake they were come hither

Now the while this war was continuing before Acre, no priest, or deacon, or clerk could tell or describe the great hardships and the sore distress which the Christians endured there until the two kings came—he of France and he of England—who cast down the walls of Acre to the ground, with the good folk that accompanied them thither, who loved God and believed in Him

On a Friday (well do I remember that day, and 'twas in the month of September)[77] there befell our people a grievous misadventure—grievous and most dire The Saracens were continually assailing them, and never for one day did they slacken On this day the Christians armed themselves and drew themselves up in ranks, divided into divers companies that had been ordered The Hospital[78] was drawn up along the seashore, where were many of the Saracen folk, and the Temple[79] with them in the foremost rank, for theirs was always the beginning of the battle The Count of Brienne, with them of his household, who were ranged in the middle of the host—the Landgrave and the men of Germany, who were a great company—these were stationed near to the Mosque,[80] for well did they deserve this honour   [81] King Guy and the men of Pisa and other warriors of high emprise had their station upon Toron, on the right, for to watch the Turks On came the Saracens, with great noise There had ye seen many a goodly battalion The Templars and the Hospital charged and met the foremost ranks and discomfited and brake them The Turks fled and the knights pursued, and all our own men pursued likewise The Saracens were discomfited, but so great were their numbers that no Christian knew which way to turn The Turks durst not turn back, and already were they come nigh to the mountain, when the Devil devised a plot whereby many of our people perished They died, and were done to death, because of an horse that escaped from one of the Germans, who pur-

---

[74]Eraid II
[75]Lewis of Thuringia
[76]Henry I, of Bar-le-Duc
[77]4 October, 1289, according to other authorities
[78]The Knights of Saint John of Jerusalem
[79]The Poor Knights of the Temple
[80]*La Mahomerie,* a place outside Acre, where a mosque had once stood
[81]Lacuna

sued after it and bade his companions follow also But when they were not able to
overtake it, the horse fled away toward the city, and the Saracens—more than
an hundred thousand of them—thought that our men were fleeing and that they
had been utterly routed So they faced about, and charged them in their turn
And that day so hard were our men beset that they who were wont to guide the
host had enough to do to defend themselves, for the Turks were four and twenty to our one, striving to lay the Christians low And some with truncheons,
and some with maces, they left many of them dead upon the field There was slain
Andrew of Brienne—may God assoil his soul! For never died a better knight,
nor one who had brought succour to so many And there was the Marquis of
Montferrat so close pressed by the savage foe that, had King Guy not succoured
him, he had perished that day And in that selfsame hour was slain the Master
of the Temple—he that spake that brave word that he had learned in a good
school For when both craven folk and bold cried out to him, "Get thee hence,
Lord! Come!" (and he could have come had he been so minded), "May it please
not God," quoth he, "that ever I be in any other place than this, nor be the reproach brought against the Temple that any man hath beheld me fleeing!" Nor
fled he, but died there, for too many Turks assailed him And full five thousand
of the lesser folk died there, whose bodies remained naked on the field And
when they of the city knew that the Turks had discomfited our men, they
mounted their steeds of Araby and came forth and attacked our men so furiously that it would have gone hard with them, an they had not defended themselves
so valiantly, but our men stood fast, and there were deeds of prowess to be seen
and sore smiting of the hated folk There did the king himself fight well—that
Guy of whom we have told you—and Lord Geoffrey of Lusignan, who suffered
great hardship that day, and James of Avesnes, the brave knight, who wrought
so many valiant deeds in that land And their enemies gave way before them and
thronged back into the city

So passed that day, which Fortune had turned against us Now were the
Saracens so heartened (may God curse them, even as I curse them) that they
began to vex and to harry our Christians far worse than they had done aforetime,
and when the valiant men and the barons saw this, then they said "Sirs, we are
profiting us here not one whit Let us devise some helpful plan against this
devils' brood, which all day long tormenteth us and all night long is stealing our
horses" And this is the counsel and the plan that they devised they digged a
trench both long and deep and wide, and therein they set up many targes and
shields and pieces of timber So was the ground divided, nevertheless the Saracens continued to assail them nor gave them any rest

Now shall ye hear of a very great vexation which befell from the slaughter
whereof I have already spoken and because of which the Franks were so cast
down On the morrow, after this misadventure and after the discomfiture of the
very best of all our people, whereby our host had been thrown into such confusion, there remained many dead of the lesser folk who had come thither on
God's behalf The bodies of all these dead did Saladin cause to be taken up

and sent on to us, casting them into the river of Acre [82] Then had ye imagined a most hideous shambles, for the bodies came floating down the water until they reached the midst of the host, and from them issued so great a stench that all the host gat themselves thence until the bodies were buried, and even after they were buried, for a long time they must needs flee from the smell thereof

The Christians wrought at the ditch wherein they had intrenched themselves, and they remained within this trench whensoever the Saracens came thither, who made assault on them every day, were the weather cold or hot And the trench was the battleground of God's people and those dogs, for our men desired to complete it, and the foe strove to destroy it There, in one moment, might ye have seen   [83] more than five hundred thousand arrows which the diggers were ever putting into the hands of them that defended the trench And there had ye seen, on both sides, deeds of courage and of hardihood—seen men falling and weltering, all disboweled There were rude blows exchanged, nor did they draw apart until night came

From the first day of this siege, which the host had undertaken before Acre, even until Allhallow-tide (this I know, for I have heard it told of many), there ceased not to come folk who could well have a place there Then came the Count of Ferriéres,[84] who laid more than an hundred Turks in their biers, for so skillful a bowman was he that there was none better 'twixt here and Dons [85] Thither, also, came Guy of Dampierre, who possessed many a fair stone castle And thither, too, came the Bishop of Verona,[86] who was reputed to be a most worthy man All these came at that season, and martyrs and confessors they became, for I make bold to say that even he who was most at his ease there was constrained to suffer sore distress, both in fears and in watchings and in travail by night and by day, for no respite could they get, nor durst they rest at all until they had finished that trench which caused such woe

XXVII

OF THE COMING OF THE EGYPTIAN FLEET, OF THE TIDINGS OF THE EMPEROR'S DEATH, OF DIVERS FIGHTINGS ON LAND AND SEA, AND OF THE COMING OF CERTAIN BARONS OF FRANCE

On Allhallowe'en there befell the host a dire misadventure, and great indeed it was, and fell and grievous For whilst the Christians were enduring these miseries that ever so beset them, they that were on Toron were looking toward the coast of Caiphas [87] And they saw approaching a great fleet of armed galleys that were coming from Babylon,[88] which had so long time given succour to Acre The fleet came on in good order, and swiftly—in the twinkling of an eye—the tidings went through all the host that it was approaching in battle array And

[82]The Nahr Namein, anciently the Belus
[83]There is evidently a lacuna here
[84]William
[85]This place has not been identified
[86]Adelardo Cattaneo, Bishop of Verona 1188-1214
[87]South of Acre, across the bay
[88]Cairo

some thought (albeit no man in the host knew aught of the matter) that it was
a fleet from Pisa, or from Genoa, or Venice, or Marseilles, or Sicily, that was
come to attack the city In the mean time, whilst they were thus conjecturing,
the galleys were ever drawing nearer, until they were so close at hand that they
passed on inside the very harbour of Acre And as they entered in they seized
one of our transport ships, whereon were men and provisions, and this ship
they led on in their own line inside the city, then they slew our men and
took the provisions

Now hear what the Turks did to God, and how they dishonoured Him On
the day of that honourable feast—the day of the feast of all the saints that God
hath gathered to Heaven—that hated folk, for to defy us, hanged from Acre's
walls the bodies of those Christians whom they had taken in the transport ship
and had afterward slain But these justly became partakers (well may the preach-
ers tell us so) of that great and everlasting joy that shall be without end, eternal
—the joy of them whose feast was held upon that day

The fleet whereof I spake so guarded the harbour and the way by which
God's people were coming that they all shunned the port, so that no more succour came to them that were maintaining God's cause there The winter season
was drawing nigh, nor was it possible for them to make any store of victuals
Their trench had they finished, but in spite of them it was filled up again That
winter they builded siege towers and made petraries, mangonels, sows, and
clayes,[89] whereat they toiled continually And the enemy also strengthened the
city, with more than thirty thousand workmen, building gates, and turrets,
and strong new barbicans, and reinforced it so on every side that they were
ready to defy the whole world And Saladin, who had no mind to give the
city up, caused to be set up therein so many mangonels and petraries and engines
of every sort, and established there so many cunning enginers—both men
from his own lands and those from other countries—and sent such store of
Greek fire in vials, and so much artillery of other kinds, that it became known
thereafter of a certainty that never before, in castle or in city, had been gathered
so many weapons of defence, or so great store of victual at such cost Thus did
they pass that winter until the sweet springtime came And then, in that Lenten
season (as AMBROSE saith and declareth), the Germans made the first windmill
that ever was builded in Syria, in the sight of that folk accurst of God, who
looked upon it with astonishment and were sore afeared

Now to the host came tidings which at the first were good and welcome, but
thereafter were grievous, terrible, dolorous, and bitter These were tidings concerning the good Emperor of Germany, who had come with a great force to seek
God's grace at the Holy Sepulchre, who died (and a grievous loss was that) in
the passage of a certain river at a ford which he had not first sounded, such was

[89]The mangonel, like the petrary (see note, page 29), was a ballistic engine The
"cat" is described by a mediaeval Latin historian as "a certain device employed in scaling
walls, it is named 'cat' because, creeping up in catlike wise, it clingeth fast to the wall that
is to be seized" The "sow" consisted of a movable roof which protected the men handling
a battering-ram The claye, also, was a protective device, made of stakes interwoven with
osiers—a sort of large hurdle or group of hurdles

God's will Within Acre, such joy had they of these tidings when they heard them that they leaped about and beat upon their timbrels, nor gave they heed to aught else, but gat themselves up into their turrets for to tell the news to our people, whereof Saladin was well informed And he had sent them word to do this So cried they with a loud voice from the top of their walls many a time and oft, and bade the Renegadoes say "Your emperor is drowned!" Then was there in the host such sorrow, such heaviness of heart, and such distress, that they cared for nought else—save only for that company which was on its way, and the hope and promise that was spread through all the host of the coming of those mighty men, the two kings to whose realms we belong, him of France and him of England These came at last unto that land, then was the host heartened again

And now was news brought, but a little after Eastertide, that the fleet was coming from Tyre, and, lo, already is it in the haven! Then might ye think of ants pouring forth from an ant-hill, before and behind, for even so forth rushed the Turks that were within the city, more than ten thousand armed men, all bedight—both themselves and their galleys—with silken stuff and tapestries, with baccaran and samite Forth went they all to meet the fleet, which was approaching swiftly with the north wind, cleaving the waters as it came adown the coast And the enemy in their fleet were watching these ships that they had come to combat and to overwhelm, and the Christian fleet was likewise watching them that were so boldly coming to meet it

It was the marquis, who held Tyre, who was coming in the fleet against the Turks, with fifty vessels, armed, and well covered and equipped Then had ye seen so many banners, so many valiant men of every station, bold, nimble and ready Then the Turks discharged their arbalests, and this was the beginning of the battle of the fleets There was no cowardice seen The Genoese and the men of Pisa were attacked in their barges by Turks armed with targes and with arbalests But they rowed alongside our people and discharged such flights of bolts and darts that they drave back the Turkish fleet and brought off one of the enemy's galleys into the harbour Then had ye heard great jubilation, then had ye seen women coming, holding knives in their hands, seizing the Turks by their locks and pulling these to the great distress of the capitves Then they cut off their heads and carried them to land On the fleet was continual shouting Many a time was each fleet driven back, and many a time were they dashed together, to and back they cast the Greek fire, kindling and slaking the flames, and so often as they joined together they dealt each to the other most grievous blows, and they fought their way clean to the harbour Never was such battle seen or witnessed of any man, but our folk paid the dearer price—they of the host of God who were carrying on the siege For by their grief over the loss of the galley that our men had carried away were the Turks so moved that every day their numbers waxed greater, and they made a fierce assault upon the trench the while the defenders thereof were watching the battle on the sea Nor was there a Christian in the host, high or lowly, young or old, so bold or so confident that he was not hard put to it with the Turks For they came on, unceasingly, like flies, each

striving to be the first to cast in his fagot for to fill up and to destroy the trench
There had ye seen all the plain, clean to the foot of the mountain, like a shorn
field covered with its stubble, teeming with Turks that rushed on to the assault
without ever a stay or respite, and cast themselves so thick into the trench that
they overthrew one another An hideous, swarthy folk were they, opposed to
God and to nature Never hath God made creatures more ugly or so cruel-minded
And what with those tossing waves of men, what with their headgear that all
crimson shone, they seemed a cherry orchard full of ripened fruit And of other
Turks were there so many that they might be reckoned at five hundred thousand
And yet other Turks from within the city came forth with banners flying and
harried the Christians on the other side And the host was so harassed on that
day and on many another that the Christians began to lose heart before these assaults, which were ever renewed

Now they of the red headgear had an ensign around which they all rallied
This was the ensign of Mahomet, who was portrayed thereon and in whose name
they were come forth to battle, for to overthrow Christendom These rogues defended themselves with great stones which they brought with them This was
the manner of warfare that engaged the Christians on the land On the sea, the
battle endured all that day Howbeit, thanks be to God, our fleet had the victory
at the last For day by day had been established in the galleys divers divisions of
the warriors of the host, most valiant men and well armed, which fought each in
its turn right vigorously and by main force drave the galleys of the Turks clean
back to the chain,[90] so that the Christian fleet wrought great mischief to the
Turks within the city, who then were forty thousand in number and could get no
succour by way of the sea, neither were they able to go forth on the side toward
the land, and thereafter had they so few victuals that they suffered grievously
from the dearth thereof On a Thursday, which was Ascension day, the day of
holy processions, the day on which God mounted up to Heaven as the Gospel
teacheth us, our people desired to mount up on the walls of Acre in the name of
the true Body consecrate Siege towers we had, well covered against the Greek
fire of those miscreants, and three of these were of great size, builded by three
of our great men—the Landgrave, King Guy, and the marquis with his Genoese
These three were inside their towers on that day when the assault was made And
the Lord God's people began the assault, and they that were within the city came
out upon the walls Fierce was the assault, and the defense was fierce, for men
that had so little sustenance Yea, they defended themselves vigorously and made
us to pay dear for their sufferings Never were any men such defenders as were
these limbs of the Devil Some were beating drums, others were hastening where
there was need of them And the Turks over against the mountain came running
in great companies toward the trenches, so that they were already leaping into
them so soon as our men had begun the assault, so must our men perforce attack
and defend at the same time For a long time did the assault endure, even until
the beginning of the evening But at eventide must it needs cease, for never were

---

[90] I e, the chain by which the harbour entrance was closed

our men able to force back the defenders, and the Turks cast Greek fire into the three towers, which they set on fire, so that they that were within them were constrained to descend and to watch them all burn to ashes

Those infidel dogs inside Acre had been for a long time very scant of victuals, and as the days passed their provisions wasted away So were they then brought to so disordered and miserable a pass that they ate up all their beasts—hoofs and chitterlings, necks and heads And they drave out the Christians that they had been holding—feeble folk and aged—but the young and those of lively mien they kept to drag and to drudge at their petraries And so great privations did they suffer that these cannot be told, nor their other pains and miseries and hardships—until after the feast of Saint John, when the devils sent them three ships, which foundered there And a part of the Turks who were in the ships perished, but the provision they recovered And when they had gotten these victuals, then were the dogs encouraged and ofttimes made sallies against us, whereby our people were sorely straitened

Now to this host, devoted to God's service, came a most dismal day It was the day of the feast of the holy Saint James, yet the Devil, who never resteth, openly wrought a work whereby the host was much diminished Nay, the Devil wrought it not—I erred—but God permitted it to be done, who desired to gather yet more martyrs and to receive them into His kingdom on high The best company of foot-soldiery—the best of them that were and of them that are now living—poor folk and destitute, went out from the camp of God's host without sufficient defense And it was their own misease which constrained them to do this, for little comfort hath any man in a camp At ten thousand souls were they reckoned, and they were all armed Forth went they, close drawn up in ranks and in battalions, straight toward the tents of the Turks, for there was the goal that they had set for themselves When the Turks saw them thitherward bent they durst not await them, so these came to the camp and loaded themselves with all the best things that they could find there But when the Turks beheld them thus burdened and hampered, then had they light work with them, for they hurled themselves so suddenly upon these footmen that they left there full seven thousand of them slain For no succour did these get, save of certain knights who hastened thither, but no great number of them came, and the footmen died right speedily And there was slain Torel of Mesnil, howbeit, he had first performed deeds of great prowess And there was great lamentation made for him that day This evil befell the host, and many another also

Many an assault and many an affront did the host of God endure of this hated folk And many a misadventure dire and fell did God in His pity suffer to befall, for He wished to put His people to the proof, even as we know that He did with the saints, whom He tried with many an hardship, even as gold is tried in the furnace Yea, much had they already suffered then, who had offered themselves to God

XXVIII

OF DIVERS ADVENTURES WHICH BEFELL IN AND ABOUT ACRE

And whilst they were in the midst of such sufferings, lo, about the month of August came the baronry of France, for that is the best time for the passage, before the coming of winter Thither came the Lord of Champagne, Count Henry, with a great company And thither came Count Thibaut of Blois, but he lived only three months thereafter Likewise Count Stephen[91] came, and shortly died And thither came the brave Count of Clermont,[92] who was pleasing to God and to the world There came also the Count of Châlons,[93] who was a strong man and tall and stately And there came so many other worthy men that no man knoweth the count or the number of them

Before Acre, what time these brave and honourable folk were sojourning there for their souls' salvation and for the pure love of God, there befell many an adventure the tale of which hath been put down in writing, and many a miracle was wrought there by the power of God In the host were many petraries, before and behind which folk were ever passing to and fro, and many things befell there which were held to be miracles at the time of their happening And in the city were likewise many petraries (so, in sooth, saith the history) which discharged so marvelously that none hath ever seen their like And one of them there was so powerful that it wrought us exceeding much mischief, ever dashing in pieces our own petraries and our clayes For it cast stones so great (and flying as they had had wings) that it needed two men to put them in the sling (according to the book), and when the sling had hurled the stone, and it came down to earth, after its fall it must needs be sought a foot beneath the ground Now this same petrary struck a certain man in the middle of his back, and had the man been a tree or a marble pillar, it had broken him in twain, so squarely did it hit him But the good man felt it not at all, for God willed not that he should In such a Lord ought men to believe, for such a miracle maketh them to believe

Thus, as the seasons passed, divers things befell As April was giving place to May, there happened a strange adventure in the host—that of a serjeant who was standing in the trench, armed with coif and hauberk and pourpoint richly embroidered[94] One of the enemies of God was holding an arbalest with its crane-quin[95] And he shot at the serjeant through a loophole and struck him in the breast, beneath his face The bolt missed the coif, but pierced the pourpoint, passing clean through the hauberk But the serjeant bare at his neck a writing, which (thanks be to God) preserved him from all harm, for the holy names of God were written thereon And it was perceived by them that were there, that when the bolt touched him it glanced and bounded off For so doth God deal with

[91]Of Sancerre
[92]Ralph (Raoul), Count of Clermont in Beauvaisis
[93]William II
[94]The coif was a kind of skullcap, the pourpoint a quilted doublet, both were worn under the mail
[95]A moulinet, or wheel and ratchet, used in bending the stiff bow of the arbalest

them that He hath taken into His own keeping that they need have no fear of any thing

And as the days went by, divers other things befell It chanced one day that a certain knight was outside the trench, having his back turned toward it, and attending to a certain business that no man can avoid And as he was bowed down for to ease himself, one of the Turks that were at the outpost, to whom he was giving no heed, withdrew himself from the others and pricked toward the knight Now it was a churlish and a most unseemly thing for him to seek to do the knight a mischief whilst he was thus busied But already had he left the outpost far behind and was coming, lance in rest, toward the knight for to slay him, when they of the host began to cry "Flee, lord! Flee! Flee!" With difficulty did he raise himself, howbeit, he stood upon his feet, nor did he finish his business The Turk came on so fast as his horse could bear him, thinking surely to stretch the knight on the ground But (thanks be to God!) he failed of his purpose For the knight sprang to one side and took up two stones in his hands (now hear how good an avenger is God), and when the Turk had turned his horse about again for to fulfill his fell intent, the knight leveled his aim at him, and whilst the Turk was yet coming he hit him with one of the stones that he held, underneath his turban and right upon the temple, even as he had aimed And at an instant the Turk fell dead The knight took the horse and led it away by the bridle And he that told me these things saw how the knight mounted the horse and rode away even to his own tent, where he had it well kept and guarded

And yet again, as time went by, did divers things befall Many folk were attacking the walls, but ofttimes they grew aweary of the assault Howbeit, some there were who never ceased from gathering stones [for to fill the trenches] and bringing them thither The barons, also, were bringing them thither on their war-horses and sumpter beasts And many a woman was bringing them, rejoicing in the task Amongst the rest was one woman who had great joy in bringing them, and a certain Saracen, one of the defenders of the city, saw this woman in act to discharge her burden from her neck And as she came forward, he shot an arrow at her and it hit her, and the woman fell, wounded to the death And all the people came a-running and stood round about her as she lay writhing in her dying throes Her husband came seeking her, but she besought the good people there, brave men and brave women, that, for the sake of God and for their own souls' sake, they make of her body a fagot to fill the trench to which she had brought the stones, for she desired not that her dead body ever be put to any other use And she was having it borne thither when God bare away her soul Such a woman, saith the history, should every one keep in remembrance

· Thus, as the season passed, did divers things befall Yet another adventure befell in the host—out of a score, and even more, of others, but never could I recall them all or number them One day, forth from Acre sallied the Turks, against our people whom they saw going out to forage, as the use is amongst men of war And with them forth came an admiral, a great man and of high lineage —Bellegemin was he called—a valiant man and bold and of great renown And

the barons who guarded the host went to meet the Saracens But that day was
the host thrown into great confusion, for they were not enough that guarded it
For so many folk were gone forth after forage that they had put the host in
great danger, both in the front and in the rear Right fierce was the assault, but
our folk drave them back   [96] all save the admiral, who stood his ground stubbornly, for he sought to burn our engines, could he but get himself near enough
to them, on this had he set his heart A vial bare he in his hand, which was filled
with Greek fire—to burn those engines did he yearn with exceeding pain! But a
certain knight, desirous to pay him for his pains, came up and smote him, the
Turk he stretched upon the ground and he emptied the vial on his secret parts
so that these members were burned with the Greek fire, which his men sought to
quench but could not

And as the days went by, did divers things befall And more than once it
came to pass that those false and mistaught folk who were holding Acre against
God came up on the top of their walls, bringing from the churches the crosses
that had been left there And these they beat and insulted, and they spat upon
them and struck them in the despite of the Christian faith, for nought else on
earth do they so hate One day, when a Turk was standing upon the wall and
beating a wooden cross that he had found, and when he had a long time thus
beaten and insulted it, he was not willing to leave the matter there, but sought to
defile the cross But a certain courteous arbalester bent his bow and set the bolt
to the string, desiring that the Turk who was insulting the cross should be made
to pay according to his deserts Then he aimed, and he hit the Saracen in the
midst of his belly, piercing body and bowels, so that he fell dead, feet in air,
whereat their people were exceeding wroth And thus did God will that the cross
should be avenged which the man had so dishonoured

Then, as the season passed, did divers things befall One day there befell an
adventure which AMBROSE recounteth in his writing A certain Turk came out
for to shoot at our men, nor would he withdraw himself from them And a certain Welshman, defying him, went forth in his turn to shoot The Welshman was
called Marcaduc, nor was he a king's son or a duke's, and the Turk was named
Grair, a bold man and stout and very powerful Forthwith they let fly the one at
the other, the Welshman at the Turk and the Turk at the Welshman And the Turk
began to enquire whence the Welshman came, and of what land he was Then
quoth the Welshman "Of Wales am I, and thou art a fool to have come down
hither" Said the Turk to him "Well knowest thou how to shoot, wilt venture
an even chance with me? Let me shoot, and do thou wait for me, nor bend thyself aside at all And if I miss, then shalt thou shoot, and I will wait for thee,
nor bend at all aside" And so did he press and pray him that the Welshman consented unto him The Turk shot at the Welshman, but he hit him not, for he
drew his bow amiss and the arrow was not discharged Then said the Welshman
"Now will I shoot Wait for me" But the other answered "That will I not! Let
me shoot yet once more, and I will let thee shoot twice at me, nor myself shoot

---

[96]Lacuna of one line

again " "So be it," quoth the Welshman But whilst the Turk was seeking a good arrow in his quiver, the Welshman, who was standing nigh at hand and whom the bargain liked but little, loosed his own shaft and pierced him through the heart Then said he "Thine own word didst thou not keep, nor do I keep my word with thee, by Saint Denis !"

XXIX

OF THE FLOATING TOWER THAT THE PISANS MADE, OF THE ARCHBISHOP'S BATTER-ING-RAM, OF THE DEATH OF THE QUEEN OF JERUSALEM, OF THE COMING OF ANOTHER FLEET FROM EGYPT, AND OF DIVERS COMBATS BETWIXT THE PILGRIMS AND THE INFIDELS

Now the Pisans who were in the host, and other folk that were well acquainted with the sea, builded a tower mounted upon galleys, and two ladders long and broad, and all the vessels did they cover with hides, and the same did they to the tower And they laid siege to the Tower of Flies[97] and shot and cast into it many arrows and other missiles They that were within the tower defended themselves well, selling their lives right dear, and forth from the city came in their galleys more than two thousand Saracens ready for battle, for to help the other pack And these discharged at our men arrows and bolts and cast great stones at them—great and exceeding heavy—and keen darts, and they brake both lances and shields And when our men that were in their own tower began the assault, then did the others defend themselves right well There had ye seen our men drawing their bows and sending many a good shaft over the walls, and arrows raining down, and the Turks constrained to hide themselves There had ye seen brave bands of valiant men making their assaults, one company after another The ladders were raised against the walls and made fast, with great travail and great loss, for ever did the foe cast down great beams of wood on the heads of the Christians, as they were setting up the ladders, yet did these never quail But the Turks were ever coming back in greater number, until at last they set on fire the tower of the Christians, and down came they that were therein Here the foe hurled their blazing Greek fire about, combating most fiercely, but on the sea there was a great slaughter of Saracens So was the tower speedily consumed, and the ladders likewise and the vessels that bare them, whereby the Turks were greatly comforted again And seeing our reverses, the hated folk cried with a loud voice and howled at the host that was aiding God

By this loss was the host of the Lord God sore disheartened, but it was heartened again by the coming of that great company of barons that had arrived in Syria The Archbishop of Beauvais (with him let us begin) caused a battering-ram to be made before Acre for to break in pieces and to rase the walls thereof It was builded at a very great cost, well bound with iron, and very closely covered above and below, before and behind, so that it need not fear a petrary, for only the best of that which is used in building such engines would the archbishop put into it Another ram did Count Henry build, well covered and of very great

---

[97]This tower was built on a rock in the middle of the harbour of Acre

price. And the high barons and counts made many engines, the number of which I know not But as for that one whereof we have told you, which first the archbishop made, we will now tell you what befell it before the walls when it came thither

The barons of the host devised the manner of this assault and considered aforehand how they would employ the engines that they had made Every one of them caused his own engine to be drawn up to the walls, and the archbishop had the ram brought up whereof I spake before, which was of so costly structure that by right and in reason it ought not to have had dread of any living thing For it was builded, as it were, inside an house, and a great mast, straight and without knots, stood in the midst of this, bound with iron at both ends And underneath the ram were they whose task it was to dash it against the walls, who had no fear of any danger But the Turks, who loved our people not one whit, brought thither much dry wood, and flung much Greek fire upon it, and with their petraries hurled against it whole pillars of heavy freestone or of marble, and they cast upon it beams and trees, and threw thereon in butts, in buckets, in bottles, and in urns sulphur and tar and pitch and tallow, and after that again great logs of wood, and the Greek fire upon the top of all—these did Mahomet's people heap thereon, until the miners fled from underneath the ram and abandoned it Now the Turks, who were continually casting these things at the ram, were discovering themselves upon the walls Then had ye seen the archers shooting, and arbalests discharging many a goodly bolt Then had ye seen violent attacks and many folk wounded on either side Then had ye seen good vassals running for to defend and to rescue the ram and to overthrow the burning heap, and hurling down from the ramparts and laying low Turks with fair painted bucklers But the enemy yet hurled and shot their missiles until they crushed the ram and brake its iron roof and all its other furnishings And yet again they hurled the fire upon it until they left it utterly consumed But dearly paid they for the ram, for there they lost fourscore of their best men, likewise an admiral But great loss did they also cause to our men in their turn And when the burning ram could not be quenched or removed, then did the assault cease But the Saracens began to hoot at us

Immediately after the end of August the Queen of Jerusalem died, in the host, which was a great misfortune, for she was not an aged woman A worthy lady was she esteemed, so may God shew mercy to her soul! Likewise died the young daughters of King Guy, two maids most fair, and through the death of these his children, who were the rightful heirs to the land, did the king thereafter lose that kingdom in whose defense he had received so many blows upon the helm

In October—after September and towards the calends of November—there came from Alexandria yet another fleet, with great pomp and pride At fifteen sail were they reckoned by them of the host who afterwards counted them These vessels were coming to the succour of the Turks who were inside Acre, who had endured many great privations and long watchings And following after this fleet came three dromonds of exceeding great size, and our seamen with their galleys were watching against their coming And when they that were in the Turkish vessels espied our people they were afeared and sore troubled, nor was there one of them so brave or so masterful that he did not wish most earnestly that he were elsewhere Now it was evening, and very dark, and the wind blew so vehemently that the Christian fleet durst not attack the heathen, for so violently did the tempest toss that every one was hard put to it to look to himself But as the Saracen fleet came sailing on most swiftly for to rescue the other heathen folk (and well-nigh running foul of the harbour chain as they came), then were they put to sore shame which they could not avoid, and they foundered their vessels For on the rocks inside the harbour of Acre God caused their ships to founder And all the host cast stones upon them, and the ships were broken in pieces and the most of the people drowned Then came the Christians down to the shore, shouting and slaying the dogs, and they took a great galley which by force had reached the shore, wherein was great store of victual taken, but all the heathen pack therein were killed But the other vessels passed through the chain and into the harbour, where the Turks were bravely awaiting them These stretched out lances and spears to them and lighted so many lanthorns that the Saracens were able to get themselves to land And of these Saracens that were now come did they make an exchange, putting out of the city all them that were unfit for fighting, and keeping these who could render service

At the great feast of Saint Martin,[98] when there was already sore dearth of victual, the host was bidden assemble on the morrow, in the name of Holy Mary's Son, for to go forth toward the mountains and combat the Turks Then were benisons said and general absolution given The Archbishop of Canterbury shrived them, together with other bishops Then were chosen and appointed barons and warriors who should guard the host And, lo, in the morning all the host was mounted, and there was numbered full many a battalion— the fairest Christian folk that ever earthly man had seen—so strait drawn up in serried ranks as they had been men chained together Broad and wide was the forefront of the host and well able to withstand fierce onsets And the rear ward was so filled with good knights that scarce could a man see the last thereof, unless he went and sat upon an hilltop Ye had not been able to toss a plum but it had lighted on folk clad in burnished steel Then away they marched, straight toward the Dok,[99] and, or ever ye had had the time to roast a cock, Saladin knew of a surety that he would have battle, if he were willing to wait the coming of the Christians But that night he bade his host break camp and left the mountain in which he had encamped with all his company Then to our host came a spy, who told them that the hated folk had abandoned the mountain and were departing thence, fleeing in great disorder Almost had our people pursued after them, but great folly had it been to follow them, for they could not have overtaken them So, finding no occasion of battle, they bent their

[98]11 November
[99]Tell Daûk, a hill near the Nahr Namein

course direct toward Caiphas,[100] where was said to be some store of victual, whereof there had ofttimes been sore lack during the siege So were they come to Recordane[101], and, quicker than the goshawk that chaseth a duck, came the Turks for to harass them They saw the Turks returning, pricking on to attack the host, beating their drums and shouting and howling That night the pilgrims encamped there, even until the morrow morn when day brake And yet had they fain held their course toward Caiphas, but the victual was no longer there whereof it had been told them, for the Turks had carried it all away when they departed that morning And now as they looked about them they beheld (so it seemed unto them) all the Turks in the world compassing their camp round about And the earth was so covered with them, up and down, on the right hand and on the left, that our host had very fain been otherwhere Never was seen such gathering of men But at an instant was our host all armed and arrayed in order of battle But the Saracens, those coward dogs, durst not attack them or combat so brave a folk So the pilgrims turned them about for to go back to the place whence they had come out, but many a great annoy had they or ever they reached their tents again

At the head of the river that runneth toward Acre, there where it riseth, was there great slaughter of knights on both sides ere the two hosts drew apart In that day's march the King of England's men, with the Temple, made the rear ward, and cause a-plenty had they to keep ward that day, for never hath God made snow, or sleet, or May shower when the drops come down, that falleth thicker or faster than fell the darts upon the host continually until our folk gat themselves thence But all in good order they withdrew themselves and turned back toward Acre Now our own host were keeping them to the left bank of the river, and the other host to the right, along the two sides of the river they marched and were ever harassing each the other And unto our people came other folk who gave them succour, and the serjeants that were keeping ward on foot with our rear ward, who kept behind the host, went ever with their faces turned toward the Turks, and these had much to suffer ere the host was come into safety

Very early in the morning, when the day began to break, our people had set forth to return to the siege of Acre But the Turks had laid an ambush by the bridge of the Dok, whither they themselves were already come and where the Christians must pass over And they were making ready to break down the bridge, when our host came upon them and attacked them But the Turks had so fully occupied the bridge that the pilgrims knew not by what way they could pass over, so many of the enemy did they see thronging the place Then forth pricked Geoffrey of Lusignan on his warhorse, which was all fresh, and five good knights pricked forth with him then and there, and they smote the Turks so fiercely that more than thirty of them fell into the stream, where they were drowned in the sight of the rest of the enemy folk Yea, so sore did they smite them that they all by main force passed over the bridge, and our men went back to the siege again, whereof the rest of the host were exceeding glad

---

[100]The modern Haifa, some fifteen miles south of Acre
[101]Tell et Khirbet-Kurdaneh

XXX

OF THE DEARTH THAT WAS IN THE HOST, HOW THE MARQUIS TOOK TO WIFE THE SISTER OF THE QUEEN OF JERUSALEM, ALBEIT HE HAD TWO WIVES ALREADY, AND HOW THE BUTLER OF SENLIS WAS CARRIED AWAY

Now the season of passage was well-nigh over for that year and there were but few coming—or wise men or simple—for they had let the season of the passage go by. Howbeit, there were some few that came. But as the number of our people waxed greater, their provision of victual decreased, and it grew ever less as the days passed by, nor had they any new supply save when some vessel came. The rich folk had some store of food, but the poor folk had none, who every day complained because of the dearth that so oppressed them, and some had fain departed because of their misease and sufferings.

Now the supply of victual was detained at Tyre when they came, for the marquis caused it to be held there so that it might not reach the host. And now shall ye hear yet more concerning this false marquis, how he had sought and endeavoured to bring it to pass, through the chief men and by means of his own wealth, that he himself should obtain the kingdom. And he so devised and contrived and wrought with his wiles that a sister of the queen who had but lately died, the wife of Hainfroi du Toron,[102] an high baron, was separated from this Hainfroi, and that he took her himself to wife, promising that he would bring his own battalion to the host without fail. So he wedded her in his own house, in despite of God and against all reason. Much did the Archbishop of Canterbury murmur at this, but the Bishop of Beauvais married her to him. And he did great wrong in consenting to do this, for the marquis had already wedded two ladies, both young and fair. The one of them was now at Constantinople—a woman fair and gentle and noble. The second was now in her own country. And now had he gotten him a third one. And because of this, the good archbishop and others, clerks and bishops, gainsaid this marriage and excommunicated him and said (as those that durst say it) that he had committed a threefold adultery and that God was not present at such a wedding or such a union.

When the marquis had wedded her whom he had so long time coveted, then did he celebrate his bridal and make a wedding feast. Three wives had he now, all living: one in his own land, another with the host, and a third yet in store. Evil must needs come of such a marriage, and come it did that day, and great loss also. For when they that were bidden to the feast had drunk deep they went out into the fields for to divert themselves, as if they were going to joust. But certain Saracens, who were lying in wait there, cast themselves upon them and pursued them. And at their shouting they of the host issued forth, but the Saracens missed not their stroke, for they took the Butler of Senlis,[103] and no man knoweth what they did with him—whether he died, or what befell him. But taken or slain were full a score, these had great joy of the feast! They of the host were sore dismayed, and the wise men among them were yet more troubled. Howbeit, many yet believed that the marquis spake the truth and that he would

---

[102] Probably of Toron des Chevaliers. See note, p 103
[103] Guy of Senlis, Butler of France. The royal butler was an official of very high rank

cause the victual to be brought to the host according to his promise But he departed immediately, both he and his people and his bride, nor ever, though he himself had great store of victuals, did he send any provision to the host, where was great lack thereof—save to them that of their frowardness had forwarded his marriage

XXXI

OF THE MOST GRIEVOUS STATE OF THE PILGRIMS BEFORE ACRE, OF THE COMFORT THAT GOD GAVE THEM, AND OF THE COMING OF THE KING OF FRANCE AND HIS BARONS

My Lords, concerning the death of Alexander, whereof was so great rumour, concerning the message of Balan,[104] concerning the adventures of Tristan,[105] concerning Paris and Helen, who for their love endured such pain, concerning Arthur of Britain and his valiant company, concerning Charles the Great or Pepin, concerning Agoland[106] or Wittekind,[107] concerning the ancient gests which minstrels do so celebrate—concerning all these can I tell you neither false nor true—can neither affirm nor gainsay But concerning those things which so many folk have themselves seen, which they themselves suffered—they of the host about Acre—concerning the miseries that they endured of heart and head—the grievous heats, the bitter colds, the sicknesses and woes of every kind—concerning these can I tell you truly, and well behooveth you to listen

It was in winter, in the season of Advent which was bringing back the rains and the winds, that there arose great plaint amongst the host about Acre, sore heaviness of heart and bitter lamentation both of middling folk and lowly, because of the dearth that was come upon them For it waxed worse from day to day, and they complained without ceasing It had gone well with them, in sooth, until the time of the Nativity, but then did their distress begin, their famine and their languishing And as the Yuletide passed, the dearth waxed greater every day Heavy indeed was a single measure of wheat, such as a man might carry under his arm, for it cost an hundred bezants[108] in the host Cold comfort did new rumours bring, corn and meal were very scarce, twelve shillings[109] was the worth of an hen, and an egg sold for six silver pennies,[110] so evil were the times But for bread, they that had none did fight one with another, and they cursed the marquis, who had brought them to this pass

My Lords, think not that I am jesting that meat might not utterly fail the host of God, their goodly steeds they butchered and devoured them most greedi-

---

[104]A character of the *Chanson d'Aspremont* (12th century)
[105]"The story of Tristan seems to have been current from the earliest times It was the subject of a number of metrical tales in the Romance language, which were versified by the French minstrels from ancient British authorities" Dunlop, *History of Prose Fiction*
The *Tristan* of Béroul was written about 1150, that of Chrétien de Troies about ten years later
[106]A Saracen king, in the *Chanson d'Aspremont*
[107]Leader of the Saxons against Charles the Great
[108]£56 (?)
[109]*Doze solz*, £1 10s (?)
[110]*Sis deners*, 1s 2d (?)

ly Great press of people was there round about at every butchering, and yet did they pay dear All that winter did this grievous case endure, and a little piece of the flesh was sold for ten shillings, yea, a dead horse sold for more than ever did a living one The flesh seemed savoury to them, and they ate even the entrails Then did they curse the marquis, who brought them to this pass

Evil were the times, sore was the need, for lowly folk and them of high estate, nevertheless, whoso had money and could get meat, even were he willing to give of it, he durst not share it amongst the many folk that came for it, and for this reason every one kept that he had And they cursed the marquis, who had brought them to this pass

Had it not been for the herbs that they had planted and the seed that they had sown, whereof each one made his pottage, never had this wasting away been withstood There had ye seen so many fair serjeants, most gentle men and valiant, who had been reared in the midst of riches, who now because of hunger and distress, wheresoever they saw grass growing, would fall to eating it, like cattle grazing Then would they curse the marquis, who had brought them to this pass

Then came upon them a sore sickness, hearken ye while I tell you thereof Because of the rains which then were falling, so great that never yet was their like seen and that the whole host was well-nigh drowned in their waters, they began every one to cough and to wax hoarse and their legs and their faces swelled, and daily a thousand in the host were lying on their biers And because of the swelling that they had in their faces their teeth fell out from their mouths, and many there were that recovered not because they gat no sustenance Then cursed they the marquis, that brought them to this pass

My lords, necessity ofttimes causeth things to be done for which many a man is blamed and upbraided There were in the host many men from many lands who were ashamed to beg their bread And these stole bread from the bakers until they were well-nigh stuffed therewith [111] One day a certain man was caught in such a theft and led away by him who had caught him to his own house, where, as best he could, the man bound both his hands behind his back but found nought whereto to fasten him And they of the house, who were baking, were hasting to and fro nor gave any heed to the prisoner But God, who keepeth watch over His own, brake the bands that bound his arms Now the man was sitting on an heap of loaves, and whilst the servants were looking other ways he was continually eating of the bread, and he took a loaf under his arm, for he was in the shadow of a settle Now was he no longer in great misease, and when he saw his time and occasion he fled away so fast as ever he could And he came to the host and recounted his adventure to the serjeants that were his companions, who were dying of the prick of hunger The bread he had brought them they divided and ate, whereby they were strengthened again for a little but not for long For the famine brake forth again and their distress so increased that they cursed the marquis, who had brought them to this pass

---

[111]This clause is obscure in the original

They that remained in the host underwent many torments there, nor could any man tell you the measure of the misery that they endured and suffered at the siege after they were come thither Now hear what misfortune, what loss, what shame, and what disgrace it is that a man whom God hath made in His own image should deny Him because of his own sufferings ! But in the host so great was the dearth of every kind of food that many of our people went over to the Turks, rejecting their own faith and denying that it was ever true, or ever could be, that God deigned to be born of a woman The cross, likewise, and baptism did they utterly deny

Two companions were there in the host, poor serjeants, who possessed nought save one penny Angevin[112] between them Evil in sooth was their case, for they had no more food nor any other possessions save their armour and their clothes Now the question was on what wise and in what manner could food enough be bought to keep them through that day? And they drew lots with hairs of their pelisses to determine what they should do And in the end they resolved to buy beans therewith, and they gat thirteen of these But one of them they found worm-eaten, and that they might exchange it one of the men must needs go back more than seven furlongs And only with great difficulty was he that went on this errand able to make the exchange Back came he and they ate the beans, being well-nigh mad with hunger But when the beans were gone their distress was doubled Then did they curse the marquis, who had brought them to this pass

A certain thing was sold in the host of God which they called carob-beans [113] These were sweet to the taste, and a man could get a mess of them for one silver penny, and they were well worth the seeking With these and with little nuts were many folk kept alive, but they who lay sick and who drank of the strong wine, whereof there was great plenty—these were so overcome of the wine that they ate nothing, save things that liked them least, so that they died by threes and by fours Howbeit, they that went forth and exercised themselves recovered They lived, but no more food had they, and these cursed the marquis, who had brought them to this pass

Sore misery was endured in the host or ever it was revictualed, for there is no worse madness than that which cometh of the pangs of hunger and of lack of bread And every day doth hunger the more grievously torment him that hath not wherewithal to satisfy it Thus, of sheer necessity, did they eat flesh in Lent, and so sinned This was at the beginning of the season of fasting, when every man rightly fasteth But they did penance for this thereafter when God had sent them better times And when they so ate flesh, and were mindful of their sin, then did they curse the marquis, who had brought them to this pass

So all that winter did the grievous dearth endure that was suffered of the folk of that host, who were seeking God and waiting what he would do—even from Yuletide until Lent (this know I of a certainty and not by conjecture), so that there where God caused the host to encamp would one man scarce look

---

[112]About 2d (?)
[113]Saint John's bread, *Ceratonia Siliqua*

upon another Charity was grown so cold that greed had waxed exceeding arrogant, and after greed was come even the most bounteous grew greedy and without bounty And because of this folk were dying in great misery, who cursed the marquis, that had brought them to this pass

So long endured this wretchedness that there was great murmuring because of it But God wished to teach His people that they ought to love and to fear Him The Bishop of Salisbury called together his sons and brethren in God and preached them a sermon, giving them a good example And the Bishop of Verona, who was well worthy of his mitre, was not slothful in preaching, but spake most profitable words And he of Fano, in Lombardy, a bishop of very holy life, preached in his turn most effectually Nor was it any long time ere in the host was a collection made for the folk that were in too great misery And this came to a great sum, for every one did his part right well and strove to relieve the needy Then had ye seen the poor folk thanking God as they ate that which the rich had given them There had Guauquelin of Ferrières open hands, not closed by greed, and Robert Troussebot, likewise, who put all his substance into the collection, and Count Henry of Champagne, who wrought many a good work there, and Sir Jocelin of Montoire, who meriteth a place in this history, and the courteous Count of Clermont, who was a good spender there, and the Bishop of Salisbury, who was no whit close-fisted, and the rest of them that knew God and succoured many folk The collection was wisely bestowed and fairly distributed to the small and to the great, to knights and to serjeants, and to all the poor who were seen to have the greatest need thereof, to every one according to his condition and his necessity And God saw His people inclining to do good and perceived that charity had entered into their hearts, and because of this their concord He looked down upon them with the eyes of His compassion

Peradventure have ye already heard of the miracle that the heavenly King wrought, and in sooth all they that have heard it ought to rejoice thereat To the harbour of Acre came a barge, neither very long nor very broad, and it was laden with corn Now shall ye hear how God succoured Christendom and out of dearth brought great abundance For never was the dearth so very great, there was ever enough victual in the host But the merchants were keeping it hidden so that they might sell it the dearer But when God, who is Himself charity and the fountain of humility, saw His people in great discouragement and faintness He commanded that the distress and the faintness should straightway cease and that the price of corn should fall

It was on a Saturday, before nones, that the barge came with these provisions, nor was there any great talk of the vessel that had arrived save of them that sold wheat and thought only of their own gain The barge came on a Saturday, I ween, in the afternoon, and 'twas God Himself that brought it And on Sunday He took the corn that was lying in the granaries, which the merchants sold for an hundred bezants, and He changed it from an hundred to four It needed, in sooth, such a merchant as He is to intermeddle in the matter, who wrought so great and so speedy a fall

And now hear ye how God punished a certain man for his misdoing, nor was this any great grievance In the host at Acre was a certain Pisan who held his corn so dear that he would not sell a single measure thereof save at a price most unreasonable And God, who knoweth the hearts of all, caused him to bear an heavy burden of punishment For a fire destroyed his house, so that all that he had therein, all that he had so unjustly gotten, was consumed and burned to ashes, nor could any avail aught against it And when men saw this work of God, then was charity increased yet more Then did all good men shew themselves bountiful one toward another in all things There had ye seen the poor filled again and giving thanks to God And all they that had used flesh in Lent confessed themselves and did penance, for they had done this because of their necessity Three strokes of a stick upon his back did each one of them receive (nor was the stick very large) at the hands of the Bishop of Salisbury, who chastised them like a good father And on Low Sunday, after that God had thus wrought, came King Philip of France to the host in good sooth And with him came the Count of Flanders,[114] whose death was so bruited thereafter, and thither came the valiant Count of Saint-Pol,[115] whose shield sat featly to his neck, and thither came William of Garlande, who had a very great company, and thither came William of Barres, a good knight, valiant and nimble, and thither came William of Mello, a knight in whom I am well pleased, and thither also came the Count of Perche[116] who gave to the cause even all that he had And then came the marquis with the French, as I have heard But why should I multiply words? There was not left a nobleman of France that came not, early or late, at this season

---

XXXII

AMBROSE TAKETH UP HIS HISTORY AGAIN WHERE HE HAD LAID IT DOWN HOW THE TWO KINGS WERE AT VARIANCE CONCERNING THE ASSAULT ON THE CITY, HOW KING PHILIP BEGAN THE ASSAULT WITHOUT KING RICHARD AND HOW HE WAS DRIVEN BACK OF THE SICKNESS OF THE TWO KINGS, AND OF THE COMING OF OTHER PILGRIMS OF THE ARTILLERY OF THE CHRISTIANS, AND OF THE DEATH OF AUBRY CLÉMENT

The King of France was there, together with the host of Christendom, from Easter even until Whitsuntide, the high feast that men so richly keep Then had the King of England already taken Cyprus, and so came to this land But now it behooveth me to follow the history and overtake again my matter, relating the siege of Acre So will AMBROSE finish now his tale and fulfill his task, knitting again his knot and joining it, and telling of the two kings who came to Acre to the siege and how they comported themselves there, relating of the substance of the history all that which cometh to his mind, and recounting how Acre was taken, even as he saw it with his own eyes

[114]Philip of Alsace
[115]Hugo IV
[116]Rotrou III He died shortly after reaching Acre

When King Richard of England was come to the Holy Land, even as I have told you already, then worthy indeed of mention are the courtesy, the prowess, and the bountifulness that he shewed there The King of France had promised and agreed with his people that each month each one of them should receive three gold bezants from his treasury, and there was much talk concerning this And when King Richard at his coming had heard this great news he caused a ban to be cried throughout the host that to every knight, of whatever land he be, who wished to take his pay, he would give four bezants, and this did he promise them This was the rightful wage, which is wont to be paid there Then was all the host rejoiced when this word was heard Then said the small folk who had long time been there—both the small and the middling "Lord God, when will the assault be made? For now is come the most valiant of kings and the mightiest warrior of all Christendom Now let God's will be done!" For in King Richard was their hope

Then the King of France, who had come thither after Easter and had comported himself right well, sent word to him that it were well that they now begin the attack, and that they bid the summons be cried for the assault But King Richard was sick, his face and his lips all wasted by a sickness accursed of God, which men called "leonardie"[117] He sent the king word of his sickness and that his fleet or his baronry were not yet come, but a wind had held the vessels back (which they call there the wind of Arsûf)[118] and had kept them at Tyre, that his petraries were on their way thither, that they would presently be there, and that so soon as his following should arrive he would right willingly and with all his might set himself to the taking of Acre But never a moment (so help me God!) for all this would the king of France delay to have the assault cried And very early in the morning they armed themselves throughout the camp, for greatly did they desire to make the assault There had ye seen so many folk in arms that scarce could they be counted Then had ye seen so many goodly hauberks, so many gleaming helms of divers forms, so many a steed of noble frame, so many white caparisons, so many chosen knights! Never before had we seen so many good knights, valiant and doughty, proud, bold, and of wide renown, so many pennons, so many banners wrought in so many fashions! Then did they appoint and set apart those who should keep ward over the trench lest Saladin enter the camp from the rear with his fell folk And then did God's people march toward the walls, and they assailed them vigorously, discharging their arrows And when the Turks that were within Acre saw that the Christians were attacking them, then had ye heard them sounding both cymbals and timbrels and drums, as if God were causing it to thunder Nor did they that beat these instruments perform any other services save from the palace to look down upon the host and

---

[117]Apparently some kind of intermittent fever In this verse the MS has *leonardie*, in a later passage, *naudie* The Latin translation has *arnoldia* and *arnaldia* Gaston Paris thinks that the reading should be *renardie*, which would be a very fair French equivalent of the Greek *alopecia* (literally "fox-sickness") We know that the disease was characterized by loss of the hair

[118]See note, p 39

to make a noise and cause a smoke to arise, for to shew the Saracens who were without that they must come to the succour of the city Then had ye seen these come a-running to fill the trench with fagots But this could they not accomplish, for Geoffrey—he of Lusignan, whose prowess was ever new—came to the barrier where they were, which they had already taken from our people, and by main force he drave them back, laying more than ten of them on their biers with the axe that he was holding So many good blows did he strike that never since the days of Roland and of Oliver hath any other knight deserved such praise Thus was the barrier won again which the Saracens had taken But there was great confusion, fierce battle, and loud cries But as for those that were assailing Acre and had already compassed the filling of the trenches thereof, now must they needs draw back and take some other counsel, and this was that they betake themselves to their camp nor discharge any more arrows or other missiles [119] Then straightway ceased the assault, and the people began to cry and to murmur and to rue the coming of the two kings on which they had so waited And each one said before his tent "Fair Lord God, what a sorry essay!" So our folk went and laid aside their arms, the while the Saracens were howling, and whilst our men were yet disarming, the Saracens had already set on fire the engines of the King of France and his clayes Thereat did such vexation seize his heart (this was known, and I have heard it told) that he fell sick, nor was he able thereafter to ride an horse

In such case was the host—sad, woebegone, cast down, disconsolate—seeing the two kings lying sick that should have taken the city And the Count of Flanders was dead, which caused great sorrow in the host But what should I say more? The sickness of the kings and the count's death did so distress the host that therein was no joy nor any mirth, save for the fleet of transport ships which came thither just at that season Then came the Bishop of Évreux, and brave men with him that were his vassals Thither also came Roger of Tosni with a great following of knights, and the brethren of Tornebu,[120] all good sons of one father Thither came Robert of Newbroke, on franker man could I not pin my trust And thither came Jordan of Hommet, who was Constable of Séez [121] Thither came the Chamberlain of Tancarville[122] in that same season Count Robert of Leicester was already come, for there did he desire to be Thither, too, came Gilebert Talebot, one of the bravest of our men And my Lord Ralph Taisson came, nor should he go unmentioned And the Viscount of Châteaudun came, and Bertran of Verdun And thither came the brethren Tozeleis, bold knights and full of courtesy Then, too, came Roger of Hardencourt, companion of the king and of his court And thither came they of Préaux [123] these likewise were of the companions of the king Thither came Garin Fitz-Gerout,[124] who had with him a

---

[119]The reading of this sentence in the MS is very doubtful
[120]John, Richard, and Thomas, of Tornebu in Normandy
[121]In Normandy
[122]Near the mouth of the Seine
[123]William, John, and Peter
[124]Or Fitzgerald The Latin has *Garinus filius Geroldi* He died in 1218

goodly company And he of La Mare[125] came also thither, in fair and noble state And many another, whom I name not here, came to the help of God

The two kings were lying sick before Acre, which they held in siege God willed not that they should die, but that they should save the city But the King of France was recovered long time before the other king And the petraries hurled their stones at the walls both night and day nor rested ever The king had Evil Neighbour,[126] but inside Acre was Evil Cousin, who was ever doing her some mischief, howbeit, the King was ever having her mended, and so many times did he set her up again that at last she brake the principal wall in pieces The Accursed Tower[127] likewise did she sorely scathe And the Duke of Burgundy's petrary also did her business there right well, and that of the noble Lords of the Temple smote many a Turk right in the temple bone [128] And that of the Hospitalers struck many a blow that was right pleasing to them all Now there was one of the petraries set up that was called God's Petrary, for the making of which a certain good priest had preached, delighting all the host, and so much money did he get that with the fruit thereof he laid low more than two perches of the wall that stood about the Accursed Tower throughout its circuit And the Count of Flanders had one, whilst he was yet alive, such that none better need be sought This did the King of England now have, and along with this he had a little one which was esteemed a very excellent engine These now played against a tower over the gate, where the Turks were swarming And so sore did they beat and batter it that they pulled down the half thereof And the king had caused two new ones to be builded in so costly fashion that wheresoever they were brought forward they cast their stones from beneath a roof And he caused a belfry[129] to be made whereof the Turks stood in great fear, which was so covered and overlaid with hides and planks and cords that it feared neither flying stone nor Greek fire nor any other earthly thing And two mangonels had he bidden build, whereof the one was so powerful that when its stone went flying into Acre it passed on clean to the Butchers' Quarter The king's petraries cast stones night and day without ceasing, and so true is it as that we are now standing here that one of them killed twelve men with a single stone, which was carried to Saladin and shewn to him For such stones as this one—round stones from the seashore—had the King of England brought to this land from Messina for to slay Saracens withal But the king was yet lying upon his bed, exceeding sick and heavy of heart Yet would he go out to see the battles that were fought with the Saracens and other heathen pack hard by the camp and the trenches, and his grief that he could not himself join battle with them was far greater than the pain which made his body to tremble

---

[125]Not identified

[126]*Male Veisine* This petrary is mentioned by other chroniclers Pieces of artillery were frequently christened with appropriate names

[127]*La Tur Maudite* It stood at an angle of the main wall, next to the harbour

[128]*E cele as preuz seignors del Temple*
      Feri meint Turc joste la temple

A good example of the poet's weakness for "homonymous rhymes"

[129]A movable tower, several storeys high, mounted on wheels and covered with raw hides

Now Acre was very hard to take, and much must perforce be spent there for to build the many engines, which scarcely yet sufficed, for when our men were not looking, the Saracens would set them on fire The King of France, at great cost and at great expense, had builded a ca-[180] and a claye richly covered, whereof ensued great loss The king himself would sit beneath his claye and ofttimes shoot with his crossbow at the Turks who came forth for to defend the walls One day, whilst his people were guarding the cat and them that were working therein, lo, the Saracens fetched and cast upon the cat and upon the claye so much dry wood, and thereafter threw so much Greek fire thereon with a petrary which they trained directly on the cat (Ambrose himself beheld this thing), that the cat was perforce destroyed and the precious claye was likewise burned and broken in pieces there, whereat the king waxed so angry in his heart that he began to curse all those who ate his bread, since they took not vengeance on the Saracens And that night he caused an assault to be cried for the morrow And on the morrow was the weather marvelous hot

So in the morning were they all afoot, brave folk and of great valour That day were the trenches guarded by men that were no cowards, for all round about them were the best knights in the world And of such was there great need that day, for Saladin had said that he would shew himself there and be the first to enter into the camp He came not, but his people came and, dismounting, began to attack the French Then had ye seen a valiant defense with blows of mace and sword-strokes But presently was the battle halted, for the Turks that were outside the city went mad at the sight of those who were within Acre, who were sending their signals with Saladin's ensign It was the admiral Saphadin with his people, who pressed so sore against the trench that they filled it perforce, but our people drave them back And they who had gone against Acre assailed the walls right vigorously—God render them their meed!

The miners of the King of France, who had given him their promise, digged underneath the ground until they were come to the foundation of the wall, which they propped up with stanchions and then set these on fire, so that a great piece of the wall fell down, howbeit, ill had well-nigh befallen our men, for ere it fell it leaned outward, so that every man there was sore afeared Then, lo, a great multitude hastened thither when they saw the wall yielding There had ye seen so many banners, ensigns with full many a device had ye seen in that great press of the fell heathen folk, there had ye seen them coming on, hurling Greek fire at our men, there had ye seen the ladders drawn this way and that which our men were laying to the walls And there was done a deed of great daring—'twas Aubry Clément performed it—he who said that on that day would he die, or else would enter Acre Nor did he deign to lie, but on that day became a martyr For up to the wall-top he went to fight the Turks, who strove to cast him down, and so many fell upon him that he died For they that should follow him, who were already on the ladder, so overburdened it that it bent, and in bending it brake asunder, and they fell headlong into the trench, and the Turks hooted and

---

[180]See note, p 51

shouted And some there were of our men that died, but some were drawn out thence But in sooth for Aubry Clément was the whole host grieved full sore, and for to mourn him and lament him must they needs give over the assault for that day

XXXIII

OF THE ATTACK ON THE ACCURSED TOWER HOW KING RICHARD, ALBEIT SICK AND SUFFERING, YET ASSAULTED THE CITY AND AVENGED THE DEATH OF AUBRY CLÉMENT

No great time had passed after the death of Aubry Clément ere they began to undermine the Accursed Tower, which I have already mentioned and named, and to put stanchions underneath it, for it was already cracked and battered The Turks also were digging from within, working their way toward them so straight as they could, until the two parties were met together, when they made a truce between them Now there were with the Turks certain Christians, bound with chains and with fetters These spake with our men and so wrought that they gat themselves outside the wall And when the Turks that were inside the wall perceived this, then know ye of a surety that they were sore vexed thereat, and they stopped the hole and repaired it, through which these men had passed

King Richard yet lay sick, even as I have said already, but he desired that the attack on the city of Acre be made under his own command So he caused a most costly claye to be drawn to the trenches, therein were his arbalesters, who did their business right well And he had himself carried (as God seeth me), wrapped in a great quilt of silken stuff, inside the claye for to work mischief on the Saracens And many a crossbow bolt did he let fly with his own hand, which was very skillful, at the tower whence the Turks were shooting and against which his own petraries were discharging And his miners were ever digging and setting stanchions beneath it, and they so wrought and the petraries so battered it that it began to bend downward toward the ground

Then the King of England bade his crier cry throughout the host, from a wall that stood hard by the tower, that whosoever should draw one stone out of the tower, to him would be given two gold bezants, then he promised three, then four Then had ye seen the serjeants running forward! But many of them were wounded   [131] and so many of them were overthrown that they durst remain there no longer or trust to the protection of their targes The wall was very high and very wide, nevertheless, they gat themselves so close to it that they drew from it more than one stone Then had ye seen the Turks pressing so eagerly thither, for to cast stones on them that were sapping the wall, that they left themselves uncovered One Turk there was who had armed himself in the rich armour of Aubry Clément, and he exposed himself rashly that day But King Richard hit him full in the breast with a great bolt, so that he fell dead on the instant Then had ye seen the Turks exposing themselves for to assuage their grief over

---

[131]Lacuna of one line

his death and laying themselves bare to bolts and arrows, shooting, and dealing mighty blows Never yet had they made such defense¹ And greatly do they marvel at it who recall it There was armour of no avail, be it never so tough and stout and sure—double pourpoints, double hauberks—these were no better than light gay-coloured cloth against the bolts from the arbalests, for they were very powerful And the Turks within the wall were digging toward our miners, until these were constrained to flee and to get themselves away Then began the Saracens to hoot at them

But when this tower, which had so long been battered, was at the last overthrown and the smoke had cleared away so that many a breach could be seen, then did our squires put on their armour, like the brave and nimble warriors that they were Then was the Count of Leicester's banner to be seen, and my Lord Andrew of Chauvigni's, in that place Thither also came, in noble array, Lord Hugo le Brun,[132] and the Bishop of Salisbury, and others of divers conditions It was at the hour of supper that they came and ranged themselves before the tower The valiant squires began the assault   [133] And they that were guarding the walls cried out when they saw these mounting them Lo, all the city was in confusion when this thing was known Then had ye seen Turks coming like the drops of rain, and our squires moving swiftly, for they desired to get themselves inside Acre Then had ye seen the two bands come together and fall each on the other, smiting and cutting and overthrowing! The squires were but few, and the Saracens waxed ever in number, and they cast burning fire at our men And these, beholding it coming, durst not await the fire but must perforce get them down again Nor do I know how many died there in the course of this undertaking

Then did the men of Pisa arm themselves, who were folk of great emprise, and they mounted up to the top of the wall But the Saracens withstood them so stoutly, and the battle betwixt the Pisans and that pack was so fierce and fell, that never was seen so sharp an attack or so firm a defense But the Pisans, too, must perforce get them down, howbeit, if the undertaking had been more widely known, Acre had been taken that selfsame day But the more part of the folk that were in the host were sitting at their supper, and the attack had been made very suddenly So the assault must needs be given over

XXXIV

HOW A COVENANT WAS MADE BETWIXT KING GUY AND THE MARQUIS OF MONTFERRAT HOW THE INFIDELS, BEING IN SORE STRAITS, SOUGHT PEACE, AND HOW PEACE WAS GRANTED THEM

Now in the host was a parliament held, whereof came a concord betwixt King Guy and the marquis, which had been greatly sought and desired The King of France held with the marquis and maintained his cause, and Richard, King of England, held with the king of this land, who had been made King of Jerusalem Therefore was it determined, since they loved not one the other, and since they

---

[132]Count of La Marche, and brother of Guy of Lusignan
[133]Lacuna of one line

strove together for the kingdom, that King Guy should remain king, but whatsoever lands were fiefs of the kingdom, and the revenues thereof, these should they divide between them, and the marquis should immediately have Tyre and Beirut and Sayette,[134] for the sake of a firm and stable peace, and if, as time passed, King Guy should be the first to die, then should the marquis have the crown, and Geoffrey of Lusignan should have Jaffa and Ascalon [135] [But if it should come to pass that King Guy, the marquis, and his wife should all die, then should King Richard] do with the land what seemed him best, for it should be his But all his life long did the marquis bear a grudge against the two brothers

An haughty folk were they within the city, and marvelously proud Had they only not been a race of misbelievers, a better people was never seen Nevertheless were they now sore afraid, beholding this great marvel—how all the world was seeking and striving to compass their destruction—how their walls were pierced and broken asunder and dashed in pieces—how their people were wounded and slain and their number diminished Howbeit, there were yet full six thousand of them within the city, amongst these Mestoc and Karakush,[136] but they sufficed not, nor had they any hope of succour Moreover, they knew that all the host was full of bitterness because of the death of Aubry Clément, and because of their sons, their brethren, their uncles, their fathers, their nephews, and their cousins, who had died at the hands of the Turks, wherefore the Christians hated them exceedingly And they knew of a surety that our people would either die there or take them by force, nor could aught else befall They had caused a wall to be reared and to be builded clean across the city, and I tell you of a certainty that they had thought to defend themselves to the utmost, but God caused them to follow a counsel whereof the outcome was most honourable to our people, but to them most mischievous and deadly, so that by this means Acre became ours without a bowshot or the casting of a stone

The Saracens that were within Acre took counsel together and determined that they would ask of our people safe conduct and would send to Saladin, who had bound himself with a promise that if he should see them in too evil a pass he would make peace for them on their own terms Thus did the engagement stand Safe conduct did they ask of our people, then they sent word to Saladin that, for their own sake, he must not suffer his high name for prowess and for honour to be lost, or the great religion of their ancestors, which Mahomet established, to be impaired by the Christians or to be abased, but that he should take counsel right speedily, nor give thought to aught else than to deliver the brave men whom he had caused to enter into Acre, which they had so long guarded for him that they were now at the mercy of the Christians' swords And they besought him for their unhappy families, which they had not seen in the three years since the hosts were called forth Let him, then, take thought for them and theirs, that they perish not through neglect, and let him fulfill his promise, otherwise—and let him

---

[134]Sidon
[135]A considerable lacuna occurs here The words enclosed in brackets are supplied by Gaston Paris from the *Itinerarium Ricardi*
[136]Two of Saladin's principal emirs or "admirals "

know this without any fail—they would themselves make with the Christians the best accord that they were able

Saladin heard the complaint of his people, who were so hard beset—their evil state, their distress, their discouragement, and their weakness He spake to them as best he could, and he told them that he had had a message from Baby-lon,[137] and that speedily would come a great multitude of men in ships and galleys, which he had summoned long before for to succour his good people of Acre, whom he would not yet forsake, and that the Mollah[138] had sent him word that he would arrive within the week And he promised, by the faith that he professed, that if succour came not, then, to save them, he would make peace with Christen-dom So the messengers were come and gone, but many a mishap befell the peo-ple of Acre Our petraries brake down their walls, ceasing not day or night, and such fear had the Turks that they came up on the walls by night and let them-selves fall down thence, for fear of worse mischance And messengers went and came and told Saladin and assured him that his people were already so good as dead if peace or succour came not

In sooth did Saladin perceive the grievous mischances and great losses of his people, and their dire disasters So took he counsel of his baronry and enquired of them what he should do in this matter of his people's request And his great men and his admirals, who were kinsmen and friends of them that were defend-ing Acre and who wished to get them out of the city, answered him openly that there was nought else to do but to make peace—the best peace that he could—before worse things befell And when the soldan had heard what each one of his barons counseled, and when he knew that he could not relieve the misery of Acre, then—willing or not—he perforce told the messengers, whom he knew to be worthy men and wise, that he gave them leave to surrender the city since they could not defend it And then and there, or ever the messengers departed, were determined the terms which they should offer to the Christians when they should come to parley Back came the messengers, nor did they wear wry faces Then met together the council of our men and they of the city who came to offer their terms Straightway were the people bidden to keep silence

Through an interpreter the Turks caused the terms to be told which they would offer And they were these that they would restore the Cross wherein Christians believe, that they would give over to them the city, and, of their pris-oners of high station, two thousand, and five hundred of the lesser folk whom they had long been holding, that Saladin would cause to be sought and searched out through all the land the arms and other possessions of these captives, and that when the Turks should go out from Acre each one would carry with him nought save his own shirt And there was yet another condition—they would pay two

---

[137] Cairo

[138] *L'amulaine* "In Arabic, *moula-na,* 'our lord,' a name given before the time of Saladin to the Fatimite caliph of Egypt However, the title of *Moulana* ceased to exist after Saladin had destroyed the Fatimite rule and slain the last Caliph of Egypt, so it must be admitted that Ambrose was misinformed in this particular matter " Gaston Paris, *L'Estoire de la Guerre Sainte*

hundred thousand bezants to the two kings who were there, and in surety for this
the kings should hold the Turks of highest estate and the wisest according to
repute and to common report that were to be found in all Acre Our people took
counsel together and examined the terms that were offered, and when our council
found them good they granted the peace [139]

XXXV

**HOW THE INFIDELS HAD DESECRATED THE CHURCHES OF ACRE HOW KING PHILIP
FORSOOK THE HOST AND WENT BACK TO FRANCE HOW KING RICHARD LENT
AND GAVE OF HIS OWN MONEYS TO THE FRENCH OF THE ARRO-
GANCE OF THE MARQUIS OF MONTFERRAT HOW SALADIN
KEPT NOT HIS PROMISE, AND HOW THE SARACEN
HOSTAGES WERE PUT TO DEATH**

The day when Acre was surrendered, as I have understood the matter, it was
four years (this know I of a certainty) since the Saracens had taken it, and I
have clearly in memory that it was surrendered on the day after the feast of Saint
Benedict, in despite of that accursed folk whom may God curse with His mouth!
I cannot refrain myself from saying this For then ought ye to have seen the
churches that were left in Acre—how the Turks had broken and defaced the
images, overthrown the altars, and beaten crosses and crucifixes, for to do despite
to our belief and to satisfy their own misbelief—and had made of them their own
mameries![140] But they paid dear for this thereafter

Now about the time, methinketh, when the Turks should give over the Cross
(after that Acre had been given up), lo, throughout the host of the King of
France, in whom the people had such confidence, ran the rumour that the king
wished to return to France And in sooth was he making preparation for his
voyage Alas, God's grace! What a return! How ill was it conceived that one
who ought to direct so many folk should wish to leave them! The king went
away because of his sickness—so he himself said, whatsoever others may say
But none hath borne witness that sickness giveth discharge from the service of
that sovereign King who directeth and leadeth all kings I do not say that he was
not at the siege, that there he made not great expense of iron, of wood, of lead, of
tin, of silver, and of gold, that he succoured not many folk, as befitteth the highest earthly king that men know in all Christendom But for that very cause ought
he to have remained and done without faltering all that was in his power to do for
that poor and defenseless land which hath cost us so dear

The news was published, certain and manifest, through all the host that the
king was returning, for every day was he making his preparations Then, lo, all
the baronry of France was filled with rage and fury, seeing the head, of which
they were the members, so set in his purpose that he would not remain for their
sake—not for all their tears or all their complaints And when they could not
gain their end, albeit they strove with him never so stoutly, then do I tell you truly

---

[139]2 July, 1191
[140]*Mahomeries* i e, temples of Mahomet, mosques

that they upbraided him, and it lacked but little that they had forsworn both their king and their lord, so did they hate his seigniory

The King of France was at the point to depart, nor would he suffer any man to persuade him to tarry longer there ere he returned to France And because of his example there returned also a great number of barons and of other folk And on this occasion he left the Duke of Burgundy as his deputy and in his stead, together with the men of his land And he sent a request to King Richard that he would lend him two galleys, then did the king's men go down to the harbour and they fetched him two goodly vessels, swift and well supplied Freely were these given by the king, but ill were they recompensed

And King Richard, who for the help of God remained in Syria, sent a request to the King of France, whom he mistrusted, for their fathers had mistrusted each the other of yore and had ofttimes wrought mischief the one upon the other And King Richard said that King Philip should give him surety and should swear upon holy relics that he would do no evil to King Richard's land nor any wrong to himself, so long as he should be upon God's business in this his pilgrimage, and that, when King Philip should once be within his own land, he would send him word by his messengers from France full forty days before he stirred up any quarrel or war against him or did him any injury And King Philip sware thereto, and he gave as surety certain men of high estate whom we yet remember the Duke of Burgundy, Count Henry, and other hostages five or more in number, but the names of these I cannot give

The King of France took his leave, but one thing will I tell you—more curses did he get on his departure than blessings He and the marquis went their way by sea to Tyre, taking with them Karakush and the rest of that portion of the Saracens that had been assigned to them, whereof the king thought to get as ransom an hundred thousand bezants of their substance wherewith to keep and to maintain his own people until Easter But all the hostages were abandoned of their own people, and the more part of them died of grief, so that not one farthing was then received for them, nor aught else of any value save the half of the spoil that the French had gotten in Acre And the French reproached him often because they had received no other payment, and great quarrels arose therefrom Howbeit, thereafter the King of England, to whom the duke had recourse, lent to the duke on their hostages (wherein they gat a very great advantage) five thousand silver marks of his own money, with which they paid their men But this was a long time afterward

King Richard saw clearly that now the whole burden and cost of the undertaking was laid upon him because of the departure of the King of France, who would no longer stay Then bade he withdraw from his own treasury gold and silver in great plenty, and this he gave most generously to the French for to hearten them, for they were sore disheartened, likewise gave he to folk of other tongues, wherewith they ransomed whatsoever they had put in pawn

The King of France was departed, and King Richard made his preparations, for he would not be forgetful of God So had he the host summoned and called

together But he tarried there yet a fortnight, and then another week, for either
Saladin would not fulfill his promise to our men, or the thing was displeasing unto
God But whatsoever may be said concerning the matter, it was for this reason
that the host tarried there so long In the mean time the king had his mangonels
and his petraries brought on board, so that he might be ready to depart, for the
summer was already passing, and for that reason he gat all things in readiness And
he caused the walls of Acre to be rebuilt, so great or greater than those that he
had caused to be broken down And he was wont to go, for to divert himself, and
watch the workmen at their work, for greatly was he set on recovering God's
heritage for Him Therefore did the stay irk him, for surely would he have recovered it had not envy wrought against him

Now was the time come for the fulfillment of the agreements, the oaths, and
the pledges that the Saracens had made to the Franks But the Christians knew
not that the Saracens were idly putting them off For they were ever demanding
a new term and a further respite that they might search for the Cross Then had
ye heard our people asking for tidings of the Cross and when it would come! But
God was unwilling to protect those for whose sake the Cross was to be surrendered And one would say "It is come!" And another would say "Such and
such an one, who hath been in the host of the Saracens, hath seen it" But they
lied, and this was evident at the last For Saladin suffered the hostages to perish
without succouring them, for he thought by means of the Cross to obtain a more
favourable peace

In the mean time, whilst they were thus delaying, the Christians sent messengers to the marquis at Tyre, bidding and beseeching him that he come and restore the hostages and receive the portion that would fall to the King of France,
that is, the half of that which had been promised

The Bishop of Salisbury, Count Robert, and one of those brethren, the good
knights of Préaux—Peter, the loyal and the brave—these three bare the message
The marquis, being filled with madness, answered them that he would not do this,
for into the host he durst not go because of King Richard of England, whom he
feared more than any other man on earth Above all, if it should so chance that
he gave up the Turks that he was holding, he desired the Cross to be divided so
that he might have his portion thereof, then would the hostages be given up,
nor would he delay any longer The messengers listened to this drunken speech of
the abominable marquis, and know ye well that they esteemed him the less for it
But they contended with him as best they could, saying that one of them would
remain there as an hostage, then could he come before the king in all safety But
he sware an oath that never would he turn his feet thither So they came away
without taking their leave, and they returned to the king at Acre and told him all,
nor mistold anything The king was filled with indignation and with shame, and
he sent for the Duke of Burgundy, and for Sir Droon of Amiens, in whom was
such valour and such virtue, and for Robert of Quinci also And when the king
beheld them before him he set forth to them the unreasonableness of the marquis,
and his arrogance, and the reason why he would not come to the host, and why

he kept back the hostages, and how he desired to share in the kingdom without wearing helm or bearing shield, and how he had intercepted the supplies of victual so that no provision passed through Tyre that was not seized and held by him Quoth the king "Here is madness! Sir Duke, it behooveth you to go thither For if madness once enter our minds we shall accomplish nothing profitable" Then forth set the Duke of Burgundy and Sir Droon of Amiens, and Robert of Quinci, that valiant knight and deft To Tyre they went, to the marquis, and in God's name and in the name of the King of England they adjured him that he come to conquer again and to regain the land of Syria, since he demanded his share of it They spake to him wisely and courteously, but he answered them like a madman, saying that never would he set foot in the host but would keep to his own city, wherein he feared no living man Yet a long time did the three messengers dispute with him, and in the end these noblemen brought back his hostages to the host at Acre, where the other hostages were

So came the hostages that had been held in Tyre, but already was the term gone by—a full fortnight, yea, even more—whereon the Saracens had said that they would fulfill the promises which they had made to the Christians But the soldan failed them, and he behaved himself as a false and a dishonourable man when he delivered his own men to death, nor ransomed them and set them free Then did he lose his renown which had stood so high, for there had not been a court in the whole world wherein it had not been celebrated But God bringeth down His enemy when He hath suffered him for a season, but His friend He upholdeth and raiseth up and directeth and exalteth his works But Saladin should He no longer uphold or exalt, for all that he did and wrought against the Christians and all his spoiling of them came to pass only because God wished to work through him and through his work to restore His people that had gone astray, whom He desired to bring back into the right way

When King Richard perceived and knew without any doubt whatsoever that Saladin was only putting him off, he was the more displeased and grieved that he had not already set his host on their way And when he understood the case and saw that Saladin would do nothing and that he had no regard whatsoever for them that had defended Acre for him, then was the matter laid before a council wherein the high men of the host were assembled And these decided that they would slay the greater part of the Saracens and keep the rest—those that were of highest birth—for to redeem those of our own people who were held as hostages And Richard, the King of England, who had slain so many Turks in that land, cared no longer to weary his head in the matter, but that he might abate the haughtiness of the Turks, that he might root up their religion, and that he might avenge Christendom, he caused two thousand and seven hundred of them, all in chains, to be led outside the city, where they were all cut down So were avenged their blows and their arrow-shots—great thanks be given to the Creator

XXXVI

HOW KING RICHARD MADE READY TO MARCH TOWARD ASCALON OF THE LOSSES
THAT THE PILGRIMS HAD SUFFERED DURING THE SIEGE HOW THE TURKS AT-
TACKED THE HOST, AND OF THEIR MANNER OF FIGHTING HOW THE PIL-
GRIMS WERE VERY LOATH TO LEAVE ACRE, HOW THEY PASSED
OVER THE BELUS, AND HOW THE TURKS ATTACKED THEM
IN THE MIST HOW SALADIN SEIZED THE PASSES,
WHILST THE CHRISTIANS ENCAMPED AT CAI-
PHAS HOW THEY WENT ON FROM
CAIPHAS TO CAPERNAUM

Then was the host summoned and called together by the criers at that hour when the sun hideth himself And it was cried abroad that they should march out and at the time appointed should ride forth and cross the river of Acre in the name of God, who giveth all good things, for to go straight to Ascalon and to conquer the seacoast So they laid in store of biscuit and of meal, of wine and of meats, for commandment had been made that they should carry with them provision for ten days, and that the sailors should come with their vessels all laden, following the host along the coast, and that the transport ships likewise should come speedily after them, laden with victual and with men armed and ready Thus were they bidden to go and to proceed in two divisions, the one by sea and the other by land, for in no other wise could Syria be conquered again, now that the Turks had it in their power

Now the host had been before Acre two winters and one whole summer, well-nigh until mid-August, with great suffering and at great cost, when the king caused the slaughter of those that had well deserved death because of the evil that they wrought toward God and toward the pilgrims, whereby were made so many orphans, so many maids were left destitute, so many wives widowed, so many an heritage lost, so many an high lineage brought low, so many bishoprics and so many churches left solitary and shepherdless And as for the number of the princes and the counts who died there, a good clerk hath written an account of these—of all those who died in the host and were men of any renown, without mention of the middling folk and small, of naming whom an end could never be made had he sought to record them all, for that had needed too much labour and too much writing He hath found and saith in his writing, in the scroll that he wrote with his own hand, that in the host there died six archbishops, the patriarch,[141] and twelve bishops, besides priests and clerks the number of whom none knoweth of a certainty And there died there forty counts, of whom the clerk kept record, and five hundred noblemen of the land, who had gone to seek God God assoil them and deign to receive them into His kingdom! For all them that died there, for all them that went thither, for the high folk and the low, for all these in one company ought we fervently to pray that God receive them amongst His friends into that heavenly glory where it is marvelous bliss to be, even as He hath promised them, and for their weal and for our own let each one of us recite a paternoster

---

[141]Heraclius

When that pack had been put to death which, the while they were shut up within Acre, had caused us so many vexations, then did King Richard bid his tents be carried forth and pitched outside the trenches, there to await the host which was already moving And he caused the serjeants of foot to be ranged round about him in their lodges because of the false Saracen folk, who were riotously assailing us and ever attacking our men when they were least on their guard But the king, as was his wont, was ever the first to spring to arms, and he would prick straight at the hated folk, performing many a deed of valour there

One day it came to pass that they drave back our men and began the mellay Quickly these armed themselves—the king and they that were with him—likewise a certain count of Hungary[142] and a great company of Hungarians Forth they went against the Turks, and some there were who acquitted themselves right well, but they pursued the Turks too far and fared most ill The Count of Hungary, who was highly esteemed in the host, was taken, and a certain knight of Poitou, named Huguelot, who was the king's marshal, was carried away captive Then the king charged with all his might, thinking to rescue Huguelot, but he was led too far away For the Turks have a great advantage, whereby they work us much mischief the Christians are heavily armed, but the Saracens bear no arms or armour save a bow, a mace, a javelin, a sword, or a very sharp lance, and a knife that weigheth very little And when one pursueth impetuously after them, they have horses whose like is not found in all the world, seeming as fleet as swallows And since the Turk, when he is pursued, cannot be overtaken, he hath the custom of the poisonous and tormenting fly—chase him, and he will ever flee thee, turn back, and he will chase thee Even so on this day did that fell folk cause the king much annoy He charged, and they fled, he turned back, and they followed, now would they seem to lose, and now to gain

King Richard was within his tent, awaiting the coming of his host But very slothfully came they forth and they that passed the trenches scarce waxed in number Yet was the city of Acre so full that hardly could they be contained therein Full three hundred thousand men there were, both within the city and without Loath and slothful were the folk to go, for most delightful was the city, with its good wines and damsels fair, of whom were some that were most beautiful With wine and women had they much traffic and took their pleasure foolishly withal, so that in the city was much unseemliness and so much sin and so much wantonness that good men were sore ashamed of that which the rest did

Forth came the host, as it was summoned Like as a candle in a sconce goeth out when the wind striketh it, even so in the host perforce must the folly be quenched which had fain remained in it, for all the women stayed behind in the city of Acre and remained there—all save the good old charwomen and the pilgrims' washerwomen who washed heads and linen and were as deft as monkeys in removing fleas So, in the morning, was the host drawn up and ranged in goodly ranks The king was with the rear ward, that they might not suffer loss through heedlessness But that day's march was very short So soon as the

---

[142]Probably Count Nicholas, who came to Acre in 1189

accursed folk had seen the host moving, then might ye have seen them raining down from the hills, twenty here, thirty there, for their hearts were very bitter because of the slaughter that they had seen of their kinsmen, who were lying there dead Wherefore they violently assailed the host and followed it and harassed it, but—thanks be to God—they did us no great mischief So our folk straight departed thence, and they passed over the river of Acre and set up their tents and their pavilions and tarried there for to await the rest of their people, whom it was hard to draw out of Acre, for with such difficulty were they drawn away that they could not be made to come forth all together

This Christian host whereof I speak passed over the river on a Friday [143] And the morrow was a feast day, whereon none doeth any work with his hands —the feast of one of the Lord God's disciples, the apostle Saint Bartholomew And on the Monday thereafter, without any error, was it just two years that Acre had been besieged, which was now possessed of the Christians And on Sunday the host marched forth, in the name of God who leadeth and directeth all, very early in the morning And the horsemen mounted throughout the host and drew up their battalions There had ye seen chivalry! 'Twas the fairest company of bachelors, the most valiant and choicest, that ever was seen before or afterward There had ye seen so many confident folk, so many goodly suits of arms, so many serjeants valiant and bold and renowned for their great prowess, there had ye seen so many a pennoncel, so many a goodly gleaming lance, there had ye seen so many banners wrought with so many devices, so many goodly hauberks and fair helms (so many and so goodly are there not in five kingdoms), and there had ye seen a marching host that well might fill men with fear King Richard made the vanguard, with men who were no cravens The Normans were about the standard, who ofttimes guarded it thus The duke and the French—that brave folk—they were with the rear ward But so slowly did these begin to march that ill must needs befall thereof The host was marching along the shore,[144] and the cruel Saracen folk were in the sand-hills on the left and could well watch the doings of our men And a mist had arisen which caused our people much annoy The line had waxed thin and in one place was it well-nigh broken, where the waggoners were marching who were carrying the victual for the host Down came the Saracens, straight on the waggoners they rushed, slaying there both horses and men And of the provision took they a large part, and discomfited and thrust apart them that were leading the train and drave them clean into the tossing sea There they yet assailed them, and they cut off the hand of a certain serjeant named Evrart, one of the Bishop of Salisbury's men But he altered not the fashion of his countenance, but when his right hand was cut off he took his sword in his left hand and, holding his ground, defended himself against them all Then was the whole host thrown into confusion (but King Richard as yet knew nought thereof) and the rear ward halted, all troubled and dismayed Then John Fitz-Lucas came pricking to the king and immediately told him the tidings Then the king rode back at full speed from the vanguard with the trustiest of his household and charged the Turks beside the hill Swifter than a thunderbolt he hurled himself into the midst of them, nor know I how many of them he slew before they recognized him, and an evil neighbour had they had in him an he had known of the matter but a little sooner And there a certain Frenchman wrought so well— 'twas he of Barres, the valiant William—that he laid many a Turk flat on the ground And that day did he so expose himself to danger that the king clean forgave him a grudge that he had long borne against him, nor cherished he any bitterness toward him thereafter Back into the mountain they drave the Turks, nor know I how many of them they slew there And Saladin was close at hand with the forces of heathendom, but after that his folk had retired they all halted and remained quiet, so that our host, which they had so disordered, all in good order went their way until they were come to a river that crossed their path, and to cisterns, which they tried There they pitched their tents and their pavilions in a great open space that they saw, where Saladin had lain the night and where it was very evident that a marvelous and numberless host of those unspeakably savage folk had been

On that first day of their march such handsel had the host of the Turks that the Turks had in sooth rather gained from them Such is oft the lot of them that are making conquests God did this for their salvation, that the host might not continue to march so heedlessly, but should be in closer order and better ranged when it was attacked Thereafter they took good heed to themselves and conducted their march more prudently But ever heavier grew their task, for already that rabble, Saladin and his pack, were moving along the other side of the mountain toward the narrow passes through which they knew that our men must go And they had so contrived that our host would be or slain or taken, or at the least would so far fall into their hands that they would be utterly discomfited Our men turned aside from the river, but only a short day's march did they make, and they went and pitched their tents below Caiphas,[145] for to await the coming of the lesser folk

Under Caiphas, along the coast, had the proud and valiant host encamped in two divisions, all the way betwixt the seashore and the tower Two days did they tarry there, busying themselves about their harness and their provisions, casting away that which they could not use, and retaining that which pleased them For they that were on foot, the lesser folk, arrived there with great difficulty, burdened as they were with victual and with their fighting-gear, so that many must perforce remain there, where they died of heat and of thirst

When the host of God had rested beneath Caiphas and had made their preparations, they departed thence on a Tuesday[146] and drew up their battalions The Temple made the vanguard and the Hospital the rear ward And whoso had seen the ranks forming had deemed them warriors most skilled, for the host was far better ordered than it had been the first time Because of the rest that they had taken they made a long day's march that day But all along the shore they

---

[145]The modern Haifa, opposite Acre, on the south side of the bay
[146]27 August

found high bushes and great brambles which caused the footfolk sore annoy and smote them in their faces All the land was desert, and there had ye seen many a goodly chase of the multitude of game that they found there along the shore, which leaped forth from under their very feet, so that they took an abundance thereof

To the castle of Capernaum, which had been torn down by them whom we hate, came the king, and he dismounted and dined there, awaiting the host And they who would dined also, then they went on even to the Casal of the Strait,[147] which was not wide, but very narrow Thither came they and dismounted and pitched there their tents and their pavilions Now every evening, after the host had encamped, ere yet they had laid them down to sleep, there was one man who cried—and the whole host cried after him, for his voice was heard afar—and he cried "Holy Sepulchre, help us!" And all cried after him and raised their hands to heaven and wept many tears And he cried yet again, until he had thrice cried And thereby were they not a little comforted

XXXVII

OF THE VERMIN THAT TORMENTED THE HOST HOW THEY MARCHED FROM THE CASTLE OF MERLE TO CAESAREA OF THE RIVER OF THE CROCODILES, THE DEAD RIVER, AND THE SALT RIVER

By day the host was peaceful, but when the night was dark, then had they many a fierce assault of stinging worms and of tarantulas, which grievously tormented the pilgrims and stang them so that they immediately swelled up But the rich men gave them of the theriac that they had, so that they were straightway healed The tarantulas gave them much annoy, but their wise men gave thought to the matter, and when the vermin were coming and the folk perceived it, then had ye heard the noise within the host! (I take AMBROSE to witness thereof) Such uproar! Such hubbub! Such discord and such din! They beat on helmets and on casques, on barrels, on saddles, and on saddle-pads, on shields, on targes, and on bucklers, on basins, pans, and kettles, and the vermin fled before the great noise that they heard And after the more part of the host had become familiar with them, the vermin withdrew themselves

At this casal, where the host had halted, they fortified and prepared themselves against the cruel, hated folk who then made many an assault upon them The place was broad, and wide the ground [148] Two full days' space must the king and the host take to await there the coming of their provision Then came the ships thither, barges and galleys together, which accompanied the host along the

[147]The term "casal" (Mediaeval Latin *casale*) means "manor," "hamlet," "village" "The country as distinguished from the towns was divided into *casals* or villages, inhabited by 'Syrians,' 'Beduins,' or, as they are otherwise styled, *rustici*, who paid a quarter or a third of the net produce of their harvests to their lord" Archer and Kingsford, *The Crusades, 92*

[148]"The name of this casal indicates that it was situated in a defile   it is therefore surprising that the poet should say a little further on, *'larges iert li leus e la place'* Doubtless we should understand that the space between the mountains, very narrow at the casal itself, grew wider immediately beyond it" Gaston Paris, *L'Estoire de la Guerre Sainte*

seacoast and carried their victual Back to the casal were they come, but the king had returned to Merle,[149] where he had lain the night And there had he ordered all for the morrow's march—that he himself would have the vanguard, so that they need have no cause for fear in the front, and that they of the Temple should make the rear ward and guard it, for the Saracens were drawing nigh unto the host, and all day long they harassed it That day the King of England charged the foe and there he won great glory, and but for the slackness of certain ones that day had he wrought many a deed of prowess For the king and his men pursued the enemy, but some there were that shewed themselves very slack And that evening were they greatly upbraided for this, even as they deserved, for an they had but followed the king a glorious feat of arms had then been seen Howbeit, he drave back the Turks, and the host marched along the sands in good order but very slowly, for the day was exceeding hot, nor was that day's march short, but long and very difficult And the heat so tormented them that a great many of them perished from it, and these were straightway buried And they that could go no further, of whom there were ofttimes many, they that were worn and spent, they that were sick and disheartened—these, like a prudent man, did the king cause to be carried in the galleys and the barges even to the end of the day's march That day they marched in sore distress, and the harbingers[150] went even to the city of Caesarea But the enemy's folk had already been there and had laid waste the town and wrought great mischief and destruction there But when our people came, they fled away, and our men went down and pitched their tents and their pavilions at the side of a river which they found there This is the river which even unto this day is called the River of the Crocodiles [151] Two pilgrims bathed themselves in the river, and the crocodiles ate them

To Caesarea, which is girt about with a long wall, where God wrought many a wondrous work, for much did He frequent that coast with His beloved company —thither did the king bid his transport ships follow after him And he caused a proclamation to be made at Acre for to bring in the laggards, enjoining them in the name of God to get them on board the transport ships and to come to the host And a great part of them came before the host departed thence And, lo, one evening the goodly fleet arrived at Caesarea and joined itself with the barges which day by day sailed along the coast And the host had plenty of victual from the ships, spite of the heathen pack

Just at the hour of terce[152] (this AMBROSE knoweth without any error) the host was armed and marched away, well ranged and ordered, and it was determined that on that day it would make but a short march because of the Saracens who came raining down upon them every day when they brake camp That day also they pursued hard after the host, but they left behind them there an admiral,

---

[149]A castle belonging to the Templars

[150]*Li herbergeor,* officers sent ahead to prepare a lodging or camping place

[151]The Latin version says that "two soldiers had once been devoured there by crocodiles, while bathing" Ambrose's account may be based on some old legend rather than on an event occurring during the crusaders' passage, as crocodiles have hardly been known to exist in Syrian rivers since very ancient times

[152]1 September

who was so renowned for his great hardihood and his great strength that no man (so they said) could overthrow him and none durst attack him, for he had a lance so heavy that no two in France were heavier This was Ayas Estoi—by that name I heard him called And the Turks so mourned for him that they cut off their horses' tails And very fain had they carried his body away, had the Christians suffered it Straightway the pilgrims departed thence and went on till they came down to the Dead River,[153] which the base and treacherous Saracens had covered over But it was again uncovered, and our men drank thereof and lay there two nights

Then from the river marched the valiant host, after they had rested there two days All leisurely they went, and in no haste, through a land impoverished and desolate That day they went along the mountainside, for the seashore found they so wild, so broken, that they could not pass that way And that day was the host more closely ranged than ever it was on any other day The rear ward did the Temple make—who that evening scratched their own temples,[154] for they lost so many horses that day that they were well-nigh disheartened And the Count of Saint-Pol likewise lost many an horse there, for so sorely did he suffer by the harassing and harrying of the Turks, and so freely did he expose himself that day, that all the host gave him great praise And that day the King of England, who went to seek the Turks and closed with them, was wounded in the side with a dart, by a Turk whom he had attacked, howbeit, he was not hurt grievously but continued to charge against them Then had ye seen darts flying, horses dying or wounded! Of arrows had ye seen such a shower that four feet of bare ground had ye not discovered in all the space round about, where the host of God was ranged And all day long endured this torment which the host must suffer, until the evening, when the Turks withdrew themselves to their encampment And our men pitched their camp beside a brackish stream and lodged there Then had ye seen the press about the fattest of the dead horses, which had been slain that day The serjeants bought the flesh of these, paying right dear, and there were grievous quarrels over it But when the king heard of the matter he caused a ban to be cried, proclaiming that if any man's horse had died and he gave it to the worthy serjeants, then would the king have a living horse given him in exchange Then did the serjeants have them without stint And they took and flayed them and ate the choicer parts of their flesh

XXXVIII

HOW THE PILGRIMS MARCHED THROUGH THE FOREST OF ARSÛF AND ENCAMPED BESIDE THE RIVER OF THE CLOVEN ROCK HOW THEY WENT ON IN BATTLE ARRAY AGAINST ARSÛF, AND HOW THE BEDOUINS AND OTHER INFIDELS ATTACKED THEM

Two days were they resting there, and on the third, just at the hour of terce, they marched away, all arrayed for battle, for it was said that the heathen pack, the black-faced misbelievers, were within the Forest of Arsûf, and that on that

---

[153]There are several streams, bogs, or fens of this name along the eastern coast of the Mediterranean

[154]See note, p 70

day would they set it on fire and make so great a burning that the host would be
roasted therein But the host went on its way through the Forest of Arsûf, all in
good order, nor do I think that ever any man will see or ever hath seen in any
place goodlier marching than was this Never made they any halt, but went their
way all quietly They passed by the mountain of Arsûf that day and went clean
through the forest and came out into the open country There they encamped
upon a plain above the River of the Cloven Rock,[155] in spite of the circumcised
folk who had come down, thick as the drops of rain, from every side, and the
number of these, according to him who saw the host and surveyed and watched
and estimated it as best he might, was three hundred thousand, or peradventure
he miscounted them a little And our Christians were not more than an hundred
thousand, so were they estimated And by the River of the Cloven Rock lay the
host of God—His household There they encamped on a Thursday and they
rested there the Friday And on the Saturday,[156] at the dawning, then had ye
seen our folk making ready every man to defend his own head For that day were
they made to understand that they could not go on without giving battle to that
rabble which was drawing nigh to them on every side and forming its battalions
Therefore the Christian host so disposed itself against the heathen that there was
no cause to dispraise their ranks or to order them again Richard, the brave King
of England, who knew much of armies and of warfare, determined in his own
wise who should go in the front and in the rear Twelve battalions did they form
and order in divisions, of such men that in all lands which heaven covereth no
more serviceable warriors might be found, all in their hearts determined and resolved to do God's service The Temple made that day the vanguard, and the
Hospital the rear ward, Bretons and Angevins followed the Temple, an I mistake not They of Poitou, and King Guy, were next thereafter, as I have been
informed The Normans and the English came riding after these, bearing the
Dragon [157] And behind came the Hospital, who made that day the rear ward The
rear ward was filled that day with the high baronry, ordered in good array, side
by side and so closely ranged that, had ye tossed an apple, ye had not failed to hit
or beast or man And it reached from the Saracen host clean down to the seashore There had ye seen so many banners, and so many folk of cheerful countenance there was the Count of Leicester, who would not in any wise have been
elsewhere, and there was Huon of Gournai, with many men of renown, and there
was William of Borriz, who was reared in that land, and there was Gauquelin of
Ferrières, with folk of divers stations, and there was Roger of Tosni, with a great
company of knights, and there was the valiant James of Avesnes, whom God received that day into His own kingdom, and there was Count Robert of Dreux,
with many folk that followed him, and there was the Bishop of Beauvais, who
had joined himself to his brother, and he of Barres and he of Garlande,[158] they

---

[155]*Sor le flum de Rochetaillee* "This is the *Nahr el-Fâlek*, to the north of Arsûf, a little
stream which owes its existence to an artificial cleft in the rock and serves as drain to a
vast morass" Clermont-Ganneau, quoted by Gaston Paris

[156]1191 September

[157]The ensign of the Normans

[158]Garlande was a fief lying inside the city of Paris

also had a great following, and William and Droon of Mello, nor were their people few They of one lineage marched together and supported one another, and the host was so bound together that hardly could it be broken asunder Count Henry, the Lord of Champagne, guarded the host over against the mountain, that day did he watch over the flank of the army and ever rode along the ranks, and the serjeants of foot were behind the host and closed the line of their march The provision and the other stuff, the waggons, the sumpter beasts, the packs—all these were down beside the shore, that they might suffer lesser loss

So marched the people in all confidence, slowly and leisurely, so marched the ranks The Duke of Burgundy, with the king and with other valiant folk and bold and proud, rode before the host and behind and on the right hand and on the left, for to watch the Turks and their doings and to lead and to direct the host And great travail must they endure, for just an hour before terce came all the Turks against them, more than two thousand of them, shooting their arrows from their bows and encompassing the host of God And after these came certain black folk—Blackamoors[159] are they called in sooth—and Saracens of the Heath,[160] hideous and blacker than soot, on foot, with bows and bucklers, nimble folk and very swift These caused our host so great annoy that neither rest nor respite did they get There had ye seen, along the plain, of Turks so great and proud a company, so many pennoncels, so many ensigns, so many banners with divers devices, so many fair battalions rightly ranged! Yea, more than thirty thousand had ye seen in full array, coming so furiously against the host, on horses swift as thunderbolts Beneath their feet arose great clouds of dust Before the admirals came their trumpeters and those that bare timbrels and drums, nor had these any other task save to beat their drums and make great noise and hoot and shout and howl Then could ye not have heard even God's thunder, so many were the drums a-beating there! The heathen pack pressed hard the host and assaulted them and closed with them For two leagues round had ye not seen an empty spot or space so big as my lap, nor aught else save their accursed brood Seaward and landward, so close they hemmed the host, with so great force and so great fury, that they caused grievous loss of horses which they slew, for many of these in sooth fell dead But a great help that day were the good arbalesters and the good serjeants that drew the bow, who kept themselves behind the host But these feared lest their line should be broken, for they were so hard assailed that they thought not to live another hour or to escape thence hale and whole And know ye of a truth that the cowards amongst them perforce flung down their bows and arrows and sought refuge within the host And the brave men that remained and that protected the host in the rear had such a pack about their heels that they walked backward that day more than in any other fashion Nor in all the host was there any man so bold that he had not wished with all his heart that his pilgrimage were over But at this I marvel not at all, for the host was so harried, on the right hand and on the left, that never hath God let a man be born that hath seen folk so

---

[159]*Noirez*

[160]*La Berue*, a term of Arabic origin

hounded or host put to such proof   There had ye seen the knights, when they had
lost their steeds, on foot along with the serjeants, drawing the bow , and I am able
to tell and to declare unto you (and many know whether I am lying) that neither
rain nor snow nor hail, when it descendeth in the depth of winter, ever flew thicker than their shafts flew there, which laid low our horses   And ye could pluck
and gather them up by armfuls, even as men gather up the straw amid the stubble, so many were the folk that were shooting at us   And they cast themselves
upon our ranks with such violence that they lacked but little of having broken
them   Then did the Hospital send word to the king that the enemy were pressing their division too hard nor could they longer withstand them unless they
charged   And the king sent back word that they should hold themselves fast and
withstand the onset   So, perforce, they withstood, and with great difficulty
they held their way

Exceeding hot it was that day, for God had so ordained   Sore was the heat,
and fierce that folk that pursued after our own, nor will I refrain from saying
that there is not in all the world a folk so brave—had they but seen the multitude
and the press of the fell paynim, and the rage and the fury wherewith the Devil
had possessed them—that they would not have been afeared an they had seen our
grievous condition nor known the custom of the foe   For even as on the anvil the
smiths strike in long turns, even so did they violently smite the rear ward, which
was guarded that day by many a valiant knight   [161]   But they took not heed to
themselves, as they ought to have done, and our men did them much mischief,
driving them back with their maces   Then had ye seen great empty places round
about men that might have been elsewhere but were very loath to acknowledge
that, for the Turks, they would yield ground or would turn back one single step.
But here did they full otherwise, for fiercely they fought their way   And the
Turks hurled themselves into our troops with fury and with violence   Nor was
this at all marvelous, so that any should marvel at it, for of all the forces of
Heathendom—from Damascus even unto Persia, from the sea even unto the sunrising—there remained no people, bold, confident, and renowned, victorious, valiant, and daring, that Saladin had not sought out and hired, or besought and en-
ticed and won over and held, because of God's people who were come against him,
whom he thought now to discomfit   But all these could not suffice, for the flower
of chivalry, the seed of warrior youth—a folk all skilled in warfare—had been
culled from the stock of all Christendom to war upon the paynim—a valiant,
chosen band !   And whoso had overcome this company, well might he say thereafter that no living thing durst resist him

---

[161]Lacuna of several lines

XXXIX

OF THE VICTORY OF THE CHRISTIANS, AND OF THE DEATH AND BURIAL OF JAMES OF AVESNES

Thick was the dust, sore was the heat, but God's people were filled with valour The Devil's folk were arrogant, but the host of God was brave and well able to defend itself There was a press of Turks, closer crowded than an hedge The Christians went their way, and these clave to their backs, but little mischief could they do them Then had ye seen how the Turks raged, that retinue of the very Devil of Hell! They called us "iron folk," because we bare so much armour, whereby our own men were the more secure, fearing their malignity the less So the Turks put back their bows into their quivers and came at us with their maces, and in a little while more than twenty thousand of them were hammering the Hospital, when one of our knights cried "O Saint George![162] Wilt thou suffer us thus to be confounded? Now ought Christendom to perish, when against this pack none offereth battle!" This was Brother Garnier of Nablûs,[163] the Master of the Hospitalers He came to the king, spurring apace, and said to him "Sire, too great shame and dishonour it is that we be driven thus, for every one of us is losing his horse!" And the king said "Patience, fair Master! A man cannot be everywhere"

Back went the master to his company, and the Turks were yet pressing our men in the rear, so that there was neither prince nor count that had not great shame thereof And they cried "Sirs, let us charge! Cravens indeed shall we be esteemed! Never was seen such shame, nor ever yet from misbelieving folk hath our host suffered such reproach! And if for any scruple we should not now defend ourselves we may well have waited too long!" God! What loss, what mischief, what desperate straits in that hour befell the host! Yet had very many of the Saracens died then, an our own sin had not confounded the charge that was then purposed In the mean time they were preparing this charge, to which all were agreed, and already had they taken their measures, which were good ones had they but been regarded For it was agreed that before they charged, in three several places should be set six trumpets which should sound so soon as our men were to turn against the Turks—two before the host, two behind, and two in the middle And if they had held to this plan, then would they have had all the Turks But they lost them through the fault of two men who could not hold themselves back from charging, but hurled themselves ahead of all the others and left two Turks lying dead The one of these men was a knight, the Marshal of the Hospital, the other was Baldwin of Caron,[164] who was bold as a lion Companion was he to the King of England, who had brought him from his own land These twain began the onset in the name of the Almighty King "Saint George!" they cried in a loud voice, and all God's people turned their horses round about to face the cruel folk and proud Then

---

[162] "Perhaps from this period [Saint George] tended to become the patron saint of England" Archer and Kingsford, *The Crusades*, 334

[163] The Hebrew Shechem, called Neapolis by the Greeks and Romans

[164] Carew (?)

charged the Hospital, all in a body, which had suffered so long, then charged the Lord of Champagne and his dear company, then charged James of Avesnes there, he and they of his lineage with him, and then charged Robert, the knight of Dreux (this know I right well), and the Bishop of Beauvais with him, these twain charged together And there charged the Count of Leicester, on the left toward the seashore, and all they of the rear ward, not a man of them was a coward And thereafter charged the Angevins, the Bretons, the men of Maine and of Poitou, and all the other divisions together And I will tell you what seemeth me to be true the valiant men who were charging there closed with the Turks so vigorously that every one of them picked his own man and thrust the point of his lance into his body, so that he must needs void his saddle This seemed to the Turks a new thing, for now our men fell upon them like thunderbolts Then had ye seen the thick dust fly! And all they who had dismounted and were shooting at us with bows, wherewith they so harrassed our folk, these now had their heads cut off, for so soon as the knights overthrew them the serjeants slew them And so soon as the king saw that the host had broken its ranks and closed with the Turks he thrust his spurs into his horse, waiting no longer, and came on full speed to help the foremost lines Swifter than a crossbow bolt, with all his household brave and eager, he smote so violently a division of the heathen that was crowded together on his right that they were all dumfounded at the sight of the valiant men, and perforce must they void their saddles, stretched out thick as the sheaves of corn had ye seen them lying all along the ground And the brave King of England pursued after them and charged them, and so well wrought he in that hour that round about him, on either side, before, behind, was a great open highway filled with Saracens that had fallen dead there, and the rest drew back, and the windrow of the dead reached full half a league in length There might ye see Turks falling headlong and Saracens unhorsed There might ye see the dust a-flying, which caused our people great annoy, for when they came forth of the great press they knew not one another for the dust that had been raised, so that their labour was doubled Howbeit, they smote on the right hand and on the left, and there were the Turks in a sorry pass There had ye seen blows given and received and folk, all bleeding, fleeing from the field There, too, had ye seen banners falling down, and many a pennoncel of divers shape So many good sharp swords, so many lances keen, so many a Turkish bow, so many a mace could ye have gathered there in many a place, with these and with the bolts and darts and arrows could ye have laden more than a score of waggons There had ye seen so many bearded Turks lying dead, piled thick as stooks in harvest There had ye seen an hard fight fought by them that yet held themselves upright, but they that were overset and they that had lost their horses hid themselves in the thickets and climbed up into the trees, and when our men drew them thence ye should have heard them howl as they were slain And some there were that abandoned their horses and fled away toward the sea and cast themselves from the cliffs, more than ten fathoms downward Verily, the heathen were routed utterly, so that for full two leagues had ye seen none but fleeing folk, who a little

time afore had been so arrogant, for all our men had turned against them
And they that guarded the standard (these were the Normans, that steadfast
folk) turned very slowly against the foe, so that (as my heart suspecteth) the
rest of the battle might have gone very ill or ever any great hurt were done
to them

The warriors who, with God's help, had made this charge stayed themselves
thereafter, but so soon as they had come to an halt, the Saracens recovered
themselves More than twenty thousand of these came, holding their maces
in their hands, for to rescue them that had been overthrown Then had ye
seen how our men were buffeted! At those who were betaking themselves back
to the host the Saracens were ever discharging their arrows, and they smote
with their maces, breaking heads and arms, so that our men bowed down over
their saddlebows But these valiant warriors recovered themselves so soon as
they had gotten their breath again, then they charged gallantly, riding into the
ranks of the foe and breaking them like nets There had ye seen saddles turned
and Turks wavering and retreating, but so hard pressed were our folk that
they could not advance a bowshot further, and had they made an halt, dearly
had they paid therefor

And there was the admiral Dequedin,[165] one of Saladin's kinsmen, who
had portrayed upon his banner a device of a strange sort, it was a banner bearing a pair of breeches—this was his veritable device And he was the Turk
who with all his heart most hated Christendom He had in his company more
than seven hundred Turks, choice men of Saladin's own household troops, warriors very hard to conquer And each squadron in its turn had a yellow banner
with a pennoncel of other colour And he came with so great speed, with
such clattering of hoofs, with such eagerness to strike the true believing folk
who were returning to the standard, bearing their arms, that there were not
amongst all these any so valiant and so skilled in war that in that hour they
had not much to learn Then had ye seen our men awaiting him! Then had
ye seen many a shock of arms, many a forceful sundering, for back came our
men to the host, since the Saracens pressed them so close that but few durst
turn against them, and all their bodies trembled, so violent were the blows
upon their helms Then the brave William of Barres made a charge that all
men praised, for he and his men hurled themselves betwixt our people and
that press of noisome savage folk and smote them so sore that I know not how
many of the Turks fell there And Richard, King of England, over against the
mountain charged in his turn—he and his gallant company—and he rode Fauvel
of Cyprus (there was not another such horse 'twixt here and Ypres), and
such deeds of knighthood wrought he upon the ugsome enemy folk that with
great wonder men beheld how he and his joined battle They drave back and
held the Turks until our people had gotten themselves back to the standard
and ordered their ranks anew So they rode and marched onward until they
were come to Arsûf, where they gat them down and pitched their tents and their

---

[165]Takieddin

pavilions, for it was in sooth the hour for seeking a lodging That evening, whoso desired to find booty, he went to the place where the battle was fought, and verily, there found he spoil a-plenty And they that went thither and counted the Saracens that were slain said that there died on this field that day two and thirty barons of the land, admirals, whose bodies their men came to seek thereafter, and seven hundred Turks whose corpses lay there, besides those that were wounded and fell dead along the country-side, but that of our men not a tenth part of that number had died—nay, not a tenth of a tenth

But, ah, God! What a great mischance, what a sore disaster befell us there where our men were what time the Saracens recovered themselves! For when they came against us again they compassed about and cut off a valiant man, the brave James of Avesnes—whom may God make a saint in His own kingdom! This misadventure befell us through his horse which fell beneath him, but so well wrought he in defending himself that those told us and informed us, who after the end of the battle were sent forth to seek his body where it lay amid the paynim pack, that in a little space of ground about him the good men who went thither found fifteen Turks all cut in pieces, on whom the warrior had avenged himself And three of his kinsmen died there with him, nor was any succour whatsoever given them by certain others, of whom there was much talk thereafter It was one of the barons of France, so they said—the Count of Dreux—he and his people that were with him And so many men were heard speaking ill of him then that the history cannot gainsay it

Before Arsûf was the host encamped, who had checked the paynim folk, and they had caused an utter checkmate had they but been in the right position And, lo, the news was noised abroad of our people that were lost—nay, not lost, but found, for they had proved themselves in God's cause, James of Avesnes and his household, who had been slain and cut in pieces And the host of God was very sorrowful and so troubled and so confounded that never for the death of any man, since Adam tasted the apple, was heard so great a plaint, or such lamenting and such mourning For right well served he God, without guile Already had he looked into Paradise and chosen there his place beside Saint James the Apostle, whom he held to be his patron and our own—James of Avesnes, the Martyr, who deigned not to retreat before the Turks

Before Arsûf lay the host, stretched out along the great river, and all that night they rested there, for they had had sore toil of giving and receiving blows, nor would they remove thence before the third day, when they were well recovered On a Saturday was the battle, and the Sunday was in sooth the precious feast of the glorious Mother of God, which men celebrate in September, for the history so recordeth it Then the Hospitalers armed themselves, and the Knights of the Temple, they took the brave Turcopoles, and many other folk went with them, and, lo, they came to the field where those lay that had died in the battle Through all the field they searched and sought, nor would they eat or drink till they had found the body of the well proved knight, James of Avesnes And at the last they found it, but first they washed the face, else never had he been recognized, so many mortal blows had he received whilst he was defending himself, holding his ground against the Saracens They covered the body, and lifted it up, and went their ways again to Arsûf There had ye seen a great company of men-at-arms and knights that came to meet the body, with such lamentation that under heaven is none who, seeing them, had not been filled with exceeding great pity And one, with tears, proclaimed his prowess, another praised his bounty That day was the King of England there, and King Guy, when they laid him in earth in the minster of Our Holy Lady—may she pray her sweet Son for the soul of him whose body found there a lodging place! And after mass the clerks most fervently performed the further office in their order [166] And the great men took the body in their arms and laid it in the earth Nor ask me if they wept

XL

OF THE DESPAIR OF THE SARACENS, AND HOW SALADIN REPROVED HIS EMIRS HOW THE EMIR OF ALEPPO MADE ANSWER TO HIM HOW SALADIN CAUSED THE STRONG HOLDS TO BE RASED

Now let us, for a season, leave off speaking of this affair and telling the tale thereof, but in no wise will it be forgotten, for it is all a part of our matter and presently will we take it up again And now will we speak of the hated folk that had made this attack upon us

This people, devoid of all good, had been driven back in such wise as I have already recounted to you Nor had they accomplished that whereof they had boasted to their soldan in their great arrogance, when they said to him that, without doubt or fail and without any vaunting, Christendom would that day be taken, conquered, and slain But otherwise was the event! Had ye but seen it from the mountain-top, along the way by which the Turks were fleeing! For they who saw it thence have told us that when their men and ours came together, we drave them back so violently—both themselves and their stuff— that as they fled full many a camel dropped dead, and many horses brown or pied, and mules and hinnies by hundreds and by thousands, and so many of their men did they lose when our folk charged upon them that, had their host been further followed and a little harder pressed and pursued, then had the whole land been made our own and peopled by Christians

When this battle had been fought and the host of the Turks had withdrawn themselves, and when Saladin, who was over against the mountain, perceived the outcome—when he beheld his people discomfited, the best and choicest of his men—then began he to speak thus to his admirals

"Ha! Where is now my household—those braggarts—those madmen? Now Christendom rideth through Syria at her will, nor findeth any one to turn her back Now know I not which way to turn Where are now those great threats? Where are those sword-strokes, those blows of maces, which they had boasted that they would deliver when they should have joined battle? Where are now

---

[166]Lacuna of one line

those goodly beginnings of great conquests and mighty battles, where are the dire discomfitures of our enemies, that we find in the books that our forefathers wrote concerning them? Where are the victories that they were wont to gain over the Christians, whereof the tale is daily told to us? Ill goeth this affair! For now are we the world's orts and its offscum, in battle and in warfare, beside the men that we were of yore are we of no account, yet they availed much"

The admirals of the Saracens heard how Saladin upbraided them on this wise, nor ever a man of them lifted his head, save one—Zenghi of Aleppo—who set himself firmly on his Arab steed and thus spake

"Righteous Soldan, now listen to me Right roundly hast thou rated us and upbraided us exceedingly But wherefore dost thou misprise us when thou knowest not the occasion of this happening? For there was no default of fighting on our part, nor of bold attacking, nor of shooting or smiting the Franks with steel and with iron, nor of enduring their grievous strokes But nothing can withstand them, for they have such armour—so strong, so firm, so closely fitted—wherewith they are covered in such wise that no more hurt can we do to them than to a weather-bitten rock And whoso hath to do with such a folk, what counsel can he take? And yet is there a greater marvel—a certain Frank that is of their company, who slayeth and maimeth our people, never another such have we seen Every day was he himself in the forefront, for every need was he found ready, like a good knight well proved He it is that hath hewn such gaps in our lines And they call him Melek[167] Richard, and rightly should such a Melek possess both lands and wealth, and conquer and dispend"

Then Saladin, being full of bitterness as ye have heard me tell, called to him his brother Saphadin and said to him

"Now do I wish it to be evident how great confidence I have in my people Get thee on horseback, go and without demur cause me the city of Ascalon to be rased—no longer booteth us to defend it, and rase the town of Gaza—let it be broken like a piece of wood, but cause Daron[168] Castle to be spared, that my people may be able to come by that way And rase me Castle Galatie,[169] that the Franks may not avail them thereof And let Fig Tree Castle[170] be rased, that they may not rally there And rase me the White Guard,[171] so that thence we may have no cause to fear Rase Jaffa, and that utterly, and the Casal of the Plains,[172] and the Middle Casal[173] Rase me Saint George[174] and Ramleh,[175] that great city which we took, and Bel Mont[176] high

---

[167]The Arabic word for "king"
[168]The southernmost of the castles of Palestine
[169]Karatieh, near Ascalon
[170]*Fuer* Its location is uncertain
[171]*La Blanche Guarde*, Tell es-Safieh
[172]Yazûr (?), between Jaffa and Jerusalem
[173]*Casel Maien*, near Yazûr
[174]The ancient Lydda
[175]A little way north of Jerusalem, Ramah in the Old Testament
[176]Not identified

upon the mountain side, Toron,[177] and Castle Ernaut,[178] and Fairview Castle,[179] and Mirabel[180] Rase also, for so seemeth me good, the castles of the mountain, so that not one of them remain standing—castle, or casal, or city—but that all be cast down to the ground, save only Kerak[181] and Jerusalem Thus do I will it, and thus shall it be done "

So Saladin commanded, and his brother took his leave of him, well understanding the commandment that had been given him Then boldly spake a certain Turk named Caisac,[182] a Saracen of high estate and great renown, and he said to Saladin

"Sire, no man ought to yield him to his anger and his spite as thou art doing Rather, send now thy scouts and spies and guards into the plains of Ramleh and upon the heights so that, whatever way the Franks shall turn, the spies may return hither, knowing whither the Christian host purposeth to go And peradventure will they go to some place where we can work them mischief By Mahomet, whom we worship, or ever a man upbraid another, first ought he to consider the time and the occasion! Nor shouldst thou misprise us, for such are the chances of war that ofttimes men suffer discomfitures Nor will I refrain myself from saying that if I have a goodly company I think to keep myself so close on the heels of the Franks that they will repent them of having come hither "

Then chose they thirty admirals, great warriors and of lofty lineage, and each one of them had in his company five hundred of the bravest of the Turks These Saladin bade depart and go down to the river of Arsûf, and all went thither, and they waited until the Christians should ride forth again

XLI

HOW THE PILGRIMS WENT ON FROM ARSÛF UNTO JAFFA HOW KING RICHARD THOUGHT TO GO TO THE HELP OF ASCALON HOW THE FRENCH BROUGHT IT TO PASS THAT THE HOST REMAINED AT JAFFA AND FELL INTO SIN HOW KING RICHARD WAS CAUGHT IN AN AMBUSHMENT, BUT WAS SAVED BY WILLIAM OF PRÉAUX

The host of God, which had fought so well and had a little abated the arrogance of the Saracens, on the third day, fearing nought, went forth from Arsûf all in order ranged, and on through the land that had been so hardly tried, for to avenge the great shame that was put upon God The Templars that day kept the rear ward where they marched, for the churl saith that "he that is on his guard cannot be made a laughing-stock" But now they guarded to no purpose, for never a Turk did they see that day, nor ever did the enemy appear until our men were come to the river, where they encamped There the Turks thought to annoy them, but nought could they accomplish Many a charge

---

[177]See note, p 103
[178]Near Jerusalem
[179]*Bel Veeir* Near Jerusalem, but not absolutely identified
[180]North of Ramleh
[181]About ten miles east of the southern end of the Dead Sea
[182]The correct form of the name would be Caisar (Alam ed-Din Kaïsar)

they made and many a shaft let fly, but at the last they withdrew themselves And our people pitched camp by the river of Arsûf and rested there In the morning the lesser folk, who could scarce be held back, departed with the foragers so that they came betimes to Jaffa Now Jaffa lieth beside the sea, but the cruel Saracen folk had already so overthrown it and so ruined and utterly demolished it that the host could not lodge themselves therein, so they encamped on the left side of the city in a fair olive grove But wherefore should I make a long tale? More than three whole weeks went by ere all the host was thither come from Acre, for so the affair befell

Before Jaffa in the olive grove, amidst the goodly gardens, there the host of God planted their banners   [183] And there were pasture lands, there were so many grapes and figs, pomegranates, almonds, growing in plenty round about —large fruits, wherewith the trees were laden—that the host took them without price and were greatly refreshed by them And now came the fleet to the harbour, the ships went and came from Jaffa unto Acre and thence back again, bringing them victual, whereat the paynim pack was sorely vexed And Saladin, who durst not offer battle, now caused the walls and towers of Ascalon to be rased One day, about the hour of nones, came tidings to the host, brought by poor folk of low estate who by night had escaped thence, that Ascalon had been mined and sapped and its walls overthrown And some held this tale to be true, even as it was reported, and others deemed it but a lie, a jest, or a dream, that Saladin, for any straits wherein he might be or for any price, would ever imagine such an act of weakness, until King Richard sent to get word thereof, in a swift sailing galley, Lord Geoffrey of Lusignan, who suffered many hardships in God's behalf, and William of L'Étang, a valiant knight and true, and other folk that with them went These waited before the city until they knew of a surety that the Turks were rasing it, then back they came and told their tale The barons took counsel together for to determine what they should do in the matter and whether they should go to the help of the city

In front of Jaffa and outside the city was the council gathered There were many words exchanged and counsels given of divers purports, for every man hath his own mind, nor are all men of the same age And the one would fain do one thing, wherein the other would find much to gainsay Yet was there no need that they should thus disagree, rather ought they all to have been of one accord Some waxed red in the face and declared that they would go to Jerusalem, whilst others would fain deliver Ascalon from the Turks if they could, for that was a good place wherein to seek shelter There might ye hear each one reproving the other's opinion, yet were they all men of high emprise Then spake the King of England, who all his days had been nourished up in war, and to the duke and to all the French assembled there he said

"Sirs, meseemeth that we are of divers minds, and this can bring great mischief to pass The Turks are causing Ascalon to be rased, yet dare they not offer us battle Let us go to the rescue of Ascalon! All the world ought to hasten thither, and methinketh this is a good thing to do"

[183]Lacuna of one line

Now why should I tell you the rest of the tale?—save that the French made answer (whereof thereafter many of them repented them sore) that it were better to remain at Jaffa and cause the place to be restored, and that from thence was the shorter road whereby to go upon their pilgrimage [184] But very evil counsel did they give when they would not go to Ascalon, for had they rescued the city at that season, then had the whole land been saved But they continued speaking thus till at the last it was determined to restore Jaffa

Now when the matter was thus agreed to, then did the host tarry at Jaffa. They gathered a great levy for to repair the castle, they caused the trenches to be digged again and the walls to be raised up anew all about the city Lo, then was the host at ease within the town, and, lo, from day to day crept sin into the host, lewd living, lust, and wantonness, for the evil women came back into the host, who behaved themselves most unseemly In the ships they came, and in the barges Ah, God's mercy! What sorry shields, what evil arms were these for conquering anew God's heritage and His Holy Land! And how miserably did those demean themselves who returned to their sin and by their incontinence brought all their pilgrimage to nought

It was now toward the end of September, and Jaffa (an I mistake not) was already somewhat restored, when the host was led forth from the gardens, and round about Saint Habakkuk's[185] the princes and the dukes pitched their pavilions But sorely was the host diminished from that which it had been at the beginning, for ever were they going back to Acre and sojourning in the taverns there And when the king knew of the slothfulness of the pilgrims and of their indolence he sent word to the pilgrims at Acre, by the King of Jerusalem (this is well known), that they must come straightway to the host and keep their covenant with God But very loath were they to go thither, for all King Guy's command, until King Richard, who both before and after gave himself much labour on their account, came himself to Acre and preached to them so effectually that he led much people back with him The queens, also, and their maids he brought back and he established them in Jaffa, and that all these folk might come thither, the host must perforce be kept there two months, or six weeks at the least—for which thereafter did we pay right dear

When the king had withdrawn the people from Acre and had brought them to the host, it was exceedingly strengthened thereby and was increased far more than it had decreased before But now shall ye hear to what proof was the host put during that very season, as he saw it who telleth this history Lightly might the whole host have been destroyed, for when an host loseth its captain, in a strange and far country as is the land of Syria, then it loseth its way utterly and falleth all to pieces And this I say because of the King of England, who had gone forth to seek the Saracens and to spy upon them that he might take them unaware But his spying had an evil issue, for too scant a retinue had the king at this time, furthermore, he had by chance fallen asleep And those enemies of nature, the

---

[184] Jaffa is about 37 miles from Jerusalem, Ascalon about 39
[185] A monastery near Jaffa

Saracens, who were on their guard, were close at hand and gat themselves so nigh to him that scarce was he awaked in time My Lords, marvel not if the king arose in all haste, for a single man whom so many folk beset is in no wise at his ease. But God granted him such good fortune that he gat him to horse, and his men with him—such as there were of them, but they were very few And when the Turks saw them mounted they turned them about, and the king pursued after them, and they fled straight toward their ambushment And they that were lying in ambush came forth impetuously and had fain laid hold on the king, but he put his hand to his brand of steel, and he was mounted on Fauvel that day The Turks were already closing with him . each one of them desired to lay hand on him, but none durst risk the stroke of his sword Yet peradventure had they taken him, had they but known at that time who he was Howbeit, one of his men, a brave and loyal knight, William of Préaux, spake unto them saying "O Saracens, I am Melek" Now Melek signifieth "the king" Then the Turks seized him in hot haste and caused him to be taken straight to their host And in this rencounter was slain Renier of Maron, who had the heart of a valiant knight, and his nephew, whose name was Walter, he also had a valiant heart and loyal Alain and Lucas of L'Étable died there also, this is sooth And when the news was known [186] joyous and content, so saith the book But to pursue the Turks would profit nought, for they were speedily drawing far away, carrying William captive with them And they thought, those hated folk, that they were carrying away the king, but such a thing was not pleasing to God, who was watching over him The Turks who thought that they had the king were already on the heights, and our men came back to the host But for William had they sore sorrow, both the king and all the host

When God of his bounty had on this wise spared the king that he might lead the host, then certain ones who knew that he was courageous and who feared for him began thus to speak

"Sire, for God's sake, do not thus, nor let it list thee to make such reconnoitrings! Guard thyself and Christendom Good men hast thou a-plenty, go no more, then, alone on such a business When thou desirest to do mischief to the Turks, take with thee a great company, for in thine hands are our lives—or our death, if aught befall thee For when the head is parted from the members, the members are no more sufficient to themselves but straightway fail and languish, and presently disaster cometh"

So many an honest man bestirred himself and spared no pains to admonish the king in this matter But he—sooth to tell—whensoever he gat wind of any skirmish (and but few were kept from his ears) ever closed with the Turks, to their great hurt, and wrought so well that at the end there were many of the foe or slain or taken captive, and his was the greatest honour And God ever brought him out of the great perils and jeopardies wherein the enemy put him

---

[186]A lacuna of several lines From the Latin translation it is evident that the missing passage described the anxiety of the Christians over Richard's prolonged absence and their joy at his return

XLII

HOW KING RICHARD RESTORED THE CASAL OF THE PLAINS AND THE MIDDLE CASAL HOW HE PURSUED AND OVERCAME THE INFIDELS OF THE PROWESS OF THE COUNT OF LEICESTER

When the host had fully armed itself with great difficulty, it was called together and proclamation was made in the name of God the Son of Saint Mary that they should go to the Casal of the Plains and that they should fortify it again, the better to guard the head of the host Then seemed it good to the king to command that certain folk remain at Jaffa for to fortify that city and to guard the port, so that no one should depart thence save merchants going after victual The Bishop of Évreux, in sooth, and the Count of Chalon[187] with him, and Sir Hugh Ribole—these were they that remained there for this purpose, and these caused the work to be performed Then, lo, the host mounted and set forth, nor ever fairer company was seen or one more nobly arrayed, but short indeed was that day's march Betwixt the two casals they descended and pitched there their tents And I know of a truth, by many proofs, that it was on the Eve of All Saints that we encamped there But the host of the Turks was at Ramleh, and from thence they made fierce attacks and dire assaults upon us

Full fifteen days or more our host lay betwixt the Casal of the Plains and the Middle Casal, which the heathen had torn down The Middle Casal the king caused to be builded up again, stronger than it had been ere it was rased, and the Templars restored the other casal But the Turks were ever tormenting us, and one day there came riding against the host—so meseemeth—full a thousand of them in one body Then our host was all confusion, like an ant-hill all a-swarm Then the king and the others mounted and hasted them forth so speedily as they could, and the Turks turned about and fled May the living Devil take them! For their horses went so swiftly every way whithersoever they turned them that the king could in no wise overtake them, and all in vain did he pursue and follow them And when he had long followed after them nor ever come up with any of them, of a sudden he beheld Ramleh openly and all the host of that base and recreant folk Then turned he back again to his own host, and with him came his men, haughty and bold.

On the sixth day of the great feast,[188] that Allhallow-tide that every one keepeth, forth from the camp came the squires a-seeking provender And for to guard them on this day went the valiant Lords of the Temple The foragers departed from the host and scattered themselves about the country-side, seeking rich grass, which many a time they purchased dear, for ofttimes did they buy it with their blood The Templars were guarding the foragers, but even as they were least expecting them, lo, after them came four companies of Saracens with great fury At full four hundred were they reckoned, all on horseback and well armed From over against Bombrac[189] they issued forth, straight at the Templars,

---

[187]William II

[188]6 November, 1191

[189]Not definitely identified Clermont-Ganneau supposes it to be Ibn Ibrâk, a little to the east of Jaffa

and assaulted them and compassed them round about, for there is no nimbler people in the world Strait and close did they press them, coming at once from every side And when the Templars beheld them so nigh they gat them off their horses and upon their feet, and there they wrought great deeds of prowess, their faces all turned toward those savage folk, each with his back against his brother's, as were they all sons of one father But so hard did the Saracens press them that they left three of our men dead There had ye beheld fearful blows given, there had ye heard the helmets ring and seen the fire fly forth from the steel and witnessed fair defense and fierce assault The Turks had thought to take them unaware, and yet they hoped to have them in their hands, so close encompassed were they holding them, when from our host came riding out in all haste certain of our folk And it was said (and this is sooth indeed) that Andrew of Chauvigni was the first, with fourteen other knights, to come to the rescue of the Templars in that hour Full drive he rushed upon the Turks, performing many a valorous deed, and his companions likewise A goodly fight was this, nor did it remain long hidden from the king That day was he rearing the walls of the Middle Casal and was intent upon that business, and he had sent for two counts who are worthy to be named in all good tales—him of Saint-Pol and him of Leicester, likewise had he commanded William of Caieux to come with them, who filled his place that day right well, there, too, was Otto of Trazignies, these all were of lofty lineage Lo, on a sudden came the sound of the cries that the foragers had raised And the king sent a message to the counts wherein he bade and ordered them to go and succour the Templars whilst he himself should make haste to don his armour and come after them, armed, so fast as ever he could So straight they rode their ways, and as they drew nigh unto the battle, lo, out from a river-bed issued full four thousand of the enemy folk, who divided themselves into two companies The one band bare down upon the Templars, the other turned against the barons And the barons ranged themselves in order and closed their ranks, whilst the Turks drew yet nearer to them Then did the Count of Saint-Pol challenge the valiant Count of Leicester to stand an hazard that was both bold and mad either the Count of Leicester should close with the Turks on their right hand and himself would guard him continually, or he himself would close with them and the count should guard him whithersoever he might go and whatsoever he might do And the count accepted the hazard With his household he departed and charged full tilt into the ranks of the swart folk and closed with them so violently that his prowess was extolled, and he rescued two knights at great cost of danger to himself And already was the battle at its height when King Richard, that brave warrior, came upon the field and beheld our men in the midst of the press of cruel paynim folk But a few men had he with him, howbeit, it was a goodly band and choice

Then certain of them began to say to him "Thou art running into sore disaster, for never wilt thou be able to rescue those of our people who are yonder, and it were better that they perish alone without thee than that thou also perish there Therefore is it best that thou turn back, for if any mischance should happen and evil befall thee, then would Christendom be slain"

The king changed colour, and then said he "I sent them thither, thither I bade them go, if then they die there without me, may I never more bear the name of king!" So he pricked his horse in the flanks and gave it the rein Swifter than the sparrow-hawk, he cast himself into the ranks of the horsemen, clean into the midst of the Saracen folk, cleaving them asunder with such fury that if a thunderbolt had passed that way it had not destroyed more of their men And he drave them, and overthrew them, and turned them to flight, and overtook them again, and hewed off hands and arms and heads And they fled away like cattle And many of them fainted, and many a one of these was taken captive or slain And the Christians continued to follow and pursue after them and chase them until it was time for them to turn back So passed that day

XLIII

HOW KING RICHARD DEMANDED OF SALADIN THAT HE YIELD HIM THE KINGDOM OF JERUSALEM HOW SAPHADIN CAME TO TREAT WITH KING RICHARD AND HOW THE PARLEY CAME TO NOUGHT OF THE MARCH OF THE PILGRIMS AGAINST RAMLEH, AND YET MORE CONCERNING THE PROWESS OF THE COUNT OF LEICESTER

In the mean time, whilst they were yet fortifying the two casals which they were restoring, and when the king perceived that his people were all inflamed against the Saracens (whom may God curse!), then summoned he his messengers, wise men and of high estate, and sent them to Saladin and to his brother Saphadin, and of them made he marvelous demands, exceedingly great and noble and magnificent to wit, the whole kingdom of Syria, from end to end with all that lieth between, together with all that appertained to the realm what time the Leper King[190] held it, and the tribute of Babylon,[191] even as that king had received it For all this did he claim as his heritage by birth and by conquest The messengers sought out the soldan and told him their message right well And he told them that he would not do this, and that the king was asking too much of him And he sent word to the king by Saphadin his brother, a very wise Saracen, that he would yield up to him peaceably and without battle all the land of Syria from the river[192] even unto the sea, without laying claim to aught thereof, but with this understanding would he do this to wit, that Ascalon be not restored either by Christians or by Saracens This word sent he to him by Saphadin Howbeit, the king perceived not that these false enemies were but delaying and holding him off whilst they were tearing down the castles, so did they hoodwink him Woe worth the day that they held this parley! For Saphadin so far deceived him that the king suffered himself to receive gifts from him, and messengers came and went, bringing these presents to the king, because of which the king was sorely blamed and many an ill word was said of

---

[190]Baldwin IV
[191]Egypt
[192]The Jordan

him But Saphadin made him to believe that he earnestly desired peace, and the
king, had an honourable peace been offered him, had straightway accepted it
for the advantage of our faith and because the King of France had gone his
way, whom he mistrusted, knowing that the king loved him not at all And so
the messengers came and went and kept the king in talk, until at the last he
perceived the craftiness of the false Saracen folk, who were indeed exceeding
false and faithless And this was because of Kerak of Montreal,[193] for he desired that they first rase it, then would he and they make peace, and because they
would not do this, he gave over the getting of peace through this parley

Now when peace could no longer be, behold, from the right hand and
from the left came the Turks and made violent assaults upon the host, for
greatly did they desire to work us mischief And the king joined battle with
them and shewed by his example, to those who blamed him because of the
gifts wherewith the Turks had deceived him, that he cherished nought but loyalty toward God and toward Christendom Many a time did he meet the Turks
and many a Turk's head did he display in the host, for many in sooth had he
cut off Nor was the host longer troubled because of the gifts that he had received And the land might well have been delivered by him, but he was kept
therefrom by such as were ever pilfering his purse

Now when the casals were builded up again and strengthened and fortified, and when the king had put therein his guards that were ever watching
from the heights, then was the host called and summoned at that hour when
the sun hideth himself And on the morrow, when they were mounted, they
ranged their men well in troops and rode straight toward Ramleh And so soon as
we had begun to march and Saladin knew of a certainty that he must perforce
get him out of Ramleh, then caused he the whole town to be rased, and, first of
them all, fled he away toward Toron of the Knights,[194] trusting himself only to
the mountain But our host rode along the middle of the plains on goodly steeds
with barley fed In two days came the host betwixt Saint George and Ramleh,
there they went and pitched their camp, awaiting more men and victual And
there again had we to suffer fierce assaults of the noisome hated folk And
grievous rains that fell delayed us much and did us great hurt And these
rains pursued us until we gat ourselves to shelter within Saint George and
within Ramleh There we pitched our tents or found lodging, and we abode
there full six weeks in sore straits and in great unease

And even as we were sojourning there, there befell a fierce battle which
must not be forgotten, nigh to Saint George on the left hand, betwixt the valiant
Count of Leicester and certain Turks that were holding themselves hard by and
ofttimes coming to harass the host And now the count with a little band of
men came forth from the host for to drive them away, and on his head he
wore an helmet of steel Before him went three knights, who foolishly rode for-

---

[193]Montreal was a stronghold near Kerak The Lordship of Kerak and Montreal was
one of the important seigniories of the kingdom because the great caravans from Egypt to
Damascus passed through its territories, paying toll

[194]*Thoron as Chevalers* (Hill of the Knights), a castle near Emmaus, once the property
of the Templars

ward and charged full tilt against the Turks But all three had remained there, had not the count, who would not forsake them, let his horse run also Against more than an hundred Turks he charged, and went on without stopping, until he had driven them across a stream But too vigorously and too far had he ridden, for now came full four hundred Turks, bearing lances and bows, who put themselves betwixt him and the host, and sought to seize him Already had they overthrown and grievously smitten and wounded Garin Fitz-Gerout and laid him on the ground Then had ye seen brave deeds of arms there where Sir Garin fell But even worse befell the count, for, after Garin, they overthrew him also and smote and wounded him grievously Down from his horse they also cast Droon of Fontenil, and Robert Neel a moment after And so many came against the count—Turks, Persians, and Renegadoes—that they fair swallowed him up in the midst of them, so that they could scarce strike him There had ye seen many a fair fight There was Henry Fitz-Nicole put to an hard test along with the count And there was Robert of Newbroke—never man lay, as a babe, in his cradle who was gentler than he, and he was a man of great stature, and of such prowess and valour that he dismounted in the midst of the great press of fell paynim folk and gave his own horse to the count, saving both himself and the count from dishonour Ralph of Sainte-Marie was also in the count's company, and had not Ernaut of the Wood[105] been there, it had gone worse with the count Henry of Mailloc and William his brother suffered many a stroke on their helmets there with him With him also was Saul of Breuil Nor ever yet was seen by eye of man, methinketh, so great prowess as these shewed who held together against so many Turks as were found there For never one of them knew any counsel whereby he might deliver himself, and sooth it is (thus saith the book) that the count had fought so long and received so many strokes—both he and his companions—that they could no longer defend themselves, for the Turks had well-nigh slain them Their arms about their horses' necks, the Turks were carrying them away straight toward Toron, when out of the host, unto which they were approaching, came pricking full speed a troop of our brave men Therein was Andrew of Chauvigni, and Henry of Graye, and there was Peter of Préaux— good knights all, and good fighters And many other famous men were there, whose names have not been told me And every one of them, as he came on, laid low his Turk upon the ground But the Turk that Peter smote, who perished there both body and soul, was so exceeding strong that, albeit Peter strove with all his might—both he and all they that were with him—they could not carry him off alive, and only with great difficulty did they slay him

---

[105]*Del Bois Ernaus*

XLIV

HOW ANDREW OF CHAUVIGNI SLEW AN EMIR HOW SALADIN WITHDREW HIMSELF TO
JERUSALEM HOW THE HOST SUFFERED FROM THE COLD AND THE RAIN, AND
HOW THE TURKS PUT TO DEATH CERTAIN OF THE SICK FOLK HOW THE
PILGRIMS THOUGHT TO LAY SIEGE TO JERUSALEM BUT WERE
DISSUADED THEREFROM BY THE SYRIANS HOW KING
RICHARD PUT TO FLIGHT A TROOP OF SARACENS

Now listen, my Lords, whilst I tell you of a strange joust, and valiant in
sooth is he that jousteth as my Lord Andrew jousted! An admiral he met, and
he thrust his lance clean through his body so that the point appeared on the other
side But as he came, the admiral had held his own spear so true that the point
thereof went into Andrew's arm and brake it, even thus did it befall him But
the admiral fell down dead

There had ye seen a noble rescue, there was fiercely brandished many a lance
and many a spear Ill indeed had it gone with our first warriors an the others had
not come to their aid But had ye seen the defense that was made by the brave
Count of Leicester—how he smote them on the right hand and on the left, until
they had killed two horses under him! And certain ones who were there have
told us that never in a man of his age had they seen greater valour, nor had they
seen better fighters than these, nor so little loss as on that day befell in succouring
him For from the host so many a one ran forth to help that never one of our
men perished there, and all were delivered and brought back   [196] So they discomfited the enemy and brake their ranks and for a long time pursued after them,
until for very weariness they let them go, then came they back to their tents

Now Saladin knew of a truth, for lightly could he perceive it, that our men
were making ready and every day preparing themselves for to go against the Holy
City And so soon as report had been made to him and he knew that our host
was within two leagues of him, nor had he any more hope of peace or truce from
them, then, for to spite us, he caused four or five of the turrets of Toron to be
broken down and departed thence, fleeing (so they said) straight toward Jerusalem, and the Turks left the plain to us and took themselves to the mountain

When the host of the Turks had retired and our own host had drawn nigh,
then was it cried throughout the host and commandment given that they should go
to the foot of the mountain and encamp there, and that victual should be brought
to them there And even so did they do Thereafter they mounted and ordered
their battalions and rode on until they were come before Bettenuble [197] There was
the weather cold and cloudy, and then came great rains and violent tempests,
which sorely diminished the number of our beasts For it rained there so exces-
sively that there was no measuring or counting of it The rain and the hail were
ever smiting us, and our tents were beaten down, and we lost so many horses
there, at Yuletide and before and after, and so much of our biscuit was corrupted
by reason of the rain that wetted it, and so much of the provision of salt flesh
rotted because of the storms which beat upon it, and so many hauberks rusted so

---

[196]Lacuna of one line
[197]Beit-Nûba (Beit-Nabala ?)

that they could scarce be scoured, and so many garments molded, and so many folk were wasting away for lack of nourishment, that their bodies were in sore misease, but their hearts were greatly at ease for the hope that they had that they were going to the Holy Sepulchre So greatly did they desire Jerusalem that they all had brought with them full provision of victual for the siege Then had ye seen folk coming to the host all filled with joy and kindled with valour And they that had lain sick at Jaffa and otherwhere, with firm and cheerful mind had themselves laid on litters and carried in great numbers to the host Then came the enemy to the road by which they were bearing these men, comforting them as they went, and the enemy spied upon them, then they fell upon the sick folk and slew them These were true martyrs, and it was meet that they should pass out of this world in perfect trust and in so firm an hope as they all had, both the simple and the wise, that they were now accomplishing their pilgrimage

Now in the host was joy complete, and all manner of rejoicing There had ye seen hauberks waved about and men turning their heads and crying "O God, grant us Thine aid ! O Virgin Lady, Saint Mary ! O God, suffer us to adore Thee ! For now shall we behold Thy sepulchre !" There was no angry man found, nor any sad, nor vexed, nor sorrowful, but everywhere was joy and gladness, everywhere were they rejoicing, everywhere were they crying out together "O God, now are we going the right way, Thine own grace doth direct us !" Yet some there were who paid small heed to these words, but sought to delay the journey these were the wise Templars, the valiant Hospitalers, and the Poulains,[198] the people of that land And these said to the King of England that of a truth, according to their belief, if Jerusalem were besieged at this season, then would Saladin attack them whilst our own people were at the siege and the Turks would occupy all the road betwixt the sea and the mountain, then, in sooth, should we be in a sorry pass an the paynim pack cut off all victual from the host But even if they were not able to cut it off and could do us no mischief there, and even if the city should be taken, yet would it be a perilous emprise if the land were not immediately filled with such men as would abide there, for all the pilgrims, the simple and the wise, so soon as they had accomplished their pilgrimage, would go back to their own country, each to his own place, then would the Holy Land be lost again, when the great host was scattered

On the third day of the new year,[199] in the morning, destiny brought a certain adventure to pass The Saracens, that ugsome, swarthy folk, had already in the evening before ambushed themselves in the sand hills above the Casal of the Plains and all that night had they lain there, spying on us But in the morning they came forth upon the road that led from the camp, where they perceived two serjeants who were passing that way These they attacked and smote them sore

---

[198]Literally, "Foals" "Half-castes, or *Pullani* These   represent, if we may trust Suger, those who were born of a Syrian father or mother, James de Vitry, on the other hand, defines them as the offspring of the earlier conquerors by the Apulian wives for whom they sent over in the first days of the kingdom, practically, however, the word means simply the Eastern Franks" Archer and Kingsford, *The Crusades*, 296-297

[199]3 January, 1192

until they were all hewn in pieces But God willed that they should be avenged,
for the King of England, who knew of this ambushment, had lain that night at
the Casal of the Plains for to watch the spying of the Turks, and there also was
Geoffrey of Lusignan, and this was the third day of the new year Then did they
let their horses run, and they had thought to rescue the two serjeants, but these
were already dead and cut in pieces And the Turks, who knew King Richard and
his banner and his nimbleness and his manner of fighting, departed thence by
crooked ways and by-paths, full four score of them were there thus retiring, who
went toward Mirabel, and the rest other ways Seven or eight of these were tak-
en or slain, then the king pricked his goodly steed with the spurs, pursuing the
four score Turks that fleeing went toward Mirabel And that day was he riding
Fauvel, which bare him on with so great speed that presently he overtook the
Saracens, and or ever his own folk could come up with him or join themselves to
him, already had he unhorsed and overthrown two of the foe and slain them And
had the pursuit been better ordered, yet more of the enemy had been taken, howbeit, our men gat a score of them, or slain or taken captive, then came they back

XLV

HOW THE PILGRIMS GRIEVED OVER THEIR TURNING BACK HOW THEY WENT BACK TO RAMLEH AND WERE FORSAKEN OF THE FRENCH HOW THEY MARCHED FROM RAMLEH TO IBELIN AND FROM IBELIN TO ASCALON OF THE DEARTH THAT WAS IN ASCALON HOW SALADIN GRANTED A FURLOUGH TO HIS ARMY

After the feast of the Epiphany the great men and the captains came together
to a council,[200] and they enquired of the wise men who were born in that land
whether they would counsel them to go back or forward And these made answer
—and first of all, they of the Hospital and of the Temple—that, after their opinion, toward Jerusalem they should not go, but rather, if they trusted them, should
they fortify Ascalon again, for to guard the passage and to intercept the Saracens
who passed that way, bringing victual from Babylon to Jerusalem Therefore
was it determined that they should go back to Ascalon and fortify it anew And
when this news was known and published and noised abroad, that the host would
return (I say not retire), then was that host so disheartened—that had been so
heartened to go forward—that never since God made the world was seen an host
so gloomy or so dull, so sad, so troubled, so disconsolate, so full of sorrow and of
sore distress, for nought remained of the joy that they had had aforetime when
they had thought to see the Holy Sepulchre, in face of the sorrow that possessed
them now And some there were that would not hold their peace, but cursed the
long delay and the hour that they had ever seen their tents pitched there But an they
had known the dolour and distress that then prevailed within Jerusalem, and the
weakness of the Turks, who suffered grievously because of the snow that was in
the mountains, which caused great numbers of their horses and other beasts to
perish—this is so true as that ye are standing here—had they but known the sorry

---

[200] 13 January, 1192

pass to which the Turks were brought in body and in substance, then soothly with but light endeavour and expense had they on that occasion destroyed the Turks and taken the city

Now it was on Saint Hilary's Day that the host had such heaviness and vexation because of their return   Every one of them cursed the day that he was born and each day that he had lived, since he must needs turn back   The host was most disconsolate and worn and very weary   How to carry back the victuals that they had brought they knew not, for all their horses were enfeebled by the great colds and by the rains and weakened much by fevers   And when they had loaded the victual upon them and the sumpter beasts were wading through the mire, they fell to the ground upon their knees, and the men cursed themselves and commended themselves to all the devils   My Lords, think not that this is some idle tale, that ever should so good men and choice be seen in such an evil pass! Amongst the lesser folk, also, were many sick, whom their own sickness held back in great dolour and distress, and surely many of these had been left behind that day had it not been for the King of England, who caused them to be sought out and searched for everywhere until all were brought away   Then all departed thence in order, and on that day, the day of our turning back, we came at last to Ramleh

At Ramleh was the host, sore disheartened as I have told you, and because of the utter discouragement that they suffered (nor could they suffer greater) was all the host at this time disjoined, for many of the French withdrew themselves and in bitterness of heart departed   Some went away to Jaffa and sojourned there for a season, and others went back to Acre, where victual was not so dear, others went to Tyre, to the marquis, who had long besought them to come, and yet others, filled with despite and annoy, returned with the Duke of Burgundy to the Casal of the Plains and abode there full eight days And the king with the remnant of the host, which was sore diminished and full of wrath, and with Count Henry of Champagne, his nephew, and with them of his own company, went straight to Ibelin [201] But so wretched did they find the roads that in the evening, when they came to camp, there was nought but vexation in their hearts

At Ibelin lay the host, all dolorous and heavier of heart than aught that liveth   But in the morning, ere yet the sun was risen, forth went those that should go to pick their resting-places   Their tents they struck, then rode the host all armed, but never a worse day's march hath been recorded by any living man   For the journey of the day before was as nought to the journey that they made this day, through many a rugged pass they went, where their provision was lost because of the sumpter beasts that there fell down   So did God will, who thus was trying them and proving unto them perforce that whoso will not suffer misease for His sake may never hope to be at ease with Him   And at the last they came to Ascalon, between midday and nones   And they found the city laid so waste, so ruined and so overthrown, and over such heaps of rubbish must they climb, that with sore difficulty did they enter there, thus, with the grievous travail that

---

[201] Yebnah, about ten miles southwest of Ramleh

they had suffered that day, there was none of them that had not great longing and desire for rest. But at the last they found there rest a-plenty

Ascalon lieth beside the Sea of Greece[202] (thus have I heard it named), nor ever have I beheld, to my thinking, any city better situate, an it but had a port or way of entry, for all about it is a very pleasant country But the sea is there most violent and so exceeding dangerous that no vessel can tarry there For this cause must our people endure there great unease, for during the space of eight days, forsooth, could never a vessel come there to land or fetch victual to sustain the host, nor ever did they taste any food save that which they had brought with them, because of the storm and the tempest Neither by land durst man or beast move themselves or come to them, because of the cruel Saracen folk, until, at the last, on a calm day, provision came to them along the coast from Jaffa Then the battle of the waves began anew, and the tempest was so violent upon the sea that food waxed very scarce again For the barges and the galleys that had gone after provision were at this season broken in pieces and the more part of their people were drowned And all our goodly transport ships were likewise shattered These the king thereafter caused to be broken up and long ships to be builded of the timber thereof, wherein he purposed to sail thence But this was not to be

Now Saladin knew full well through his spies that our people were come down to the seacoast, then bade he his Saracens depart each to his own country and repose them there until the month of May, when it would be time to fight again Nor did these need to be prayed, but departed right gladly, since they had been four whole years in Syria in great distress, enduring many a grievous heat in summer time and many a bitter cold in winter, which befitted not their nature, in such sort that many a one of them must perforce remain there for ever So ought ye to have heard how so many of the Turks lamented, admirals and other of their principal men, so many Kurds, so many Persians, so many folk from countries far away who had been aforetime in so many great wars nor had suffered any loss of yore But now had ye seen them on their departure bitterly mourning their great losses and bereavements, whilst every one of them lamented them of his own lineage that he had lost in Syria! Nor ever yet had any man been so hated or so reviled of the Saracens as was Saladin because of the Turks whom he had suffered to perish, without deliverance and without succour, before the walls of Acre, where so many of them died But in the end the armies went their ways, all save Saladin's own people, those that were of his own demesne

---

[202]That part of the Mediterranean lying between Greece and Syria. In ancient times the name "Parthenian Sea" was used in much the same sense

XLVI

**HOW THE FRENCH CONSENTED TO RETURN TO THE HOST HOW ASCALON WAS RE-
STORED HOW KING RICHARD DELIVERED A THOUSAND CHRISTIAN CAP-
TIVES HOW HE BADE THE MARQUIS OF MONTFERRAT COME TO AS-
CALON AND HOW THE MARQUIS REFUSED TO GO THITHER**

It was about the time of Candlemas that from our host and theirs the folk
departed, going their divers ways to divers places Then did the king send
word to the French, who had gone away afore, to come to Ascalon and join
themselves to the rest, so that with their counsel it might be determined and ordained whither the host should go and what course they should follow, for
better it were that they go on together than that they abide in sinful discord
And they sent back word that they would come, but would remain with him
only until Eastertide, with this understanding, that if they should then desire
to depart and should so determine, then should he grant them leave to go and
cause them to be conducted in all safety by land to Acre or to Tyre And the
king granted their request and did what each one of them desired And, lo, the
host was one again, and joy shone forth anew

When the host was on this wise united again in good accord at Ascalon
(how soon, alas, was that union severed!) they all sojourned together there
Then did they make ready and prepare to build up again the walls of the city
But so poor were the barons who had sojourned there since their coming back,
and the poverty of some was so evident and so well known, that no man alive
could behold it that he would not have pity of them Nevertheless, all set them
to the work, and they laid bare the foundations of a gate, all toiling together so
that they themselves marveled at the work which they had accomplished [203]
From hand to hand they passed the stones—the good knights, the serjeants, and
the squires, all laboured there without rest or respite, and so many came, both
clerks and laymen, that in a brief time they accomplished much And after this
they sent for the masons to finish the work, but much time it needed to fulfill
this task

In Ascalon had been of yore (but now were they all destroyed) three and
fifty towers goodly and strong, to say nought of the lesser turrets And there
were five of these that were called by their own names after them who had
builded them Hear ye, then, who they were that first laid their foundations,
even as those told us who knew the truth of the matter For in the very ancient
days there reigned a man called Ham, high and mighty and of great renown,
the son of Noah was he, that made the ark whereby all flesh was saved And
this Ham begat two and thirty sons (he that remembereth them all can name
them) who reigned after him and founded Ascalon And these sons sent through
all the lands over which they held sway, through all the cities and the towns,
seeking help to build the towers And they say that the damozels builded the
Tower of the Maids, and the Tower of Shields was builded by the knights who
were living at that time, and the Tower of Blood they builded with the blood-
money paid for crimes and deeds of violence, and the Tower of the Admirals

---

[203] Apparently, two or more lines of this passage have been omitted in the MS

was builded and fortified by the admirals themselves, and the Bedouins, also, builded their tower, goodly and strong and of great worth These are the names that those five towers bare, and these are the things that were told us by them that knew And other folk, all according to their station, builded the other works

When the masons were come, they were straightway engaged for the work The king, the first of all, gave freely for their cost, and the men of high estate presently did likewise, each one took his own share of the burden; and wheresoever the others failed him or the barons were doing nothing, there did the king take over the work, beginning it and finishing it And when the barons waxed weary of working or were not able to provide their portion, then would the king cause succour of his own to be brought to them for to hearten them And so much did he put into this labour and so much did he spend that, as was well known, the cost for three parts of the city was paid out of his own moneys It was by the king that the city was now builded, and by him thereafter was it pulled down again   [204] because of the French, who failed him when he and his valiant men leaped into the sea from his galleys, at Jaffa There was his prowess proved, even as we shall shew you in due time and in a fitting place, and we shall prove this thing so well that never, so it follow our remembrance, will history relate one lying word in the matter—so may God grant to me His glory!

Now listen to a strange adventure which is indeed worthy to be put into writing, a very miracle without any doubt Saladin was sending away to Babylon in one band, convoyed by the men of his own household, a thousand Christian captives, Franks were they, and Syrians Already were they come so far as Daron, but God, who brought back Lazarus from death to life, wrought help and succour for them also Now hear ye in what manner he did this King Richard with his doughty men had ridden forth from Ascalon one day, betwixt midday and nones, and gone on to see Daron, which afterwards he took by siege, for the Saracens who brought victual from Babylon to Jerusalem were wont to make their refuge in Daron, in peace, nor fearing battle or annoy, ere Daron yet was taken There now were those miserable men who were to be led away to die in ignominy But why should I prolong the tale? So soon as the king drew near, and his brave people with him, so soon as the Turks beheld his banner, great fear had they and were utterly confounded And some there were that betook themselves within the castle, whilst the captives tarried without, whom they durst no longer hold when they saw the king coming So the prisoners gat them inside a church, and there those poor folk waited Then came the king and delivered them, and all the Turks he put to death whose retreat he was able to cut off with his horse's body And that day he took twenty Turks alive, besides them that were slain, and there he gained many a noble steed But an God had not led him thither with His own hand, on the morrow had all the captives been conducted thence and led on to Babylon, and all would have died in captivity but for the king and his men

---

[204]There is evidently a lacuna of several lines in the MS at this point

When the Lord God had thus delivered His people who had been predestinate to death, when He had sent King Richard in Saint Leonard's[205] stead, who brake the prisoners' bonds, for which so great thanks were given to God, then did the king send word to the marquis to come to Ascalon and take his place in the host, even as he had besought him to do many a time before, and to merit that portion of the kingdom which had been allotted to him, according to the oath and promise that he had made before the King of France Such word did he send to him But the marquis sent back word that never would he set foot within the host until he should have spoken with the king Thereafter did they speak together—'twas at Casal Imbert, an I mistake not

XLVII

HOW THE DUKE OF BURGUNDY FORSOOK KING RICHARD HOW THE PISANS QUARRELED WITH THE GENOESE HOW KING RICHARD AND THE MARQUIS OF MONTFERRAT MET AT CASAL IMBERT OF THE GREAT BOOTY THAT THE PILGRIMS TOOK HOW THE FRENCH WERE CALLED TO TYRE

Whilst our people were at Ascalon, which they were fortifying, ordered in their several divisions, then arose words betwixt the king and the Duke of Burgundy which sorely hampered that business The French were demanding their pay of the duke and were pressing him for it, for he had not wherewith to pay them So then went he to try the King of England and to find out whether the king would lend him yet more moneys besides those that he had lent in the summer to the French on their portion of the spoil of Acre But the king would not make any further loan, and for this reason and for others were words spoken there a plenty, which are not written down here And in the end the duke departed thence, full of bitterness, and certain of the French with him, and they came straight to Acre There they found the Genoese fighting with the men of Pisa, for the Pisans of their honesty held with King Guy, and the Genoese inclined toward the marquis in their allegiance, because he was sworn to the King of France So was there great turmoil in Acre and the city was at an evil pass, and the people were a-killing and a-slaying and made great noise and shouting Then the French armed themselves, likewise did the duke and they that were with him When they of Pisa saw this then they defended themselves right boldly and put the duke to great shame, for they killed his horse under him and set him in despite of himself on his own feet Then they ran to close the gates, for they desired not to shut in with themselves folk from whom the town would stand in jeopardy For already had the Genoese informed the duke by a messenger that they would yield the city to him So came he with his galleys and with his people armed, and thought to surprise the city Then had ye seen the Pisans lay hand to the mangonels and the petraries, like brave and doughty warriors! Three days they strove thus, and then the Pisans sent in

---

[205]Saint Leonard is said to have belonged at one time to the court of Clovis I He devoted his life to the physical and spiritual welfare of prisoners and captives

all haste for the King of England He was already come by land to Caesarea, as
I learned, for to go and speak to the marquis, and the messengers met him
there Then rode they all and hasted, and he came with them to Acre in the
darkness of the night And when the marquis knew of a certainty that the king
was come thither, then could he in no wise be held back, but went with all speed
to Tyre, for the wind was then a-blowing from Arsûf And the Duke of Burgundy had gone thither before him with his French And when the king learned
this at Acre, where he had lain the night, he mounted betimes on the morrow
morn and took the whole matter in hand, then was the tumult laid and peace
obtained from either side And he reconciled the Genoese to the Pisans, for
he bethought him that great mischief might ensue an he brought not peace to pass

When they of Genoa and they of Pisa were in this wise brought into accord, albeit they had been so many days at war, then did the king send word to
the marquis that they would meet at Casal Imbert and would speak together,
for to know whether they could now bring it about that they should be in accord the one with the other So they came and met together and long time spake
they there—the king and the marquis—each to the other But all came to
nought, meseemeth, for the marquis straightway brake word with the king,
both because of the Duke of the Burgundians and because of his other companions who led him away from the peace until they utterly prevented it   [206]

And when the king knew of this thing, then was counsel given him that
inasmuch as the marquis had no mind to earn his portion of the kingdom or
perform God's service, then should they seize his revenues and deprive him of
them And thence arose that great discord betwixt the king and the barons of
France and the marquis, who drew the French to him then as he had done
aforetime, and who so troubled the whole land that the king for full three quar-
ters of the Lenten season (an I mistake not) never durst depart from Acre[207]

On the third day before Palm Sunday[208] certain bachelors of the host set
forth from Jaffa straight toward Mirabel, and this was a very profitable thing
for many of them, for they found great booty there, all of which they brought
away And thirty Saracens they slew, and fifty took they alive, and they came
back to Jaffa with them The half of the spoil they kept, the price whereof they
scarce could tell, the other half was given to the count[209] The serjeants' portion
was thereafter sold (as I have heard the tale) for more than fourteen hundred
Saracen bezants of full weight

On the Saturday thereafter, from Ascalon this time in sooth, forth rode in
ordered ranks all they that had horses for the sake of certain booty whereof they
knew, which had been spied upon And well did they acquit themselves this
day, for they that were with the expedition said that they rode clean over into
Egypt, four leagues beyond Daron And there they took horses and mares, and
verily they took there seven hundred sheep, and cattle, asses a score, and thirty

---

[206]Lacuna of several lines
[207]Another lacuna
[208]27 March, 1192
[209]The Count of Leicester

camels And there took they, to my knowledge, more than nine score of the misbelieving folk, both men and women and children And then with joyous mien straight back they came to Ascalon

Ye have heard of the discord, which I have already described, that prevailed between the barons who had fallen out one with another The duke and the marquis sent word from Tyre to the host at Ascalon—to all the French that were therein—bidding them all come immediately to Tyre, to the marquis, and all hold themselves fast to him, so they all bound themselves to him because of the homage that he had done to the King of France Then was the whole affair discovered and revealed and made known—all the plotting and the perfidy and the cruel, deadly hatred whereof the false marquis had been guilty, and the oath that he and the French king sware each to the other what time the king departed from the host And because of this the French withdrew themselves at this season from the King of England, who was seeking only the good of the land, even as ye shall hear me relate an it please you to attend a little

On the Tuesday[210] of Holy Week wherein men do penance, the king came back to the host, heavy of heart and with sorrowful countenance, and on the Wednesday the barons of France accosted him, asking that he furnish them a convoy, even as he had promised and agreed with them And this he straightway granted, and he gave them of his people of Poitou and Maine, of his Angevins and barons of Normandy, and himself convoyed them in his own person, weeping and beseeching them whensoever they halted that they would abide with him at his own cost and remain together with the rest, but never were they willing to remain And when he could accomplish nothing, nor would they listen to his prayer, then came he back to Ascalon and swiftly and in all haste sent word to Acre, to all his justiciaries in that place, that they see to it that the French might not tarry there

XLVIII

HOW SALADIN SUMMONED HIS ARMY OF THE MIRACLE THAT BEFELL AT THE HOLY SEPULCHRE HOW EASTER WAS CELEBRATED HOW THE PRIOR OF HEREFORD CAME TO CALL KING RICHARD BACK TO ENGLAND HOW THE MARQUIS CONRAD WAS CHOSEN KING OF JERUSALEM

It was on Maundy Thursday that sin had thus removed from our host the baronry of France And, lo, the host was all in sore despair, disheartened, sad, and full of heaviness, and grievously diminished by the loss of more than seven hundred knights renowned in arms, valiant and mighty men, who durst no longer tarry with the host Then had ye seen so many folk a-weeping because of the discord that they suffered ! But when the Saracens knew thereof, then know ye well that they greatly rejoiced thereat, and they that heard him said that Saladin bade letters be written and word be sent to all his admirals of all the lands whereof he had become lord through conquest, commanding them to return to Syria, for now the Franks would never take that land—rather, there prevailed such discord

---

[210] 30 March, 1192

amongst them (whereof he was well informed) that he thought by his wit and his wealth to have both Tyre and Acre again And these obeyed his commandment, but slow and sluggishly they came Howbeit, enough of them were gathered so that, methinketh, they were all too many

'On Holy Saturday (thus saith he whose tale I follow) was the soldan Saladin at the Holy Sepulchre in Jerusalem And there were many unhappy Christians, in fetters and in irons, both Latins and Syrians, who were softly weeping there, and in their weeping they prayed God's mercy for Christendom, which was fallen into orphanhood And whilst they were thus shedding tender tears and pouring forth their prayers, lo, there came a spiritual fire, in such fashion as it is wont to appear in the lamp, and so quickly as a man can lift and raise his eye did they all see—both young and old, both Saracens and Christians—that the lamp was lighted even as it was accustomed to be Then verily were the people moved when such a miracle was seen And the Saracens marveled, and they said and thought within themselves that it was by enchantment that the lamp was so lighted But Saladin, desiring to know the truth of the matter, commanded the lamp to be put out, and immediately his people put it out But their intent availed them nought, nor could they bring it to pass that the lamp should not be lighted again And once more he bade the lamp be put out, but the Lord God willed that the truth should there be made evident, to the honour of His name and His city, and He lighted it yet again the third time And when Saladin beheld the faith of the Christians and their confidence, then said he to his Turks that verily and without any doubt either would he himself die right soon, or at least the city would not remain his much longer And he lived thereafter according to my knowledge and my reckoning, only until the Lent which followed

On Easter Day, that precious feast, the king held full court and free for to comfort his people in the host, and he caused his pavilions to be carried and pitched outside Ascalon, and every man might enter therein and take such meat as him listed The court lasted but a day, and on the morrow, with no more delay, the king caused the labour to begin anew upon the walls and the work to be taken up again which the French had abandoned when their people departed And again at his own cost did he have all things done that were to do Now lately have ye heard me tell—ye whom it liked to listen to my tale—of the convoy of his barons of Poitou, of Normandy, Anjou, and Maine, who a little time before had convoyed the French even to Acre and were now come back And now shall ye hear how the French behaved themselves at Tyre, whither they were gone, during the season that they abode there, and what profit came of their undertaking, and what they went about to do there, and what travail, what pains, what miseries they suffered there on God's behalf It hath been said by those who saw them there that they spent their nights in dancing and ware garlands and wreaths of flowers upon their heads, and that they sat before the tuns drinking until matins, then they resorted to the houses of evil women, breaking down doors, speaking mad words, and swearing great oaths Such was their manner of life I say not that all did such villainies or spake such evil, for the honest folk that were there and remained there against their will and were sore grieved at the discord that God would not suffer to be appeased—these were very indignant because of such things, but the evil folk amongst them rejoiced in the defection of the barons and of the King of France

When the valiant king Charlemagne, who conquered so many lands and kingdoms, went to wage war in Spain, whither he led that brave company that was sold to King Marsile by Ganelon, whereby France suffered great loss, and likewise when he was in Saxony, where he wrought many a deed of prowess and discomfited Wittekind and destroyed the Saxons at the hands of many valiant warriors, and when he led his host past Rome after that Agoland with a great army was come to Reggio in Calabria's rich land, also, when Syria in the other war was lost anew and conquered yet again, and Antioch besieged, and in all the great wars and battles fought against the Turks and all the paynim pack, wherein were so many defeated and slain—in those days and in the days that were yet before was never any strife or any questioning who were the Normans or who were the French, who were of Poitou or who of Brittany, who of Maine or who of Burgundy, who Flemish or who English Then were no mutual revilings or wranglings one with another, but all won honour together and all were called FRANKS, were they brown, or ruddy, or swart, or pale And when, through sin, they fell into discord, and their princes reconciled them again, then were they all of one accord so that discord endured but a brief season Even thus ought these of our day to have done and so to have directed their affairs that men might take example from them, rather than to have contended one with another

After Eastertide, at the season of the passage, there came to King Richard a messenger who caused great distress to the host This was the Prior of Hereford, a priory of England, who had come to Syria seeking him and bringing him tidings that were neither good nor welcome, and a letter, written and sealed, which was indited in great need This letter said that his governors whom he had established in England had been removed from their castles, and that in this removal divers persons had been killed throughout the land, and this had the prior himself seen Furthermore, the letter said that the king's brother had driven the king's chancellor out of England, and that neither in chamber nor in vault nor in treasure-house—save only in the churches—did anything of the king's remain that his brother had not caused to be seized and taken, and that he had waxed so bold in his evil-doing that against the chancellor—albeit he was a priest, a bishop, a seignior, and a master—he had wrought such villany and such annoy that the man had fled away to Normandy And yet was there another thing, for so did he desire to supplant the king, who was now upon his pilgrimage, that he sought to receive the oaths of all the baronage of England, and he had striven to lay hands on the king's revenues which came to the Exchequer

"Fair Sire," quoth the prior, "for this cause do I beseech you that ye come back to your own land and avenge you of them that have done you such wrong, else will they yet increase their wrong-doing, and into that land which they are pilfering piecemeal will ye never enter without battle"

My Lords, marvel not if the king, who had so laboured in God's behalf in that far country where he had such travail and such pain, was greatly troubled in his heart For such news dishearteneth any valiant man and maddeneth him, when he thinketh to lose his high estate And, lo, these tidings were noised about, nor do I think that ever were there seen in any place folk more distressed or more sorrowful because of any man's departure from the host For they would all have parted company, had the king left them, and would have been in exceeding jeopardy, all in discord as they were, nor had there ever again been any accord twixt them of Tyre and them of Ascalon But on the morrow, between tierce and nones, the king assembled all the baronry and recited in the hearing of all the message that had come to him from England how they sought to take from him his land, and how they had deposed the chancellor set up by him, who guarded and upheld the land, and how for this cause he must needs go back And he said that if it should so befall that he in sooth must needs go back, then would he leave in Syria, at his own cost, three hundred chosen knights, and likewise would he leave two thousand serjeants, worthy and valiant men and true He said, moreover, that he desired to know of them, and bade them answer him, who of them all wished to go back with him And he left it to their choice whether to go or to remain, for he desired to constrain no man

The men of high estate who were there present spake together concerning this matter even as the king requested them Every one of them sought to discover what they ought to say and to do in the case And in their counseling they considered how there was now in that land and kingdom no sovereign head, but rather was it divided into two parts, whereof King Guy was in no wise able to maintain his own, nor would the marquis for any assurance return to the host but kept himself with the men of France, so that all was in disorder And when they had considered this they came back to the king and told him, without any concealment, that unless he should establish in the land a lord who had knowledge of warfare and to whom all would cleave, from whatsoever land they might come, then would they all go away with him and would forsake that land And the king, desiring at once to be upon his journey, straightway asked them whether of the twain they would have for king and whether they would not have—King Guy or the marquis Then all they of whom he thus enquired kneeled down before him—the small folk, the middling, and the great—and prayed and besought him to make the marquis their lord, for of all the men of the kingdom was he the best able to help it and to bring it succour And when the king saw that all desired him and that no man opposed him, then did he upbraid certain ones that were there who had spoken evil to him of the marquis And when every one of them asked for the marquis, then did he grant their request, and he bade men of high rank go and seek him out and bring him back with great rejoicing, and the French with him, so that all might be of one accord

Now this election whereof I have told you was not held to be a light matter, but all desired it, both the simple and the wise Then did the messengers make themselves ready Count Henry, Lord of Champagne, and with him in his company my Lord Otto of Trazignies These were men of high lineage, and with them was William of Caieux Then set they their helms upon their heads and set forth to bear their message to the marquis and bring him tidings of good cheer (and good tidings in sooth they seemed to him and to the French who were in Tyre) Then the messengers mounted and went their way, and ye shall hear what things befell when they came thither

XLIX

HOW THE MARQUIS SOUGHT AN ALLIANCE WITH SALADIN HOW HE REJOICED THAT HE HAD BEEN CHOSEN KING HOW THE MESSENGERS OF THE OLD MAN OF THE MOUNTAIN PUT AN END TO HIS JOY

True it is, without any doubt, that when the baronry of France had departed with the marquis, King Richard besought him again and again, as we have seen and have told you, to come to the host and help him to conquer the land with the others, but that he would never come, wherefore he deserved that misfortune befall him Now shall ye hear what he purposed and the wrong that he thought to do to God Against the honour of the crown and against the host of Ascalon had he promised peace to Saladin and sworn that he would come over to him and would hold of him the half of Jerusalem Thus had he already brought it to pass with his villainy (as was made known) that he should have Beirut and likewise Sayette and the country round about, and together with these the half of the whole kingdom This peace did Saladin desire, but the admiral Saphadin would never consent thereto, nay, we heard thereafter that he said to the soldan his brother, "Sire, may it please not God the Father that ye ever make peace with Christendom through any one of them that seeketh it of you, save only the King of England (better Christian is there not on earth!), nor do I counsel peace nor desire it" And thus the matter rested But it became known everywhere and was enquired about and debated, for Stephen of Turnham was in Jerusalem on a mission to the soldan what time the marquis' messengers came thither, whose names certain folk remembered Balian of Ibelin, who was falser than a goblin, also Renaud of Sayette These came to seek and to purchase a peace—but a foul one, not a fair They ought to have been hounded from the place

The messengers of whom we have told you and whom we have seen departing on their mission journeyed day by day on the way they had determined, until they were come with all speed to Tyre There straightway they dismounted and went right to the marquis and told him what they desired of him Courteously did they salute him, but he and they that were with him greeted them with loud laughter Then Count Henry spake and said, in all good will "The king, O Marquis, and the host of Christendom which is at Ascalon, have bestowed on you the crown and the kingdom of Syria Come, then, with your mustered host and bravely conquer your realm"

And the history saith in good sooth that such joy had the marquis in his heart that he cried, in the hearing of all his baronry and with both his hands raised to heaven (whereat many were grieved thereafter) "Fair Lord God, who didst make me and didst set my soul within my body, Thou that art the true and righteous king, as Though knowest, Lord, that I am worthy to rule Thy kingdom well, now let me go and be crowned, O Lord, but if thou perceivest me not to be such, then consent Thou not to my crowning"

The news was known and noised abroad through all the city that the marquis was to be made king, and that all the host desired it. Then in sooth was there marvelous rejoicing, and the host was glad and very fain to don harness and to make ready to go, and to borrow gold and silver for their costs, according as each desired aught for himself. There had ye seen arms seized and helmets and skull-caps furbished anew, there had ye seen many a squire burnishing many a good sword, there had ye seen many an hauberk rolled and knights and serjeants rehearsing the strokes wherewith they would smite the hated paynim folk. There in sooth were men of great prowess, had God but deigned to be with them—who knew their nature better than did we. There, verily, had ye seen many folk in great joyance, so is it very meet that we should learn and know (and truly it behooveth us to learn it) that in the hour of joy none ought to rejoice to excess, neither in time of grief should he grieve overmuch. Now all were of good cheer and light of heart because of this thing, and Count Henry and the barons who had brought the message were gone to Acre for to make their borrowings, where they were now preparing and making ready to go back to the host. But now befell in very sooth a grievous thing at Tyre. It chanced that the marquis had supped with the Bishop of Beauvais, in all ease and with much merriment, and had taken his leave of him and was departing from his house. And he was already arrived before the Change. Now shall ye hear how joy is changed, and how quickly it is turned to sorrow. For even as he was blithely passing, lo, two varlets with two knives—lightly clad were they and without cloaks—came running straight toward him, and as they rushed upon him they smote him in the middle of his body so that he fell. And of these that had thus foully wounded him—who were men of the Assassins—the one was straightway slain, but the other gat himself inside a minster. But never a whit did this profit him, for he was taken thence and was dragged through the city until his body was utterly destroyed. Howbeit, or ever he was dead, they that were there present asked him wherefore they twain had done this thing, and what wrong the marquis had done to them, and who had sent them. And he answered them, the caitiff vile (and thereafter was this found to be true), that to this end had they long sojourned in the marquis' neighbourhood but had found no occasion to slay him until that day, when so many a tear was shed, and that they had been sent by the Old Man of the Mountain,[211]

---

[211]*Li Vils de Mouse* (in Joinville, *Li Viex de la Montaigne*) Gadamûs, in Lebanon, was the headquarters of the order of the Assassins. The chief of the order, or Old Man of the Mountain (Sheikh al-Jebal), at the time of Conrad's death was the celebrated Raschid-ad-dîn Sinân

who hated the marquis For every one that he hated with deep hatred he causeth to be slain in such wise as ye shall now hear told, an it please you to listen longer

Now the Old Man of the Mountain hath this custom, which is handed down from heir to heir he causeth to be nourished in his house many young lads until they have attained reason and acquired instruction and training And they learn courtesy, and they frequent wise men of high estate until they know all the tongues of all the lands throughout the world But their faith is so gloomy, so cruel, so dark, that whensoever the Old Man of the Mountain summoneth them to his presence and commandeth them, in exchange for the remission of their sins and for his friendship, to slay some man of lofty station, then in accord with their most earnest teaching do they regard this as a work of exceeding merit Then are great knives given to them—bright and polished and goodly ones—and they go their ways and spy upon the great man and acquaint themselves with him and become a part of his household, keeping their tongues well oiled until they have taken his life Then do they think themselves to have earned the high joys of Heaven— which can in no wise be And even such, my Lords, were these twain of whom we have told you, who thus slew the marquis

His men took him very softly in their arms and raised him from the place where these had stricken him down, and they bare him away to his lodging Then had ye heard such lamentation that all the people came a-running thither Yet a little time he lived, and then he died But first had he made confession and had spoken privily with the marchioness his wife, whose eyes he saw all wet with tears, telling her that she must strive to guard Tyre right well, nor yield the city up to any one save to the King of England in person or to the lawful lord of the land And so he died, and they buried him , and clerks and laymen grieved alike At the Hospital was he buried, and there was great mourning made , never was greater known—but thus had God decreed And, lo, the news was spread abroad; and, lo, the great rejoicing was brought to an end, which had so little time endured in that land that had sworn fealty to him who so soon left it—a land so filled with sorrow and with woe that no man could describe it

L

HOW THE FRENCH ACCUSED KING RICHARD OF HAVING SUBORNED THE MURDERERS OF THE MARQUIS HOW COUNT HENRY OF CHAMPAGNE WAS CHOSEN KING OF TYRE OF THE EXPLOITS OF KING RICHARD AGAINST THE TURKS HOW COUNT HENRY MARRIED THE WIDOW OF CONRAD OF MONTFERRAT

Now hear ye in what manner the Devil worketh, and how his work revealeth itself in evil, and how it multiplieth, and how he increaseth it, and how he then multiplied and increased it from a single word that was spoken by certain accursed and envious folk who hated King Richard and disparaged all his acts— folk that ought to have been driven thence And these said that the king with bribes had sought and had brought about the death of the marquis, and they sent word to the King of France that he had great cause to fear and that he should beware of the Assassins, for that by these had the marquis been slain, and into the sweet land of France had the King of England sent four of them for to slay the king himself God! What a foul thing was this to say and how basely wrought they that sent such a message, whereby so many folk were thereafter troubled and disquieted and grieved! For because of this their wickedness was King Richard afterward cast into prison, through treachery and through envy of the good deeds that he had wrought in Syria

When the marquis had been buried and they had made mourning for him and had done for him all that they ought, then were the barons of France gathered in their tents without the city—of high and lowly more than ten thousand in all And those of high estate spake together, and they sent word to the marchioness that she should deliver the city to them in all peace and quietness, that they might hold it in ward in behalf of the King of France And she made answer with no delay that when the king came back, then would she right willingly yield it up to him, an there were no other lord chosen before that time And they were filled with indignation against her In the mean time, whilst they were yet seeking and striving to get possession of Tyre, as I have told you, lo, the good Count Henry came into the city and dismounted there—so saith he whose word I am telling And so soon as the people beheld him, they waited for no later term, but chose him straightway for their king, even as God had ordained And they came to him and laid hold on him and besought him to accept the seigniory and the kingdom of Syria and to marry the marchioness, who had remained a widow and heir to the kingdom And he made answer immediately, nor put the matter off, that, inasmuch as God had called him and they had chosen him to govern the land, he first desired the consent of the King of England, his uncle, and he sent at once to find out the king's mind and his will concerning the choice of the baronry

It was in May, when flower and leaf are renewed, that tidings came even to King Richard of the thing that had befallen the marquis, whereof we have told you And the king was on the plains of Ramleh, where he was riding over the heath, pursuing a band of Saracens that fled before him as before one that they feared above aught else, for since God formed the world hath no man waged such war upon the Turks nor by any one man's hand have so many of them died Many a time did he make a raid upon them and bring back to the host heads of Saracens as they had been beasts of the chase—or ten or twelve, or twenty, or thirty at a time, whereat Heathendom was sore distressed And living captives, too, would the brave Richard bring back when he was so minded Nay, never died so many together at one man's hand, that is sooth

And, lo, the messengers came pricking, who were seeking the king They rode up to him and greeted him on the count's behalf, and they told him of the marquis' fate, and how the people had requested that the count be made lord of the land, for lowly and high had chosen him for lord and desired him to take the marchioness to wife, but he would undertake nought against the king's desire and unless it were for the good of Christendom

The king remained long lost in thought at the tidings concerning the marquis, who by great misadventure had been so foully slain But great joy had he when he knew the people so eager to do his nephew this high honour And thus did he make answer in the matter

"Serjeants and lords, greatly do I desire that he be king, an it please God, when the land shall have been conquered But let him not wed the marchioness—her whom the marquis took away from her lawful lord, and lay with her, against God's law and against all right, and so wrongfully did he keep her that the count, an he heed me, will never in his life take her in wedlock But let him receive the seigniory and the kingdom of Syria, and I will give him Acre also in demesne and the revenues of its harbour, and Tyre, and Jaffa, and the jurisdiction of all the conquered country, for greatly do I desire that he hold it all And tell him to come to the host and to bring the French with him, so soon as ever he can, for I wish to take Daron from the Turks, an they dare await me there"

The messengers marked well what they had heard from the king, and they went their ways, taking their leave without any further speech, and back to Tyre they came, unto the count, and told and recounted to him the word that they brought from the king But why should I prolong my tale? Great joy was there in Tyre for the count's sake when the messengers returned thither Then had ye seen the great and eager throng of the high lords about him, all urging him to take the marchioness to wife But, for all their urging, he durst not undertake this against the will of the King of England But she was heir to the land, and the count had greatly desired her Howbeit, the matter was so managed that the marchioness herself (though strongly had she been dissuaded) brought the keys of the city to the count, this is sooth And the French went in all haste and fetched the priest and made the count to marry the lady—and so, by my soul, had I myself done, for she was altogether fair and lovely, methinketh, moreover, as God seeth me, that the count was very lightly put in the way to wed her So came the marriage feast and such rejoicing that, meseemeth, never heard I or saw the like in all my life It was a festival free from wrangling, envy, or dissension, and all the land was at ease and full of good hope because of the count, who was nephew to the King of France and nephew to the noble King of England The count sent through all the land, to Acre, to Jaffa, and to other places, to seize the castles and the towers and to cause all to do him homage And he bade the host be called and summoned, summoned likewise were the barons, for to go and take Daron

LI

HOW COUNT HENRY WAS RECEIVED AT ACRE HOW GUY OF LUSIGNAN WAS MADE KING OF CYPRUS HOW KING RICHARD RECEIVED DIVERS TIDINGS FROM ENGLAND HOW DARON WAS TAKEN

When the count had celebrated his wedding and had gathered all his people to him, then, on the advice of his baronry and of the French lords of his own lineage, he determined to lead all his people to Acre for to equip and prepare themselves there and to buy barley for the horses and victual for the men, that they might ride on to Ascalon Then left he good guards at Tyre, to watch from the high places both over the city and over the country round about that evil folk might not enter there The count took with him his wife, who was whiter than a pearl Then, lo, the host set forth from Tyre, and at Acre were the tidings known that the count was coming And then did every one consider himself in such good case because the count was made king, that hardly could they be kept from making merry night and day There had ye seen a noble welcoming, processions ranged in order, all the streets bedecked with tapestries, in every window and before the houses censers all filled with incense! And all the men of Acre, three score thousand or more, came forth, all armed, from the city for to meet him, so soon as they saw him This was in token, also, of their yielding themselves to him and acknowledging him to be their lawful lord The clerks led him to the minster and brought forth the relics to him and caused him to kiss the Holy Cross; and he and many more made offerings there Even to the palace did they convoy him and they lodged him therein There had the count a noble lodging—would that I might always have the like!

When the count stood seized of Tyre, and of Acre, Jaffa, and Arsûf, then was King Guy without a kingdom—he who had received so many blows upon his helmet and had paid such a price for his realm And now he saw himself despoiled thereof, who had suffered such wrongs, such grievous misadventures, and not because of his sins alone, for no king was ever gifted with better qualities, save for one single quality that he had—that which men call simplicity He was the king who by his prowess had laid siege to Acre after the Saracens had taken it Now it chanced that long afore this the Lords of the Temple had purchased the land of Cyprus of the king who had conquered it, but thereafter was the bargain annulled, so that in the end was King Guy made emperor and lord thereof, wherewithal he was something comforted

Now about the time when the marquis was done to death with knives at Tyre —both at that season and before and after—on divers occasions we saw how messengers came to the King of England who caused him much vexation For some would disquiet him, others again would assure him, one bade him come away, another bade him remain there in God's service So they spake, each after his own mind, one told him that his land was all at peace and free from war, another said that in very deed was it in utter confusion, so that what some said the others gainsaid Therefore was it no wonder that he knew not what counsel to take or that he was very fearful because of the going back of the King of France; for the adage saith that an evil morning hath he who hath an evil neighbour

In the mean time, the French that were in Acre, of whom I but newly spake to you, were making ready and girding themselves for war—even Count Henry and all his barons—for to be present at the siege of Daron And the king came forth from Ascalon, in the name of God who giveth all things good, for he would not longer wait, but caused his petraries to be put on board and taken to Daron by sea And he made his good people to arm themselves, and he took serjeants in his pay, whom he paid right generously, and he set men in all the castles round about, bidding them guard and watch them well and see to it that no caravans passed through by night, or Turks betaking themselves to Daron as they were wont to do, whereby they had wrought us much mischief So King Richard, in whom so much valour dwelt, mounted his horse, and with only the men of his own domain he came to Daron on a Sunday, so was he now before the place There were all his barons gathered, but so few people had they that neither they nor the king knew on which side to lay siege to it For if they should spread themselves all about it, and if the Turks should make a sally, or if their own host should be attacked, then would they not be sufficient for their own defense but would surely be discomfited Wherefore they betook themselves all to one side   [212] And the Turks harried and harassed our men, until they all withdrew themselves again into the castle, where they prepared their defenses, using great care and labour, and barred well the gate thereof, which they held to be exceeding strong

When the gate was closed behind the Turks and their people had shut themselves within, then, lo, the petraries came and were let down out of the vessels and set on shore piecemeal And the valiant King of England himself, together with his companions, bare on their shoulders (this did we ourselves see) the beams and timbers of the petraries—all on foot and with faces dripping sweat—well-nigh a league along the sand, like horses or sumpter beasts Then were the petraries set up and delivered to the constables The king had one of them under his own command, wherewith the great tower was assaulted The Normans, valorous folk, had likewise one that was all their own, and the men of Poitou, an I err not, had one of them in common All these played upon the castle, and the Turks were sore affrighted by them, even though they had a very great defense in their strong castle and in their stores But the king caused the place to be assailed both night and day without surcease and so troubled them that they were at their wit's end Seventeen towers and turrets had Daron, goodly ones and strong, but one there was that rose above the rest and was of stouter frame, and round about it ran a deep moat, whereof the one side was paved, but the other was of the living rock But fear possessed the paynim folk, who could not escape thence And King Richard caused his men to dig beneath the ground all secretly until they were come to the pavement and brake it by force Thereafter they digged beneath the wall, casting the earth behind them And the petraries played against the Turks and brake in pieces one of their mangonels, which they had raised upon the chiefest tower, whereat they were sore dismayed Verily, this was a castle assailed in many ways There had ye seen the Turks defending themselves at the crenelles

---

[212] A lacuna of some five lines The Latin paraphrase tells how the Turks made a sortie

and the loopholes, and they hit our folk in their faces, for their bolts rained thickly down But so soon as ever they moved themselves, our own bowmen, who were straitly watching them, let fly against them and wounded so many of them that for very terror they durst move themselves no more, and in sooth were they in an evil case Then was their gate burst asunder, and burned, and beaten down by the king's petrary Then had ye seen folk attacked with vigour and with fury, but a folk disordered and ill directed, for night and day had they been so long tormented that now were they disheartened utterly

Thus did King Richard and his barons sit down before Daron, and for three days did they assail it continually both night and day without any respite And on the fourth day, a Friday, the Turks of whom I have spoken perceived that they could no longer suffer or endure these fierce assaults whereby they were so discomfited, and that many wounded men and maimed lay everywhere within the castle, and that our men were attacking them above ground and below, and that the king was at the point of taking them with but little more effort Then made they no long delay, but spake only of saving themselves And by three Saracens sent they word to King Richard that they would yield themselves, on the understanding that they might themselves depart with lives and bodies safe, likewise their wives and their households But the king told them to hold their peace and to defend themselves if they could So back went they to the castle And, lo, even then the largest petrary struck and hurled down one of the turrets, which wrought great damage to their defense, for it fell against the chiefest tower—God so willed, and so it befell And this tower was all mined underneath and all their people had fled thence Then from all sides did our men rush forth, and they armed themselves and attacked the Turks, and these forsooth all gat themselves together into the chief tower But then had they a very evil thought, for they hamstringed their horses so that the Christians might not have them or be able to ride them And the people of God went up into the castle, and of them that first entered there was Seguin Barré the foremost, and one Espiard, a squire, was not far behind Seguin The third was Peter the Gascon And others of them may there well have been, whose names I could not learn

Then entered the banners, and of these were there divers sorts The first that entered was that of Stephen of Longchamp, howbeit, it was no longer whole, but rent in many pieces, and after this was raised that of the Count of Leicester, and over above the wall to the right was that of Andrew of Chauvigni, and next beside it high upon the wall was planted that of my Lord Raimond, the prince's son [213] And they of Genoa and they of Pisa had banners there of divers fashions Our own banners had these raised upon the walls and those of the foe had they cast down Then had ye seen Turks cut down and cast from the ramparts, overtaken and seized and stricken and smitten and slain, so that within the castle (and this is indeed true) were found three score dead bodies—bodies of them that missed the great tower and failed to rally there in time

---

[213] Count of Tripoli, son of Bohemond III, Prince of Antioch

The Saracens that were in the great tower looked round about them, and they saw their castle occupied, and their companions taken and slain; and they saw bucklers lifted and raised against the tower for to cover them that were cutting the wall beneath, whilst they themselves were above And they saw that they were forsaken of the admiral that ought to have succoured them—Caïsac was he called, a Saracen of great renown And when they perceived that they would get no succour, then did they all straightway yield them to the valiant King Richard, without condition, as captives and as slaves, taken, beaten, checked, and mated And full two score Christians were there, who had been kept in bonds, that now had their lives saved and warranted and assured And the king caused the Turks to be watched and guarded in the tower all the night of Friday, and in the morning, on a Saturday, the day before the high and precious feast of Pentecost, he had them all brought down from the castle, and straightway without further waiting he ranged them in such sort that he straitly bound the hands of all behind their backs, whereat they howled exceedingly Thus, then, was Daron taken, to the great honour of them that took it, who had been sore vexed and very wroth an they had not taken it or ever the French came

LII

HOW DARON WAS GIVEN TO COUNT HENRY HOW KING RICHARD WENT AGAINST THE EMIR CAÏSAC HOW THE KING HEARD OF THE TREACHERY OF HIS BROTHER JOHN HOW THE ARMY MARCHED TOWARD JERUSALEM HOW KING RICHARD THOUGHT TO GO BACK TO ENGLAND AND HOW WILLIAM OF POITIERS REBUKED HIM

Then, lo, with Count Henry came the French a-pricking, who had thought to arrive there in time, but too late were they come thither And the king and his people went forth to meet the count, his nephew But wherefore should I make a long tale of this? Enough, to tell you what great joy they all had together Then the king, whilst many folk were looking on, gave Daron to the count and bestowed on him as handsel his own conquest And there we rested through the day of Pentecost, and on the Monday we departed thence toward Ascalon, and passing by Gaza came straight to Herbia,[214] where the king and his company lodged that night, but the rest of the people rode on till they were come to Ascalon, where the French held high festival

A little time thereafter came to the king at Herbia a spy who was come from spying upon the Saracens round about Fig Tree Castle, and he said that in that castle were a thousand or more—this knew he of a surety—who were putting the place in fit state to defend it against the Christians And the valiant king without delay mounted and called his host together, and that night lay they (an I remember aright) at the Canebrake of the Starlings[215] And on the morrow was the morning fair, and they set forth with the sunrising and marched until they were before Fig Tree Castle, which the Turks should have defended against them But

---

[214]*Furbie*
[215]*La Canoie as Estornels* (Wâd el-Kassâba)

that did they not, for our men found there but two Turks, whom they brought away with them, the rest had first torn down and destroyed the gates with Greek fire and then had abandoned the castle, fleeing thence in all haste so soon as they knew that the host was coming, for they bethought them of Daron, whereof they had had tidings—how it had been taken and their people lost, and for this cause did they forsake the castle And our people rode on until they beheld the castle without defenders, then clomb they the heights round about for to see an they might discover any Turk whom they could attack And when they found none there, back came they to their resting-place Then they returned all their way to the Canebrake of the Starlings

At the Canebrake was the host encamped (as I have heard the tale) after that they were come back from Fig Tree Castle Then (saith he who retelleth this history), came to the king a messenger, who was an inhabitant of the king's own land, a clerk was he, John of Alençon And this man told the king that strife and dissension and war had sprung up throughout all England because of the barons and because of his brother, who, spite of all that his mother might say to him, would work nought but his own will, and that the affair had gone so far and had taken so evil a turn, because of the emissaries of the King of France that he sent to England for to turn the king's brother from the right path and to bind him to himself, that the messenger himself durst well affirm that unless the king came back right soon, then very speedily would the land that he held be reft from those to whom he had committed it And so indeed was it at the season of his return, and even yet the fruits of this evil abide, as it is to be seen in Normandy, which thence waxed poor and was wasted and brought to beggary When the king had heard these tidings, which were neither good nor welcome, then was he lost in thought, downcast, and sad And he said to himself "If thou return not now, then verily hast thou lost thy land" Then was his mind all distraught, so that he declared resolutely that in sooth would he return, and when the good people heard him, know ye of a truth that they rejoiced not thereat Some in the host knew these tidings and others knew them not And one said "He will go", another "That will he not" His enemies greatly longed for his departure, but his friends desired it not For his honour had been sore abased had he left this land otherwise than in the way he ought and had he wrought no more good therein

Now while they were yet there, all the barons assembled—French, Normans, men of Poitou, English, folk of Maine, Angevins—and took counsel together what they should do, until in the end they declared that, whatsoever King Richard might do, whithersoever he might go, they themselves would all go together to Jerusalem Then a certain man, I know not who, gat him privily from the council and came to the people of the host and told them what all the chief men and the counts had said at this parliament to wit, that they would lay siege to Jerusalem Then verily did joy enter into the host, and in both great folk and small such hope sprang up, such cheer, such lightness of heart, such exultation, that in the host was not one Christian soul, highborn or low, or youth or aged man, that rejoiced not with exceeding joy, save only the king himself, who was in no wise cheered but laid him down all saddened by the news that he had heard But in the host so merry were the folk that they fell to dancing nor laid themselves to rest till midnight was past

It was in June, when the sun on his rising wasteth and drieth up the dew, when every creature rejoiceth, that the host marched forth of the Canebrake and came down through the plains toward Ibelin of the Hospital, hard by Hebron and nigh to the valley where Saint Anna was born, the mother of the Holy Maid who is God's mother and His hand maiden There saw I the host all joyous because of the task that had been resolved upon, that they should go against Jerusalem and lay siege to the city Howbeit, there were a many, both of poor folk and of rich, who ardently longed for that city but never entered therein Hear ye, then, what now befell the pilgrims—verily a strange martyrdom and fierce persecution Into the host came little flies that were so small and tiny as sparks, which we call gnats By these gnats through all that region was the host so assailed (so help me Saint Celerin!) that they stang the pilgrims' hands, their necks, throats, foreheads, and faces, in such wise that there was not a space so broad as a man's hand that was not covered with little swellings from the stinging of these flies, and that every one, old man or youth, seemed to be a leper, and they must needs make veils for to cover their necks and their faces This pain did they endure there, but ever did they comfort them with the thought of that which they had undertaken and with the hope whereof they were possessed But the king was troubled and sad because of the news whereof ye have heard, and ever was he pondering in his tent and to his pondering gave he all his care

One day when he was sitting, silent and pensive, in his tent, he saw passing before the entry a chaplain from his own country, William of Poitiers it was, who would fain have spoken to the king an he had dared accost him, but never a word durst he say, for this was not the fitting time or place So the chaplain wept hot tears and was in sore distress, but even yet durst he not tell the king what things the people of the host spake concerning him and how they blamed him, saying that because of the news from England he wished to leave the Holy Land poor, and waste, and helpless, or ever he himself had helped it Then the king called the priest and said to him "Tell me the truth, by the faith that thou owest me! Whence cometh this grief because of which I have seen thee weeping thus? Tell me without delay" And the priest made answer—nor did he longer wait— yet weeping, and in a low voice

"Sire, I will not tell thee a word until thou hast assured me that thou wilt hold no grudge against me" And the king assured him with his word and sware an oath thereto that never would he bear him any malice in any wise or at any time Then said he "Sire, they are misspeaking thee, and through all the host runneth the rumour of thy departure May that day never come when thou shalt essay such a thing! Never may such reproach be brought against thee—neither near at hand nor far away, neither here nor otherwhere! Remember, O King, the great honours that God hath bestowed upon thee on so many occasions, which shall be spoken of for ever, for never any king of thine own time hath suffered less loss O King, remember how men say that never, what time I saw thee Count of Poitiers, hadst thou any neighbour so arrogant, so puissant, so renowned, whom, an he came against thee in war, thou didst not overcome Remember the great fighting bands of the Brabanters[216] that thou discomfitedst so many a time with a few men and weapons Remember the glorious adventure and thy great victory at Hautefort, which thou didst rescue after that the Count of Saint-Gilles had besieged it, whom thou didst vanquish and drive dishonoured from the field Remember thine own realm which thou, without taking up shield or donning helmet, didst receive in peace and quietude—a thing the like of which befell none before thee Remember all thy great emprises, the multitude of captives whom thou hast taken, Messina, which thou didst seize, the deeds of prowess that thou wroughtest what time thou overcamest the Grecian rabble, who had thought to take thyself in battle and from whom God delivered thee, putting them to great shame Remember also the glory that God in His bounty extended to thee, when, in fifteen days, thou didst complete the conquest of Cyprus, which none other durst essay (for, save through God's help, the emprise had not succeeded), and remember how thou tookst the emperor captive and cast him into prison King, take heed that thou be not caught in a snare! Remember, too, that great and mighty ship that could never enter Acre's harbour, since God caused thee first to meet it, which thou tookest with tiny galleys, together with eight hundred armed men, what time the serpents were drowned Remember how many times God hath succoured thee and succoureth still Remember Acre, and the siege to which thou camest in time to take the town, where God suffered thee to expend so much of that which was thine that the city was yielded up Good King, hast thou then not understood why thou wert spared of the sickness which prevailed at the siege, the 'leonardie,' whereof the other princes died and against which no physician born could help them? King, remember these things, and so guard this land whereof God hath made thee the guardian, for all the land did He commit to thee when the other king departed hence Remember the Christians that thou didst free from their bonds at Daron, whom the Turks were carrying off and who were going away into captivity when God so caused thee to come thither betimes King, well shouldst thou keep in mind how God hath shewn thee so many kindnesses, whereby thou hast mounted so high in glory that thou fearest neither king nor baron King, remember now Daron, which thou tookest in four days—not a moment longer was thy stay there Remember the great jeopardy wherein the enemy put thee what time, for thy sins, thou fellest asleep, and remember, noble King, how God quickly freed thee from the snare But now are we all delivered up to death Now do all say, both great folk and small—all they that love thine honour —that thou wert wont to be the father of Christendom, and her brother, and if now thou leavest her without succour, then is she betrayed and dead"

---

[216]The name of certain companies of mercenaries and bandits from the duchy of Brabant

LIII

HOW KING RICHARD PROMISED TO REMAIN IN THE HOLY LAND UNTIL EASTER HOW THE HOST MARCHED FROM ASCALON TO BLANCHEGARDE, TO CASTLE MA- TRON, TO CASTLE ERNAUT, AND TO BEIT-NABALA HOW KING RICHARD SURPRISED THE TURKS AT THE FOUNTAIN OF EMMAUS

The clerk had said his say and had the king to school, and such a sermon had he preached to him The king uttered not one word, neither did they that were sitting in his pavilion open their mouths But the king gave all his thought to the sermon that had been preached to him, then was his mind enlightened On the morrow, lo, about the hour of nones the host was come back again before the walls of Ascalon And every one thought without any doubt—both the barons and all the men of the host—that the king would now make ready for his departure and that then would he go his way But he had changed his purpose because of the message that he had received, first from God, then from the priest, who had caused him to judge his own case aright And in the end (for why should I make of this a long tale?) he said to the count his nephew, to the barons, and to the Duke of Burgundy, that neither for any need that might arise, nor for any messenger or any message, nor for the sake of any earthly quarrel, would he depart ere Eastertide or so forsake the land Then he called for his crier, Philip, the publisher of his bans, and caused it to be cried throughout Ascalon, in the name of Him who giveth all good gifts, that the king declared absolutely and in his own person that until Eastertide would he remain in the land nor depart thence, and that all should hold themselves ready, with all that which God had bestowed upon them, and that against Jerusalem would they go, and that they would straightway lay siege thereto Now when this cry was heard, then were all the people so rejoiced as is the bird at the coming of the day Then all prepared themselves without delay And every one in his own place addressed himself to God in the firmament on high, saying (so may God amend me!) "O God! Now can we worship and adore Thee and give thanks to Thee, for now shall we behold Thine own city! Too long have the Turks dwelt therein Blessed now be all our waiting, all the tarrying, all the delaying that each one of us hath made here, and all the pain that each hath here endured!" Then had ye seen men eager and in haste to don their harness And into all the lesser folk was such joy entered that every one of them bare his own victuals on his back and said that willingly would he bear victual enough for a whole month to come, so desirous were they to bring this work to its fulfillment What more should I say, save that whoso serveth God, him doth it nothing cost

It was about the time of Pentecost—on a Saturday,[217] methinketh—that the host was led forth together again from Ascalon, as I have told you—and lightly led, forsooth, for that which each was now doing liked him and pleased him well So the host set forth in the morning, nor do I think that ever was host seen more valiant or better accoutred Howbeit, that day they marched but a little way, because of the heat And there might ye have seen men of high rank performing

---

[217] June, 1192

works of honour, of humility, of courtesy, and of charity, for such as had horses
or other beasts which they could offer suffered the poorer pilgrims to be carried
thereon and themselves walked behind—both high barons and bachelors And
there had ye seen waving in the wind so many banners fair and costly and pennoncels of divers fashions So many mothers' sons had ye seen there, so many
a lineage, so many brethren and nephews, so many goodly hauberks and pourpoints, so many folk armed at all points, so many lances and so many spears (so
many were not seen in all the days of our forefathers), so many swords costly
and bright, so many goodly and well-favoured serjeants! There had ye seen so
many folk a-marching, so many horses pied or iron-grey, so many hinnies, so
many goodly mules, so many knights, valiant and confident, that they might well
—after my thinking—have faced two score times as many Turks And so they
rode and so they marched until they had passed over a stream of sweet water,
and then before the castle of the White Guard the host laid them down, for that
first night, under God's ward But on the Sunday there died within the host a
good knight, also, within less than two furlongs' distance thence, a brave and able
serjeant, from the bites of two several serpents—may God look down upon their
souls and heed them, for they died journeying in His path

Two days did we tarry there, and then on the third day we departed thence
And all the host marched in close order, the roads all filled with warriors iron-
clad, meeting no man nor encountering any hinderance, straight on to Toron of
the Knights One night lay we there, nor on the morrow moved we thence till we
had eaten, but then the king brake camp, with the people of his own domain,
and himself in person went before And presently he caused his tent to be pitched
upon the height, a little to the right of Castle Ernaut And on the morrow came
the French, and the others with them, and on they went to Bettenable Fair was
the weather, nor was there any mist There the host halted and rested, in that
place whence they had come in the winter, for to await Count Henry, and I
will tell you wherefore The king had sent him to Acre to the misled folk who
would not come to the host, and because of this must we needs tarry a month
or more[218] hard by the foot of the mountain, where the palmers were wont to
pass when they came back from that high and holy city whereof we were disinherited Now in that season when we were resting in this valley whither we had
withdrawn ourselves there happened divers adventures and alarms and discomfitures, which we saw befall, yet must perforce contain ourselves It chanced one
day that a certain spy (of those that were sent out to spy and to enquire) came
down from Monjoie[219] unto the king (and I saw how joyously he came) and said
that there were Saracens in the mountain—this knew he of a surety—who were
watching and guarding the roads because of the host And the brave king mounted ere it was day and departed with him that had told him this thing, and he went
seeking the Turks, to their woe, even so far as the Fountain of Emmaus And he
surprised them there at daybreak and slew a score of them whom he overtook

---

[218]11 June—3 July, 1192
[219]An eminence from which pilgrims got their first sight of Jerusalem

But he took captive Saladin's herald, his crier, him only did he spare And three camels gat he there, and certain lusty Turkomans with them, and two goodly mules well laden with rich garments of great price and with spices and aloes in little sacks And he pursued the Saracens through the mountains with all speed until he overtook one of them in a valley, whom he cast down dead from his horse And when he had slain this caitiff, he looked and saw clearly Jerusalem And they told us thereafter that they of Jerusalem were so sore afeard that if the king had had the host with him and if they had seen the host, then surely had Jerusalem been delivered and possessed again of the Christians For all the Saracens had gone forth of the city and fled away, thinking that the host was coming, so that there was none left to hold the city and none that durst remain within it, spite of all threatenings and constrainings Yea, Saladin had already sent word and commanded his best courser to be brought, since he durst no longer tarry there, when he learned through one of his spies that of a truth the great host was not coming, for it was not God's good pleasure at this time that the host be led thither

And on that selfsame day (this was well remembered) when the king made his foray and discomfited the paynim folk, two hundred Turks descended from the mountain into the plain, coming toward the tents of the French, and they stormed the camp ere any was yet moving therein And already before this had they slain hard by the camp (and great shame it was) two serjeants who had gone forth a-foraging And at their cries the French rushed forth straight toward the place where the serjeants had already died, so, likewise, did the Temple and they of the Hospital But the Turks held them in check at the foot of the mountain, for much did they mistrust the plain And there they rallied so well that they struck one of the knights dead—for which the French were bitterly reproached But prowess is better than gold or precious balm, and a great prowess was wrought there by a knight of the Hospital—a goodly feat of arms, had he not broken the rule of his order, but courage made him to snap the bait of danger Robert of Bruges was he called Already had he pushed beyond the gonfalon, as he spurred forward at the sound of the cries, and outstripped all his brethren   [220] and that they should not separate themselves from the host But he was so eager to spur forward that he must needs separate himself from the others A marvelous steed he rode, and right vigorous Straight he spurred at a Turk whom he spied, a doughty warrior richly dight With such violence he came that with the stout lance which he held he pierced the Turk's yellow coat of fence, putting an ell of the lance through the midst of his body, so deft was he And the Turk fell to earth, but his body was not abandoned Thereupon arrived in all haste the Master of the Hospitalers, Garnier, that courtly knight, who said to the brother "Down from thy horse now, brother, and learn how thou shouldst heed the rule" So must the brother perforce go back all the way to their tent on foot, and there he stood, awaiting judgment, until the high

---

[220]A lacuna of several lines, apparently describing the order of the Master of the Hospital forbidding the knights to engage in single combats

barons besought the master, kneeling before him, that he bestow on them this boon that he forgive the brother, for the sake of the prowess that he had wrought, the offense that he committed in breaking of the rule So in the end the master had compassion on him "But take heed," quoth he, "that thou snap not the bait again "[221]

LIV

HOW CERTAIN KNIGHTS CONDUCTING A CARAVAN FROM JAFFA TO BEIT-NABALA WERE ATTACKED BY THE TURKS, BUT WERE SAVED BY THE COUNT OF LEICESTER OF THE FINDING OF A PIECE OF THE TRUE CROSS HOW THE FRENCH DESIRED TO ATTACK JERUSALEM, AND HOW A SCORE OF KNIGHTS PURPOSED TO ATTACK EGYPT

On a Tuesday,[222] an I mistake not, a certain caravan was to come to the host, all laden with victual and well armed And on that day—so we heard—should it be conducted by my Lord Ferri of Vienne He must needs guard the caravan in Count Henry's stead, who himself should have had the rear ward, but he had been sent to Acre And my Lord Ferri had besought Baldwin Le Caron and Clarembaud of Montchablon to guard the caravan for him that day, that the folk might not commit any foolishness But foolishness they wrought that day, and some there were that paid therefor There were Manasses of Lille, who had a dapple-grey horse, and Richard and Tierri of Orques, who were in Ferri's stead, Philip, and the companions of Baldwin Le Caron, Otto, and certain squires that were with them in this battle Kinsmen and friends were these, and they proved it that day in the hour of need Now whilst they of the great company were going their way, having no fear of any one, all at their ease like folk that bear no burden, the rear ward were burdened, yet since the other company were moving speedily, they too like valiant folk and confident followed featly after Then, lo, forth from an ambushment sprang Turks on horseback and came, each for himself, pricking adown the road from the high land, straight toward the rear ward Clean through the midst of the convoy they rode, mounted on their swift steeds, so violently that they clave it in twain And there did they unhorse brave Baldwin Le Caron, but he had the heart of a warrior, so he laid hand to his good sword, which the Turks felt many a time that day and greatly feared And in this mellay they overthrew Richard of Orques, and then Tierri, but Baldwin defended himself so well that his men gat him again upon an horse that they had taken from the enemy There had ye seen many a combat fell, and many a goodly stroke and quick return, many a sword gleaming, many a thrust that failed not, many an encounter fierce and rude, and many a steed with empty saddle There had ye seen the Turks attacking and our men valiantly defending themselves as best they could When the Turks overthrew any one of them, then would the rest draw themselves back from the midst of the press and get him to horse again, helping each the other like good

---

[221]There appears to be a considerable lacuna in the MS at this point The *Itinerarium Ricardi* gives further details of this skirmish, in which the Count of Le Perche was put to shame and only the opportune arrival of the Bishop of Salisbury prevented a total defeat

[222]17 June, 1192

men and true But the mellay was very unequal, for they of our party were so drowned, as it were, in the press that it cannot be gainsaid that more than one count fell there and suffered sore hurt For the Turks' arrows were ever flying and wrought great loss amongst the horses And by such an arrow-shot it chanced that Baldwin was again unhorsed Then did one of his own serjeants dismount, who had defended himself right well, and Baldwin gat him upon this man's horse But, as he himself related, within a very brief time he saw the serjeant beheaded who had lent him his horse There, then, were they halted And there was Philip taken captive, Baldwin's companion, who had won great praise from all that were there, and with Philip they led away a brave serjeant whom they took by force, and Richard's brother[223] they slew Then had ye seen sharp fighting As in the lists enclosed for wager of battle, even so were Baldwin and his companions, for Clarembaud of Montchablon had abandoned and forsaken them and fled away in hot haste so soon as he saw the Turks coming Then had ye seen Baldwin withstanding them, as ever closer they hemmed him in! And with their maces so violently smote they him that he was all but overcome and the blood ran from his nostrils and his mouth and his sword was all blunted, nicked, and shattered Then cried he with a loud voice to the brave Manasses of Lille, who ever discomfited the Turks "Manasses! Wilt thou forsake me, then?" And my Lord Manasses tarried not at all, but came thither to rescue him Then had ye seen so many Turks rushing upon Manasses that they thrust him down from his horse, and they so beat and smote and wounded him that they clave the great bone of his leg clean to the marrow. And lost already in that press were Baldwin and he both, when God sent to them at that moment the valiant Count of Leicester, who had known nought of their case afore And as the count came, lance in rest, straight at a Turk he rode, striking him so hard that the paynim pitched headlong over his horse's neck, and Ançon, a companion of Stephen of Longchamp, lopped off his head so that it bounded to the ground And my Lord Stephen himself wrought manfully there both then and afterward, and so did the number of our men wax greater as the news was known, that when the Turks beheld them increasing, away to the mountains fled they, save those that were overtaken And our men that lay there wounded were lifted very gently upon their horses and borne back to the host Thus passed this adventure, which well deserveth to be written down

Now on the third day before the feast of Saint John, thither where the host was encamped were tidings borne whereby the host was mightily comforted An holy abbot brought them, giving great comfort to all the people From Saint Elias'[224] the holy abbot came, on bread and roots he lived, a flowing beard had he that was left unshorn, and surely did he seem an holy man And to the King he said that he knew a place, which he had long kept secret, wherein a cross was hidden whereof God had made him the guardian And therein was wrought a portion of the Holy Cross itself, that had been divided into many parts, and this good Christian man (who was not exceeding old) had, all alone, taken and hidden it

[223]Tierri of Orques
[224]An abbey near Jerusalem

until the land should be conquered again But for his valour had he paid right
dear, for more than once had Saladin demanded this cross of the abbot, but the
abbot had ever hoodwinked him Nevertheless had Saladin put him to the torture
for the sake of it and caused him to be fast bound But never, for all the evil that
they wrought on him, could they make him to tell where this cross was or to give
it up; rather, he said that he had lost it what time Jerusalem was taken And when
the king had enquired into the matter he caused the holy abbot of whom ye have
heard me tell to be put on horseback Then the baronry also mounted, and there
was a great company of bachelors, and all close ranged they gat them on their
way and rode and journeyed, following the abbot all along the road even to the
place whereof he had spoken, where this cross was hidden And that day was
the cross in sooth exalted, for so many people were coming for to kiss it that
scarcely could they be quieted Then straight back to the host they bare it, who
were greatly comforted thereby, and many a tear was shed whilst they adored it

Now when this cross had been exalted thus, whereby the host was greatly
cheered, and when they had kept it a long time, then the poor common folk began
to cry, saying "God, fair sweet Lord! What do we here? What will be done?
Shall we go against Jerusalem?" And in such sort did they lament that in the end
the king and the high barons heard thereof and spake thereof together, and in
divers ways did they devise, to know what counsel they should take and whether
they should go against Jerusalem And the French sought the king again and
again and said to him (certain ones of them, at least) that they were of a mind
to besiege Jerusalem But the king said ·

"This thing cannot be, nor ever shall ye see me leading my people to an emprise whereof I shall but get reproach, for little care I who misjudgeth me now in
the matter Know ye of a surety and without any doubt that whithersoever our
host goeth, Saladin knoweth our purpose and what force we can employ We are
far from the seacoast, and if he and the Saracen host should come down into the
plains of Ramleh and should cut us off from our victual so that we could get none,
this would not be a good thing for them that might be at the siege, nay, dear (methinketh) would they pay therefor And the circuit of the city (so hath it truly
been told me) is so great on every side that we must needs have there so many
people   [225] that we never could save the host an it were assaulted by the Turks;
rather would it be lost and utterly destroyed And so if I led the host thither, and
laid siege to Jerusalem, and some misadventure should befall, whereby loss were
incurred, then should I ever be blamed therefor and shamed and misprized And
I know of a truth and of a certainty that there be folk both here and in France
who have wished and who would wish and greatly desire that I do some thing of
this sort, which would everywhere be evil spoken of And we—folk from strange
countries, who know not their highways here, their roads, their paths, their perilous passes and dangerous defiles—we can accomplish nothing profitable, lacking
the knowledge which would give us the power to conquer the land But through
them that are of this land, who desire to recover their fiefs—through these ought

---

[225]A lacuna of one line

we to work, and after the counsel of the Templars, or in accord with the Hospitalers, and through those who were aforetime in this land, who knew it then and know it now To these would I have the matter referred that they might make decision thereof, whether it be better to undertake and to go about this siege, or to go on to take Babylon,[226] or to go against Beirut or Damascus So shall we cease to be in disaccord, for never in such disaccord have any folk been "　　[227]

In the end they came to this resolve of the Templars took they four or five for to abate the discords that were amongst themselves, and so many also of the Hospitalers, and of the Syrian knights, and so many also of the barons of France, until there were twenty of them in all who should put themselves on their oath, and the rest bound themselves to accept loyally what these should decide And these decided that it would be for the greatest good of the land to conquer Babylon And when the French heard this, then in sooth brake they their word, for they declared that they would go to the siege [of Jerusalem] but would not proceed to any other place And when the king heard again this discord, to which God would not bring any accord, and when he knew that it arose from them of France, then said he without any reservation that an the French had heeded him, then had they gone against Babylon

"Behold my fleet," quoth he, "waiting at Acre, where I had it already prepared to carry their equipage, their harness, their carriages, their biscuit, and their meal, and the host would have followed along the seacoast, and I would have brought at my own cost, in God's name, seven hundred knights and two thousand serjeants with them, and I would have led them all the way thither And let them know, furthermore, of a truth that no worthy man would ever have lacked help of my moneys at any time But inasmuch as they will not do this, I am all ready for to go to the siege, howbeit, let them know (by Saint Lambert of Liège) that I will not lead them, but only go thither in their company "

Then he bade his people assemble without any more delay in the tent of the Hospital and there determine what aid they would render in the siege, if they were to go against Jerusalem And they came thither and sat them down and made rich promises, and some made great offers there who had but very little money in their coffers But an exceeding great folly had they wrought an they had begun the siege at this season, after that they who had sworn to counsel them had in all good faith advised them against it

LV

HOW KING RICHARD AND THE FRENCH SURPRISED A CARAVAN

Whilst they were yet promising what they would contribute toward the siege, lo, Bernard the spy, a man who was born in Syria, with two others—outlandish men like himself—came back from Babylon, all clad in Saracenic raiment Nor

---

[226]Cairo, Egypt
[227]Lacuna of several lines, probably describing the effect of Richard's speech

in any other business did these serve, save only to spy upon the Saracen host, and I dare wager before you all that never saw I folk who more resembled Saracens or better spake the Saracen tongue Each one of them had received from King Richard three hundred marks of silver what time they departed These said openly to the king that he should mount with all speed—he and his people—and they would lead them to certain caravans which they had espied coming, heavily laden, toward Babylon And so soon as the king heard this he rejoiced greatly in his heart, and he sent word to the Duke of Burgundy to come to this emprise and to bring the French with him And this did he, howbeit, first they said that they desired the third part of the booty and the spoil, and the king granted it to them Then they mounted, and the king mounted also And there were counted there five hundred knights well armed and a thousand serjeants brave and nimble, whom the king brought thither at his own cost, and he himself rode on before Now this was on a Sunday evening, and all night long they marched by the light of the moon, nor ever halted they one moment till they were come to Castle Galatie And there they gat them down, these hardy folk, all armed for battle as they were, and sent to Ascalon for victuals, and there they tarried till the squires came back But so soon as our people began to move again—the king and they that were with him—lo, a certain spy turned him about and went back to Jerusalem, and going straight to Saladin, he told him that he had seen the king mounting for to go and seize his caravans Then Saladin, no longer waiting, took five hundred Turks, all chosen men, of the best that he had, and these he sent forth for to find the caravans, and they bare bows and light lances And when they were joined with them that were conducting the caravans, then did they number two thousand horsemen, besides them that went on foot Then, lo, there came to the king a spy, spurring straight toward Castle Galatie and greatly did he press the king to come quickly himself, letting the host remain quiet, for that to the Round Cistern and all round about it was a caravan come, and whoso should halt it would get much booty Now this spy was born in that land, and the King could not trust him But he immediately sent a Bedouin and two Turcopoles, brave men and quick of wit, and he caused the Turcopoles to wrap their heads about after the fashion of the Bedouins and the Saracens And it was night when they set forth, and up amongst the hills they went—upward, then down again—until upon a certain height they spied I know not how many Saracens keeping watch there Then the Bedouin, taking the spy with him, drew nigh to them step by step, and the Bedouin bade his two companions keep silent, lest they be perceived of the Turks, and thus were the Turks deceived And they that were upon the height asked our men whence and from what side they were come Then the Bedouin spake freely to them, saying that they came from the coast of Ascalon, where they had gotten them booty Then said one of the Turks "Nay, in sooth are ye come for to do us a mischief! Thou thyself art come from the King of England " Then answered the Bedouin "Thou liest!" And then was he minded to go his way, and he went on toward the caravans And the Turks with their bows and lances followed and pursued after them, until for very weariness they let them go, thinking that they were in sooth of their own people But the Bedouin turned him about and went back so soon as he knew of a certainty that the caravan was come thither, which was accounted him a very prudent act So back to the king he came and told him that he knew of a truth that he could have the caravan The king, in the name of Saint George, bade barley be given to the horses Then the men themselves ate, and thereafter they mounted And all that night they rode until they were come to that very place where the caravan and the Turks lay, and there they halted Fair was the weather, as in summer time The king and all they that were with him armed themselves and ordered their ranks The French made the rear ward, and the king was in the vanguard, and he caused it to be cried throughout the host that he who would not forget honour must not be mindful of gain, but they should strive always to discomfit and break through the Turks and smite them with their brands of steel In the mean time, whilst they were ranging and ordering their battalions, lo, another spy came pricking in great haste to the king and told him that since daybreak they of the caravan had prepared for battle and were on their guard And when the king had heard this he sent ahead archers, Turcopoles, and arbalesters, for to harry the Turks and to hold them back until he could come up to them And whilst these were harrying them, the battalions moved ever nearer until they were come very nigh to them And when the Turks perceived them they withdrew themselves to the foot of the mountain for to have it at their backs, all ordered for battle as they were Howbeit, they were none too eager And the king had divided his battalions into two companies And our archers harried the Turks and shot their arrows thick as the drops of dew, so the caravan was halted And the good king, as giving an earnest of the battle, threw himself so violently upon their foremost rank, and he and his band smote them so furiously, that I tell you of a surety, never one of them did they meet whom they did not overthrow and cast to earth Nor ever a Turk gat him thence save as he turned his back and fled Nor was there any rallying thereafter, but even as greyhound might chase the hare across the moor, even so along the mountain-side did our men with theirs, putting them to such confusion that they fled all scattered, discomfited, and routed, and the caravan was abandoned And our men, riding at full speed, were yet pursuing them to right and to left And one that was further informed of the matter hath said that so long and so far endured the flight of the Turks over the wide heath that they fell dead from thirst, and as for them that were overthrown, the knights cast them down and the serjeants slew them Then had ye seen saddles turned, and ranks ill ranged, there had ye beheld mighty warlike blows dealt by the valiant King of England But think not that I shall now begin to tell his praises here, for so many men themselves beheld these deeds of prowess that I must needs refrain therefrom There had ye seen the king chasing the Turks, his steel brand in his hand, and as for those whom he overtook as he pursued, no arm could guard them from his stroke, which clave them to the teeth And they fled him even as sheep that spy the wolf And now whilst the foremost of our men were thus pursuing the Turks across the mountain and pressing them hard, some thirty of the Saracens, full of rage and spite, turned aside by a bypath and came upon Roger of Tosni His horse they killed under him and lacked but little of taking himself captive Then, lo, straight at the paynim folk rode one of his companions, Juquel of Mayenne, who was immediately overthrown, and Roger, who was himself busied with fighting, went on foot to rescue him Then had ye seen our folk come rushing up, pricking thitherward from the right hand and from the left! Then came the Count of Leicester; then came Gilbert of Malesmains, and one or two others with him, and Alexander Arsis came, with fifteen or twenty other knights Thither came also Stephen of Longchamp, who, in the very midst of the paynims, rendered such aid to Roger that he gat him speedily to horse again Then had ye beheld the discomfiture of those unnatural folk! Mighty sword-strokes had ye seen, lopping off feet and hands and heads, thrusting through eyes and mouths, so many dead bodies lying there like logs that they hampered our men and caused them to stumble Well did the men of Poitou fight, and Normans, English, and Angevins, and the good king, bold and valiant, wrought greater prowess there than all the rest together There had ye seen such destruction of the Turks as never man saw in all our fathers' days So crushed were they, so spiritless—as was most clear and evident— that a little lad of paltry force might lightly have slain seven of them, or ten Then had ye seen the camel-drivers coming to the serjeants and to the knights and yielding themselves prisoners, and they led before them by their bridles the great camels, all heavy-laden, and the mules, the hinnies also, which bare such wealth of precious things, such riches—gold, silver, silken stuffs and samite from the land of the Seignior of Damis,[228] and figured stuffs, and fabrics from Bagdad, and Grecian textures, and purple stuffs, and quilted coats, counterpoints, and raiment quaint and fair, and goodly tents and pavilions cunningly wrought, biscuit, wheat, barley, and meal, electuaries and other medicines, basins, leathern bottles, chess-tables, silver pots, and candlesticks, pepper and cumin, sugar and wax, so many spices of every kind, so many goodly suits of arms, stout, light, and proof, so many other precious things, such riches and such wealth—that they in sooth declared that never in the time of any war had so great a booty been taken in that land

Now when the paynim pack was slain and the rich caravan taken, a right rich spoil had they gotten, but sorely were they troubled then to get together the swift-footed camels, so that all the host was thrown into confusion thereby For so swiftly did these flee away, when our men were pursuing them on horseback, that God never made aught else so speedy—neither stag, nor hind, nor fallow deer, nor gazelle—that it could overtake them an they had but a little start And they who in the end gat the camels together and counted them without the help of the serjeants, reckoned at four thousand and seven hundred the camels that had been taken, but so many were the mules and hinnies, and so many the sure-footed sumpter asses, that they were never able to number them; they were, in sooth, but a burden And it was said that in this pursuit there were slain, of both great folk and small, full seventeen hundred Turks that rode horses, besides those on foot that were killed or ever they could get themselves away

---

[228]Unidentified It is possible that Ambrose here uses the form *Damiz* for *Damas* (Damascus) in order to furnish a rhyme for *samiz* (samite)

LVI

HOW COUNT HENRY JOINED HIMSELF TO KING RICHARD OF THE GRIEF OF THE
HOST WHEN THEY COULD NOT MARCH AGAINST JERUSALEM HOW THE DUKE
OF BURGUNDY MADE A SONG ANENT KING RICHARD, AND HOW KING
RICHARD MADE ONE CONCERNING HIM OF THE RETREAT OF
THE CHRISTIANS, AND HOW SALADIN GATHERED HIS
ARMIES AND MARCHED AGAINST JAFFA

Then went they on, by such day's marches as they had already determined,
until they were come before Betafe,[229] this town is four leagues distant from
Jaffa There did they divide their spoil, and departing thence on their return,
they came to Ramleh in another day. There were they met by the host that was
coming from Acre, Count Henry and his people, so were all come together in the
host again Then had ye seen exceeding joy because of the great marvel that they
beheld, of the beasts which filled the camp And the king divided the camels
(such goodly ones eye never saw before) amongst the knights who guarded the
host, likewise amongst those who had gone on this emprise Mules and hinnies also
did he richly bestow upon them, and all the asses, both great and small, he caused
to be given to the serjeants Then was the host so filled with beasts that with
great difficulty could they be kept therein But the young camels they killed, and
ate the flesh thereof right willingly, for it was white and savoury when it was
larded and roasted

When the beasts had thus been divided and apportioned amongst the host,
then many began to complain because these were causing a dearth of barley And
then did the folk begin to murmur, who were very bitter because they were not
besieging Jerusalem, for which they had great longing, nor would they be quieted
And they that had taken oath and had determined that the host should not go
thither repeated to them now the reasons therefore, and they said also that if
they should lay siege to the city, so little water would they find thereabout that
neither beasts nor men could get drink—however little the Turks might avail to
hinder them—without great danger and sore toil For this was about the time of
the feast of Saint John, when the heat, as is its wont, drieth up everything in the
land And the Saracens had in sooth torn down and broken all the cisterns round
about the city, so that within two leagues' space, in a land where we had neither
peace nor truce, was no water to be found, save with great travail (this was
found to be true) in a little brook that floweth adown Mount Olivet into the
Valley of Jehoshaphat, this is Siloam So was it not advised by these that the
host should compass the city about or lay siege thereto in summer time And
when this counsel was revealed and made known—that they should not go to
Jerusalem but should turn back again—then had ye seen the folk so sorrowful
that they cursed the long delay that they had made, and the tents that they had
set up, since Jerusalem would not be besieged nor could be taken, for they would
not have asked to live another day after Jerusalem should have been taken

My Lords, marvel not if God had all in vain tried our pilgrims with sore

---

[229]"Beit-'Affè, 40 kilometers (ten leagues, not four) from Jaffa" Clermont-Ganneau
(quoted by Gaston Paris)

travail, as we have told you For sooth it is that many a time we saw, what time
they were encamped at eventide and weary with their marching, how the French
would get themselves apart from the other folk and pitch their tents all by themselves in another place So was the host divided, for in sooth could not the one
part—save by lying—agree with the other But one would say. "Thou art such
and such !" And the other to him "Such and such art thou !" And Hugo, the
Duke of Burgundy, who did much to make the matter worse, with great and exceeding arrogance made a song about the king, and a right villainous song it was
—yea, full of villainy, and this song spread throughout the host What could the
king do, save in his turn to make another song concerning them that through envy
thus assailed and mocked him? Verily, of folk so overweening never shall good
song be sung, nor work be wrought by them whereon God may look, well-pleased,
as He did in that other pilgrimage when Antioch was besieged and our folk gat
themselves therein by force, whereof history yet telleth the tale—the tale of them
to whom God accorded the victory—of Bohemond and of Tancred (noble pilgrims
they !) and of Godfrey of Bouillon and of the high princes of great renown, and
of the others that were there, who laboured in God's service until He recompensed their serving after their own liking and their hearts' desire Their works
did He exalt and multiply, so that themselves and all their lineage are yet extolled

Ten days or twelve—an I mistake not nor remember amiss—after the caravan had been taken, the host rested there in such sort as ye have heard me tell.
And when it was evident that it could in no wise come to pass, for all the travail
whereto they might submit themselves, that they should go to seek that sepulchre
which lay but four leagues distant, then had they sore grief in their hearts So
came they back again[280] in such heaviness and with so sad faces that under heaven
was no folk more downcast and distressed Their rear ward they established, but
so soon as they had departed, down from the mountain rushed the Saracens and
pursued after them until they had slain one of our serjeants But our men, sitting on their good steeds, drave them back and chased them in their turn And they
rode and they marched until they come to a place betwixt Saint George and Ramleh And on the day when we made that march was it just five years that this land
had been lost in the war The French were on the left side, and the king and his
men on the right And on the morrow, when they marched again, were they
separated in the same fashion Back came they before the Middle Casal and
pitched their tents and rested there, but some there were who departed and went
back to Jaffa because of the hardships and the poverty that they had suffered in
the host

Now when Saladin knew of a surety that our people could take no other
course and could do nought else but go back, great joy had he then and made good
cheer, and he had letters written in all haste, and gat him many a speedy messenger, and sent word to the Turks that loved him that the Christians were departing and that they were all in disaccord and divided beyond all hope of accord,
and that whosoever would have a portion of his wealth should come, an he so

[280] 5 July, 1192

desired, to Jerusalem and enter his pay Then, lo, so many folk assembled both within and without the city that they were reckoned at full twenty thousand—Turks on horseback and well armed—besides them that were on foot, who could not lightly be numbered All these knew our state, and well did they shew this to us . [231] so soon as our people returned to the place where they rested

Day by day, in their discouragement, men left the host and departed, returning unto Jaffa, for too wretched was the life that they had been leading And when the king saw them thus withdrawing themselves and perceived that he could do nought to bring the host into the right way—what should I say more? He sent word to Saphadin, bidding him speak to Saladin and let him know betimes if he might yet have the truce which Saladin had offered him on the plains of Ramleh, even as we have recounted it to you, until such time as he should be come back again from his own country So Saphadin went to enquire of the soldan But Saladin had known of our retreat, even since the first day, and he would now in no wise grant the truce, save only so that Ascalon were destroyed Now were tidings of this brought back to the host and came even unto the king, who feigned not to heed them, nor did he change his countenance nor would he in any wise listen to them But he bade both Templars and Hospitalers mount in hot haste, and three hundred other knights with them, and he commanded these to go and destroy Daron, but to cause Ascalon to be straitly guarded, so that no loss befall it through any heedlessness And they went and destroyed Daron and came back to the host And the host returned again to Jaffa, pensive and with downcast mien And from Jaffa they went immediately to Acre, but much people remained behind at Jaffa, both sick and hale, who afterward were in great fear there So was the host come back on a Sunday to Acre—by the same road over which it had gone thence—mazed and disheartened, but so goeth it with them who follow sin

So soon as Saladin and Saphadin his brother knew that we were departed from Jaffa, as we have told you, and that we went away in such exceeding sorrow as we have described to you, then was summoned and mustered the army of the proud paynim folk, and at that time and season had the soldan of Turks on horseback more than twenty thousand, he had, also, the admiral of Bile,[232] and he had the son of the Assassin,[233] and admirals full an hundred and six, and footfolk from the mountain so many that they covered all the plain And, lo, all this host came down from Jerusalem and encamped below in the plains of Ramleh, and there had ye seen many a goodly steed

---

[231]Lacuna of three lines
[232]Unidentified
[233]I e., of the Old Man of the Mountain

LVII

HOW SALADIN ATTACKED JAFFA AND TOOK THE CITY, BUT NOT THE CASTLE HOW KING RICHARD SUDDENLY CAME TO JAFFA BY SEA AND DELIVERED BOTH THE CASTLE AND THE CITY

On a Sunday, on the selfsame day when we came back to Acre, was the host of the fell paynim folk encamped before Jaffa, and on the Monday they began the assault Our men went forth of the city and met them in the gardens without the walls All day long did our men withstand them, so that never on that day did the enemy get them nigh to the castle, so grievously were they harried, nor on the morrow, which was Tuesday, nor on the third day But on Thursday was the whole city compassed round about and the folk within were sorely beset And Saladin caused four petraries to be set up, strong and light, and two mangonels for to hurl missiles

Then had ye heard the lamentations of the Christians that were within the city—more than five thousand of them, both those that were hale and those that lay sick—who all lamented, saying "Ah! King of England! Wherefore art thou gone away to Acre? O Christendom, how art thou now undone!" Then had ye seen folk assailed with such vigour and such violence, so many wounded or slain, so many boldly defending themselves and mounting and descending so continually, that under heaven is there no living wight that had not had great pity of them The petraries were ever playing, nor did the mangonels ever rest And they that were within the city also had petraries, but they knew not how to make use of them The Turks played upon the very strong gate that looketh toward Jerusalem, until the arches thereof fell down, whereby our folk were sore distraught And the wall to the right of it was cleft, so that two perches thereof came tumbling down But on the Friday[234] then in sooth had ye seen fierce battle when the Turks entered into the city, for hand to hand they fought Howbeit, the Turks, whose number waxed ever greater from the battalions that issued from the host, were in the end so increased that they brake the ranks of our men and drave them up the hill even to Toron, before the tower There had ye seen an hideous sight— sick folk lying in the houses, whom the Turks slew There was many a good martyr found There had ye seen many folk leaving the rest and fleeing toward the seashore And the cruel Saracens took and spoiled the houses, and all the wheat they bare away, but all the wines they spilled And some of them attacked Toron, where God's people were, who defended themselves valiantly, and the rest ran down to the sea, unto the ships and barges that were there, wherein our men wished to get themselves for to preserve and to safeguard their lives But many of them that were last died there And there did men see Auberi of Reims, who should have guarded the castle, so shamefully play the craven that he clomb into a barge for to flee away over the broad sea But the brave men cried after him so lustily that they constrained him to return, and they brought him by force to Toron Then said he "Here let us die in God's behalf, since nought else can be" All about them, on the right hand and on the left, at the foot of Toron were so

---

[234] July

many Turks attacking that they wist not on which side to defend themselves
There had ye seen arrows falling thicker than hailstones Foot to foot they
fought, all pell-mell All day long the fray endured, but our people had never
withstood the violent assaults or the fierce charge, had God not caused the newly
made patriarch to remain there, who would not through fear of death refrain
from rescuing them who were fighting even unto the death But he sent word
unto Saladin—to that generous, that valiant Saracen—and unto Saphadin, praying them to grant a truce, were it only until the morrow And he engaged himself—if ere the hour of nones they should not have seen men coming from Acre
or from Ascalon, or the King of England's men whom they had sent to seek—
to yield his own person as hostage, together with others of high lineage, to be
put in chains and in bonds until every one of those Christians who were combating on Toron should pay to Saladin ten bezants of gold as surety, and the women
likewise should give each one five bezants, and three for the little children And
even as he demanded, so did Saladin command that the engagement be accepted
and observed So came his messenger, and the truce was granted and the matter
thus arranged To the Turks they delivered two hostages, who went with the
patriarch these were Auberi[235] and Tibaud of Troies—a valiant man and bold, a
serjeant of Count Henry who had brought up his father And others might there
well be, whose names I could not learn

   Ye have heard me tell (and it is well worth the telling again because of the
great good that came therefrom) of the host that returned to Acre all heavy and
disconsolate and crushed with woe, and how all thought now to depart and were
going straight to their vessels, and how King Richard himself, as we saw with
our eyes, had now taken his leave of the Temple and of the Hospital and had
looked to his galleys that they might be well prepared And on the morrow
would he go on board (as saith the book) for to proceed to Beirut—he and his
household And he had already sent seven galleys, which attacked them that
were in the castle, who fled away nor would have awaited him an they had seen
any more galleys Now whilst the king was in his tent one evening at vespers, lo,
a barge came full speed toward Acre and landed there And they who came
forth of the barge hastened to the king nor tarried at all, and they told him that
Jaffa had been taken and our folk besieged on Toron, and if these were not succoured by him they all would be destroyed and slain (even as I have told you)
And the brave king, of his generosity, abandoning his own purpose, said to them
"In sooth will I go thither!" And immediately he bade the host be summoned
But in no wise would the French listen to him, but they made answer—those envious ones, who looked coldly on him—saying that never would they turn their
steps thither nor to the host would they ever go Nor did they, with him or with
any other man But they died, in sooth, not long after Nevertheless, they who
feared God, of whatsoever land they were—Templars and Hospitalers and many
other good knights—made ready and gat them to horse and journeyed by land
straight to Caesarea, and the valiant King of England went in galleys by sea

---

235Of Reims

So richly had he and his armed themselves that never might goodlier sight be seen There was the Count of Leicester, and there was Andrew of Chauvigni, and there was Roger of Saci, there too was seen Jordan of Hommet, who died in that same year And there was Ralph of Mauléon, who beareth a lion on his banner, there was Auçon of Fai, who many a Saracen engaged, and there were they of Préaux—companions, these, of the king—and many other famous men who were not named to me These were going on God's service, with them of Genoa and them of Pisa, who had great part in this emprise Now hear ye how the affair befell they that were going by land to Jaffa, and who thought to go all the way thither, had rested at Caesarea, and scarcely were they come thither when it was told them that Saladin was causing the roads to be guarded on their account, so that they were so good as besieged there, it was the Assassin's son, who lay between Arsûf and Caesarea And on the sea our other people were held back by a contrary wind—both the king and the rest that were in the galleys—so that for three days they lay off Caiphas nor moved thence And the king cried "Have pity, O God! Wherefore holdest Thou me here? For 'tis on Thy service I am bent!" And God in His bounty sent them a wind out of the north, which bare him with all his fleet to the port of Jaffa on a Friday, late in the night, and on Saturday, at nones, would the truce be expired Then had the Christians been in evil case and deadly, doomed to death and dole, had God not thus delivered them through the king, as we will tell you briefly

The brave king and his illustrious men had lain in their galleys through all the night of Friday even until the morning of Saturday, then he armed himself, and his men did likewise Now shall ye hear of the warrant whereby the safety of the city had been warranted, and of the treachery that the Turks had contrived against them that thought their safety warranted by the bezants which they had promised The Saracens demanded that they should pay in the morning, and in the morning began they to make their payments But even as they made them, the Saracens cut off their heads one by one And they thought that they were acting very cunningly, but fie upon the faith of a cur! Already had they slain seven and had cast them into a ditch, when they that were on Toron perceived it And they that were there have said that then might ye have seen a very sweet sight upon Toron, before the tower, because of the fear which they had that they were now doomed to death Then had ye seen many folk weeping, kneeling down and praying, making confession, reciting their *mea culpa,* whilst they that were without gat themselves within, into the great press of people, that they might put off their dying so long as possible For every creature, when death close pursueth it, seeketh a little season of respite and delay They were awaiting their martyrdom, and in all sooth can we tell you that there were tears shed which had for God a very pleasant savour, for they came, in the bitterness of death, from the utmost depths of their hearts which they lifted up to Him, whilst they waited for death nor had any other expectation save to die

Then did the Turks perceive the galleys which were already in the harbour All down to the strand they came, until the shore was so filled with them that they could scarce abide there Bucklers they bare, and targes, and they shot at the barges and clean over to the king's galleys Then had ye seen the fierce recklessness of them that were on horseback, how they hurled themselves into the sea, shooting at our men for to keep them from getting themselves to land! But the brave King Richard drew all his vessels together, as it were, for to speak to his company Then said he to his chivalry "Ye gentle knights, what shall we do? Shall we go hence, or shall we get us to land? Or how shall we be able to do this?" Then such was the case that certain ones there were who answered that to their mind it were of no avail to gain the shore or to seize the port, for all thought that surely were the people of the castle already slain But in the mean time, whilst they were yet enquiring whether they could get them to land, lo, the King of England saw a chantry priest leap suddenly from the shore into the sea, who came a-swimming straight toward the king And him he took into his galley. Then quoth the priest "O gentle king, perished are the folk that here await thee, an God and thou have not compassion on them!" "How, good friend?" quoth the king "Are any yet alive? Whither are they gone?" "Yea, sire, before yonder tower are all assembled, awaiting death" And so soon as the king perceived that this was so, no longer did he tarry, but straightway said "God hath caused us to come hither for to endure and suffer death, and since it now behooveth us to die, then shame on him who will not go yonder!" Then he bade the galley draw near to the shore and, with his legs unarmed, he leaped into the sea—by good fortune, only up to his girdle—and came apace to the dry ground, the second or mayhap the first to land, such was his custom Geoffrey of the Wood[236] and Peter of Préaux, valiant companion of the king, and all the others leaped in after him and went against the Turks with whom the shore was filled and attacked them And the brave king in his own person slew many with his arbalest, and his people, bold and ready, pursued them all along the strand The Turks fled before the king, whom they durst not confront, and he laid hand to his brand of steel and went running after them and pursued them in that hour so hard that they had no leisure to defend themselves They durst no longer await him or his well-proved company, who were smiting them like folk gone mad And so did these smite and press them that they cleaned the shore of Turks and drave them all back; and after this they took tuns and timbers and great planks and old galleys and barges, and therewith builded they a bulwark across the shore betwixt them and the Saracen folk And there the king put knights and serjeants and arbalesters, who skirmished with the Saracens The paynim howled and hooted, but they withdrew perforce in their own despite Then the king went up by a winding stair which leadeth to the House of the Templars There entered he the first of them all and gat him by force into the city, and he found there more than three thousand Saracens who were despoiling the castle and carrying away all that was therein Then Richard, the bravest king in all the world, so soon as he was on the top of the walls, caused his banners to be displayed and to be lifted up until the beleaguered Christians saw them And so soon as they espied them, "Holy Sepulchre!" cried they all

---

[236]Giefroi del Bois

Their weapons they seized and did their armour on, nor tarried any longer Then
had ye seen the paynim host assailed with fear when they beheld our men descending! Then had ye also seen full many a Turk laid low, whom the king struck
down to earth None durst await his stroke, lest his life be lost thereby Then
were our folk come clean down into the midst of the streets There had ye seen
the enemy put to confusion, cut in pieces, and slain And there were avenged the
wounds of those sick folk that could not move, whom the Turks had found within the city and had put to death There had ye seen our people descending like
the rain, putting the Saracens to shame But why should I make a long tale thereof? So soon as ever our men overtook those that were yet in the city nor had
the time to get them thence, straightway they slew them So was the town delivered and its people saved from great shame

LVIII

**OF THE FLIGHT OF SALADIN HOW THE BODIES OF THE TURKS WERE CAST AMONGST
THOSE OF THE SWINE THAT THEY HAD KILLED HOW THE WALLS OF JAFFA
WERE RESTORED HOW THE TURKS SOUGHT TO SURPRISE KING RICHARD
IN HIS TENT, AND OF THE COMING OF COUNT HENRY OF CHAMPAGNE**

The king went out of the city after them, who had already wrought such
prowess that day Only three horses had he, nor ever, even at Roncesvalles, did
any man, young or old, Saracen or Christian, acquit himself in such fashion as
he For when the Turks beheld his banner they trembled on every side There
had no coward cared to be, for never hath God made snow or rain to fall thicker or
faster, even when they fall most grievously, than the bolts and arrows which
rained down in the midst of the Christians Then was the news brought and told
to Saladin that his people were thus assailed, and he, the caitiff, who was worse
maddened than a wolf, waxed feverous with fear Nor durst he tarry longer there
but caused his pavilions to be struck, and his tents, and to be carried back into
the plains And the king and his proud and valiant men followed and pursued
after them, smiting them and treading hard upon their heels, with their arbalesters shooting at them and slaying their horses And so close did they press the
Turks and so sorely did they wound them with their arrows that they retreated
full two leagues Then straightway the king caused his own tent to be pitched in
that very place where Saladin had not dared await him There encamped Richard
the Great

When that two days' fight was ended and when the host of the Turks had retreated, then was that host abashed and sore ashamed because they had been driv-
en back by folk on foot, who had but a little force against so great a multitude as
they were, but God had put forth His hand that His people might not come to
harm Then, lo, Saladin called together his Saracens and Turks of highest estate
and asked of them "Who pursueth you? Is, then, the whole host come back
from Acre, that it hath thus put my folk to flight? Are they on foot or horseback,
they that came down upon you?" Then up spake a certain traitor who knew the

matter and had seen the king "Sire, never a beast have they with them, neither horse nor mule, save that the king, that doughty warrior, found three steeds in Jaffa, so many are there or can be—not another one! And if there be any one here who would fain undertake the thing, then could he seize the king's person with scarce any pains, for he lieth all alone in his tent"

Now it was on a Saturday (according to the history that I am reciting to you) that the city was recovered and delivered from the Saracens, who indeed had wrought marvels there which shall always be spoken of for they had taken Jaffa a second time, and had put to death the sick Christian folk that they found there, and it was proved of a truth that they found so many swine in the city, which they killed and destroyed, that the number thereof was infinite, for it is in sooth known that they eat not the flesh of swine and are therefore very fain to kill them, nor hate they more any other earthly thing in their despite against the Christian faith So had they mingled and laid side by side the dead folk and the swine But our people, being moved by God to do this thing, took up the bodies of the other Christian folk and laid them all in earth, but the Saracens that they had slain on the Saturday they cast out together with the dead swine, which stank so that our folk could no longer endure it

Then did the king bid them toil on Sunday and on Monday upon the walls of Jaffa, and on the Tuesday also, wheresoever they saw it broken, until in the end they had reared it anew so well as could be done without lime or mortar, so be it there were any need of defense But the host abode without in their tents, where they must needs keep straiter watch

The Mamelukes of Saladin, they of Aleppo, the Kurds, and all the light-armed bachelery of the hated paynim folk came together to a parley, and they declared that they were sore shamed because they had yielded up Jaffa to folk so few as ours were, and to folk that had no horse This said they everywhere one to another, until in the end they made a compact together and boasted one to another that they would seize the king in his tent and take him to Saladin Thus was their compact made

Lo, in a galley came Count Henry of Champagne from Caesarea, he and his company For the host had come to Caesarea, but there, despite itself, had it been stayed by the Saracens, who were watching the streams and the passes so that the king might get no succour Nor had he any, of all their company, save only of the count his nephew Nor had he, for to carry him through that day's fighting that had been prepared for him, more than fifty knights, or at the most three score, with serjeants and arbalesters brave and skillful in their business, and men of Genoa and men of Pisa who had offered themselves there in God's service, and other folk about two thousand Nor even then, after he had rescued the city, had he full fifteen horses, good and bad together, such lack of these had he thereafter that his people had surely perished and been undone if God had not protected him against the Turks and their designs

Now shall ye hear a great marvel, whereat all the world marveleth, for certainly had all our people been taken on Wednesday through that complot whereby the enemy thought to seize the king, had not God taken care of him That night, about the hour of matins, the Saracens mounted and drew up their ranks, then they laced their aventailes[237] and rode forth by the light of the moon And then did God perform one of His glorious acts of mercy, and when He doeth such a kindness, fitting it is that it be recounted Behold them, then, riding adown the plain in serried ranks Then the Lord God Himself caused a dispute to arise betwixt the Kurds and the Mamelukes, whether of the twain should dismount and await our people on foot so that our men might not be able to retreat into the castle and find shelter there And each company said "Ye shall dismount!" "Nay, ye shall!" "Nay, ye yourselves, that is but right, for we are the better horsemen!" So came they, quarreling amongst themselves, and the strife of each with the other endured until they saw the daylight clear, even as God had purposed And the king was yet asleep in his tent

Now listen ye to the high adventure of a certain Genoese who had arisen and gone out upon the heath at the very peep of dawn [238] And as he was turning about to go back he heard the Turks coming and saw the glistering of their helmets Then straight he bowed his head, but lifted up his voice and cried to our people to do their armour on and all to rush to arms And the king was wakened by the cry, albeit he had laboured hard that day Forth of his bed he leaped upon his feet and donned, I ween, an hauberk white and tough and stout He bade his companions instantly awake, nor is it any marvel if, in so sudden a surprise, they had much ado to clothe and to arm themselves And I can well assure you that they had such haste, both the king and many others beside, that with legs unarmed, bare and uncovered save by the shadow of the clouds—yea, some even naked and unbreeched—they fought perforce that day, receiving many blows and wounds; and 'twas their state that troubled them the most of all

Now whilst our folk were arming themselves, the Saracens were drawing ever nearer Then the king mounted, and he had with him not more than ten men on horseback And the history telleth us clearly that Count Henry of Champagne was there on horse with his company, and there was the Count of Leicester, Robert, who was worthy to be there, and Bartholomew of Mortemer was there, mounted, I ween, and there was Ralph of Mouléon, who never had his fill of fighting, and there was Andrew of Chauvigni, stout and valiant in his saddle, and there was Girard of Fournival, on horseback with the king, and there was Roger of Saci, sitting on a sorry nag, and there was William of L'Étang, who had a foundered horse, and there was Hugh of Neuville, a serjeant bold and noble And Henry Le Tyois bare the king's banner in the midst of their band

And now behold our people drawn up in order against the cruel infidel host, and ranged by battalions, each with its own command The knights were on the left hand, along the shore, over toward Saint Nicholas',[239] fronting the Saracen folk, there was it meet that they should be, for thitherward moved the more part of the Turks, beating their drums and yelling And before the gardens were set

---

[237]The front of the hood of a hauberk
[238]5 August
[239]A church near Jaffa

folk of divers nations, there were Pisans and there were Genoese, nor were it now possible to tell or to recount the assaults that these suffered of the hated folk The Turks began to shoot their arrows, and to hoot and to shout and to yell There had ye seen marvelous fighting, and our good folk hard beset They kneeled upon their knees, setting their targes and their shields upright before them, their lances in their hands And the king, who was well skilled in arms, caused to be hidden under all the targes, betwixt two men, an arbalester and a man for to bend his bow and give it back to him when he had bent it, and by this means was the host well defended Thus were they ordered But it must not be doubted that they who were in such jeopardy, opposed to the multitude of Turks that they saw, had fear for their own heads But it is so true as that ye are now here that the king went amongst them, encouraging them and exhorting the knights, and John of Préaux went with him, likewise preaching to them And they said· "Now will it soon be shewn who will strive to do valiantly so long as God preserveth his life For now is nought else to do save to sell our lives dearly and to await our martyrdom, since God hath so decreed for us Now are we in the right way, since He Himself of His bounty giveth us that which we came to seek Here is found our true recompense"

Then the ranks stood fast, and the squadrons of the Turks came on And our folk ever kept their legs planted in the sand and all their lances in rest, ready to receive them Then advanced the battalions of the false Saracen folk with such impetuosity, with such clatter of hoofs, that an our folk had moved at all, the Turks had broken through their line, for there were, an I err not, a thousand in each battalion But when they were hard upon our men and saw that they moved not, they turned and rode close along our front Then the arbalesters let fly, and the Turks durst not await them, for they hit both their bodies and the bodies of the horses and overthrew them. But presently back came the squadrons, and yet again were they drawing near, stopping short, and wheeling them about, and thus did they many times And when the king and his men saw that even though they were so many and were on horseback, the Turks would not do otherwise, then with lance-head lowered, each man thrust himself with all his might full into the midst of the great press of misbelieving enemy folk, and so violently did they assail them that all the ranks trembled, even unto the third line Then did the king look about him, and yonder on the left saw he the brave Count of Leicester fall, who had been stricken down from his horse, though valiantly had he fought, but the brave king went and rescued him Then had ye seen so many Turks come charging straight toward the Lion banner! Then, lo, was Ralph of Mauléon led off captive of the Turks, but the king put spurs to his noble steed and gat him out of their hands again Mightily wrought the king in the midst of the press against Turks and Persians, never in one day hath any man, be he weak or strong, performed such deeds of prowess For he charged into the midst of the Turks, and clave them to the teeth, and so many a time did he charge them, and so many blows did he deal them, and so wore he himself with smiting, that the very skin of his hands cracked

Then came a Saracen pricking, outstripping the other Turks, riding a courser swift and mettlesome This was the valiant Saphadin of Arcady,[240] he that wrought such deeds of prowess and of bounty and of largess Spurring he came, as I have said, with two Arab steeds which he delivered to the King of England, praying and beseeching him, because of the king's prowess which he knew and the great valour that he possessed, to mount them, with this understanding that if God brought him safe and sound out of this pass wherein he saw him now, the king would grant to him some guerdon Thereafter had he rich reward for this The king was very fain to take them, and he said that many another such would he right gladly receive from his most mortal enemy, an ever again he were brought to such straits as he was now in

Then hotter waxed the fight, never was its like seen before All the ground was covered with the arrows of that folk perverse, which men gathered up by armfuls So many wounded folk were there to see that the rowers fled back into the galleys, whence they had come forth He that fleeth in such an hour greatly dishonoureth himself! Then arose a cry from the city that the Turks were coming thither in a body, thinking to take our people by surprise both in the front and in the rear And the king, with two other knights, rode thither, bearing his banner And so soon as he was entered therein, in the middle of the street he met three Turks in costly harness, he smote them like a king and gave them so rude an encounter that he straightway gat him two other horses there, and the Turks he slew And the other paynim drave he by force out of the city Then passed he on and caused the gate whereby they had entered to be stopped from side to side and from top to bottom, and he set guards to guard it Straight to the galleys then went he, whither his people had gone in great fear and distress And Richard, son of prowess, brought back courage to them all and caused them to row again to land, and he gat his people once more together, so that there remained only five men in each of the galleys And with the rest back came he to the host, which had had no repose Then made he that adventurous charge—none other such was ever made! For so deep he charged into that heathen horde that they swallowed him up, nor could any of his own folk longer see him And it lacked but little that they had followed after him, breaking their ranks, then had we all been lost Howbeit, the king was not dismayed, but he smote before him and behind until with the sword that he held he had made him an highway there, whithersoever he would go, were it man or horse he smote, he cut them all down There, at one stroke an I mistake not, he clave off the arm and head together from an admiral in iron armour, sending him straight to hell And after this stroke, which the Turks beheld, so wide room did they make for him that he came back, thanks be to God, unharmed But his body, his horse, his trappings—all were so covered with arrows which the swarthy folk had rivaled in shooting at him that he resembled an hedgehog So came he back from the battle, which endured all the day long from morning until eventide—so cruel and so fierce a battle that if God had not sustained His people, ill had it gone with them But in sooth was He with us

---

[240]The name seems to be used here vaguely, merely indicating some distant land

—that saw we, when never a man had we lost there that day, save one or two only. But the Turks lost more than fifteen hundred horses, which were lying on the hills and in the vales, and more than seven hundred men also, who all lay there dead Nor for all this their travail did they carry off the king, who before the eyes of their hated folk had wrought his great feats of knighthood, so that they were all dumfounded at the prowesses which they saw performed by him and by them that were with him, who put themselves in jeopardy of death

LIX

HOW SALADIN RALLIED HIS MEN HOW HE THREATENED KING RICHARD WHILST HE LAY SICK, AND HOW THE FRENCH REFUSED TO COME TO THE KING'S AID HOW KING RICHARD MUST PERFORCE MAKE A TRUCE FOR THREE YEARS WITH SALADIN OF THE COURTESY WHICH KING RICHARD AND SALADIN SHEWED EACH TO THE OTHER HOW KING RICHARD SUF-FERED NOT THE FRENCH TO GO TO JERUSALEM

When the Lord God had thus of His bounty delivered the king and the Christian people from the paynim folk and the host had departed, then were told the words that the soldan Saladin had addressed to the Saracens in his bitter anger at his discomfiture "Where," asked he, "are they that have taken the king? Where is he that bringeth him hither to me?" And a Turk from a far country made answer "Sire, I will tell thee, nor in aught will I lie Never yet hath such another man been seen—so valiant, so cunning—or one better proved in arms For every need will he be found ready Greatly have we travailed and mighty blows have we dealt, but never have we been able to take him, for none dareth to await his stroke, so bold is he and so dexterous "

My Lords, think it no fable that the Turks knew him right well, or that they would have taken him that time but for God's help and his own great cunning For so many prowesses wrought he that day, and such travail had he and the other brave men that were with him, that they fell sick—being yet nigh to that folk whom may God curse!—both from the labours of that day's emprise and from the carrions wherewith the city was so defiled, and so was their natural strength broken that it lacked but little that they had died—both the king and the others that were there

Now whilst the king lay sick and in sore misease, Saladin sent him word that himself and his Saracens would come and take him where he lay, so be it he durst await their coming And straight the king sent word back to him that Saladin should know and be assured that he would await him in that very place where he now was, nor ever, in any place, so long as he could stand upon his feet or raise himself upon his knees, would he flee one single foot for him Thus was taken up the gage of war But God knew well how little ease he had the while he spake so nobly Then did he send Count Henry (so saith the tale) back to Caesarea for the French who had come hither afore, and for the other folk that were there, to come now and defend the land And he called to mind their promise and made known to them his present evil case But never would they give him any succour, but left him in that jeopardy whence he had not escaped but for the truce which he accepted, but which was sorely blamed of many But no man ought to blame him on this account, for surely would the Turks have come to take him and himself have suffered hurt, and Ascalon would have been lost. Of a surety would Ascalon have been taken, and Tyre and Acre by all likelihood

So lay the king at Jaffa, in troubled mood, in sickness, and in pain And he considered what he would do, thinking that he must depart thence because of the weakness of the city, which was no longer strong or defensible Then summoned he Count Henry, whom his own sister reared, and he sent for the Templars and for the Hospitalers And he recounted to them the evils that he suffered of his heart and of his head, and he told them that some of them must needs go to Ascalon and guard it, and the others must remain at Jaffa and keep good watch over it, and himself would go away to Acre for to seek healing there And he said that he could not do otherwise But what should I tell you more, save that they all began to make excuses? And they all answered him flatly, saying that never without him would they guard castle or watch over any place, and they departed, saying nothing more Then was the king exceeding wroth But when he saw that all the world, which is neither loyal nor without guile, had flatly failed him, then was he troubled and distraught and well-nigh at his wit's end My Lords, marvel not if he but did the best that he knew according to the occasion that he had, for whoso feareth shame and followeth honour, he chooseth, of two evils, the lesser one So would he rather seek a truce than leave the land in danger; for all the rest were leaving him and going in a body to their ships

Then sent he word to Saphadin, who was Saladin's brother and who greatly loved the king because of his prowess, that he should procure him without delay so favourable a truce as he could and that himself would accept it And Saphadin bestirred himself mightily and parleyed so well that a truce was determined and declared by Saladin in these terms that Ascalon, which was a grievous threat to his crown, should be razed and torn down, nor should any one fortify it again within the space of three years, but then should he that should be at that time the stronger have the place and build it up again, and that Jaffa should be fortified anew and peopled again with Christian folk, and that all the rest of the level land along the mountains and along the sea, wherein no man then dwelt, should be under a firm and loyal truce, and whoso would faithfully observe this truce might safely come and go for to visit the Holy Sepulchre, and that all merchandises should pass through the land without paying tribute Thus ran the terms, and thus was the truce written down and carried back to the king and read to him And he, who was without help and very nigh to the hated folk (for their host lay not more than two leagues away), accepted the truce in this wise And if any one should tell the story otherwise, then would he lie

Now when the truce had been brought to the king and he had acknowledged it, since he saw that he could not do otherwise, then could he not keep secret that which he had in his heart, but he sent word to Saladin, in the hearing of many noble Saracens, expressly declaring to him that in all sooth had he accepted this truce for three years only—one year, for to go back to his own country, another, for to seek him out men and gather them together, and the third, for to return and take this land, an Saladin durst await him　And the soldan sent back word to him, by those whom he despatched for this purpose, that, by the law that he observed and by the God whom he adored, so highly did he esteem the great prowess of the king and his great heart and his great understanding, than an ever in his life by any chance his land were conquered, the king would be the one of all the princes that he knew or had beheld whom he would fainest see take his land from him by force and conquer it　So thought the king to do, and to recover the Holy Sepulchre, but he knew not neither did he understand what things awaited him

Now when this truce was sworn and ratified by the two parties, when the terms had been established and the charters thereof made, then did the good king cause himself to be carried to Caiphas by the sea that he might be healed and strengthened, and there he took medicine　And the French who were sojourning at Acre were desirous to return to France, but they declared that first would they go on their pilgrimage, albeit they had blamed the truce and mocked and scorned it, nor would they rescue Jaffa in its need, neither gave they any succour to the king　And when it had been made known to the king that they desired to have safe-conduct for to make their pilgrimage, then the king straight gat him messengers and sent to Saladin and to the admiral Saphadin, saying that they should not let any Christian, young or old, go to Jerusalem without letters from the king or from Count Henry, if they wished him to abide by his promise　And the French were so displeased when they heard tell of this message that the more part of them took up their carriages and went back to France

LX

HOW THE FRENCH DEPARTED　OF THE FIRST OF THE PILGRIMS THAT WENT TO JERUSALEM, AND HOW SALADIN SUFFERED NOT THE TURKS TO DO THEM MISCHIEF　OF THE SECOND COMPANY OF PILGRIMS, WHEREOF AMBROSE WAS ONE

When the multitude of the French had departed—that is, the greater part of them, those that spake evil of the king and had caused him the most hinderances, in whom he could never put his trust—then he bade it be cried abroad that his people might go to the Sepulchre, and that they should bear their offerings to Jaffa for to help build up the walls thereof　But what should I say more?　In the several companies, even as they were ordered, with a constable to each one, they all went to the Sepulchre　The first constable, methinketh, was Andrew of Chauvigni—there are worse monks at Cluny [241]　And the second was Ralph Taisson,

---

[241] *Si fu Andreus de Chavigni*
Si a peor moine a Cloignie

Andrew of Chauvigni (Chavigni, Chavignié) is repeatedly mentioned in the chronicles, poems, and legal documents of his time but there is no apparent reason for associating him with the abbey of Cluny　Ambrose, following his usual custom of devoting an entire couplet to each member of any expedition which he is describing, seems to have dragged in the second name merely for the sake of the rhyme

who greatly loved music and song The Bishop of Salisbury, who was afterward made archbishop, led the last troop, this know I for a certainty So soon as these men stood possessed of their charters, then did the pilgrims go their ways, marching in closed ranks Now hear ye how evil ofttimes, and in many a way and many a place, befalleth them who think but to do good Whilst they were thus journeying and were passing through the plains of Ramleh, lo, the barons spake together and determined that they would send word to Saladin that they were coming to Jerusalem with letters from the King of England, for to seek and to see the Holy Sepulchre They that bare this message were very valiant men and very wise, but their sin or their slothfulness brought all their valour to nought The one of these was William of the Rocks,[242] on whose head the helm sat trimly, and the others were Girard of Fournival and Peter of Préaux Adown the plains of Ramleh they rode, and they journeyed and went their way till they were come to Toron of the Knights, and there they stayed and waited for Saphadin, whom they were seeking, for they desired his safe-conduct And sooth is it that they fell asleep And so long a tarrying made they there that well into the afternoon their company, marching ever in close order, had already crossed the plain and drawn nigh to the mountain, then, looking about them, did my Lord Andrew and they that were with him see coming those that should have borne the message And when they saw and knew them, they stopped, dumfounded Then had ye heard how the high barons spake! "Ah, Lord God! In an evil hour are we come hither, an the Saracens espy us! See ye those coming yonder who ought to have carried our message on before? Not wisely do we journey here, for eventide is drawing nigh, and those savage Saracen folk are not yet withdrawn from their host If we go further toward them nor send them word aforehand, then will they fall upon us and we shall lose our heads, for we and all our folk set forth unarmed"

So were the messengers chidden, none the less they besought them to go on and sent them forth again upon their errand, and pressed them to make haste. So these went toward Jerusalem, and they found outside the city more than two thousand Turks encamped The admiral Saphadin they sought until they found him, and they told him that our folk were coming thither and that they desired of him safe-conduct and that they bare letters from the king, and they besought him to take good care of them But Saphadin reproached them bitterly, and he said that he had undertaken a right foolish thing and foolish counsel had he given them—whoso had led their people thither on this wise, and that they loved their lives but little if without safe-conduct thus they journeyed And so they spake together until already night was falling Then came their company thither, of arms and of good rede bereft And when the Saracens beheld these pilgrims, such countenance and such mien did they shew them that I tell you in all sooth that in that company was none so bold that he had not very fain been back in Acre or in Tyre Underneath a wall that night they lay, and know ye well that they were in great fear On the morrow came the Saracens before Saladin and kneeled down at his feet And they prayed and besought him, saying "Ah, righteous

---

[242]*Des Roches Guillames* Guillaume des Roches, afterward Seneschal of Anjou

soldan! Now were it most just and expedient to avenge us of the slaughter which these made of our own people before Acre Sire, let us avenge our fathers, our kinsmen, our sons, and our brethren, whom these have slain and cut in pieces Now can every one of them be avenged And he made answer, as was fitting, that he would speak with his friends concerning the matter So these came together before the soldan and examined the matter straitly There were the high Saracens, Mestoc, with Saphadin and Bedredin Dorderon[243], and these said: "Sire, we will tell thee that which befitteth thy majesty Verily were it a sore shame and a dire disgrace to the paynim law, if these Christian folk, who are here in our power and have such trust and confidence in us, were slain in this manner whilst there is a truce betwixt us and the King of England How couldst thou longer hold thy land if thou shouldst commit such breach of faith, for any cause or any reason? And who would trust us more?" And Saladin straightway summoned his serjeants and sent for Saphadin, to whom he gave the commandment that the Christians should be guarded and should have his safe-conduct both for their going to the Sepulchre and for their returning, whilst they made their pilgrimages And even more honour did they shew the pilgrims until they went back to Acre

And even as these were returning, they of our own band set forth At the very break of day the soldan had set his people to guard the roads whilst the pilgrims were passing, so that we ourselves passed through in all safety, and we clomb the mountains and came to Monjoie Then had we great joy in our hearts because we beheld Jerusalem And we kneeled down upon the ground, as rightly do all they that come hither, and we saw the Mount of Olives, whence the procession set forth when God went to His Passion Then came we toward the city where God conquered His heritage They that had come on horseback were able to kiss the Holy Sepulchre, and the horsemen who were in our company told us that Saladin caused to be shewn to them, and suffered them to kiss and to adore, that true and veritable cross which had been lost in the battle But we who were on foot saw what we could We saw the tomb wherein God's own body as laid when He had suffered death There was wont to be made some manner of offering, but the Saracens were ever taking these offerings when our people had laid them there Therefore but little offering did we make there, but we divided our money amongst the captives who were there in bonds, both Franks and Syrians To these did we bring our offerings, who said "May God restore it to them!" For there were they in slavery Then made we another journey, straight to Mount Calvary on the right, where He died who had humbled Himself to be born, where the cross was set up and the holy flesh pierced with nails, whereat the rock brake asunder and was cloven clean to Golgotha That place we saw and kissed, and thence went we to Mount Zion, unto the church which now lay all in ruin A place we saw, on the left hand, where the Mother of the Heavenly King passed on to Heaven, unto God His father, who had made her to be His mother This place we kissed, weeping, and thence went we in haste to see the holy table where

[243]Bedreddin Duldur (Stubbs)

God sat and ate This we straightway kissed, but no long space tarried we there; for the Saracens would steal our pilgrims and hide them in the caves by threes and fours—this was our fear and dread Then down we went, both men on foot and men on horseback, through the Valley of Jehoshaphat unto Siloam, for thus had we been counseled and advised There saw we the tomb of that body whereof God suffered birth, this kissed we fervently, with pitiful and devout hearts Then went we in great fear into that same cave where God was when those took Him who slew His precious body This place we also kissed without delay, with pity and with deep desire, and wept warm tears And cause enough were there to weep, for here were the stables of the horses of that devilish folk who had thus defiled God's holy places and ill entreated our pilgrims Then we departed from Jerusalem and came back to Acre

LXI

OF THE THIRD COMPANY OF PILGRIMS OF THE EVILS THAT BESET THE PILGRIMS ON THEIR RETURN HOW KING RICHARD RANSOMED WILLIAM OF PRÉAUX HOW KING RICHARD BADE FAREWELL TO THE HOLY LAND, AND OF THE SUFFERINGS THAT YET AWAITED HIM HERE ENDETH THE HISTORY OF THE HOLY WAR

As for the third band, this in sooth did the bishop lead, he who thereafter was made archbishop of the city of Canterbury, and truth it is that because of his prowess, his great renown, and his high dignity, Saladin caused to be paid to him all the honour whereof I now will tell you For he sent his people to meet him, through whom he prayed him to sojourn with him at his expense But the bishop excused himself and made answer to the Saracens, saying that inasmuch as he was a pilgrim he might not in any wise or in any place suffer his costs to be defrayed And when he would not suffer his costs to be defrayed, then did Saladin straitly command his household to shew all honour both to him and to his people, and many a goodly gift did these bestow upon them And Saladin caused the bishop to be led about the places which our Lord God frequented, then he invited him to a parley that he might see what manner of man he was He suffered him to look upon the True Cross, then he caused him to sit down before him, and a long time did they continue speaking together And the soldan began to enquire concerning the qualities of the King of England, and what our Christians said of those that himself possessed And the bishop answered him saying "Sire, concerning my lord I can well tell you that he is the best knight in the world and the best warrior, and bounteous and full of good qualities I take no account of your sins, but an thine own qualities were put with his and joined to them, then may we lightly say that not in all the world—within all the circuit thereof—could other two such princes be found, so valiant and so well approved" The soldan listened to the bishop, then said he "Well know I that the king hath great prowess and hardihead, but he rusheth forward so recklessly! Whatsoever high prince I might be, I would fainer have valour and understanding in good measure than hardihead without measure" When Saladin had thus for a long time spoken to the bishop through interpreters and had gladly listened to him, he bade the bishop ask a gift of him—whatsoever thing he wished or desired, of such sort that the soldan could give it—and be assured that he would have it And the bishop thanked him and said "By my faith, it is a great thing, if one understand it But, an it please thee, I will wait and will take counsel of God this night concerning the matter, and tomorrow will I return" And the soldan agreed thereto And on the morrow the bishop made his request, and it was a great thing that he obtained to wit, that at the Sepulchre which he had visited, where there was no service of God save that of the Syrians after their own fashion, two of our Latin priests also should serve with the Syrians every day both morning and evening, with two deacons also to render them aid, and that they should live of the offerings, and likewise at Bethlehem should it be done even as at Jerusalem, and at Nazareth also And the soldan declared that it should be so, so long as he possessed the land So the good bishop caused priests to be sought out and had them sing mass And well might the bishop boast that he had given back to God the song that then was silent there And when they had visited Jerusalem and had done all things that they desired, they took their leave of Saladin, and departing from Jerusalem, they returned to Acre

When the people were come back, when all both great and small had returned from the Holy Sepulchre, then were the ships made ready and the pilgrims entered therein And when they gat a good wind they sailed away Presently were the ships scattered and broken into little companies And some of the pilgrims came in safety unto the haven whither they were bound, and others underwent great dangers and were brought to an evil pass in divers places, and yet others died upon the sea and found bitter burial there Bitter? Nay, sweet, for sweetness found they in the kingdom which is on high And some fell sick, nor ever were made whole And others had left behind them their fathers, their cousins-german, and their brethren, who died in battle or of sicknesses, whereof they were in sore heaviness For as the martyrs whom men saw depart from this world suffered divers martyrdoms, even so did they that undertook this pilgrimage endure divers sufferings and many and divers misadventures But many folk that were without understanding said many a time thereafter in their folly that these had nothing wrought in Syria, since they had not taken Jerusalem But they had not well enquired into the matter, but blamed an emprise whereof they knew nought, in a place where they had never set their feet But we ourselves, who were present there, who saw and knew these things and were perforce acquainted with these evils—we should never lie concerning that which the others suffered for the love of God, which our own eyes beheld And I make bold to tell you, calling those to witness that were there, that full an hundred thousand men died there because they had no commerce with women, holding themselves fast to the love of God, nor in any wise would these have died save for their abstinence And further I dare say to you and do engage my word, that from disease and famine died more than three thousand at the siege of Acre and within the city itself And such worthy men as had their own chaplains and heard their service daily (such as a bishop or a most holy archbishop) and died in the midst of such a life when sickness laid hold on them—these shall be with God, at His right hand in the high and heavenly Jerusalem, for such as these by their good acts that they performed have won that other Jerusalem

When Richard, King of England, had been in the Holy Land so long that it was now time to return, then made he ready for his passage And his ship was so prepared for him that there was nothing lacking whatsoever—men, or arms, or provision Then, as a worthy and a noble man, did he give proof of his worth and his nobility, for in exchange for William of Préaux, who had suffered captivity on his behalf, he gave up ten Saracens of high estate, who would have brought him great riches, this did he to have William back again And he caused it to be cried abroad that he would make payment of whatsoever he owed, so that there might be no plaints and no exactions, and he caused all his debts to be acquitted and discharged Then,[244] when he took his leave, might ye have seen folk a-weeping softly as he went, and praying for him, sadly reciting all his deeds of prowess, of valour, and of largess, and they cried "Ah, Syria! How dost thou now remain forlorn! O God! If now the truce be broken, as it hath been broken many a time afore, who is there who would then defend us when the king is gone away?" Then in sooth had ye seen many folk weeping

And the king, exceeding sorrowful, waited no longer, but bidding them all farewell, put out to sea He bade the sails be raised to catch the wind, and all that night he steered his course by the stars And in the morning, when the dawn grew bright, he turned his face toward Syria and said (so that his own people heard him and all the others understood) "Ah, Syria! Unto God do I commend thee! And may our Lord God in His good pleasure and of His might grant to me yet sufficient dole of days that I may succour thee!"

But his ship sailed swiftly away, nor did he himself know the great hardships, the evils dire and grievous, that yet awaited him, or the sore travail that was in store for him because of that message of treason prepensed which was sent from Syria to the King of France concerning the Assassins Because of this was he seized and cast into prison, in spite of God's safe-conduct, being on a pilgrimage And thereby were they able to take away his heritage and his castles in Normandy, through covetousness and envy Thereafter was he ransomed in a great sum, for which he must needs strip all his people and take the crosses and the reliquaries, the chalices, the vessels, and all the gold and silver plate from all the minsters And such need had he that never was there one of all God's saints, whereof have been right many, who (save for dying) ever suffered more evil in God's behalf than did the king within his prison in Austria, and in rich Germany But of all this knew he not as yet one word

But God, whom he had served, and his own wit, and his great bounty, his prudence, his prowess   [245] and the barons who sent their children as surety for him, until he claimed his land again of the King of France and made war upon

[244] 9 October, 1192
[245] Lacuna of several lines

him, and so well laboured and wrought he thereafter that he recovered so much of it as had been taken from him, or peradventure more Thus ever doth God perform His work so rightly that whosoever toileth in His service, to him is recompense made after his own desire

Now be it known to all that now are, and unto all them that are yet to be, that at this point the history endeth, and it assureth you in all truth that in the year wherein the Cross was taken and carried away of the Saracens there were a thousand an hundred eighty and eight years (and the book affirmeth this) since the Incarnation, when God's Son suffered Himself to be born, who now liveth and reigneth with His Father May He bring us all into His kingdom! AMEN

EXPLICIT

THE HISTORY OF THEM THAT TOOK CONSTANTINOPLE

(Li estoires de chiaus qui conquisent Coustantinoble)

BEING AN ACCOUNT OF THE FOURTH CRUSADE, WHICH

ROBERT OF CLARI IN AMIÉNOIS, KNIGHT

CAUSED TO BE WRITTEN DOWN IN THE PICARD TONGUE ABOUT

THE YEAR 1216

Done into English

by

EDWARD NOBLE STONE

1936

FOREWORD

Concerning Robert of Clari not very much has been recorded beyond his own modest mention of himself in his history We know, however, that both he and his brother Aleaume, "Clerk" (to whom, possibly, he dictated his story about the year 1216), served through the whole of the Fourth Crusade, like the chief chronicler of that expedition, Geoffry of Villehardouin, the Marshal of Champagne

But while Villehardouin was a great captain, a scholar, and a statesman, the humble knight Robert possessed little learning and even less understanding of the political intrigues that turned this campaign against the Infidel into an internecine war of Christians Nevertheless, the plain soldier's quaint narrative is not without value to the historian, nor is it devoid of interest to the lover of tales of adventure What would we not give for a record of the March to the Sea taken from the lips of one of Xenophon's Ten Thousand, or for some Roman centurion's memoirs of the Gallic War!

Like the lengthy and formidable genealogies that fill the first chapter of the Book of Numbers, a redoubtable array of names of mighty men of valour crowds the opening pages of Robert's chronicle, but once the bold and patient reader has forced his tedious way through this vanguard, he comes to a long succession of engaging episodes, some tragic, others (perhaps unintentionally) very comical And when we reach the closing chapter, wherein the author solemnly assures us that he has never recorded aught but that which was strictly true, we almost regret that he "has left untold many true things, because he cannot, in sooth, remember   them all"

The text from which this translation has been made is that of Philippe Lauer (Robert de Clari, *La Conquête de Constantinople Paris,* Édouard Champion, 1924) Readers who care to compare or to contrast Robert Clari's narrative with Villehardouin's account of the same events are referred to Sir Frank Marzials' admirable translation of the latter (*Memoirs of the Crusades, by Villehardouin and De Joinville* Everyman's Library, No 333)

E N S

CONTENTS

CONTENTS—(Continued)

CONTENTS—(Continued)

CONTENTS—(Continued)

THE HISTORY OF THEM THAT TOOK CONSTANTINOPLE

Book II, of

Three Old French Chronicles of the Crusades

THE HISTORY OF THEM THAT TOOK CONSTANTINOPLE

I

OF THE PREACHING OF MASTER FULK, AND OF THOSE THAT TOOK THE CROSS

Here beginneth the history of them that took Constantinople, and presently we will tell you who they were and for what cause they went thither. It came to pass, what time Pope Innocent[1] was Pontiff of Rome, and Philip[2] was King of France (another Philip[3] there was, who was Emperor of Germany), and the year was the twelve hundred and third[4] or fourth year of the Incarnation, that there was a certain priest, Master Fulk by name, who was of Neuilly, a parish that lieth in the Bishopric of Paris. This priest was a right worthy man and a right good clerk, and he went about throughout the lands preaching the cross,[5] and many folk followed him, because he was so worthy a man that God wrought very great miracles in his behalf, and much substance did this priest obtain to carry to the holy land beyond the sea.

Then there took the cross Thibaut, Count of Champagne, and Baldwin, Count of Flanders, and Henry his brother, and Lewis, Count of Blois, and Hugh, Count of Saint-Pol, and Simon, Count of Montfort, and Guy his brother.

And now will we name to you the bishops that went thither. Thither went Bishop Nevelon of Soissons, who shewed himself there a right worthy man and valiant in all commands and in all times of need, and Bishop Warnier of Troyes, and the Bishop of Halberstadt[6] in Germany, and Master John of Noyon, who was chosen Bishop of Acre. Thither also went the Abbot of Loos in Flanders, who was of the monks of the order of Cîteaux[7] (this abbot was a very wise man and most worthy), and other abbots and clerks so many that we cannot name them all to you.

And of the barons that went thither we cannot name all to you, but a part of them we can name. Thither went, from Amiénois, my Lord Peter of Amiens, that fair knight and worthy and valiant, and my Lord Enguerrand of Boves, with his three brothers (one was called Robert, another Hugh, and their other brother was a clerk), Baldwin of Belvoir, Matthew of Wallincourt, the Advocate of Béthune,[8] and Conon[9] his brother, Eustace of Canteleu, Anseau of Cayeux, Renier of Trit, Wales of Frise, Girard of Manchecourt, and Nicholas of Mailly, Baldwin Cavarom, Hugh of Beauvais, and many other knights of high estate,

---

[1] Innocent III, Pope 1198-1216
[2] Philip Augustus, King of France, 1180-1223
[3] Philip of Swabia, (rival) Emperor of the Holy Roman Empire 1198-1208
[4] Fulk's preaching was mostly in 1199 and 1200
[5] I e, crusade
[6] Konrad de Krosik
[7] The Cistercian order was founded in 1098
[8] Guillaume l'Avocat de Béthune
[9] Conon de Béthune won considerable celebrity as a poet

both Flemings and men of other lands, not all of whom can we name to you, and thither, too, went my Lord James of Avesnes

Thither also went, from Burgundy, Odo of Champlitte, and William his brother, who had many men in the host, and there were others from Burgundy, so many that we cannot name them all to you

And from Champagne went thither the Marshal,[10] and Ogier of Saint-Chéron, and Macaire of Sainte-Menehould, and Clérembaut of Chappes, and Miles of Brabant, these were of Champagne

Next, there went thither the Castellan of Coucy,[11] Robert of Ronsoi, Matthew of Montmorency, who shewed himself there a right worthy man, Ralph of Aulnoy, and Walter his son, Giles of Aulnoy, Peter of Bracheux, that worthy knight and bold and valiant, and Hugh his brother And those that I name to you here were of the Isle of France and of Beauvaisis

And from Chartrain went thither Gervais of Châtel, and Hervée his son, and Oliver of Rochefort, and Peter of Alost, and Payen of Orléans, Peter of Amiens, a good knight and a worthy and one that wrought there many deeds of prowess, and Thomas his brother, a clerk, who was Canon of Amiens, Manasses of Lille in Flanders, and Matthew of Montmorency, the Castellan of Corbie

Now there were so many other knights of the Isle of France, and of Flanders, and of Champagne, and of Burgundy, and of other lands, that we cannot name them all to you, all valiant knights and worthy, and these that we have named here were the richest men, and they bore banners, nor have we named all those that bore banners

And of those that wrought there the most deeds of prowess and of arms, both rich men and poor, we can name to you a part Peter of Bracheux, who was, of both poor men and rich, he who wrought most deeds of prowess, and Hugh his brother, and Andrew of Urboise, and my Lord Peter of Amiens, that worthy knight and fair, and Matthew of Montmorency, and Matthew of Wallincourt, and Baldwin of Belvoir, and Henry, the brother of the Count of Flanders,[12] and James of Avesnes these were they of the rich men who wrought there the greatest deeds of arms And of the poor men Bernard of Aire, and Bernard of Somergen, Eustace Heumont, and his brother, Gilbert of Vismes, Wales of Frise, Hugh of Beauvais, Robert of Ronsoi, Alard Maquereau, Nicholas of Mailly, Guy of Manchecourt, Baldwin of Hamelincourt, William of Embreville, Aleaume the Clerk[13] of Clari in Amiénois,[14] who was a right worthy man and wrought there many deeds of hardihood and of prowess, Aleaume of Sains, and William of Fontaines (and they whom we have named here were they that wrought there the most deeds of arms and of prowess), and many other good

---

[10] Geoffry of Villehardouin, the great chronicler of the Fourth Crusade
[11] Gui, Châtelain de Coucy He was the author of several beautiful lyrics
[12] Either Henry of Angre, brother of Count Baldwin of Flanders and Hainault, crowned Emperor of Constantinople in 1206, or Henry the brother of Count Philip of Flanders, probably the former
[13] Brother of Robert of Clari, the author
[14] Now Cléry-les-Pernois, about 120 kilometers north of Paris

folk, both knights and footmen, so many thousands that we know not the number thereof [15]

II

HOW COUNT THIBAUT OF CHAMPAGNE WAS CHOSEN LEADER OF THEM THAT TOOK THE CROSS, OF HIS DEATH, AND OF THE DEATH OF MASTER FULK

Then came together all the counts and high barons who had taken the cross And they summoned all the men of high estate that had taken the cross, and when they were all assembled they took counsel among themselves, whom they would make their captain and lord, until they chose Count Thibaut of Champagne and made him their lord   Then they departed, and went each one to his own land

And no long time thereafter Count Thibaut died, and he left fifty thousand pounds[16] to them that had taken the cross and to him who after himself should be captain and lord of these, to make such use thereof as they themselves should desire.   Thereafter also died Master Fulk, whereby they of the cross suffered grievous loss

III

HOW THE MEN OF THE CROSS SENT MESSENGERS TO THE MARQUIS OF MONTFERRAT

When the men of the cross knew that the Count of Champagne, their lord, was dead, and Master Fulk also, then were they very sad and sorrowful and sore distressed, and they all came together on a certain day to Soissons, and they took counsel among themselves what they should do and whom they would make their captain and lord, until they agreed among themselves that they would send for the Marquis[17] of Montferrat in Lombardy   Thither they sent right good messengers for him   The messengers made ready and went to the marquis   When they were come thither they spake to the marquis and said to him that the barons of France sent him greeting and that they bade and besought him, in God's name, to come and speak with them on a day that they named to him   When the marquis heard this he marveled much that the barons of France had summoned him, but he made answer to the messengers that he would take counsel in the matter, and on the morrow he would let them know what he would do concerning it   And he did the messengers much honour

When the morrow was come, the marquis said that he would go and speak with them at Soissons on such a day as they had named to him   Then the messengers took their leave and went their way, and the marquis made offer to them of his horses and of his jewels, but they would take none of these

And when they were returned they made known to the barons what they had done   Then the marquis made ready for his journey, and he passed through the

---

[15]All these "rich men" are listed by Villehardouin, of the "poor men," he mentions only Bernard of Somergen, Eustace of Huemont, Robert of Ronsoi, Alard Maquereau and Nicholas of Mailly

[16]*"l m livres"*

[17]Boniface

mountains of Mont-Joux[18] and came into France to Soissons And he made known aforehand to the barons that he was coming, and the barons went forth to meet him and did him great honour

IV

HOW THE MARQUIS WAS MADE LEADER OF THE MEN OF THE CROSS

When the marquis was come to Soissons he asked the barons wherefore they had summoned him And the barons had taken counsel, and they said to him: "Lord, we have summoned you because the Count of Champagne, our lord, who was our master, is dead, and we summon you, as being the worthiest man that we knew and the one that could bring the best counsel to our undertaking—God guide it ! So we all beseech you, in God's name, to be our lord and, for the love of God, to take the sign of the cross "

And after these words the barons kneeled down before him, and they said to him that he should not trouble himself to seek substance, for that they would give to him a great part of the substance that the Count of Champagne had left to the men of the cross The marquis said that he would take counsel in the matter, and when he had taken counsel he said that, for the love of God and to succour the land beyond the sea, he would take the cross And the Bishop of Soissons straightway made ready and gave him the cross And when he had taken it, they gave him, of the substance which the Count of Champagne had left to the men of the cross, five and twenty thousand pounds

V

THE MEN OF THE CROSS TAKE COUNSEL TO WHAT LAND THEY WILL PROCEED, AND THEY AGREE TO SEND MESSENGERS TO ENGAGE A FLEET

Thereafter, when the marquis had taken the cross, he spake to the barons "My lords," quoth the marquis, "whither will ye proceed, and into what land of the Saracens will ye wish to go?" Then the barons answered that to the land of Syria they would in no wise go, for there could they gain no advantage, but they had purposed to go to Babylon,[19] or to Alexandria, into the very midst of the infidels, where they could gain the most advantage, and it was in their mind to hire a fleet which should carry them all thither together Then said the marquis that this counsel was good and that he fully agreed to it, and that they should send good messengers, of the wisest of the knights among them, either to Pisa, or to Genoa, or to Venice, and to this counsel did all the barons agree

---

[18]Jura (?)
[19]I e , Cairo The citadel of Cairo was called Babylon, and the name was often applied to the city itself

VI

HOW THE MESSENGERS CAME TO GENOA, TO PISA, AND TO VENICE, SEEKING A FLEET, AND OF THE BARGAIN THAT THEY STRUCK WITH THE DOGE OF VENICE

Then they fixed upon their messengers They all agreed that my Lord Conon of Béthune go thither, and the Marshal of Champagne Then, when they had agreed upon their messengers, the barons withdrew, and the marquis departed to his own land and the others also, every one of them And the messengers were bidden to hire vessels to carry four thousand knights and their accoutrements and an hundred thousand footmen The messengers made ready for their journey, and they went straight on their way until they came to Genoa And they spake to the Genoese and told them what they were seeking, but the Genoese said that they could in no wise aid them Then they went on to Pisa, and they spake to them of Pisa And these made answer to them that they had not so many vessels nor could they aid them in any wise

Then they went on to Venice, and they spake to the Doge of Venice,[20] and they said that they were bidden to seek to hire passage for four thousand knights and their accoutrements and for an hundred thousand footmen When the Doge heard this he said that he would take counsel in the matter, for in so weighty an undertaking good counsel should be taken

Then did the Doge summon all the high counsellors of the city, and he spake to them and shewed them what had been demanded of him And when they had fully taken counsel, the Doge answered the messengers and said to them

"Sirs, we will gladly strike a bargain with you and we will find you a sufficient fleet, for an hundred thousand marks, if ye will, with this condition that I myself shall go along with you, and half of the men of all Venice who are able to bear arms, and with the stipulation that we shall have the half of all the gains that shall be made there Furthermore, we will furnish you with fifty galleys at our own cost, and one year from the day that we shall name to you we will bring you to that land that ye shall choose, whether ye will go to Babylon or to Alexandria "

When the messengers heard this they answered that an hundred thousand marks was too much, and they spake together until they made a bargain for fourscore and seven thousand marks, and the Doge and the Venetians swore that they would abide by the bargain Then the Doge said that he desired to have five and twenty thousand marks as earnest-money, for to begin the preparation of the fleet, and the messengers made answer that he should send back other messengers with them to France and that they would gladly cause the five and twenty thousand marks to be paid to these Then did the messengers take their leave and departed homeward And the Doge sent with them a nobleman of Venice to receive the earnest-money

---

[20]"[Henry] Dandolo, the grand old Doge, blind and bearing gallantly his ninety years " Sir Frank Marzials, *Memoirs of the Crusades*, p xix

VII

HOW THE DOGE COMMANDED THE FLEET TO BE MADE READY

Then did the Doge cause a ban to be cried throughout all Venice, that no Venetian should be so bold as to undertake any traffic, but that all should help in making ready the fleet, and so they did And they began to prepare the goodliest fleet that ever yet was seen

VIII

HOW THE MESSENGERS CAME TO FRANCE AND RENDERED AN ACCOUNT OF THEMSELVES

When the messengers came into France they let it be known that they were come Then were all the barons that had taken the cross bidden to come to Corbie And when they were all assembled there, the messengers told what they had accomplished When the barons heard it they were right glad and right well did they approve what the messengers had done, and they paid much honour to the messengers of the Doge of Venice, and they gave them of the moneys of the Count of Champagne and of the moneys that Master Fulk had obtained, also, did the Count of Flanders add thereto of his own moneys so much that the whole came to five and twenty thousand marks And these were delivered to the messenger of the Doge of Venice, and there was given to him a goodly escort to go with him even unto his own land

IX

HOW THE PILGRIMS WERE BIDDEN ASSEMBLE AT EASTERTIDE AND GO THEIR WAYS TO VENICE

Then was word sent throughout all the lands to them that had taken the cross, that they should all make ready at Eastertide to go to Venice betwixt Pentecost and August, without fail, and so did they And when Eastertide was past, they all came thither And full many were the fathers and mothers, the brothers and sisters, the wives and children, that were sore grieved for their loved ones

X

HOW THE PILGRIMS CAME TO VENICE AND LODGED IN THE ISLE OF SAINT NICHOLAS

When the pilgrims were all assembled in Venice and saw the goodly fleet that had been made ready, the goodly ships, the great dromonds,[21] the transports [22] for carrying the horses, and the galleys, greatly did they marvel at these and at the great riches that they found in the city And when they saw that they could not in any wise all lodge in the city, they took counsel together that they would

---

[21] Large, swift-sailing war-vessels
[22] "*Uissiers*," literally "door-ships" They had a large door in the stern, through which the horses were embarked and disembarked

go and lodge in the Isle of Saint Nicholas,[23] which was wholly encompassed by the sea and lay a league distant from Venice Thither did all the pilgrims go, and there they pitched their tents and lodged as best they could

XI

HOW THE DOGE COMMANDED THE HALF OF THE VENETIANS TO GO WITH THE PILGRIMS, HOW THEY DETERMINED THE MATTER BY LOT, AND HOW THEY DEMANDED OF THE PILGRIMS THE FULFILLMENT OF THEIR AGREEMENTS OF THE LEVY THAT THE PILGRIMS MADE, AND THE OUTCOME THEREOF

When the Doge of Venice saw that the pilgrims were all come, then summoned he all those of his own land of Venice And when they were all come, then did the Doge command that the half of them should dispose themselves and make themselves ready to go in the fleet with the pilgrims When the Venetians heard this, some rejoiced, others said that they could not go thither, nor could they come to any agreement how the half of them could go thither But at last they resorted to lots, for they made, two by two together, two lumps of wax, and in the one lump they put a writing Then came they to the priest and gave them to him, and the priest made the sign of the cross over them, and he gave to each one of the two Venetians one of these lumps, and he of the twain that had the lump with the writing, he must needs go in the fleet Thus they made their division

And when the pilgrims had lodged themselves in the Isle of Saint Nicholas, then went forth the Doge and the Venetians to speak to them And they demanded of them the fulfillment of the agreement concerning the fleet that they had caused to be prepared And the Doge said to them that they had done ill in that they had asked, through their messengers, that the Venetians should make ready a fleet for four thousand knights and their accoutrements and for an hundred thousand foot, whereas, of these knights, there were scarce more than a thousand, since the rest had gone to other harbours, and of these hundred thousand footmen, there were scarce more than fifty or sixty thousand "Wherefore we desire," said the Doge, "that ye pay us the sums promised, which were agreed upon with us "

When the men of the cross heard this they spake together, and they agreed among themselves that each knight should give four marks, and for each horse four, and each serjeant of horse two marks, and that he who should give the least amount should give one mark When they had gathered these moneys they paid them to the Venetians, but there yet remained to pay fifty thousand marks

When the Doge and the Venetians saw that the pilgrims had paid them no more than this they were sore distressed, so that the Doge said unto them

"Sirs," (quoth he) "ye have served us ill, for so soon as your messengers had made agreement with me and with my people, I gave commandment throughout my whole land that no merchant should undertake any traffic, but should help make ready this fleet, and they have ever since bided their time, nor have they

---

[23]San Niccolo del Lido, on the east side of the Lagoon of Venice

got any gain this year and a half past   Nay, rather have they suffered great loss,
and for this reason my men desire, and I also, that ye pay the moneys which ye
owe us   And if ye do not so, know then that ye shall not remove yourselves from
this island until we shall have been paid, nor shall ye find any one to fetch you
aught to drink or to eat"

But the Doge was a right worthy man, and, for all that he had said, he ceased
not to suffer both drink and meat a plenty to be fetched to them

XII

HOW THE PILGRIMS MADE YET ANOTHER LEVY, AND HOW THEY REACHED AN ACCORD WITH THE DOGE AND THE VENETIANS

When the counts and the other men of the cross heard that which the Doge
had said, they were exceeding sad and sore distressed   And they made yet another
levy, and they borrowed such moneys as they could of them that they believed
might have any   And these they paid to the Venetians, but when they had paid
them there yet remained to pay six and thirty thousand marks   And they said
to them that they were utterly bereft, and that the host was much impoverished of
this levy that they had made, and that they could procure no more moneys to pay
them, but that they had scarce wherewithal to maintain their own host meanly
When the Doge saw that they were utterly unable to pay all these moneys, nay,
rather, that they were in exceeding sore straits, he spake to his people and said
thus to them

"Sirs," (quoth he) "if we let these people go unto their own country, we
shall ever be esteemed wicked men and deceivers   But let us straightway go to
them and let us say to them that if they will render us these six and thirty thousand marks, which they owe us, out of the first conquests that they shall make
and shall have for division, then will we set them over the sea"

The Venetians approved that which the Doge had said   Then went they to
the pilgrims, there where they were lodged   And when they were come thither
the Doge said unto them

"Sirs," (quoth he) "we have taken counsel together, I and my people, to the
effect that if ye will promise us loyally to pay us those six and thirty thousand
marks that ye owe us, from the first conquests that ye shall make on your account, then will we set you over the sea"

When the men of the cross heard that which the Doge had said to them and
shewed them, then were they right glad, and they fell at his feet for joy, and
they promised that they would be very fain to do that which the Doge had advised them   And such rejoicing did they make that night that there was none so
poor that he made not a great illumination, and they carried on the tips of their
lances great torches of candles round about and within their lodgings, so that it
seemed that all the host was one bonfire

XIII

HOW THE PILGRIMS MADE YET ANOTHER LEVY, HOW THE DOGE PROPOSED THAT THE PILGRIMS GO AGAINST ZARA, AND OF THE SETTING FORTH OF THE FLEET

Thereafter came the Doge to them, and he said to them "Sirs, it is now winter, and we could not pass over the sea, nor is it I that have been lax in the matter, for I would have set you over long ere now, but ye yourselves have been lax therein But let us make the best of the matter" (quoth the Doge) "There is a city near at hand, Zara[24] is the name thereof They of that city have done us much hurt, and I and my men wish to avenge ourselves of them, if we can And if ye will trust me, we will go thither this winter and abide there until about Eastertide, and by then we shall have made ready our fleet, and we will go thence beyond the sea, with God's help And the city of Zara is a right goodly city, and full of all manner of riches!"

The barons and the men of high estate that had taken the cross agreed to that which the Doge had said, but not all the men of the host knew of the plan—none save the men of highest estate Then did they all in common prepare for their voyage and make their fleet altogether ready And they put forth to sea And each of the men of high estate[25] had his own ship for himself and his people, and his own transport to carry his horses, and the Doge of Venice had with him fifteen galleys, all at his own cost The galley wherein he himself was, was all vermilion-coloured, and it had a pavilion stretched above it of vermilion samite,[26] and there were four silver trumpets which sounded before him, and timbrels[27] that made a most joyful noise And all the men of high estate, and clerks and laymen, both small and great, made so great a rejoicing at their setting forth that never yet had such rejoicing and such an armament been seen or heard And the pilgrims caused the priests and the clerks to go up into the castles of the ships, who chanted the *"Veni Creator Spiritus"* And all, both great and small, wept for fulness of heart and for the great gladness that they had

And when the fleet set forth from the haven of Venice, and [28] dromonds, and the rich ships, and so many other vessels, that it was the goodliest thing to behold that ever hath been since the beginning of the world For there were full an hundred pair of trumpets, both silver and brass, which all sounded for the departure, and so many timbrels and tabours[29] and other instruments that it was a fair marvel to hear

---

[24]This is the Italianized form of the Slavonic name Zadar, which, in turn, is derived from the old Roman name Jadera Both Robert of Clari and Villehardouin use the form Jadres This city was long the capital of Dalmatia It has been held, at different times, by Venice, Hungary, Austria, and France It now belongs to Italy

[25]"Haus homes," literally, "high men" The author uses this term repeatedly to designate the rich and powerful members of the higher nobility, for whom, as a class, he entertained a very lively dislike In Middle English the expression "heigh mene" is used in a similar sense In this translation the phrase has been paraphrased in various ways, depending on the context

[26]A silken fabric, often interwoven with gold

[27]An instrument of percussion, resembling the tambourine

[28]A half-line is missing from the MS

[29]Small drums

But when they were come forth upon the sea, and had spread their sails and hoisted their banners upon the castles of the ships, and their ensigns, then verily did it seem that the whole sea was all aswarm, and that it was all ablaze with the ships that they were steering and the great rejoicing that they made

Then they went their way until they came unto a city the name whereof was Pola [30] There went they on land, and refreshed themselves And they tarried there a little time, until they were well refreshed and had bought fresh victuals to put in their ships Thereafter did they put forth to sea again And if they had made great rejoicing and revel before, now made they as great or greater, so that the folk of the city marveled much at the great rejoicing, and at the great fleet, and at the great pomp that they manifested And they said (and this was in very deed the truth) that never had so fair a fleet, nor one so magnificent, been seen or assembled in any land, as was gathered there

XIV

HOW THE PILGRIMS AND THE VENETIANS WENT AGAINST ZARA, HOW THEY ATTACKED IT IN DESPITE OF THE POPE'S BAN, AND HOW THEY TOOK THE TOWN AND DIVIDED IT

So the pilgrims and the Venetians sailed until they came to Zara on the night of the feast of Saint Martin [31] When the men of the city of Zara saw the ships and the great squadrons coming, then were they sore afraid, and they caused the gates of the city to be shut, and they armed themselves as best they could, as if to defend themselves When they were armed, the Doge spake to all the notable men of the host, and said to them, "Sirs, this city hath done much evil both to me and to my people, fain would I avenge myself thereof So I beseech you that ye come to mine aid" And the barons and notable men answered and said to him that they would aid him gladly

Now the men of Zara knew full well that the men of Venice hated them Therefore had they procured a letter from Rome to the effect that whosoever should make war upon them or should do them any hurt would be excommunicated And they sent this letter by trusty messengers to the Doge and to the pilgrims who had come thither When the messengers came to the host, then was the letter read before the Doge and before the pilgrims When the letter was read and the Doge had heard it, he said that not for all the Pontiff's excommunication would he refrain from avenging himself on them of the city Thereupon the messengers went their ways

Then spake the Doge a second time to the barons, and he said to them, "Sirs, be it known to you that not in any wise would I refrain from avenging myself of them, not for the Pontiff himself!" And he besought them that they might aid him The barons made answer all that they would aid him gladly—all save Count Simon of Montfort and my Lord Enguerrand of Boves These said that they

[30] Near the southern point of Istria Its Roman amphitheatre, dating from the second century, is the only one whose outer walls have been preserved intact
[31] 11th November, 1202

would in no wise go against the commandment of the Pontiff nor did they at all desire to be excommunicated So they turned away, and went to Hungary to abide there through the winter

When the Doge saw that the barons would aid him he caused his engines to be set up to assault the city, until they of the city saw that they could not hold out against them , then they came to terms and surrendered the city to them Then did the pilgrims and the Venetians enter therein, and they divided the city into two halves, so that the pilgrims had the one half thereof and the Venetians the other

XV

HOW A CONTENTION AROSE BETWIXT THE VENETIANS AND CERTAIN OF THE PILGRIMS, AND HOW THEY ALL OBTAINED ABSOLUTION FROM THE POPE

Thereafter it chanced that a great contention arose betwixt the Venetians and the baser sort amongst the pilgrims, which lasted a full night and half a day. And so great was this contention that scarcely were the knights able to separate them But when they had separated them, they established so good a peace between them that never thereafter did they fall out one with the other

Then the notable men who had taken the cross, and the Venetians, spake together concerning the excommunication wherewith they had been banned because of the city that they had taken, until they took counsel among themselves to send to Rome to obtain absolution And they sent thither the Bishop of Soissons and my Lord Robert of Boves, who obtained from the Pontiff letters whereby all the pilgrims and all the Venetians were absolved When they had their letters, then did the bishop return as speedily as he could, but my Lord Robert of Boves returned not with him but went his ways beyond the sea, straight from Rome

XVI

HOW THE PILGRIMS LOST HEART IN THEIR UNDERTAKING

In the mean time, while the men of the cross and the Venetians abode there that winter, they considered that they had made great expenditure, and they spake together and said that they could in no wise go to Babylon, nor to Alexandria, nor to Syria, since they had neither victuals nor substance wherewith to go thither, for already had they spent well-nigh all that they had, both in the sojourn that they had made there and in the great payments that they had made for the fleet And they said that they could in no wise go thither , and if they should go thither, they would accomplish nothing there, for they had neither victuals nor substance wherewith to sustain themselves

XVII

HOW THE DOGE ENCOURAGED THE PILGRIMS, AND OF THE OCCASION WHEREOF THE MARQUIS TOLD THEM OF GOING AGAINST CONSTANTINOPLE

The Doge of Venice perceived right well that the pilgrims were not at ease; and he spake to them, and said to them

"Sirs, in Greece is there a very rich country, and abounding in all good things, if we could find a reasonable occasion for going thither and getting victuals in that country, and other things, until we should be fully restored, this would seem to me a good counsel, and so might we in sooth go on beyond the sea"

Then arose the marquis and said

"Sirs, I was last year at Yuletide in Germany, at the court of my Lord the Emperor [32] And there saw I a young man who was brother to the wife[33] of the Emperor of Germany And this young man was the son of the Emperor Isaac of Constantinople, from whom one of his own brothers had taken away the empire by treachery Now whosoever could have this youth" (quoth the marquis), "he could right easily go to the land of Constantinople and get victuals and other things, for this youth is the rightful heir thereto"

XVIII

OF THE EMPEROR MANUEL COMNENUS AND OF HIS DEALINGS WITH THE FRANKS

And now will we leave off telling you of the pilgrims and of the fleet, and we will tell you of this young man and of the Emperor Isaac, his father, how they fared before

There was an emperor in Constantinople whose name was Manuel [34] And he was a right worthy man, this emperor, and richest of all the Christians who ever were, and the most bountiful, nor ever did any one ask of him aught of that which was his (one who was of the religion of Rome and who could speak with him) that he caused not an hundred marks to be given him Thus have we heard men testify concerning him

This emperor loved the Franks much, and much did he trust them One day it came to pass that the people of his land and his counselors chid him sore, even as they had chidden him many a time before, because he was so bountiful and loved the Franks so exceedingly And the emperor made answer to them

"There be but two persons who ought to give, God and I But if ye so counsel, I would dismiss the Franks and all of them that are of the religion of Rome who are about me and my army"

And the Greeks were right glad thereat and said

"Ah, lord! Now will ye act right well, and right well will we serve you"

And the emperor commanded that all the Franks should depart, and the Greeks were passing glad thereat Thereafter the emperor bade all the Franks,

[32]Philip of Swabia
[33]Daughter of Isaac Angelus, Byzantine emperor 1185-95 and 1203-04
[34]Manuel Comnenus, Byzantine emperor 1143-80

and the others whom he had dismissed, come and speak with him privily And so did they And when they were come, then said the emperor unto them

"Sirs, my people leave me not in peace except I give you no gifts and drive you forth of my land But do ye all depart together, and I will follow you, both I and all my people, and so see ye to it that ye are in such and such a place" (which he named unto them), "and I will send you word by my messengers that ye are to go your ways, but ye shall send me answer that ye will not go, for all me or my people, but rather ye shall make a great shew of attacking me, then shall I see how my people prove themselves "

And all this they did And when they had departed the emperor summoned all his people and followed them And when he drew near to them he bade them straightway go their ways and take themselves forth of his lands, and they who had counseled the emperor to drive them forth of his land were right glad, and they said to the emperor

"Lord, if they will not straightway go their ways, give us leave that we slay them all !"

And the emperor answered, "Gladly !"

And when the emperor's messengers came to the Franks they delivered them their message most arrogantly, that they should straightway go their ways And the Franks made answer to the messengers and told them that they would not go, not for all the emperor and his people The messengers returned and reported what the Franks had answered Then did the emperor bid his people arm themselves and help him to attack the Franks, and they all armed themselves, and they went against the Franks And the Franks advanced to meet them, and they had ordered well their battalions And when the emperor saw that they were advancing against him and against his people, to combat them, then said he to his people

"Sirs, be mindful now to acquit yourselves well ! Now can ye well avenge yourselves of them !"

And when he had said this, the Greeks were filled with great fear of the Latins (for men do call all those of the religion of Rome, Latins), and the Latins made great feint of attacking them When the Greeks saw this they turned and fled, and they left the emperor all alone When the emperor saw this, then said he to the Franks

"Now come ye back again, and I will give you more than ever yet I have given !"

And he led back the Franks, and when they were come back, then summoned he his people, and he said to them

"Sirs, now can it well be seen whom one ought to trust Ye fled away, when ye ought to have aided me, and ye left me all alone, and if the Latins had so wished, they might have cut me all in pieces But now do I command that no one of you be so bold or so daring that he ever again speak of my bounty, nor of the love that I bear to the Franks, for verily do I love them and trust them more than you, and therefore will I give them more than I have yet given them !"

And the Greeks were never thereafter so bold that they durst speak thereof

XIX

HOW THE EMPEROR MANUEL BETROTHED HIS SON TO THE SISTER OF KING PHILIP OF FRANCE

This Emperor Manuel had a very fair son by his wife, and he purposed to make for him as high a marriage as he could, and by the advice of the Franks he sent word to Philip, the King of France, that he should give his sister in marriage to this his son   And the emperor sent his messengers to France, who were very notable men, and they journeyed thither in very rich array, nor ever yet had men been seen to journey in richer or more magnificent array than did these, so that the King of France and his people marveled at the magnificence that the messengers displayed

When the messengers came to the king, then told they him the word that the emperor sent him   And the king said that he would take counsel in the matter   And when the king took counsel concerning it, then did his barons advise that he send his sister to so noble a man and so rich a man as was the emperor   Then did the king make answer to the messengers that he would gladly send his sister to the emperor [35]

XX

HOW KING PHILIP'S SISTER JOURNEYED TO CONSTANTINOPLE, AND HOW THE EMPEROR'S KINSMAN, ANDRONICUS, OFFERED VIOLENCE TO QUEEN THEODORA OF JERUSALEM

Then did the king accoutre his sister most richly and send her with the messengers to Constantinople, and much people with her   And they rode and journeyed without resting until they came to Constantinople   And when they were come thither, then did the emperor shew the damsel great honour, and he had great joy both of her and of her people

In the mean time, when the emperor had sent for this damsel, he also sent elsewhere across the sea a certain kinsman of his, Andronicus by name, for Queen Theodora of Jerusalem, who was his sister, that she might come to the crowning of his son and to the feast   The queen put to sea with Andronicus, to come to Constantinople   But when they had gone some long way upon the sea, what did Andronicus do but begin to lust after the queen, who was his own cousin, and lie with her by force   And when he had done this, he durst not return again to Constantinople, but he took the queen and brought her by force to Konieh,[36] to the Saracens   And there he abode

---

[35]Agnes of France, sister of Philip Augustus, became, successively, the wife of Alexius the Younger, of Andronicus Comnenus, and of Theodore Branas
[36]In the south central part of Asia Minor

XXI

HOW THE EMPEROR MANUEL DIED, HOW ANDRONICUS, BY CRAFT AND VIOLENCE, MADE HIMSELF EMPEROR, AND OF THE ADVENTURES OF THE YOUTH ISAAC ANGELUS

When the Emperor Manuel got word that Andronicus had dealt thus with his sister, he was sore grieved thereat, nevertheless, for all this did he not forego his purpose to make high festival and to crown his son and the damsel But no great time thereafter the emperor died

When Andronicus, the traitor, heard tell that the Emperor Manuel was dead, he sent word to Manuel's son, who was now emperor, and besought him in God's name to lay aside his displeasure, and he persuaded him that this was but a lie that had been told against him, so that the emperor, who was but a lad, laid aside his displeasure and sent for him And so this Andronicus came back, and was ever about the lad, until the lad made him bailiff of all his land, and he waxed exceeding proud because of the bailiwick that he held

And it came to pass, no long time thereafter, that he seized the emperor by night and murdered him, and his mother also When he had done this he took two very great stones and caused them to be bound about their necks and then he let them be cast into the sea Thereafter he caused himself by force to be crowned emperor When he was crowned, he seized all those of whom he knew that they took it in evil part that he should be emperor, and he put out their eyes, and grievously entreated them, and caused them to die an evil death And he took all the fair women that he found, and lay with them by force, and he took the empress to wife, who was the sister to the King of France, and he wrought so many and so great iniquities that never any other traitor or murderer wrought such as he wrought

When he had wrought all these iniquities, he enquired of one of his master bailiffs who helped him to bring about all these calamities, if there were left any of them who took it in evil part that he should be emperor And this man answered him that he knew of none such, save that it was said that there were three goodly youths who were of the house that was called the House of Angelus, and they were notable men, but by no means rich, rather, poor men, nor had they any great power When the Emperor Andronicus heard that there indeed were three youths of that house he commanded that bailiff of his, who was a most wicked man and a traitor, even as he himself was, to go and take them and hang them or cause them to die an evil death The bailiff went forth to take these three brethren, but he took only one of them and the two escaped As for him who was taken, they put out his eyes, afterward he became a monk The two others fled, and the one of them went into a land that is called Wallachia, the name of this one was Isaac And the other went to Antioch and was taken by the Saracens in a foray that the Christians made

He who fled to Wallachia was in such straits there that he could not sustain himself, and at last, because of dire poverty, he returned to Constantinople and hid himself in the house of a widow woman in that city Now he possessed not a chattel in the world save a mule and one manservant, and this servant, with the mule, trafficked in wines which the beast carried about, and in other things, whereby his master Isaac and he did live At length came tidings to the emperor, the traitor Andronicus, that the man was indeed come back to the city Then commanded he his bailiff, who was sorely hated of all the people because of the evils that he wrought every day, that he should go and take this Isaac and hang him Accordingly, this man mounted his horse one day, and took much people with him, and went his way to the house of the good woman And when he was come thither he caused them to call at the door, and the good woman came forth and wondered much what he desired, until at last he commanded that she should lead forth him that was hidden in her house And the good woman answered and said

"Ah, lord! By God's grace, there is no man hidden therein!"

And he commanded her yet again that she should cause him to come forth, else, if she did not so, he would seize them both When the good woman heard that, she was filled with great fear of this devil who wrought so much evil, and she went into the house and came to the young man and said to him

"Ah, fair Sir Isaac! Ye are indeed a dead man! For here is the emperor's bailiff, and much people with him, who are come to seek you for to use you despitefully and to slay you!"

The young man was sore dismayed when he heard these tidings, nevertheless, he came forth, for he was in no wise able to save himself from going out to the bailiff Then what did he do but take his sword and put it underneath his surcoat And he went forth of the house and came before the bailiff and said to him "Sir, what is your pleasure?"

And the bailiff answered him most despitefully and said to him "Thou foul varlet! Now shalt thou be hanged!"

So Isaac saw that, will he, nill he, he must perforce go with them, but right fain would he avenge himself on some one of them And he drew as nigh as he might to the bailiff, then drew he his sword and smote the bailiff in the middle of his head, so that he clove it clean down to the teeth

XXII

OF THE FURTHER ADVENTURES OF ISAAC, AND HOW HE WAS CROWNED EMPEROR

When the sergeants and the folk that were with the bailiff saw how the young man had thus cloven the bailiff asunder, they fled away When the young man saw them fleeing, he took the horse of the bailiff whom he had slain and mounted it, yet holding fast his sword, which was all bloody And what did he do then but set out on his way to go toward the Minster of Saint Sophia And as he was going his way he cried mercy to the folk that were along the streets, who were all sore affrighted because of the hubbub that they had heard, and the young man said to them

"Sirs, by God's grace, slay me not! For I have put to death that devil and murderer, who hath brought all manner of shame on them of this city and on others!"

When he came to the Minster of Saint Sophia he gat himself up upon the altar and embraced the cross, because he would safeguard his own life Then the shouting and the hubbub waxed very great in the city, for so went the shouting up and down the whole city that everywhere therein it was known how Isaac had slain this demon and murderer When they of the city knew this they rejoiced greatly thereat, and they ran, every one for himself, toward the Minster of Saint Sophia, for to see this young man who had wrought this bold deed And when they were all gathered there, then began they to say one to another

"This is a valiant fellow and a bold, for that he hath ventured so bold a deed!"

And then said the Greeks one to another

"Let us seize the occasion! Let us make this young man emperor!"

And thus did they all agree among themselves Then sent they for the Patriarch, who at that very season was in his palace, that he should come and crown a new emperor whom they had chosen When the Patriarch heard this he said that he would do nought of the sort, and he began to say

"Sirs, ye do ill! Be ye at peace! Ye do not well at all, ye that have undertaken such a thing If I should crown him, then would the Emperor Andronicus put me to death and hew me all in pieces!"

And the Greeks answered him that, if he would not crown him, then would they cut off the Patriarch's head, so that the Patriarch, by force and because of the fear that was in him, came down from his palace and went to the minster, where Isaac was standing, in a very mean robe and very mean garments, for that selfsame day had the Emperor Andronicus sent his bailiff and his people to take and to destroy him Then did the Patriarch array himself, and he crowned him with all speed and haste, whether he would or no When Isaac was crowned, then did the tale thereof spread all up and down the city, until Andronicus knew it and knew that Isaac had slain his bailiff, nor even yet could he ever believe it until he sent thither his own messengers And when his messengers came thither, then saw they that it was indeed true, and they went straightway back to the emperor and said, "Lord, it is all true!"

XXIII

HOW ANDRONICUS SOUGHT TO FLEE FROM THE CITY

When the emperor knew that this was true he arose and took many of his people with him and went even to the Minster of Saint Sophia, through certain passages that led from his palace even to the minster When he was come to the minster, then did he go on until he was over the vaults of the minster, and he saw him who had been crowned And when he saw him, he was sorely grieved thereat, and he enquired of his people if there was any of them that had a bow And they brought him one, and an arrow And Andronicus taketh the bow, and he bendeth it, and he thinketh to pierce Isaac, who had been crowned, through the midst of the body But as he bent it, the bowstring burst in twain, and he was sorely vexed and troubled thereat So back went he to his palace, and then said he to his people that they should go and shut the gates of the palace and should arm themselves and defend the palace And thus they did And in the mean time he went forth of the palace and came to a secret postern-gate, and thereby went he out of the city And he went on board a galley, and certain of his people with him, and he put out to sea, for he desired not that the people of the city should take him

XXIV

HOW ISAAC REWARDED THE FOLK THAT HAD MADE HIM EMPEROR

Thereafter, the people of the city went to the palace and brought the new emperor with them And they took the palace by force, and they led the emperor within it And then they seated him on the throne of Constantine, and after he was seated on the throne of Constantine, they did reverence to him, even as to an holy emperor The emperor was very glad of the great honour that God had this day bestowed upon him, and he said to the people

"Sirs, now behold the great marvel of this great honour which God hath bestowed upon me, for in that very day that they sought to take me and destroy me, in that selfsame day am I crowned emperor! And because of the great honour that ye have done me, I give you all the treasure that is in this palace and in the Palace of Blachernae "[37]

When the people heard this they were all exceeding glad because of the great gift that the emperor had given them, and they went and brake into the treasury and found there so much gold and silver that it was in sooth a marvel And they divided it amongst themselves

XXV

OF THE CAPTURE AND THE SHAMEFUL DEATH OF ANDRONICUS

Now on that same night when Andronicus fled, there arose so great a tempest on the sea, and so great a storm of wind and of thunder and of lightning, that neither he nor his people knew whither they were going, and at last the storm and the blast drave them back again to Constantinople, nor did they know a word of it But when they saw that they were come back to land and could not proceed on their way, then said Andronicus to his people

"Sirs, look and see where we are"

And they looked and saw plainly that they were returned to Constantinople, therefore said they to Andronicus

"Lord, we are dead men! For we are come back again to Constantinople!"

---

[37]Situated on the Golden Horn

When Andronicus heard this he was so sore dismayed that he knew not what to do, and he said to his people

"Sirs, for God's sake take us elsewhere, away from this place!"

And they answered that they could not proceed on their way, even though one were to cut off their heads And when they saw that they could not on any wise proceed on their way, they took Andronicus, the emperor, and brought him to a tavern, and they hid him behind the wine-butts The tavern-keeper and his wife regarded closely these people, and it was in their mind that they were of the people of the Emperor Andronicus At last, by chance, the tavern-keeper's wife went about amongst the wine-butts for to see that they were stoppled tight, and looking round about her, lo, she espied Andronicus sitting behind the wine-butts in all his imperial vestments, and she knew him right well So back came she to her lord, and she said to him

"Lord, Andronicus, the emperor, is hidden here within!"

When the tavern-keeper heard this he sent a messenger to a certain nobleman who dwelt hard by in a great palace, whose father Andronicus had put to death, moreover, he had ravished the wife of this nobleman When the messenger was come thither he said to this nobleman that Andronicus was in the house of the tavern-keeper And the man was rejoiced thereat, and he taketh certain of his people and goeth to the tavern-keeper's house and seizeth Andronicus and bringeth him to his own palace

And when the morrow came, early in the morning, the nobleman took Andronicus and led him away to the royal palace into the presence of the Emperor Isaac When Isaac saw him he said to him

"Andronicus, wherefore hast thou in such fashion betrayed thy lord, the Emperor Manuel, and wherefore didst thou murder his wife and his son, and wherefore hast thou been so fain to do evil to those who were displeased because thou wert emperor, and wherefore didst thou seek to have me taken?"

And Andronicus answered him

"Hold thy peace!" (quoth he) "for I would not deign to answer thee!"

When the Emperor Isaac heard that he would not deign to answer him, he summoned many of the men of the city to come into his presence And when they were in his presence, the emperor said to them

"Sirs, behold, here is Andronicus, who hath done so much evil both to you and to others I myself could, me seemeth, in no wise do such justice to him as ye all would desire, but I release him to you, to do with him what ye will"

Then were the men of the city right glad, and they took him, and some said that he should be burned, and others, that he should be boiled in a caldron that he might live longer and suffer more, and others, that he should be drawn and quartered, so that they could not agree amongst themselves by what death or what torture they might destroy him But there was there a certain wise man, who said·

"Sirs, if ye would trust me, I would shew you how we might avenge ourselves right well of him I have at home a camel, which is the foulest beast and the most bedunged and ugliest in the world Now we will take Andronicus, and we will strip him stark naked, and we will bind him to the camel's back in such fashion that his face shall be against its rump, and we will lead him from one end of the city even unto the other Thus will all they, both men and women, whom he hath wronged, be able to avenge themselves right well "

And all agreed to that which that man had told them And they took Andronicus and bound him even as the man had devised And as they were leading him adown the city, then came those that he had wronged, and they stabbed him and pricked him, some with knives, and others with daggers, and yet others with swords And they cried.

" 'Twas thou didst hang my father ! 'Twas thou didst ravish my wife !"

And the women whose daughters he had taken by force tare his beard and wrought such other indignities on him that when they were come to the other end of the city there was no flesh whatsoever left upon his body Then took they his bones and cast them into a draught-house In such wise did they avenge themselves of the traitor.

And after the day that Isaac became emperor, it was portrayed upon the portals of the minster how Isaac was made emperor by a miracle, and how Our Lord was laying the crown upon him on the one side and Our Lady on the other, and how the angel cut the string of the bow wherewith Andronicus sought to shoot him, because, said they, his house bore the surname of Angelus

XXVI

HOW THE EMPEROR ISAAC PROCURED THE ENLARGEMENT OF HIS BROTHER FROM THE HANDS OF THE SARACENS

Thereafter there laid hold on him a great longing to see his brother, who was in captivity in the land of the heathen, therefore did he take messengers and send them to seek his brother And they sought him until they learned in what place he was held in captivity, then went they thither When they were come thither and when the Saracens heard that the young man was brother to the Emperor of Constantinople, then did they esteem him much more precious because of that, and they said that they would not give him up without great ransom So the messengers gave them as much gold and silver as they demanded And when they had redeemed him they returned to Constantinople

XXVII

HOW THE EMPEROR ISAAC SAW AGAIN HIS BROTHER ALEXIUS, AND HOW HE MADE HIS BROTHER BAILIFF OF HIS LAND

When the Emperor Isaac saw his brother he was exceeding glad of him and made great rejoicing over him, and he also was right glad in his turn, because his brother was emperor and because he had won the empire by his might This young man was called Alexius [88] And it was not long thereafter ere the emperor,

---

[88]There are four of this name mentioned in this chronicle (1) Alexius II, the "lad" who was murdered by Andronicus, (2) Alexius III, the "young man" described here, (3) Alexius IV, the "young man" for whom the crusaders sent to Germany (Chap XXX), (4) Alexius V, "the traitor Mourzuphles," the murderer of Alexius IV

his brother, made him bailiff of his land and commander thereof Then did he wax so proud of this bailiwick that he had, that the people of all the empire spake very ill of him , but they feared him because he was brother to the emperor and because the emperor so loved him

XXVIII

OF THE TREACHERY OF THE ELDER ALEXIUS, AND HOW THE YOUNG ALEXIUS, HIS NEPHEW, WAS SAVED FROM IT

Thereafter it chanced one day that the emperor went a hunting in his forest, and what did Alexius, his brother, do, but come into the forest where the emperor was and seize him treacherously and put out his eyes Thereafter, when he had done this, he caused him to be cast into prison, albeit none knew a word thereof And when he had done this, back came he to Constantinople and caused it to be noised abroad that the emperor, his brother, was dead , and he had himself crowned emperor by force

But when the tutor of the Emperor Isaac's son knew that the child's uncle had betrayed his father and made himself emperor by treachery, what did he do but take the child and cause him to be carried into Germany, to his sister, who was wife to the emperor of Germany, for he desired not that the child's uncle should have him put to death, and the child was more the rightful heir than was Alexius, his uncle

---

XXIX

HOW ALL THESE THINGS CONCERNED THE MEN OF THE CROSS AND THEIR UNDERTAKING

Now have ye heard how Isaac fared, and how he became emperor, and how his son came into Germany—he for whom the men of the cross and the Venetians had sent by counsel of the Marquis of Montferrat, their master (even as ye have heard before in this history, that they might have occasion to go to the land of Constantinople) Now will we tell you concerning this child, and concerning the men of the cross, how they sent for him, and how they went against Constantinople, and how they took it

XXX

HOW THE MEN OF THE CROSS SENT MESSENGERS FOR THE YOUNG MAN ALEXIUS

When the marquis had said to the pilgrims and to the Venetians that whosoever should possess the child of whom we have spoken heretofore, he would have good occasion to go unto Constantinople and get provision for them there, then did the men of the cross accoutre two knights right richly and well, and they sent them into Germany for this young man, that he might come to them And they sent him word that they would help him to gain that which was his right

When the messengers were come to the court of the Emperor of Germany, where the young man was, then did they tell to him the word which they had been charged to tell When the young man heard this and understood the message which the notable men of the cross had sent him, he was right glad thereat and made great rejoicing over it, and he spake the messengers fair and told them that he would take counsel in the matter with the emperor, his brother-in-law When the emperor heard this thing he answered the young man that good fortune had indeed befallen him, and he exhorted him to go thither, and he told him that he would never possess any part of his heritage save that he got it through the help of God and of the men of the cross

XXXI

HOW THE MESSENGERS BROUGHT THE YOUNG MAN TO THE PILGRIMS IN THE ISLAND OF CORFU

The young man perceived clearly that the emperor was giving him good counsel Therefore did he array himself in as goodly fashion as he could, and he departed with the messengers But before either the young man or the messengers were come to Zara, the fleet had already sailed away to the isle of Corfu, for Eastertide was already past But when the fleet weighed anchor to go thither they left behind two galleys to await the messengers and the young man And the pilgrims abode in the isle of Corfu until the young man and the messengers came thither When the young man and the messengers came to Zara they found the two galleys that had been left behind for them, so put they forth to sea and in due season came to Corfu, where the fleet was When the men saw that the youth was coming they all went out to meet him, and saluted him, and did him much honour And when the young man saw how the men of high estate were honouring him, and all the host of the fleet which was there, then was he glad as no other man ever was Then did the marquis come forth and take the young man and lead him with him into his own tent

XXXII

OF THE BARGAIN THAT THE YOUNG MAN ALEXIUS STRUCK WITH THE PILGRIMS

When the youth was there, then came together all the high barons and the Doge of Venice into the marquis' tent, and they spake of one thing and of another, until at last they asked him what he would do for them if they would make him emperor and if they would cause him to wear the crown of Constantinople And he answered them that he would do whatever they might desire Thus they spake together, until at last he said that he would give to the host two hundred thousand marks, and that he would maintain the fleet for one year at his own cost, and that he would go beyond the sea with them, with all his forces, and that he would maintain all the days of his life ten thousand men-at-arms in the land beyond the sea, at his own cost, and that he would give to all those of the host who should depart from Constantinople, for to go beyond the sea, provision for one full year

XXXIII

HOW THE PILGRIMS WERE IN TWO MINDS WHETHER TO GO TO CONSTANTINOPLE, WHY THE MARQUIS WAS EAGER TO GO AGAINST IT TO AVENGE HIMSELF ON THE EMPEROR, OF THE TREASON THAT THE EMPEROR HAD DEVISED AFORETIME AGAINST THE MARQUIS' BROTHER, OF THE BROTH-ER'S DEPARTURE FOR THE HOLY LAND, OF THE THINGS THAT HAD HAPPENED THERE BEFORE HIS COM-ING, AND HOW GUY OF LUSIGNAN BE-CAME KING OF JERUSALEM

Then were summoned all the barons of the host and the Venetians, and when they were all assembled, the Doge of Venice arose and spake to them thus

"Sirs," (quoth the Doge) "now have we a reasonable occasion to go to Constantinople, if ye approve it, for we have the rightful heir"

Now there were some that would not by any means agree to go to Constantinople, but said

"Bah! What have we to do in Constantinople? We have our pilgrimage to make, and thus is it our purpose to go to Babylon or to Alexandria And our fleet is bound to accompany us only one year, and already the half of that year is past!"

And others said, on the other hand

"What have we to do in Babylon or in Alexandria, since we have neither victuals nor substance wherewith to go thither? Better were it for us, ere we go thither, to gain provision and substance by some reasonable occasion, than to go yonder to die of hunger Then shall we be able to obtain some advantage, and he offereth to come with us and to maintain our army and our navy yet a whole year at his own cost!"

Now the Marquis of Montferrat was more eager than any other that was there to go against Constantinople, because he desired to avenge himself of a wrong which the Emperor of Constantinople who now held the empire[39] had done him

Now will we here leave off speaking of the army, and we will tell you of the wrong because of which the marquis so hated the Emperor of Constantinople It so befell that the Marquis Conrad, his brother, took the cross and went beyond the sea, and he took two galleys and went by way of Constantinople And when he was come to Constantinople he spake to the emperor and the emperor welcomed him and greeted him

Now at this time a certain nobleman of the city had besieged the emperor in Constantinople, so that the emperor durst not go out from thence When the marquis saw this he enquired wherefore it was that the man had thus beleaguered him and that he durst not contend against the man And the emperor answered that he possessed neither the heart of his people nor their aid, wherefore he was unwilling to combat the man When the marquis heard this he said that he would aid him in the matter, if he so wished, and the emperor said that so did he wish and that he would be exceeding thankful for his aid

---

[39]I e, the elder Alexius

Then the marquis told the emperor that he would call upon all them of the religion of Rome, to wit, all the Latins that were in the city, and he would have them with him in his company, and with these he would go forth to battle and form the vanguard, and that the emperor should take all his own people and follow after him So the emperor summoned all the Latins of the city When they were all come, the emperor commanded them all to arm themselves, and when they were all armed and the marquis had caused all his own people to arm themselves, then did the marquis take all these Latins with him and ordered his battalion as best he could And the emperor also was fully armed, and his people with him Then what did the marquis do but set forth on his way before, and the emperor followed after But so soon as the marquis was outside the gates with all his battalion, lo, the emperor went and caused the gate to be shut behind him

But so soon as Branas[40] (for he it was had beleaguered the emperor) saw that the marquis was coming on resolutely to attack him, he rose up—both he and his people—to go against the marquis And as they were coming on, what did Branas do but thrust in his spurs and put himself ahead of all his people, about a stone's throw, that he might make haste to charge against the battalion of the marquis When the marquis seeth him coming he pricketh to meet him, and he smiteth him, at the first blow, in the eye, and striketh him dead with that blow Then smiteth he on the right hand and on the left, both he and his people, and they slay many of the foe And when these saw that their lord was dead they began to be confounded, and they turned about and fled

When the emperor, the traitor, who had caused the gates to be shut behind the marquis, saw that they were fleeing, then went he forth out of the city with all his people and began to pursue them that fled And they gat much booty there, the marquis and others, both horses and other things a plenty In this wise did the marquis avenge the emperor of him who had beleaguered him

And when they had routed the foe they returned again to Constantinople, both the emperor and the marquis And after they were returned and had laid aside their arms, then did the emperor thank the marquis right heartily for that he had so well avenged him of this his enemy But the marquis asked him wherefore he had caused the gates to shut behind him

"Bah ! All is well now !" quoth the emperor

"Now—yea !" quoth the marquis, "through God's providence !"

And no very long time thereafter the emperor and his fellow traitors contrived a great treachery against the marquis, for he was desirous that the marquis should be destroyed Howbeit, an aged man, who knew of this thing, had compassion on the marquis, and he came to the marquis most honourably and said to him

"Sir, for God's sake get you hence out of this city ! For if ye tarry here until the third day from this, the emperor and his fellow traitors have contrived a great plot whereby they will seize you here and cause you to be destroyed "

When the marquis heard these tidings he was by no means at ease So cometh he that very night and biddeth his galleys be made ready, and he putteth

---

[40] Alexius Branas

out to sea, ere it is yet day, and departeth thence Nor did he stay his course until he was come unto Tyre

---

Now it had already come to pass, or ever yet that whole land was lost [to the Christians], that the King of Jerusalem[41] died, and all the kingdom of Jerusalem was indeed lost,[42] nor was there any other city that still held out, save Tyre and Ascalon And the king that had died had two married sisters a knight, my Lord Guy of Lusignan, had wedded the elder, to whom the kingdom had escheated, and my Lord Humphrey of Thoron had the younger And on a certain day there came together in Jerusalem all the high barons of the land, and the Count of Tripoli,[43] and the Temple, and the Hospital in Jerusalem,[44] to the temple And they said among themselves that they would divorce my Lord Guy from his wife, because the kingdom had escheated to his wife, and that they would give her another husband who would be more competent to be king than was my Lord Guy And so did they They divorced them, but when they had divorced them, then could they never agree to whom they should marry her, until at last they left the whole matter to the queen, who had been wife to my Lord Guy To her, then, did they deliver the crown, and she should give it to whomsoever she desired to be made king

Then they came together again on another day—all the barons, and the Temple, and the Hospital, and there also was the Count of Tripoli, who was the goodliest knight in the land, and who verily thought that the lady would give him the crown And there too was my Lord Guy, he that had had the queen to wife When, therefore, they were all come together, the lady held up the crown, and she looked this way and that Then she espieth him who had been her husband, and she goeth forward and setteth the crown on his head Thus did my Lord Guy become king

But when the Count of Tripoli saw this, he was so grieved that he departed unto his own land, even unto Tripoli, in high dudgeon

XXXIV

HOW KING GUY GAVE BATTLE TO THE SARACENS AND WAS TAKEN CAPTIVE, HOW HE PURCHASED HIS ENLARGEMENT, AND HOW THE MARQUIS CONRAD AND THE MEN OF TYRE DEFIED HIM

Not long thereafter the king gave battle to the Saracens, and he was taken captive, and all his people routed, and the land was so utterly lost that there was now not a city that held out, save only Tyre and Ascalon And when Saladin saw that he held the land in his hand he came to the King of Jerusalem, whom he was keeping in captivity, and he said to him that if he would cause Ascalon to be given up to him, then would he let the king go, and a great part of his people also And the king answered him

---

[41]Baldwin IV (?)
[42]1187
[43]Raymond II, Count of Tripoli, in Syria
[44]I e, the commanders of the Templars and the Hospitalers of Saint John in Jerusalem

"Only lead me now thither, and I will cause it to be given up to you"

And Saladin led him thither When they were come thither, then the king spake to them of the city and told them that they should give up the city, for such was his will And they came and delivered the city to him When Saladin had the city in his hand, then did he let the king go, and a part of his people with him, and the king, being escaped from captivity, departed with such of his people as he had and came to Tyre

---

And now, while the king had been accomplishing these things, the marquis[45] in the mean time had all the men of Tyre, and the Genose who were there, both in full accord with him And they had all sworn fealty to him and vowed by holy relics that they would hold in all things to him as their lord, and he, that he would help them to defend the city And the marquis had found so great a famine in the city that one measure of corn (of the measure of that city) was sold for an hundred bezants, which would not amount to more than a setier[46] and a half at Amiens

When the king came to Tyre, then his serjeants began to cry

"Open ye! Open ye the gate! Lo, the king cometh!"

And they that were within the city answered that they should not enter Likewise the marquis came to the walls and said that the king should not enter

"Bah!" quoth the king "How so! Am I not in sooth lord and master of them that are within?"

"As God liveth," quoth the marquis, "neither lord nor king are ye, nor shall ye enter here! For ye have brought us all to shame and utterly lost the land, furthermore, so great is the famine here within that if ye and your people should come in, the whole city would perish of hunger And I would rather," quoth the marquis, "that ye should perish, both ye and your people, who are of no great use, than that we who are within should perish, or the city itself"

When the king perceived that he could not enter there, he turned about and departed toward Acre, and he went up into a little hill and encamped there And there was it that the King of France and the King of England[47] found him

And while the marquis was in Tyre, in the midst of the great dearth which prevailed there, God sent them great comfort, in that a merchant came thither who brought a shipload of corn, and he offered the corn at ten bezants which had been at an hundred So was the marquis greatly rejoiced thereat, and all they of the city And all the corn was kept and purchased in the city

XXXV

HOW SALADIN LAID SIEGE TO THE CITY OF TYRE

But after a brief space cometh Saladin and layeth siege to Tyre, both by land and by sea, so that neither victuals nor any other thing could enter the city, and he abode there until the dearth was once more as great in the city as it had been before

---

[45]Conrad of Montferrat
[46]An old French unit of measure for wheat, varying greatly in different localities
[47]Philip Augustus and Richard the Lion-Hearted

XXXVI

OF THE GRIEVOUS DEARTH THAT AFFLICTED THEM OF TYRE, AND HOW ONE OF THE GENOESE DEVISED A PLAN FOR THEIR RELIEF

When the marquis saw that the dearth was so great in the city and that they could not get comfort or relief from any quarter, then did he summon all the men of the city and the Genoese also whom he had there, and he spake to them and said

"Sirs" (quoth he), "we are undone unless God take pity on our plight, for the dearth is so great in this city that there is scarcely any meat or corn wherewith we may any longer sustain ourselves, nor can any relief come either by land or by sea In God's name, if there be any one of you that knoweth how to offer counsel in this case, let him offer it!"

Then stood forth a Genoese and said

"If ye would trust me" (quoth he), "I would give you good counsel"

"Now, what counsel?" quoth the marquis

"I will tell you," quoth the man "We have here within this city ships and galleys and barges and other vessels, and I will tell you what I will do I will take four galleys with me, and I will have them manned with the fittest people that we have, and I will put forth to sea before daylight, as if I were seeking to escape hence And so soon as the Saracens shall perceive me, they will not take the time to arm themselves, but rather they will have such haste to pursue and to overtake me that they will arm themselves not at all, rather will they all press hard after me But ye shall very carefully have caused all your other vessels and barges and galleys to be filled with the fittest people that ye have, and when ye shall see them all pressing hard after me, and when they shall be well under way, then shall ye loose all your vessels and press hard after them, but I will turn back On this wise will we give them battle Thus will God give us counsel, if so please Him"

To this counsel were they all agreed, and they did all things even as this man had devised

XXXVII

HOW THE MEN OF TYRE UTTERLY DISCOMFITED THE SARACENS, AND OF THE GRIEF AND RAGE OF SALADIN THEREAT

When day was near at hand, and this man had right well equipped his galleys, and all the other vessels were likewise well armed, then what did he do but set forth to sea a little before the day Now the deep sea harbour was inside the walls of the city of Tyre, within which ships departed from the city or landed there And he setteth forth on his course and beginneth to move on apace When he was a little space away and the Saracens perceived him, then had they such haste to follow him that never at all did they arm themselves but let go all their hundred galleys and began to chase him When the galleys were well under way, then did the men of the city press hard after them, but he whom the Saracens were chasing turned back Then did the Tyrians engage the Saracens, who were all unarmed, and they slew many of them and put them to rout, so that of all those hundred galleys never a one escaped save two which the Tyrians did not take

And Saladin beheld all this, and he made great moan, and plucked his beard, and tare his hair for grief, the while he saw his people cut to pieces before his eyes, nor could he help them And after he had thus lost his fleet he brake camp and departed

In this wise was the city still held by the marquis, and King Guy was yet in that little hill, toward Acre,[48] where the King of France and the King of England had found him

XXXVIII

HOW KING GUY AND HIS WIFE DIED AND HOW THE MARQUIS CONRAD BECAME KING OF JERUSALEM, OF HIS DEATH, AND OF THE TAKING OF ACRE

It was not long after this that King Guy died, and his wife also So the kingdom escheated to the wife of my Lord Humphrey of Thoron, who was sister to the queen Then did they go and take away his wife from my Lord Humphrey and give her to the marquis Thus was the marquis made king, thereafter he had a daughter by her And afterward was the marquis slain by the Assassins [49] Then took they the queen and gave her to Count Henry of Champagne And afterward was Acre besieged and taken

---

XXXIX

HOW THE PILGRIMS ENQUIRED OF THE BISHOPS WHETHER IT WERE A SIN TO GO AGAINST CONSTANTINOPLE AND HOW THE BISHOPS SAID THAT IT WAS A WORK OF MERIT

Now have we recounted to you the wrong because of which the Marquis[50] of Montferrat hated the Emperor of Constantinople, and wherefore he desired and planned more eagerly to go to Constantinople than did all the others, so then, we will return to our former matter

When the Doge of Venice had said to the barons that now had they a good occasion to go to the land of Constantinople and that he approved it well, then were all the barons agreed among themselves Thereafter they made enquiry of the bishops whether it would be a sin to go thither, and the bishops answered that this was in no wise a sin, but rather a good work of great merit, for now that they had the rightful heir, who had been disinherited, they could well aid him to obtain his right and to take vengeance of his enemies Then did they cause the young man to swear on holy relics that he would hold fast to the covenant which he had made with them before

---

[48]Guy of Lusignan besieged Acre for nearly two years (1190-91)
[49]28th April, 1192
[50]Boniface

XL

HOW THE PILGRIMS SET FORTH ON THEIR VOYAGE AND HOW THEY CAME AT LAST TO CONSTANTINOPLE

Then did all the pilgrims and the Venetians agree together to go thither Then they prepared their fleet and made ready for their voyage and put out to sea So they sailed until they came to an harbour which is called Abydus,[51] and which lay full an hundred leagues distant from Constantinople Now this harbour was in the place where once stood Troy the Great, at the entering in of the Strait of Saint George [52] Thence they rowed and sailed, all up the Strait of Saint George, until they were come within a league of Constantinople Then they waited one for another until all the vessels were gathered together When all the fleet and all the vessels were come together, then they decked and adorned their vessels in such fair fashion that it was the goodliest thing in the world to look upon And when they of Constantinople saw this fleet, which was coming in such goodly array, they looked upon it with wonder, and they mounted upon their walls and upon their housetops to behold this marvel And they of the fleet also looked upon the greatness of the city, which was so long and so broad, and they in their turn marveled exceedingly thereat Then they passed on and went into harbour at Chalcedon, beyond the Strait of Saint George

XLI

HOW THE EMPEROR ENQUIRED OF THE PILGRIMS WHAT THEY WERE SEEKING, HOW THEY DEMANDED THAT HE ABDICATE HIS OFFICE, HOW THEY OF THE CITY WOULD NOT RECOGNIZE ISAAC'S SON AS THEIR LORD, AND HOW THE PILGRIMS PREPARED TO ATTACK THE CITY

When the Emperor of Constantinople knew this he sent to them, by good messengers, asking them what they were seeking there and wherefore they were come thither, and likewise he sent them word that if they desired any of his gold or of his silver he would send it to them right willingly When the nobles heard this they made answer to the messengers that they desired nought of his gold or of his silver, rather, they desired that the emperor should abdicate his office, for that he held it neither by right nor by law And they sent word to him that they had the rightful heir with them, to wit, Alexius, son of the Emperor Isaac

Then the messengers answered and said that the emperor would do nought of the sort, then went they their ways

Thereafter the Doge of Venice spake to the barons and said to them·

"Sirs, I would fain counsel you that ye take ten galleys, and that ye put the young man in one of them, and people with him, and that they go under a truce to the seashore of Constantinople, and that they ask the folk of the city whether they will acknowledge the youth as their lord "

And the men of high estate answered that this would be indeed a good thing to do So they made ready the ten galleys, and the youth, and armed men a plenty

---

[51]*Bouke* ['mouth'] *d'Ave"* (possibly a corruption of "Abydos," in Late Greek pronounced "ávithos")

[52]The Dardanelles

with them, and they rowed until they were come hard by the walls of the city
Then did they row back and forth, and they shewed the youth called Alexius to
the people and enquired of them if they would recognize him as their lord   And
they of the city made answer that by no means did they recognize him as their
lord, and that they knew not who he was   And they that were in the galleys with
him (the youth) said that this was the son of Isaac, the emperor that had been
And those within the city answered yet again that they knew nought concerning
him   Then did these come back again to the host and make known what answer
had been given them

Then was word sent throughout the host that all should arm themselves, both
great and small   And when they were all armed, then did they shrive themselves
and partake of the sacrament, for greatly did they doubt whether ever they would
come nigh Constantinople   Thereafter they ordered their squadrons, both ships
and transports and galleys   And the knights went on board the transports with
their horses, and they set forth upon their way   And they let sound trumpets of
silver and of brass, as many as an hundred pair of them, and tabours and timbrels
in great number

XLII

HOW THEY OF THE CITY MADE READY TO RESIST THE ATTACK

When the people of the city saw this great fleet, and heard the sound of the
trumpets and the tabours, which made great noise, then did they arm themselves
every one, and they went up upon the housetops and upon the towers of the city
Then in sooth did it seem to them that all the sea and the land trembled and that
the whole sea was covered with ships   And in the mean time the emperor had
caused his people to come, all armed, to the seashore for to defend it

XLIII

HOW THE PILGRIMS TOOK THE SEASHORE OF CONSTANTINOPLE

When the men of the cross and the Venetians saw the Greeks who were come
down to the seashore all armed against them, then spake they together, and at last
the Doge of Venice said that he would go first, with all his people, and that he
would seize the shore, with God's help   Then took he his ships and his galleys
and his transports and put himself before the host, in the very front thereof, and
next they took their crossbowmen and archers and sent them ahead in barges to
clear the shore of the Greeks   When they had ordered themselves on this wise,
then went they forward toward the shore   And when the Greeks saw that the pilgrims would not, for any fear of them, forbear to come to the shore, and when
they saw them drawing yet nearer to them, then did they fall back, nor durst they
await them any longer   So the fleet came to land, and when they were landed,
forth came the knights out of the transports, all mounted, for the transports were
built in such fashion that they had doors, which were easily opened, and a bridge
was thrust out whereby the knights could come forth to land all mounted

When the fleet had landed and the Greeks who had drawn back saw that the host had all come forth, then were they sore distressed Now were they but a rabble, those Greeks who had come down to defend the shore and had boasted to their emperor that never should the pilgrims come to land so long as they were there

When the knights were come forth from the transports they began to chase these Greeks, and they chased them as far as a bridge which stood nigh the end of the city, and above this bridge was a gate, through which the Greeks passed inward and fled into Constantinople

And when the knights were returned from chasing the Greeks they spake together, and the Venetians said that their vessels were by no means in safety unless they were inside the harbour And they took counsel how to get them within the harbour Now the harbour of Constantinople was firmly closed with a very thick chain, which was made fast on the one side within the city and on the other to the Tower of Galata This tower was very strong and right easy to defend, and it was right well garrisoned with defenders

XLIV

HOW THE TOWER OF GALATA WAS TAKEN, AND OF THE BEGINNINGS OF THE ASSAULT UPON THE CITY

By the advice of the notable men, this tower was invested, and at last it was taken by storm, but from end to end of the chain were galleys of the Grecians who were helping to defend the chain But when the tower was taken and the chain broken, then did the vessels enter within the harbour and were brought into safety, and they took the galleys from the Greeks who were within the harbour, and certain ships also And when their own ships and all their other vessels were brought inside the harbour in safety, then the pilgrims and the Venetians came together and took counsel amongst themselves how they might besiege the city And at last they agreed between them that the Franks should invest the city by land, and the Venetians by sea And the Doge of Venice said that he would cause engines to be built upon his ships, and ladders wherewith they could attack the walls Then they armed themselves, the knights and all the other pilgrims, and went on to pass over a bridge which lay some two leagues away, nor was there any other road whereby to go to Constantinople within less than four leagues of that place, save only this bridge And when they came to the bridge, certain Greeks came thither who disputed the passage as long as they could, until at last the pilgrims drave them back by force of arms and so passed over

And when they were come to the city, the men of mark encamped there and pitched their tents in front of the Palace of Blachernae, which was the emperor's, and this palace was at the very end of the city Then did the Doge of Venice cause most marvelous engines to be made, and right goodly ones, for he had them take the spars which support the sails of the ships, which were full thirty fathoms in length, or more,[53] and these he caused to be firmly bound and made fast to the

---

[53]Most of the dimensions recorded in this passage seem considerably exaggerated

masts with good cords, and good bridges to be laid on these and good guards alongside them, likewise of cords, and the bridge was so wide that three armed knights could pass over it abreast And the Doge caused the bridge to be so well furnished and covered on the sides with sailcloth and other thick stuff, that those who should go up the bridge to make an assault need have no care for crossbow bolts nor for arrows And the bridge projected so far forward beyond the ship that the height of the bridge above the ground was full forty fathoms or more [54] And each one of the transport ships had a mangonel,[55] which continually hurled missiles against the walls and into the city

When the Venetians had made ready their ships, even as I have told you, here, the pilgrims on the other hand, who were attacking by land, had their petraries[56] so well trained that they hurled missiles and shot arrows clean into the emperor's palace And they that were inside the palace likewise hurled and shot in their turn, even to the tents of the pilgrims Then they spake together, the pilgrims and the Venetians, and they determined on the morrow to attack the city at once by land and by sea And when the morrow came, early in the morning, whilst the Venetians were making themselves ready and ordering their vessels and drawing ever nearer to the walls to begin their assault, and when the pilgrims likewise on their side had ordered their people, lo, the Emperor of Constantinople, Alexius, came forth from the city by a gate which is called the Roman Gate, with all his people under arms, and there did he order his people and he drew up seventeen battalions, and in these seventeen battalions there were numbered wellnigh an hundred thousand horsemen Then sent he the more part of these seventeen battalions around the flank of the Frankish host, and the rest he kept with himself And all the footmen of the city that were able to bear arms he caused to come forth and he ranged them from end to end of the walls, between the host of the Franks and the walls When the Franks saw themselves thus hemmed in round about by these battalions they were sore dismayed, but they drew up their own battalions, and these made but seven battalions of some seven hundred knights, for more than these had they none, also, of these seven hundred, there were fifty that were on foot

XLV

HOW THE PILGRIMS ORDERED THEIR BATTALIONS, AND OF THE USE THAT THEY MADE OF THE GROOMS AND THE KITCHEN-KNAVES

After this,[57] when they had ordered their people on this wise, then the Count of Flanders asked for the first battalion, and it was granted to him, the second battalion had the Count of Saint-Pol and my Lord Peter of Amiens, the third battalion had my Lord Henry, the brother of the Count of Flanders, and the Germans And then they settled it that the serjeants of foot should follow the battalions of horse, so that three companies or four followed one battalion of horse, and each

---

[54]This passage is very obscure
[55]A huge engine for throwing rocks and other heavy missiles
[56]Ballistic engines for throwing stones, mounted on massive wheels
[57]16th July, 1203

one of the battalions had those of its own country behind it Thereafter, when they had drawn up the three battalions that were to fight against the emperor, then did they draw up the four others which should guard the host, so that the marquis, who was lord of the host, had the rear-guard and guarded the host behind, and Count Lewis[58] had the other next after it, and they of Champagne had the third, and the Burgundians the fourth, and these four battalions did the marquis guard

And next they took all the fellows that guarded the horses, and all the kitchen-knaves who could bear arms, and these they attired in quilted trappings and in saddlecloths and armed them with copper pots and with pestles large and small, so that they were so hideous and so horrible that the common crowd of the emperor's footfolk, who were standing outside the walls, had great fear and horror of them when they beheld them And these four battalions that I have already named to you guarded the host, for fear lest the emperor's battalions, which were all about the host, should harm or harry the host or the tents, and the grooms and kitchen-knaves were placed toward the city, over against the emperor's footfolk that were drawn up beneath the walls And when the emperor's footsoldiery saw our common folk so hideously accoutred, they had so great fear and so great horror of them that they durst not so much as move or come toward them, nor ever on that side had the host any need of a guard

XLVI

HOW THE VENETIANS FOUGHT FIERCELY AND SET FIRE TO A PART OF THE CITY

Next was it ordered that the Count of Flanders and the Count of Saint-Pol and my Lord Henry, who had the three battalions, should attack the emperor, moreover, it was straitly forbidden that, for any need that they might have, the other four should remove from their places until they should see that the others had so good as lost everything, that they might not be surrounded or assailed by the battalions that stood round about the host

In the mean time, whilst the Franks were drawn up in this fashion, the Venetians, who were on the sea, did not forget themselves, but they drew their ships up hard by the walls, so that they easily mounted the walls of the city by means of the ladders and the bridges which they had built upon their ships And they discharged their bolts and shot their arrows and let their mangonels hurl missiles, and they fought exceeding fiercely until they set fire to the city, so that there was consumed thereof a portion as large as the city of Arras [59] Yet durst they not scatter themselves nor venture into the city, for they were too few men, nor would they have been able to endure there, so, rather, they withdrew again to their ships

---

[58]Lewis of Blois (and Chartres)
[59]Situated only a few miles from Clari, Arras would be that one of the larger towns with which Robert's hearers and readers were most familiar

XLVII

OF THE EXPLOITS OF THE COUNT OF FLANDERS, THE COUNT OF SAINT-POL, AND MY LORD PETER OF AMIENS

The noblemen who were on the other side, who were to attack the emperor, had brought it about that from each battalion two of the most valiant men that were known there—and wisest—were chosen, and that whatsoever these commanded was done if these commanded, "Thrust !" then they thrust, and if they commanded, "Charge !" then they charged

The Count of Flanders, who had the vanguard, rode the first of all at full speed to meet the emperor, and the emperor was fully the fourth part of a league distant from the Count of Flanders, and he bade his battalion ride to meet the count, and the Count of Saint-Pol and my Lord Peter of Amiens, who had the next battalion, rode up a little way alongside, and my Lord Henry of Hainault[60] and the Germans, who had the third battalion, rode after them, nor was there a horse that was not covered with emblazoned trappings or with silken cloth over all its other housings And three companies, or four, or five, of serjeants of foot followed each one of the battalions, at the tails of the horses, and they rode so well ranged and close pressed that there was none so rash as to dare ride before another

And the emperor rode toward our people with full nine battalions, nor was there one of these battalions wherein there were not three thousand horsemen, or four, or five, so great were they And when the Count of Flanders had left the host full two crossbow shots behind, his counsellors said to him

"Lord, ye do not at all well to go thus to attack the emperor so far away from the host, for if ye fight there and have any need of help, they who guard the host will not be able to help you But if ye will trust us in the matter, ye will turn back to the palisades of the camp, and there will ye await the emperor more safely if he be willing to fight "

So the Count of Flanders turned back to the palisades of the camp, even as he had been advised, and the battalion of my Lord Henry also But neither the Count of Saint-Pol nor my Lord Peter of Amiens would turn back, rather, they remained in the midst of the field, all quietly, with all their people But when the battalion of the Count of Saint-Pol and that of my Lord Peter of Amiens saw the Count of Flanders turning back, then said they all together that the Count of Flanders was doing a most shameful thing in that he turned back, who had the vanguard And they cried all together

"Lord ! Lord ! The Count of Flanders turneth back ! And since he turneth back, he leaveth to you the vanguard Now let us take it, in God's name !"

And the barons agreed together and said that they would take the vanguard But when the Count of Flanders saw that neither the Count of Saint-Pol nor my Lord Peter of Amiens would turn back at all, he sent them word by messenger and besought them that they would turn back And my Lord Peter of Amiens

---

[60]Henry of Angre

sent back word to him that they would not turn back one step And the Count of Flanders sent word yet again by two messengers that, for God's sake, they should not bring this shame upon him but should turn back, for thus had he been advised to do And the Count of Saint-Pol and my Lord Peter of Amiens sent back word yet again to him that on no account whatsoever would they turn back Then came my Lord Peter of Amiens and my Lord Eustace of Canteleu, who were master leaders of the battle,[61] and said

"Sirs ! Ride ye forward in God's name, at full speed !"

And they began to ride forward at full speed, and all they of the host who had remained behind began to cry after them

"See ! See ! The Count of Saint-Pol and my Lord Peter of Amiens will engage the emperor ! Lord God !" they began to shout and to cry, "Lord God ! Be Thou this day the defender of these and of all their company ! See ! They have the vanguard which the Count of Flanders ought to have ! Lord God, lead them to safety !"

And the ladies and damsels of the palace had gone up to the windows, and other folk of the city, both ladies and damsels, had climbed the walls of the city and were watching the battalion as it rode on, and the emperor on the other side And they said one to another that it seemed as if our warriors were angels, such goodly men were they, and armed in such goodly fashion, and their horses caparisoned with such goodly trappings

XLVIII

OF THE MEETING OF THE TWO HOSTS, AND HOW THE EMPEROR'S ARMY FLED

When the knights of the battalion of the Count of Flanders saw that the Count of Saint-Pol and my Lord Peter of Amiens would on no account turn back, then came they to the count and said to him

"Lord, ye are doing a most shameful thing in that ye bestir not yourself ! Know ye, then, that unless ye ride forward we will not hold with you any longer !"

When the Count of Flanders heard this he pricked his horse with the spurs, and all the rest after him, and they pricked on their way until they overtook the battalion of the Count of Saint-Pol and my Lord Peter of Amiens, and when they had overtaken it, then rode they on beside them, all abreast, and the battalion of my Lord Henry rode behind

And the battalions of the emperor and our own battalions had by now drawn so near together that the emperor's crossbowmen were shooting into the midst of our people, and our own crossbowmen likewise into the midst of the emperor's people, and there remained but one hillock to climb betwixt the emperor and our battalions, and the emperor's battalions were ascending it on the one side and ours on the other And when our people came to the top of the hill and the emperor saw them, he halted, and all his people also, and they were so dismayed and confounded because our battalions were riding thus abreast against them that they

---

[61]See the first paragraph of this chapter

knew not what counsel to take In the mean time, as they stood there thus confounded, the other battalions of the emperor, which had been sent around the
host of the Franks, withdrew themselves and went back and all joined themselves
with the emperor in the valley And when the Franks saw all the emperor's battalions thus joined together, they stood stock-still on the top of the hillock and
wondered what the emperor meant to do And the counts and the chief men of
the three battalions sent messengers the one to the others, to take counsel what
they should do, and whether they should advance clean up to the emperor's host,
or not And they found none to counsel that they go thither, for they were far
away from the host, and if they fought there where the emperor was, they who
were guarding the host could no longer see them or, if need be, bring them any
help And on the other hand, there lay betwixt them and the emperor a great
canal, a great conduit, through which water went to Constantinople, which if they
should cross, they would suffer great loss of their men And for this reason they
found none to counsel that they go thither

In the mean time, the while the Franks were thus speaking together, lo and
behold, the emperor gat himself back into Constantinople And when he was come
thither, most bitterly was he reproached both by the ladies and by the damsels and
by one and another of his people, for that he had not attacked folk so few in number as were the Franks, with so great a multitude as he was leading

XLIX

HOW THE PILGRIMS AND THE VENETIANS SOUGHT NEWS EACH OF THE OTHER AFTER THE BATTLE

When the emperor had thus turned back, then back went the pilgrims to their
tents and laid aside their arms, and when they had laid them by, the Venetians,
who had crossed over in ships and in barges, came to ask tidings of them, and
they said

"By our faith! We had heard tell that ye were fighting against the Greeks,
and we feared greatly for you, so came we to you"

And the Franks answered them and said

"By our faith! Thanks to God, we have done well! For we went to meet
the emperor, and the emperor durst not close with us!"

And the Franks in their turn asked tidings of the Venetians, and these said

"By our faith!" (quoth they) "We have attacked fiercely, and we have entered the city over the walls, and set fire to the city so that much of the city was
burned"

L

HOW A GREAT MURMURING AROSE IN THE CITY AGAINST THE EMPEROR

And whilst the Franks and the Venetians were thus speaking together, there
arose a great murmuring in the city, and the folk of the city said to the emperor
that he should deliver them from the Franks. who had besieged them, and that
if he would not fight these, then would they go after the young man whom the
Franks had brought with them and would make him emperor and their lord

LI

OF THE FALSE PROMISE AND THE FLIGHT OF THE EMPEROR

When the emperor heard this he promised them that he would fight the Franks on the morrow, but when it drew nigh to midnight, away fled the emperor out of the city with as much people as he could take with him

LII

HOW THEY OF THE CITY SOUGHT THE YOUNG ALEXIUS, HOW HE WAS BROUGHT TO THE PALACE, HOW ISAAC AND HIS WIFE WERE RELEASED FROM PRISON, HOW ISAAC WAS SEATED ON THE IMPERIAL THRONE, HOW MOURZUPHLES WAS RELEASED AND MADE MASTER BAILIFF TO THE EMPEROR, AND OF THE REQUEST THAT THE SULTAN OF KONIEH MADE TO THE FRANKS AND HOW THEY REFUSED TO AID HIM

And when the morrow came, in the morning, when they of the city learned that the emperor had fled, what did they do but come to the gates and open them And they went forth to the host of the Franks and asked and enquired for Alexius, Isaac's son And it was made known to them that in the tent of the marquis they would find him When they came thither they found him indeed And these his friends made great celebration over him and very great rejoicing, and they gave great thanks to the barons and said that they had done right well and had shewn great valour who had acted on this wise, and they told them that the emperor had fled, and that they should come into the city and into the palace, as into that which was their own

Then came together all the high barons of the host, and they took Alexius, Isaac's son, and led him to the palace with great rejoicing and much pomp And when they were come to the palace they caused Isaac, his father, to be delivered from prison, and Isaac's wife also, whom his brother, who had held the empire, had caused to be put there And when Isaac was forth of the prison he had very great joy of his son, and he fell on his neck and kissed him, and he gave great thanks to the barons who were there and said that, first by God's help and then by theirs, he was now forth of his prison Then were brought in two golden thrones, and they set Isaac on the one and Alexius his son on the other, at his side, and Isaac was established in the imperial seat

Then said they to the emperor

"Lord, here within there lieth in prison a man of high birth—Mourzuphles is his name—who hath been there full seven years If your will be such, it were well that he be delivered from prison"

Then was Mourzuphles delivered from prison, and thereafter the emperor made him his master bailiff (whereof the emperor had but ill recompense, even as I will tell you presently)

Now it came to pass, after the Franks had brought these things about, that the Sultan of Konieh heard tell how the Franks had thus done So came he for to speak with them, there where they were yet encamped without Constantinople, and he said to them

"Verily, sirs," (quoth he) "ye have shewn great valour and great prowess, who have conquered so great a thing as is Constantinople, which is the capital of the world, and have set the rightful heir of Constantinople again in his seat and have crowned him emperor" (For they were wont to say in that country that Constantinople was the capital of the world) "Sirs," quoth the Sultan, "I would fain beg you for a certain thing which I will tell you I have a brother, younger than I, who has treacherously robbed me of my land and of my seignory of Konieh, whereof I was lord and whereto I am the rightful heir Now if ye would help me to conquer my land and my seignory, I would give you a very great abundance of my substance, and I would cause myself to be baptized, and all those that are subject to me, if I might have my seignory again and if ye would help me"

And the barons answered that they would take counsel in the matter Then were summoned the Doge of Venice and the marquis and all the high barons, and they came together in a very great council But all the counsel that they took could not bring them to do that which the sultan required of them And when they came away from the council they made answer to the sultan that they could not do that which he required, for that they yet had their agreements to fulfill with the emperor, and that it would be dangerous to leave so great a thing as Constantinople in such case as it now was, wherefore they durst not leave it When the sultan heard this he departed, sore displeased

LIII

HOW THE BARONS VISITED THE EMPRESS OF FRANCE

Thereafter, when the barons had brought Alexius into the palace, they made enquiry concerning the sister of the King of France, who was called the Empress of France, if she were yet alive And they told them, yea, and that she was married, for a nobleman of the city, Branas by name, had taken her to wife, and that she dwelt in a palace hard by Thither went the barons for to see her, and they saluted her and promised to render her much service, but she treated them most discourteously and was sore vexed that they had come thither and that they had crowned this Alexius Nor would she herself speak to them, but, rather, bade an interpreter speak for her And the interpreter said that she knew not a word of French But Count Lewis (he was her cousin) found favour with her

LIV

OF THE KING OF NUBIA AND HIS ADVENTURES

Thereafter it came to pass one day that the barons went to divert themselves in the palace, for to see Isaac and the emperor his son And when the barons were within the palace, lo, there came thither a king whose flesh was all black, and he had a cross in the middle of his forehead, which had been made with an hot iron This king sojourned in a very rich abbey in the city, where that Alexius that had been emperor had commanded that he should be and that he should be lord and master thereof so long as he desired to sojourn there

When the emperor saw him coming he rose up to meet him and did him much honour And the emperor enquired of the barons

"Know ye now" (quoth he) "who this man is?"

"Nay, lord," quoth the barons

"By my faith!" quoth the emperor "This is the King of Nubia, who is come on a pilgrimage to this city"

And they bade the interpreters speak to him, and they caused these to ask him where his own land was And he made answer to the interpreters, in his own tongue, that his land was yet an hundred days' journey beyond Jerusalem, and from thence had he come to Jerusalem on a pilgrimage, and he said that when he departed from this land he brought full three score of his countrymen with him, but when he came to Jerusalem there were but ten of them left alive, and when he was come from Jerusalem unto Constantinople he had but two yet living He said, furthermore, that he wished to go on a pilgrimage to Rome, and from Rome to Saint James,[62] and then return thence to Jerusalem, if he might live so long, and then die there And he said that all they of his land were Christians, and when a child had been born there, it was baptized, and a cross was marked in the middle of its forehead with an hot iron, even such a mark as he himself bore And the barons looked upon this king with great amazement

LV

HOW THE BARONS LODGED WITHOUT THE CITY FOR FEAR OF THE GREEKS

Thereafter, when the barons had crowned Alexius, even as I have told you, it was determined that my Lord Peter of Bracheux, both he and his people, should abide in the palace with the emperor, then, after this, the barons determined how they themselves should lodge, for they durst by no means abide in the city because of the Greeks, who were traitors, rather, they went and lodged beyond the harbour, over against the Tower of Galata, and they lodged there all together in certain houses which were there And they removed their fleet and brought it to land in front of them, and they went into the city when they would And when they would go by water they passed over in barges, and when they would go on horseback they passed over the bridge Then, when they were lodged, they took counsel together, both the Franks and the Venetians, how they would cause some fifty fathoms' length of the walls of the city to be rased, for they feared that they of the city would revolt against them

LVI

HOW ALEXIUS WAS SOLEMNLY CROWNED EMPEROR, AND HOW THE BARONS DEMANDED THEIR PAY

Thereafter, on a certain day all the barons assembled in the emperor's palace and demanded of the emperor the fulfillment of their agreements, and he answered

---

[62]Saint James of Compostella, in Spain

that he would certainly keep his word, but that he wished first to be crowned So then they set and fixed a day to crown him And on that day was he crowned in state, as emperor, with the consent of his father, who agreed freely thereto And when was crowned, the barons asked again for their pay And he told them that he would pay them right willingly what he could , and he paid to them then some hundred thousand marks And of these hundred thousand marks did the Venetians receive half, for they were to have the half of the conquests, and of the fifty thousand marks which remained there were paid to them thirty and six thousand marks, which the Franks were yet owing to them on their fleet , and with the other twenty thousand marks that remained discharge was made to all them that had lent of their substance for the payment of their passage

LVII

OF THE CONQUESTS THAT WERE MADE BY ALEXIUS AND THE PILGRIMS

Thereafter the emperor besought the barons, telling them that outside Constantinople he possessed nothing, and that but little would it boot him if he possessed nought else, for his uncle held all the cities and castles which ought to be his own Wherefore he besought the barons to help him conquer some of the land round about, then would he gladly give them yet more of what was his Then they answered that this were they right fain to do, and that all they who wished to get themselves gain should go thither So thither then went full half of the men of the host with Alexius, and the other half remained in Constantinople to receive the payment, and Isaac remained there to make payment to the barons

And Alexius departed with the host, and he conquered from that land full a score of cities and some two score castles, or more , and Alexius, the other emperor, his uncle, fled ever before him And the Franks were with Alexius for the space of three full months And in the mean time, the while Alexius was making this incursion, they of Constantinople caused their wall to be built up again, stronger and higher than it was before, for the Franks had caused some fifty fathoms' length thereof to be rased after they had taken the city, because they were afraid lest the Greeks should revolt against them

And when the barons who had tarried behind to receive the payment saw that Isaac was paying them nothing, then sent they word to the other barons that had gone with Alexius, that they should come back, since Isaac was paying them nothing, and that they should all return before the feast of All Saints When the barons heard this, they told the emperor that they would go back, and when the emperor heard that, he said that he too would go back, since they were going, for he durst not trust the Greeks So back came they to Constantinople, and the emperor went away to his palace, and the pilgrims to their lodgings beyond the harbour

LVIII

HOW ALEXIUS AND THE FRANKS FELL OUT ONE WITH THE OTHER

Thereafter came together the counts and the other noblemen and the Doge of Venice and the emperor And the Franks demanded their pay of the emperor, and the emperor answered that he had expended so much in the ransom of his city and his people that he had not wherewithal to pay them, but let them grant him yet another term, and within that space he would provide means whereby to pay them This they granted him, but when the term was past, he paid them nothing And yet once again did the barons demand their pay And again did the emperor ask yet another respite, and it was granted him

In the mean time, his vassals and his people and likewise that Mourzuphles whom he had brought out of prison came to him and said to him

"Ha! Sire, ye have already paid them too much! Pay them nothing more! Ye are now fully ransomed, so much have ye paid them Bid them depart and dismiss them from your land!"

And Alexius listened to this counsel, so would he pay them nothing

And when this term of grace also was past and the Franks perceived that the emperor was paying them nothing, then did all the counts and other noblemen of the host assemble and go to the emperor's palace and demand their pay anew And the emperor answered them that he could not pay them in any wise whatsoever, and the barons answered him that unless he himself paid them, then would they take for themselves so much of what was his that they would be paid

LIX

HOW THE DOGE OF VENICE WENT AND SPAKE WITH ALEXIUS

On these words the barons departed from the palace and returned to their lodgings, and when they were returned they took counsel together what they would do And at last they sent back two knights to the emperor and demanded of him yet again that he send them their pay And he made answer to the messengers that he would pay them nothing, for that he had already paid them too much, and that he was not one whit afeared of them, rather, he commanded them to depart and to quit his land And let them know well that unless they quitted it betimes forsooth, then would he cause them great annoy

Thereupon the messengers went back and made known to the barons what the emperor had answered them The barons, when they hear this, took counsel what they would do, until the Doge of Venice said that he would go and speak to him So he took a messenger and sent word to him that he should come and speak with him above the harbour And the emperor came thither on horseback, but the Doge bade four galleys be manned, and he went on board one of them and bade the three others go with him to guard him And he spake to the emperor and said thus

"Alexius, what thinkest thou to do?" (quoth the Doge) "Mind thyself that we have delivered thee out of a grievous captivity and have made thee lord and crowned thee emperor Wilt thou not hold at all" (asked the Doge) "to our agreement, nor fulfill any more of them?"

"Nay!" quoth the emperor "I will fulfill no more of them than I have fulfilled!"

"Wilt not?" quoth the Doge "Naughty lad! We" (quoth the Doge) "have raised thee off the dunghill, and on the dunghill will we cast thee back again! I disown thee! And know thou of a surety that I will work on thee all the evil that is in my power from this day forward!"

LX

HOW THE GREEKS TRIED TO BURN THE FLEET, AND OF THE GRIEVOUS DEARTH THAT PREVAILED IN THE HOST

On these words the Doge took himself thence and went back Then came together all the counts and all the other noblemen of the host, and the Venetians, for to take counsel what they would do And the Venetians said that they could not possibly make their ladders or their engines on their ships because of the weather, which was too keen (for this was the season betwixt the feast of All Saints and Yule)

In the mean time, whilst they were thus all discouraged, what did the emperor and the traitors that were about him do but contrive a great treachery, for they wished   [63] they seized the ships within the city by night, and they caused them all to be filled with very dry wood, and pieces of swine's fat amongst the wood, then set they fire to them And when it drew nigh unto midnight, and the ships were well ablaze, and the wind was blowing very fresh, then did the Greeks loose the burning ships for to burn the fleet of the Franks, and the wind drave them apace toward the fleet When the Venetians were aware of this, up they sprang and entered their barges and their galleys, and they wrought so well that, by God's grace, their fleet took never a hurt

Nor was more than a fortnight again past, when the Greeks once more did the same thing And when the Venetians were again aware of them, they went yet again against them, and right well did they defend their fleet against this fire, so that never, by God's grace, did they take any harm of it, save one merchant ship which was come thither, this one was burned

And the dearth waxed so great in the host that a firkin of wine sold for twelve shillings, or fourteen shillings, or fifteen shillings[64] at times, and a hen, for twelve shillings, and an egg, for two shillings But of biscuit was there no such dearth, but they had sufficient thereof to maintain their host for a season

---

[63]Four lines are missing from the MS
[64]"*Un sestier de vin xij saus xiiij saus xv saus*" Because of the great variation in the capacity of the *sestier* and the value of the *sol* at different times and places, it is impossible to give any exact English equivalent for these amounts

LXI

HOW THE GREEKS STRENGTHENED THEIR WALLS AND THEIR TOWERS, AND OF THE PLOT THAT MOURZUPHLES MADE TO DESTROY ALEXIUS THAT HE MIGHT HIMSELF BE EMPEROR

In the mean time, whilst they were wintering there, the men of the city fortified themselves right well and caused their wall to be raised again, and their towers, and they caused to be built atop these towers of stone goodly wooden towers, and these wooden towers did they overlay well on the outside with good planks and cover them over with good hides, so that they had no dread of the ladders or ships of the Venetians And the walls were full three score feet in height, and the towers an hundred And they had some two score petraries ranged within the city, from end to end of the walls, in those places where it was thought that assault would be made And it was no great wonder if they accomplished all this, for leisure had they a plenty for it

In the mean time the Greeks (they that were traitors to the emperor) and Mourzuphles, whom the emperor had brought out of prison, came together one day and devised a great treason, for they wished to set up another emperor than this one, who would deliver them from the Franks, since Alexius seemed not good enough to them And at last Mourzuphles said

"If ye" (quoth he) "would trust me, I would so well deliver you from the Franks and from the emperor that ye would never more have dread of them"

And they said that if he could indeed deliver them from these, they would make himself emperor And Mourzuphles promised that he would deliver them within eight days So they agreed that they would make him emperor

LXII

HOW MOURZUPHLES PUT TO DEATH ALEXIUS AND HIS FATHER, AND HOW THE BARONS RECEIVED THE TIDINGS THEREOF, HOW MOURZUPHLES COMMANDED THE PILGRIMS TO DEPART, AND HOW THE PILGRIMS DEFIED HIM

Then went Mourzuphles forth, nor did he forget himself, but took officers with him, and he entered by night into the chamber where his lord the emperor, who had brought him out of prison, was sleeping, and he bade a noose be cast about his neck and caused him to be strangled, and his father Isaac also And when he had done this, back came he to them that should make him emperor, and told them all And they went and crowned him and made him emperor

Now when Mourzuphles was become emperor, the rumour ran throughout the city

"Is it so? Is it not so? Mourzuphles is emperor, and hath murdered his lord!"

Then a letter was shot with an arrow into the host of the pilgrims, which said that Mourzuphles had done thus When the barons knew this, then one said that it were a shame that they should care because Alexius was dead, since he would never hold to his agreements with the pilgrims, but others said that it grieved them that he had died in this manner Thereafter no great time passed ere Mourzuphles sent word to the Count of Flanders, to Count Lewis, to the marquis, and to all the high barons, that they should get them thence and quit his land, and let them know of a surety that he was now emperor, and that he would attack them within eight days and slay them all   When the barons heard this word that Mourzuphles sent them, they answered

"Who?" (asked they) "Hath he who hath treacherously murdered his lord by night sent us such word?"

And they sent back word that now they defied him, and let him be on his guard against them, for never would they abandon the siege until they should have avenged him whom Mourzuphles had murdered, and should have taken Constantinople, and should have full quittance of the agreements that Alexius had made with them

LXIII

OF THE MEASURES OF DEFENCE THAT MOURZUPHLES TOOK

When Mourzuphles heard this he commanded the walls to be right well guarded, and the towers likewise, and that hoardings[65] be placed on them, so that the Greeks should not be in danger from the assaults of the Franks   And these things they did right well, so that the walls and the towers were stronger and more easily defended than before

LXIV

OF JOHN THE WALLACH

It came to pass thereafter, in those days when Mourzuphles the traitor was emperor, and the host of the Franks was so poor, as I have recounted to you before, and whilst they were diligently making ready their ships and their engines for the assault, that John the Wallach[66] sent word to the high barons of the host that if they would crown him king, to be lord over his land of Wallachia,[67] he would hold his kingdom from them, and would come to their aid to help take Constantinople, with an hundred thousand men at arms

Now Wallachia is a land that belongeth to the emperor's domains, and this John was a groom of the emperor, who kept one of the emperor's studs, so that whensoever the emperor sent for three score horses, or an hundred, this John sent them to him   And he himself came every year to court, ere yet he fell out of favour at the court   But at last it chanced one day that he came thither and that a certain eunuch, one of the emperor's doorkeepers, did an unseemly thing to him, for he smote him with a scourge full in the face whereof he suffered great pain

---

[65]Covered structures of timber, placed on the tops of walls and towers to afford additional protection to the defenders

[66]*"Jehans li Blakis"* elsewhere called Johannitsa (Johannizza) and Kalo-Jan

[67]"The Wallachian kingdom [comprised] Bulgaria, Roumania, and a part of what was Roumelia   Johannitsa, the ruling tsar, had inherited the anti-Byzantine traditions of the first Bulgarian empire." *Cambridge Medieval History*, vi, 31

And because of this unseemly thing that was done to him, John the Wallach departed in high dudgeon from the court and went back to Wallachia And Wallachia is a mighty land that is all compassed about by mountains, so that one can neither enter it nor come out thence save by one single pass

LXV

HOW JOHN THE WALLACH MADE HIMSELF MASTER OF HIS PEOPLE AND WON THE FRIENDSHIP OF THE COMANS, OF THE CUSTOMS OF THE COMANS, AND HOW JOHN THE WALLACH RECEIVED HIS CROWN FROM ROME

When John was come thither, then began he to draw to himself the notable men of Wallachia, as one who was a rich man and had some power, and he began to make promises and gifts to one and to another, and thus did he, until all they of that country were subject to him and he was become lord over them And when he was become their lord, then did he turn to the Comans,[68] and so wrought he, by one means and by another, that he became their friend and they were all in his service and he was become, as it were, their liege lord

Now Comania is a land which bordereth on Wallachia, and I will tell you what manner of people these Comans are They are savage folk, who plough not, neither do they sow, nor have they hut nor house, but they have tents of felt, in which habitations they hide themselves, and they live on milk and cheese and flesh And in summer time are so many flies and gnats there that they scarce venture themselves forth of their tents ere the winter But in winter they come forth of their tents and of their country, when they desire to make their forays And we will tell you what they do Every one of them hath some ten horses, or twelve, and these have they so trained that the beasts follow them whithersoever they wish to lead them, and they mount now one, now another And every one of these horses, when they are journeying, hath a little sack hanging at its muzzle wherein is its fodder, and it eateth the while it followeth its master, nor do they break their journey by night or by day And so swiftly do they travel that in one night and one day they go six common day's journeys, or seven, or eight Nor ever, so long as they are going, do they burden themselves with anything or take aught before they begin to return But when they begin to return, then do they gather booty, and seize men, and take all whereon they can lay their hands Nor ever will they go otherwise armed save that they wear garments of sheepskin and carry bows and arrows with thm Nor put they any trust in any thing save in the first beast that they meet in the morning, and he that meeteth the beast putteth his trust in it all that day, whatsoever beast it be

These Comans did John the Wallach have in his service, and he came every year to ravage the lands of the emperor, even so far as Constantinople itself Nor had the emperor power enough so that he could defend himself against him

Now when the barons of the host had heard the word that John the Wallach sent them, they said that they would take counsel in the matter And when they

---

[68]The Comans, Cumans, or Kumani were a Ugric tribe which invaded Hungary and Bulgaria in the 11th century

had taken counsel (and in sooth it was an evil counsel!), they answered that neither with him nor with his help had they any concern, and let him know of a surety that they would trouble him and work him evil if they could But for all this did he make them pay right dear thereafter! And this was a sore shame and grievous pity

But when he had failed of his purpose with them, then did he send to Rome for his crown, and the Pontiff sent a cardinal for to crown him Thus was he crowned king

---

LXVI

OF THE ADVENTURES THAT BEFELL MY LORD HENRY OF ANGRE, HOW HE OVERCAME MOURZUPHLES, AND HOW THE ICON WAS LOST

Now will we tell you of another adventure which befell my Lord Henry, the brother of the Count of Flanders During that time when the Franks had laid siege to Constantinople, it chanced that my lord Henry—both he and they of his company—were by no means very rich Nay, they had great lack of victuals and of other things, until they were put in mind of a city called Philae, which lay at ten leagues' distance from the host This city was very rich and very opulent, so what did my lord Henry do but make ready for the road and depart from the host with nine and twenty knights and serjeants of horse not a few, going privily by night so that scarce any of the folk knew thereof When he came to the city he did what he was come to do, and he tarried there one day But in the mean time, when he went thither, he was spied upon and report of him was borne to Mourzuphles When Mourzuphles knew this he bade as many as four thousand men at arms take horse, and he took with him the Icon—an image of Our Lady which the Greeks call by that name—which the emperors take with them whensoever they go forth to battle And so great confidence have they in this Icon that they verily believe that no one who carrieth it into battle can be beaten (and because Mourzuphles did not carry it rightfully, we believe, was he discomfited)

And the Franks had already sent their booty to the host And Mourzuphles waited for them on their return, and when he was come within a league of our people he lay in wait with his folk and laid his ambushments And our people knew not a word of this, but they were returning apace, nor knew they aught of this snare When the Greeks saw them, they cried out, and our Franks looked one at another When they saw the Greeks they were sore afraid, and loudly did they begin to call on God and Our Lady, and they were so dismayed that they knew not what counsel to take but said one to another

"By our faith! If we flee now we are all dead men, better doth it become us to die defending ourselves than to flee "

Then they halted and stood still And they took some eight crossbowmen that they had with them and set these before themselves And the Emperor Mourzuphles, the traitor, and the Greeks came toward them very swiftly and smote them fierce and fell, but, through God's mercy, never a one of the Franks did they unhorse

When the Franks saw the Greeks thus rushing upon them from every side, they let fall their lances and drew the knives and daggers that they had and began to defend themselves right hardily, and they slew many of them And when the Greeks saw that the Franks were discomfiting them thus, they began to be discouraged and turned about and fled But our Franks overtook them and slew many of them, and many they kept for ransom—and great gain gat they thereby

And they chased the Emperor Mourzuphles more than half a league, for they ever thought to take him, but he and they of his company hasted so that they let fall the Icon, and his imperial cloak, and the ensign with the Icon, which was all of gold and set with rich and precious stones, and it was so beautiful and rich that never was aught else seen so beautiful and rich When the Franks saw this they left off the chase, and were most exceeding glad, and they took the image and bare it away with very great joy and rejoicing

And in the mean time, whilst they were yet fighting, came tidings to the host that they were contending with the Greeks, and when they of the host heard these tidings they hastened away toward my lord Henry for to succour him But when they came thither, the Greeks were already fled and our Franks were bringing in their spoils and were bearing along the Icon, which was so beautiful and rich, as I have told you And when they drew near to the host, then did the bishops and the clerks who were in the host go forth in procession to meet them, and they received the Icon with great joy and rejoicing, and it was put in the keeping of the Bishop of Troyes And the bishop bare it into the midst of the host, to a church whither they were wont to repair, and the bishops sang and made great rejoicing over it And after that day on which it was taken, the barons all agreed that it should be given to Cîteaux,[69] and thereafter wast it carried thither

But when Mourzuphles came back to Constantinople he gave out that he had routed and discomfited my lord Henry and his people, but certain of the Greeks enquired, all unwittingly

"Where is the Icon? And the ensign?"

But others said that these had been put away in a safe place

And so did the rumours go back and forth, until the Franks learned how Mourzuphles had in this wise caused it to be believed that he had discomfited the Franks And what did the Franks do then but arm a galley, and take the Icon and lift it very high up in the galley, and the ensign of the empire also, and row this galley, with the Icon and the ensign, from end to end of the walls, so that they that stood upon the walls, and many other folk of the city, saw it and perceived clearly that these were the emperor's ensign and his Icon

---

[69]The birthplace of the Cistercian order

LXVII

OF THE WRATH OF THE GREEKS AT THE LOSS OF THE ICON, AND HOW MOURZUPHLES PROMISED TO RECOVER IT

When the Greeks saw this, then came they to Mourzuphles and began to cry shame upon him and sorely to upbraid him because he had lost the ensign of the empire and the Icon, and because he had made them to believe that he had discomfited the Franks And when Mourzuphles heard this he excused himself as best he could and began to say

"Now be ye not at all dismayed, for I shall make them to pay right dear, and well will I avenge myself of them!"

LXVIII

OF THE PLAN WHICH THE PILGRIMS AND THE VENETIANS DEVISED FOR THE CHOOSING OF AN EMPEROR AND A PATRIARCH, FOR THE JUST DIVISION OF THEIR CONQUESTS, AND FOR THE MAINTAINING OF ORDER

Thereafter it came to pass that all the Franks and all the Venetians came together for to take counsel how they should proceed, and what they should do, and whom they might make emperor if they should take the city, until they agreed amongst themselves that they would take ten Franks, of the most worthy men of the host, and ten Venetians, likewise of the most worthy men that were known among them, and that whatsoever these twenty should decide, that should be observed with the understanding that if the emperor were one of the Franks the patriarch should be one of the Venetians And it was decreed that he who should be emperor should have the fourth part of the empire and the fourth part of the city in his demesne, and that the other three parts should so be apportioned that the Venetians should have the one-half thereof and the pilgrims the other, and that all should be held from the emperor

When they had resolved all this, then they caused all the men of the host to swear on holy relics that all the booty of gold and of silver and of new cloth, of the value of five shillings or more, they would deliver to the host for just apportioning, save only tools and victuals, and that they would do no violence to a woman nor despoil her of any cloth that she wore, for whosoever should be convicted of this would be put to death And they made them swear on holy relics that they would not lay hand on monk, nor clerk, nor priest, save only it were to defend themselves, nor would they break into any church or minster

LXIX

HOW THE FRANKS AND THE VENETIANS REPAIRED AND EQUIPPED THEIR FLEET

Thereafter, when all this had been done, and when Yuletide was already past and the beginning of Lent was nigh, then did both the Franks and the Venetians repair and put in order again their ships, and the Venetians caused the bridges of their ships to be rebuilt, and the Franks caused certain other engines to be built,

which were called "cats"[70] and "carcasses,"[71] and "sows"[72] for sapping the walls
And the Venetians took timber from the houses and covered their ships therewith, joining the planks together and then covering them with vine-cuttings, so
that the petraries could not break or shatter their ships

And the Greeks strongly reinforced their city within, and without, they
caused the bretesses,[73] which were on the top of the towers of stone, to be covered over with good hides, nor was there a bretesse that had not seven storeys,
or six, or five at the least

LXX

HOW THEY MADE READY TO ASSAULT THE CITY

Thereafter it came to pass upon a Friday, about ten days before Palm Sunday, that the pilgrims and the Venetians had prepared their ships and their engines and made ready for the assault And they ranged their ships one alongside
another, and the Franks caused their engines to be put on board barges and galleys and set on their way to go toward the city, and the fleet stretched over a full
league of front And all the pilgrims and the Venetians were fully armed

And there was a hillock within the city, in that part where the assault was to
be made, which could easily be seen from the ships over the top of the walls, so
high was it And to this hillock was Mourzuphles the traitor come, the emperor,
and some of his people with him And he had bid them pitch there his scarlet
tents, and he caused his silver trumpets to be sounded, and his timbrels, and made
great ostentation, so that the pilgrims could easily see him, and Mourzuphles
could easily look down into the ships of the pilgrims

LXXI

OF THE UNSUCCESSFUL BEGINNING OF THE ASSAULT, AND OF
THE BOASTING OF MOURZUPHLES

When the fleet must needs come to land, then took they goodly cables and
drew up their ships so nigh as they could to the walls And the Franks caused
their engines to be trained—their cats, their carcasses, and the sows for sapping
the walls—and the Venetians went up on the bridges of their ships and violently
stormed the walls, and the Franks likewise attacked them with their engines
When the Greeks saw that the Franks were thus assailing them, then they made
haste to hurl huge bolts at the engines of the Franks, and they began to break and
to crush and to shatter all these engines, so that never a man durst remain within
or beneath these engines, nor could the Venetians, on the other hand, reach the
walls or the towers, so lofty were they Nor ever, on that day, were Venetians
or Franks able to do any mischief either to the walls or to the city

---

[70]Heavy timber frames, with projecting teeth, to be hoisted up and dropped on assailants
[71]*Carchloies* (?), probably for *carchois* or *charchois*, dialectic forms of Old French
carquois, "carcasses," perforated iron shells or vessels, filled with combustibles
[72]*Truis*, probably for *truies*, "sows," movable sheds which protected men undermining
a wall
[73]Wooden towers, crenelated and loopholed

When they saw that they could do them no hurt, then were they very sad and withdrew themselves And when the Greeks saw them drawing back, then began they to hoot and to shout right lustily, and they went up upon the walls and let down their breeches and shewed them their buttocks

When Mourzuphles saw that the pilgrims had turned back, then he made haste to sound his trumpets and his timbrels and to make as great a shew as he could, and he summoned his people and began to say

"Behold, sirs Am I not a good emperor? Never yet have ye had an emperor so good! Have I not done well? Now have we no more cause for concern, I will cause them all to be hanged and put to shame"

LXXII

HOW THE BISHOPS ASSURED THE PILGRIMS YET AGAIN THAT IT WAS A WORK OF MERIT TO FIGHT THE GREEKS

When the pilgrims saw these things they were sore distressed and exceeding sad, and they went back to their lodgings on the other side of the harbour And when the barons were come back and had disembarked from their ships, then they gathered together, and they were much cast down and said that it was because of their sin that they had been able to do nothing nor had wrought any mischief on the city But at last the bishops and the clerks of the host spake together and adjudged that the battle was a righteous one, and that they ought in sooth to attack the Greeks, for in olden time they of the city had been obedient to the religion of Rome, but now were they disobedient thereto, since they said that the religion of Rome was of none account, and that all they who believed in it were dogs And the bishops said that for this reason the Greeks ought to be attacked, and that this was no sin, but rather was it a good work and of great merit

LXXIII

HOW SERMONS WERE PREACHED THROUGHOUT THE HOST, AND HOW THE EVIL WOMEN WERE DRIVEN OUT

Then was it cried throughout the host that all should come to the sermons—both Venetians and all and sundry—on Sunday, in the morning And so did they Then did the bishops preach sermons throughout the host—the Bishop of Soissons, the Bishop of Troyes, the Bishop of Halberstadt, Master John Faicete, and the Abbot of Loos—and they shewed the pilgrims that the battle was a righteous one, for that the Greeks were traitors and murderers, and that they were faithless, since they had murdered their lawful lord, and that they were worse than Jews And the bishops said that they absolved, in the name of God and of the Pontiff, all those that should attack the Greeks And the bishops commanded the pilgrims all to confess themselves and freely to partake of the sacrament, and let them not be at all afraid to attack the Greeks, for these were God's enemies And an order was given that they should seek out and remove all the light women from the host, and send them very far away from the host, so they caused all these to be put into a ship and sent away, far from the host

LXXIV

OF THE CONTINUATION OF THE FIGHTING, AND OF THE VALIANT DEEDS OF ANDREW OF URBOISE AND PETER OF BRACHEUX

Thereafter, when the bishops had preached and had shewn the pilgrims that the battle was a righteous one, then did all freely confess themselves and receive the sacrament And when Monday morning came, then did all the pilgrims array themselves right well and arm themselves, and the Venetians also, and they mended the bridges of their ships and their transports and their galleys, and they ranged these side by side and set out to go forward and attack the city And the fleet had a front a full league in length And when they were come to land and had drawn as nigh to the walls as they could, they cast anchor And when they were at anchor they began to attack fiercely and to discharge arrows and hurl missiles and to throw Greek fire at the towers But the fire could not take hold there because of the hides wherewith the towers were covered And those within the city were defending themselves right sturdily and were discharging some three score petraries, and at every discharge they were hurling stones upon the ships, but the ships were so well covered with timber and with vine-cuttings that these did them no great mischief, though the stones were so large that one man could not lift one from the ground

And Mourzuphles the traitor was standing on his hillock and causing his trumpets to sound, and his timbrels, and making great display, and he was encouraging his men and saying, "Go thither! Come hither!" and sending them wheresoever he saw that the need was the greatest And there were not in all the fleet above four or five ships that could reach the towers, so high were these And every storey of the wooden towers that were built above the towers of stone, of which there were some five or six or seven, was also garrisoned with men at arms who were defending the towers

And so did they continue the assault, until the ship of the Bishop of Soissons fell foul of one of these towers by a miracle of God, even as the sea, which is never quiet, bare it on And on the bridge of the ship were a Venetian and two armed knights And so soon as the ship hath fallen foul of this tower, the Venetian layeth hold with hands and feet, as best he can, and getteth himself at last within the tower When he was within, and when the men at arms who were in this storey—English, Danes, and Greeks, who were keeping guard there—when these espied him, then rushed they upon him with axes and swords and cut him all in pieces And as the sea bare the ship forward again, again did she fall foul of the tower, and when she was thus afoul of it, what did one of the two knights do—Andrew of Dureboise was his name—but lay hold with feet and hands to the tower until he gat himself up inside it, upon his knees But when he was inside, upon his knees, the foe fell upon him with axes and with swords and smote him sore, but since he wore his armour, thanks be to God, they wounded him not, for so was God guarding him, who would not consent that the Greeks should longer endure or that this man should die Nay, rather, it was God's will, because of their treason and because of the murder that Mourzuphles had committed and because of their faithlessness, that the city should be taken and that they should all be put to shame For the knight rose up on his feet, and when he was on his feet he drew his sword When these saw him on his feet again, so dumfounded were they, and so greatly afeared, that they fled thence into the other storey underneath And when they that were in this other storey saw that those from above them were fleeing, then did they quit this storey also, nor ever durst they remain there any longer

And the other knight came in after the first, and after him came in folk a plenty And when they were within, they took strong ropes and stoutly lashed that ship to the tower, and when they had made her fast, there came in yet other folk a plenty But when the sea again bare the ship backward, then did the tower quake so violently that it seemed certain that the ship must pull it down, so that perforce, because of this fear, it behooved them to cut the ship adrift

And when they that were in the other storeys beneath saw that the tower was filling with Franks, then were they so greatly afeared that never a one of them durst remain there, but they forsook the whole tower And Mourzuphles indeed saw all this, but he encouraged his people and sent them thither where he saw that the chiefest assault was made

In the mean time, when this tower had been taken by such a miracle, the ship of my Lord Peter of Bracheux fell afoul of another tower, and when it had fallen foul thereof, then began they that were upon the bridge of the ship to storm this tower so exceeding fiercely that, by a miracle of God, this tower also was taken

LXXV

OF THE DEEDS OF PROWESS THAT WERE PERFORMED BY MY LORD PETER OF AMIENS

When these two towers had been taken, then were they garrisoned with our own men, and these remained in the towers, nor durst they remove thence because of the great multitude of folk that they saw on the wall round about them and inside the other towers and below the walls, which was a fair marvel, so many were there of them

When my Lord Peter of Amiens saw that they that were within the towers moved not themselves, and when he perceived the purpose of the Greeks, what did he do but come down on foot to the land—he and his people with him—in a little space of ground that lay betwixt the sea and the wall When they were come down thither, they looked before them and espied a false postern gate, the doors whereof had been taken away and the gateway itself walled up anew And thither he came, having with him some ten knights and three score men at arms And there was a certain clerk, Aleaume of Clari by name, who was a right good man in all times of need and was ever the first in all the assaults wherein he was engaged And at the taking of the Tower of Galata had this clerk performed more deeds of prowess with his own body, one by one, than had all others of the host save only my Lord Peter of Bracheux For he it was that outdid all others, of both high and low degree, for never was there one among them that wrought so many deeds of arms or acts of prowess as did Peter of Bracheux

Now when they were come to this postern gate they began to hack away at it right valiantly, but so thick flew the bolts and so many were the stones hurled down from the walls that it seemed in all likelihood they would be buried in the stones, so many were there cast at them And they that were below had shields and targes wherewith they covered those that were hacking at the postern gate And from above were cast down upon them pots of boiling pitch, and Greek fire, and very great stones, so that it was a miracle of God that they were not all destroyed, so many hardships did my Lord Peter and his people suffer there, and such multitude of grievous perils Yet did they hack away at that postern gate with axes and good swords, with timbers and bars and picks, until at last they made a great breach therein And when this postern was pierced through, then looked they through it and saw so many folk, both of high and of low estate, that it seemed that half the world were there, wherefore they durst not venture to enter there

LXXVI

OF THE VERY VALIANT DEED OF ALEAUME THE CLERK

But when Aleaume the Clerk saw that none durst enter there, he sprang forward and said that he would go in Now there was present a knight, his brother, Robert of Clari by name, who forbade him and said that he should by no means go in And the clerk said that he would do so, and he gat himself in on his hands and feet And when his brother saw this, he took him by the foot and began to drag him toward himself, but at last, despite his brother, whether his brother would or would not, the clerk went in And when he was within, a multitude of the Greeks fell upon him, and they that were upon the walls began to cast down great stones at him When the clerk saw this, he drew his knife and rushed upon them and made them to flee before him like cattle

Then cried he to them that were without, to my Lord Peter and his people

"Sirs, enter boldly! For I see that they are utterly confounded and are fleeing away"

When my Lord Peter heard this—he and his people, who were without— then did my Lord Peter and his people come in And there were not more than nine knights with him, nevertheless, there were some three score men at arms with him, and they were all on foot inside the walls

And when they were within and they that were standing upon the walls in that place beheld them, then were these so greatly terrified that they durst not tarry in that place, but abandoned a great portion of the wall and fled, every man for himself

And the Emperor Mourzuphles, the traitor, was very near at hand, less than a stone's throw away, and he caused his silver trumpets to sound, and his timbrels, and made an exceeding great noise

LXXVII

HOW MY LORD PETER ENCOURAGED HIS MEN

And when Mourzuphles saw my Lord Peter and his people, who were on foot within the city, then he made a great pretence of falling upon them and of spurring his horse, and he came about half-way up to them When my Lord Peter saw him coming, he began to hearten his people and to say

"Now, sirs, let us acquit ourselves well! Then shall we already have won the battle Lo, yonder cometh the emperor! See to it that there be not one that dareth to draw back, but bethink you now to acquit yourselves well!"

LXXVIII

HOW CONSTANTINOPLE WAS TAKEN

When Mourzuphles the traitor saw that they would in no wise flee, he halted, and then he turned back to his tents And when my Lord Peter saw that the emperor had turned back, he sent a troop of his men at arms to a gate that stood hard by and commanded it to be broken in pieces and opened And these men went and began to beat and to drive in this gate with axes and with swords until they brake the iron bolts, which were very strong, and the bars, and opened the gate And when the gate was opened and they that were without saw this, then they brought up their transports and led forth their horses and mounted them, and they began to ride apace into the city through the midst of the gate And when the Emperor Mourzuphles, the traitor, saw them, then had he so great fear that he left his tents, and his jewels in them, and fled forth into the city, which was very great, and long, and broad For they say there that the circuit of the walls covereth full nine leagues, so great a compass have the walls that surround the city, and within hath the city a length of two French leagues and a breadth of two And so did my Lord Peter of Bracheux get Mourzuphles' tents and his coffers and his jewels that he left behind

Now when they who were defending the walls saw that the Franks were entered into the city and that the emperor had fled, they durst tarry no longer but fled away, every man for himself

When the city had been taken in this manner and when the Franks were therein, they all remained quiet Then did the high barons come together and take counsel amongst themselves what they should do, until they let it be cried throughout the host that none should be so foolhardy as to venture into the city, for there was danger in going thither that stones would be cast down upon them from the palaces, which were very great and high, or that they would be slain in the streets, which were so exceeding narrow that they could not defend themselves therein, or that fire would be hurled down on their backs and they would be burned And because of such hazards and perils they durst not set foot therein nor scatter themselves about, rather, they all remained quiet where they were And the barons agreed upon this plan that if the Greeks desired to fight on the morrow (who numbered an hundred times as many men able to bear arms as did the Franks), then would they arm themselves on the morrow morn, and order their battalions, and await them in certain squares which lay open before them in the city, but if these desired not to fight, yet would not yield up the city, then would the Franks observe from which quarter the wind was blowing, and would hurl fire adown the wind, and so burn them Thus would they take them by force To this plan did all the barons agree

And when eventide was come, the pilgrims laid aside their armour, and reposed themselves, and supped, and they lay there that night before their fleet and within the walls

LXXIX

HOW MOURZUPHLES FLED FROM CONSTANTINOPLE, HOW LASCARIS WAS MADE EMPEROR AND FLED LIKEWISE

But when it drew near to midnight and the Emperor Mourzuphles, the traitor, knew that all the Franks were in the city, then had he great fear nor durst he tarry there any longer, but he fled away at midnight or ever one knew a word thereof When the Greeks saw that their emperor had fled away, then they pitched upon a certain nobleman of the city, Lascaris by name, straightway that selfsame night, and made him emperor And when he was made emperor he durst not remain there, but he gat himself on board a galley ere it was yet day and crossed over beyond the Strait of Saint George and went on to Nicaea[74] the Great, which is a goodly city There did he abide, and he was lord thereof and emperor

LXXX

HOW THE MEN OF THE CROSS TOOK UP THEIR ABODE IN CONSTANTINOPLE

But when came the morrow, early in the morning, lo, priests and clerks in all their vestments—English and Danes were they, and folk of other nations—came forth in procession to the host of the Franks, and cried them mercy, and let them know all things that the Greeks had done And they said that all the Greeks had fled away and none remained in the city save only poor folk When the Franks heard this they were all rejoiced thereat, and immediately thereafter they caused it to be cried throughout the host that none should take up his abode there until it should have been decided in what manner they would take them Then came together the noblemen, the rich men, and took counsel amongst themselves (and neither the lowly folk of the host nor the poor knights wist a word thereof) how they might take the best habitations of the city And straightway began they to deal treacherously with the lowly folk and to shew them bad faith and ill comradeship—for which they paid thereafter right dear, as we will tell you presently [75] So did they send and seize all the best habitations and the richest ones of the city, so that they had already seized all these or ever the poor knights or the lowly folk of the host were aware thereof And when the poor folk were made aware

---

[74]In Bithynia
[75]See end of Chapter CXII

thereof, they went then, every man for himself, and took whatsoever they chanced upon, for places enough did they find there, and places a many did they take, and many yet remained, for the city was very great and abundantly peopled

And the marquis took the Palace of the Lion's Mouth,[76] and the Minster of Saint Sophia, and the houses of the Patriarch, and the other noblemen, like the counts, took the richest palaces and the richest abbeys that could be found there, howbeit, after the city was taken no mischief was done to poor or to rich Nay, he departed who desired to depart, and who so desired, remained, but the richest men departed from the city

LXXXI

OF THE DIVISION OF THE SPOIL

Thereafter, a command went forth that all the substance of the body be brought to a certain abbey which was within the city Thither was the substance brought, and they chose ten noble knights from amongst the pilgrims, and ten Venetians who were reputed to be honourable men, and set them to guard this substance And when the booty was brought thither, which was so rich and contained such wealth of gold and of silver and of cloth of gold, and so many rich jewels, that it was a fair marvel to behold the great riches that had been brought thither—then, never since the world was established was so great wealth, or so noble, or so magnificent, either seen or won—no, not in the days of Alexander, or of Charles the Great, or before, or after. Nor do I believe, of my own knowledge, that in the fifty richest cities of the world could there be so much wealth as was found in the body of Constantinople For the Greeks also bore witness that two-thirds of all the wealth of the world was in Constantinople, and that the other third was scattered throughout the world

But those selfsame ones who ought to have guarded this wealth took the jewels of gold and whatsoever else they desired, and robbed the spoil And of the rich men did every one take either jewels of gold, or silken cloth of gold, or whatsoever liked him best, and carried them away In this wise did they begin to steal the treasure, so that no division thereof was ever made amongst the commonalty of the host, nor amongst the poor knights, nor amongst the men at arms, who had all helped to win it—save only of the coarser silver, such as silver ewers that the ladies of the city carried to the baths But all the rest of the treasure which remained to divide was carried away in such base fashion as I have told you, nevertheless, the Venetians had their half thereof So the precious stones, and all the greater treasure which remained to divide, went such base ways as we shall presently describe to you

---

[76]*"Bouke de Lion,"* "Lion's Mouth," the French soldiers' interpretation of the Greek name Bucoleon (Βουκολέων)

LXXXII

OF THE MARVELS OF CONSTANTINOPLE OF THE PALACE OF THE LION'S MOUTH

When the city was taken and the pilgrims had lodged themselves, even as I have told you, and when the palaces were taken, then were there found in these palaces riches without number And how rich was the Palace of the Lion's Mouth,[77] and how builded, I will tell you now There were, forsooth, within this palace (which the marquis now held) five hundred chambers, which were all joined one to another; and they were all wrought in mosaic work of gold. Moreover, there were full thirty chapels there, both large and small, and there was one of these which was called the Holy Chapel, that was so rich and so noble that it contained neither hinge nor socket, nor any other appurtenance such as is wont to be wrought of iron, that was not all of silver, nor was there a pillar there that was not of jasper or porphyry or such like rich and precious stone And the pavement of the chapel was of white marble, so smooth and so clear that it seemed that it was of crystal And this chapel was so rich that one could not describe to you the great beauty and the great magnificence thereof Within this chapel were found many precious relics, for therein were found two pieces of the True Cross, as thick as a man's leg and a fathom in length And there was found the lance wherewith Our Lord had His side pierced, and the two nails that were driven through the midst of His hands and through the midst of His feet And there was also found, in a crystal phial, a great part of His blood And there was found the tunic that He wore, which was stripped from Him when He had been led to the Mount of Calvary And there, too, was found the blessed crown wherewith He was crowned, which was wrought of sea rushes, sharp as dagger blades There also was found the raiment of Our Lady, and the head of my Lord Saint John Baptist, and so many other precious relics that I could never describe them to you or tell you the truth concerning them

LXXXIII

OF THE PALACE OF BLACHERNAE

Now there were yet other holy relics in this chapel, of which we had forgotten to tell you For there were two rich vessels of gold which hung in the midst of the chapel by two great chains of silver, and in the one of these vessels was a tile, and in the other a towel And we will tell you whence these relics had come

There lived of yore, in Constantinople, a certain holy man And it chanced that this holy man was mending with tiles the roof of a widow woman's house, for the love of God And as he was mending it, lo, Our Lord appeared to him and spake to him, and the good man had a towel girt about him

"Give thither," said Our Lord, "that towel"

And the good man yielded it to Him And Our Lord wrapped His own face therein, so that the likeness thereof was imprinted upon the towel; then gave He

---
[77]Bucoleon

it back to him And He told him that he should carry it away, and lay it on sick
folk, and that whosoever had faith therein, he would be cleansed of his sickness
And the good man took it and carried it away But before he carried it away,
when God had given his towel back to him, the good man took it and hid it under
a tile until the evening In the evening, when he went thence, he took the towel,
but as he lifted up the tile, he saw the likeness imprinted upon the tile also, even
as upon the towel And he carried away both the tile and the towel, and thereafter were many sick folk healed by them And these relics hung in the midst of
the chapel, even as I have told you

Now there was also in this chapel another holy relic, for there was to be
seen therein a likeness of Saint Demetrius, which was painted upon a board This
likeness gave forth so much oil that it was not possible to remove all the oil that
flowed ever downward from this picture

And there were some twenty of these chapels, and there were some two hundred chambers, or three hundred,[78] which all adjoined one to another, and they
were all wrought in mosaic of gold And this palace was so rich and so magnificent that one could not describe or relate to you the magnificence and richness
thereof

And in the palace of Blachernae also was very great treasure found, and
very rich For here were found the rich crowns that belonged to the emperors
who dwelt there aforetime, and their rich jewels of gold, and their rich raiment of
silken cloth, and their rich imperial robes, and rich and precious stones, and other
riches so great that one could not number the great treasure of gold and of silver
that was found in the palaces and in many places elsewhere in the city

LXXXIV

HOW THE PILGRIMS MARVELED AT THE WONDERS OF THE CITY

Then did the pilgrims gaze upon the greatness of the city, and the palaces,
and the rich abbeys, and the rich minsters, and the great wonders that were in the
city, and they marveled very greatly thereat, and much did they marvel at the
Minster of Saint Sophia and at the riches that were there

LXXXV

OF THE MINSTER OF SAINT SOPHIA

Now will I tell you of the Minster of Saint Sophia, how it was built (Saint
Sophia, in Greek, signifieth Holy Trinity in our own tongue) [79] The Minster of
Saint Sophia was altogether round And there were on the inside of the min-

---

[78]Once more, Robert's figures are open to question In the preceding chapter he spoke of
thirty chapels and *five hundred* chambers It is possible, of course, that the amanuensis or
transcriber, using Roman numerals, may have made a slip in one case or the other
[79]Robert's ignorance of the Greek language has already been shown in his rendering of
the name Bucoleon (see Chapter LXXX and footnote) But in an age when even churchmen
were unacquainted with Greek, such ignorance is not surprising It is doubtful whether the
author's brother, Aleaume, "Clerk," would have come any nearer to the correct translation,
"Holy Wisdom"

ster, all round about, arches which were borne up by great pillars—very rich pillars, for there was not a pillar that was not either of jasper, or of porphyry, or of other rich and precious stones, nor was there one of these pillars that had not some virture of healing For one there was that healed a man of the disease of the reins[80] when he rubbed himself against it, and one that healed folk of the disease of the side,[81] and some that healed them of other diseases. Nor was there any door of this minster, or hinge, or socket, or other furnishing such as is wont to be made of iron, that was not all of silver And the high altar of this minster was so rich that the price thereof could not be reckoned, for the table which lay upon the altar was of gold, and of precious stones all squared and ground, and all fast joined together, which a certain rich emperor caused to be made And this table was full fourteen feet in length, and about the altar were pillars of silver, which upheld a canopy above the altar, made like to a bell-tower, and all of massive silver And so rich was it that one could not reckon the price that it was worth

And the place where the Gospel was read was so rich and so magnificent that we could not describe to you how it was made Then, adown the minster hung full an hundred lustres,[82] nor was there a lustre that hung not by a great chain of silver, as thick as a man's arm, and in each lustre were some five and twenty lamps, or more, nor was there a lustre that was not worth full two hundred silver marks

By the socket of the great door of the minster, which was all of silver, there hung a tube—of what alloy wrought, no man knoweth—and it was of the size of one of those pipes such as shepherds pipe upon That tube had this virtue, of which I will tell you When a sick man who had some disease within his body— as some swelling whereof his belly was swollen within—when such an one put the tube to his mouth, then this tube would lay hold on him, and would suck out all that disease from him, and would make the poison thereof to run out through his throat And it kept such fast hold on him that it made his eyes to roll and to turn in his head, nor could he release himself therefrom or ever the tube had sucked all that disease clean out of him Nevertheless, albeit he that was sickest was longest held by the tube, when a man who was not sick at all put it to his mouth, it held him in no wise whatsoever

LXXXVI

OF THE GREAT PILLAR THAT WAS BEFORE THE MINSTER OF SAINT SOPHIA AND THE STATUE OF AN EMPEROR THAT STOOD THEREON

Furthermore, in front of the Minster of Saint Sophia there was a thick pillar, having in sooth a thickness of thrice the spread of a man's arms, and it was full fifty fathoms high And it was made of marble, and then of copper laid over the marble, and it was very stoutly bound with goodly bands of iron And above, on the top of this pillar, was a stone some fifteen feet long and as many wide And upon this stone stood an emperor,[83] cast in copper, on a great copper horse, who

---

[80]Nephritis (?)
[81]Pleurisy (?)
[82]Branched candelabra or chandeliers
[83]The Emperor Justinian
"And before that Chirche is the Ymage of Justynyan the Emperour, covered with Gold"
Sir John Mandeville, *Travels*, I

was stretching out his hand toward Heathendom [84] And there were letters graven upon him, which said that he was swearing an oath that the Saracens should never have rest or respite from him And in the other hand[85] he held a golden apple, and on the apple, a cross And the Greeks said that this was the Emperor Heraclius [86] Furthermore, both on the horse's croup, and on its head, and round about it, were ten aeries of herons, which nested there every year

LXXXVII .

OF THE CHURCH OF THE SEVEN APOSTLES

Furthermore, in another part of the city was another minster, which was called the Minster of the Seven Apostles And it was said that this minster was yet richer and more magnificent than the Minster of Saint Sophia, and so great riches and such magnificence were therein that one could in no wise describe the half of the richness and magnificence of this minster And there lay within this minster the bodies of seven apostles, and therein also stood the pillar whereto Our Lord was bound or ever He was put upon the cross And it was said that there also lay the Emperor Constantine, and Helena,[87] and other emperors a many

LXXXVIII

OF THE GATE OF THE GOLDEN MANTLE

Now in another part of the city was a gate which was called the Golden Mantle Above this gate was a golden ball, which was made by enchantment, for the Greeks said that never, so long as this ball should remain there, would thunderbolts fall within the city And over and above the ball was an image cast in copper, which had a golden mantle wrapped about it, and it leaned forward upon one arm, and there were letters graven upon it, which said

"All they" (so spake the image) "that tarry in Constantinople for one year ought to have a mantle of gold, even as I have"

LXXXIX

OF THE GOLDEN GATE

In yet another part of the city is another gate, called the Golden Gate Above this gate were two elephants, cast in copper, which were so huge that it was a fair marvel to behold them This gate was never opened, save when the emperor returned from battle after he had conquered some land And whenever he thus returned from battle, having conquered some land, then came forth the clergy of the city in procession to meet the emperor, and the gate was opened, and a chariot was brought, which was made like to a four-wheeled waggon and was called a triumphal chariot And in the midst of this chariot was a high dais, and on the dais

[84]*"Paienisme,"* the lands of the heathen, as opposed to *Crestienté,* Christendom
[85]I e, the one not raised in asseveration
[86]Emperor of the East 610-641 almost a century later than Justinian
[87]Saint Flavia Julia Helena, mother of the Emperor Constantine (died 328)

was a throne, and round about the throne were four pillars that bare up a canopy that overshadowed the throne, which seemed to be all of gold So sate there the emperor, upon this throne, wearing his crown, and he came in by this gate and was brought on this chariot, amid great joy and rejoicing, even unto his own palace [88]

XC

OF THE EMPEROR'S GAMES

Now in another part of the city was yet another wonder, for there was an open space, hard by the Palace of the Lion's Mouth, which was called the Emperor's Games [89] This space was full a crossbow-shot and a half in length, and about one in breadth Round about this open space were thirty or forty tiers of stairs, where the Greeks went up for to see the games, and there were lodges there, very magnificent and very noble, where sat the emperor and the empress whilst the games were playing, together with other nobles and ladies And if two games were playing together, then would the emperor and the empress make a wager together that the one of these games would be better played than the other, so, likewise, did all they that were watching the games

Lengthwise of this space ran a wall, full fifteen feet high and ten feet wide, and on the top of this wall were images of men and of women, of horses, and oxen, and camels, and bears, and lions, and all manner of other beasts, cast in copper, which were so cunningly wrought and so naturally shaped that there is not, in Heathendom or in Christendom, a master so skilled that he could portray or shape images so skilfully as these images were shaped And these images were wont erstwhile to play, by enchantment, but afterward they played no more at all

And on these Games of the Emperor did the Franks gaze with wonder when they beheld them

XCI

OF THE TWO MARVELOUS IMAGES

And now in yet another part of the city was another marvel There were two images, cast in copper, in the shape of women, most cunningly wrought and naturally, and exceeding beautiful And neither of the two was less than twenty feet high And the one of these images was stretching out her hand toward the West, and there were letters written upon her which said

"From out of the West will come they who shall conquer Constantinople "

And the other image was stretching out her hand toward an unseemly place and saying

"Thither" (so spake the image) "shall they be thrust forth again "

These two images were sitting before the Exchange, which was wont erst-

---

[88]This gate (in the Wall of Theodosius) was afterward walled up by the Turks because of a tradition that the conqueror of Constantinople would enter the city by it
[89]The Hippodrome

whiles to be full of wealth; for there were wont to sit the rich money-changers, having before them great mountains of bezants and of precious stones, ere yet the city was taken But there were not so many of them there, now that the city was taken

XCII

OF THE PILLARS OF CONSTANTINOPLE, AND OF THE CHURCH OF SAINT MARY OF BLACHERNAE

Yet again, in yet another part of the city, was to be seen yet a greater marvel For there were two pillars, each one of them was, in thickness, thrice the spread of a man's arms, and each was full fifty fathoms high And on the top of each one of these pillars dwelt a hermit, in little huts which were there And there was a passage on the inside of the pillar, whereby one went up thither And on the outside of these pillars were portrayed and written in prophecy all the happenings that have come to pass in Constantinople or are yet to come Nor could any happening be known ere yet it had happened, but when it had happened, then went the people thither and mused there, and then did they perceive for the first time and divine the happening Yea, even the conquest which the Franks made was written and portrayed there, and the ships with which the assault was made whereby the city was taken, nor yet were the Greeks able to see it until it had already come to pass But after it was come to pass, then went they thither for to muse and to gaze on these pillars, and it was found that the letters which were written on the ships portrayed there declared that from out of the West would come a tall people, shaven with knives of iron, who would conquer Constantinople

And all these marvels which I have related to you, and still many more which we cannot relate to you, did the Franks find in Constantinople when they had conquered it Nor do I believe, of my own knowledge, that any man, be he never so skilled in accounting, could number all the abbeys of the city, so many were there of them, both of monks and of nuns, to say nought of the other minsters in the city And they counted, in round numbers, some thirty thousand priests in the city, both monks and others

Of the other Greeks—the high, the lowly, the poor, the rich, of the greatness of the city, of the palaces, and of the other wonders which are therein—will we forbear to tell you further, for no earthly man, though he abode never so long in that city, could number or relate all this to you And if he were to describe to you the hundredth part of the riches and the beauty and the magnificence which were to be found in the abbeys and in the minsters and in the palaces and in the city itself, it would seem that he was a liar, nor would ye believe him at all

But among the rest, there was also another of the minsters, which was called the Church of my Lady Saint Mary of Blachernae, within which was the shroud wherin Our Lord was wrapped And on every Friday that shroud did raise itself upright, so that the form of Our Lord could clearly be seen And none knoweth —neither Greek nor Frank—what became of that shroud when the city was taken

Likewise, there was another of the abbeys, wherein lay the good Emperor Manuel, for never was body born on earth—neither holy man nor holy woman—that lay so richly and magnificently in its tomb as did this emperor In this abbey, also, was the marble table whereon Our Lord was laid out after He had been taken down from the cross, and there, too, were seen the tears that Our Lady had shed over Him

---

XCIII

HOW THE PILGRIMS MADE READY TO CHOOSE AN EMPEROR

Thereafter it came to pass that all the counts and all the other nobles came together on a certain day to the Palace of the Lion's Mouth, which the marquis held, and said one to another that they would elect an emperor, and that they would choose ten men from their own number And they said to the Doge of Venice that he should choose ten of his people When the marquis heard this, he wished to place in this number his own men and such as he thought would choose himself for emperor, for he wished to be emperor forthwith But the barons were by no means agreed that the marquis place his own men there, but, rather, they agreed that none of his men should be of that number When the Doge of Venice, who was a very wise and worthy man, saw this, he spake in the hearing of all, and said

"Sirs, listen now to me" (quoth the Doge) "I desire, ere we elect an emperor, that the palaces be guarded by the common guard of the host, so that, if I myself should be elected emperor, I may go thither straightway without any gainsaying and be seized of the palaces, and in like manner, if the Count of Flanders be chosen, that he may have the palaces with no gainsaying, or if the marquis be chosen, or Count Lewis, or the Count of Saint-Pol, or if some poor knight be chosen, that he who is to be emperor may have the palaces with no gainsaying, either on the part of the marquis, or of the Count of Flanders, or of one, or of another"

XCIV

OF THE MANNER OF THEIR CHOOSING AN EMPEROR, AND OF THE PRETENSIONS OF THE MARQUIS OF MONTFERRAT

When the marquis heard this, he could in no wise go counter to it but gave over the palace which he held Then they went and set as guards in the palaces men of the commonalty of the host, for to guard the palaces

When the Doge of Venice had spoken after this fashion, he bade the barons choose their ten, for himself would very speedily have his own ten chosen And when the barons heard this, then did each one wish to put forward his own men The Count of Flanders wished to put forward his men, likewise, Count Lewis, the Count of Saint-Pol, and the other rich men, so that never in this manner could they agree whom they would put forward or choose So, then, they set another day to choose these ten, and when that day was come, yet again were they unable to agree whom they would choose Nay, rather, always did the marquis desire to put forward those that he thought would elect him emperor; for he wished to be emperor, even were it by force

And this discord endured full fifteen days, nor could they come to any accord Nor did a day pass, that they did not come together for this business, until, in the end, they agreed that the clergy of the host—the bishops and the abbots who were there—should be the electors Then, when they had thus come to an agreement, the Doge of Venice went and chose his ten in such a manner as I will describe to you He called four of those that he deemed the worthiest of his countrymen, and he made them to swear on holy relics that, to the best of their knowledge, they would choose the ten worthiest of their countrymen that were in the host And these acted in such wise that when they called one of these men he must needs come forward, neither durst he speak or take counsel with any one, rather, they put him straightway into a minster, and in the same way the others, until the Doge had his ten And when they were all in this minster—the ten Venetians and the bishops—then was sung a Mass of the Holy Ghost, that the Holy Ghost might counsel them and give them wisdom to appoint such a man as should be a good and profitable one for the office

XCV

HOW COUNT BALDWIN OF FLANDERS WAS CHOSEN EMPEROR

When the Mass had been sung, then came the electors together and spake together in their council, and they spake of this one and of that, until the Venetians and bishops and abbots with one accord agreed that it should be the Count of Flanders, and there was never a man of them that gainsaid this choice

When they were thus agreed together and their council must needs break up, then they charged the Bishop of Soissons with the task of making known their choice So when they had departed, then all they of the host assembled for to listen and to hear who should be named as emperor. And after they had assembled themselves they all remained very quiet And the more part greatly feared and suspected that the marquis would be named, and they that held with the marquis greatly dreaded lest another than the marquis be named And as they all stood there, so quiet, then rose the Bishop of Soissons to his feet and said to them

"Sirs," (quoth the bishop) "by common consent of you all were we sent to make this election We have elected such a man as we knew, of our own knowledge, to be fit for the office, and one in whom the imperial power may well be vested, who is mighty to uphold the law and a man of gentle birth and high estate We will name him to you he is Count Baldwin of Flanders !"

When this word was heard, then were all the Franks right glad because of it, but certain others were there who were sore displeased thereat, such as they who clave to the marquis

XCVI

HOW COUNT BALDWIN WAS CROWNED EMPEROR

When the emperor was elected, then the bishops and all the high barons and the Franks, who were exceeding glad because of this, took him and led him away to the Palace of the Lion's Mouth, amid very great joy and very great rejoicing And when the nobles were all within the palace, then did they set a day to crown the emperor And when that day[90] was come, they mounted their horses—both the bishops and the abbots and all the high barons, both Venetians and Franks—and went forth to the Palace of the Lion's Mouth Thence they brought the emperor to the Minster of Saint Sophia, and when they were come to the minster, then was the emperor taken to a place apart, within the minster, and into a chamber there Then was he stripped of his garments, and his shoes taken off his feet, and then they put on him scarlet hose of samite, and over these, shoes that were all set with precious stones above And then they laid on him the imperial mantle—a manner of vestment was this which reached to his ancles in front, and behind was so long that he girded himself therewith and then was it cast back over the left arm, even as a priest's maniple And this mantle was very rich and very magnificent and all laden with rich and precious stones Thereafter there was laid over this a very rich cloak, which was all laden with precious stones, and the eagles which were upon the outer side of it were wrought of precious stones and shone so that it seemed as if the cloak were all alight

When he was arrayed in this manner, they led him before the altar, and as he was brought before the altar, Count Lewis bare his imperial gonfalon, and the Count of Saint-Pol bare his sword, and the marquis bare his crown, and two bishops held up the arms of the marquis, who bare the crown, and two other bishops walked beside the emperor And all the barons were right richly arrayed, nor was there Frank or Venetian that had not a robe either of samite or of silken cloth

And when the emperor came before the altar, he kneeled down, then they took from him his cloak and his imperial mantle, so he remained in his bare coat And they loosed from the coat the golden buttons, before and behind, so that he was all naked from the girdle upward, and then did they anoint him And when he was anointed, they fastened again the coat with the golden buttons, then they laid on him again the imperial mantle, then the cloak was folded over his shoulder And then, when he was thus arrayed, and two bishops were holding the crown above the altar, came all the bishops, and together they took the crown and blessed it, and made the sign of the cross over it, and set it upon his head Thereafter was hanged about his neck a very rich stone for an agraffe,[91] which the Emperor Manuel bought for three score and two thousand marks

---

[90] 1st. May, 1204
[91] A clasp or brooch

XCVII

HOW COUNT BALDWIN WAS SEATED ON THE THRONE OF CONSTANTINE

When they had crowned him, they set him on a high throne, and there he remained until Mass had been sung, holding his sceptre in his hand and in the other hand a golden apple with a little cross above it And the ornaments that he had upon him were of greater price than the treasure of a rich king And when he had heard Mass, they brought him a white horse, whereon he mounted, and the barons led him back to his palace of the Lion's Mouth, and they seated him on the throne of Constantine Then, when they had set him on Constantine's throne, all acknowledged him emperor, and the Greeks that were there did him reverence, even as to an holy emperor Then were the tables set, and the emperor ate, and all the barons in the palace with him When they had eaten, then the barons departed and all went their ways to their habitations, but the emperor remained in his palace

XCVIII

OF THE DIVISION OF THE TREASURE

Thereafter it came to pass one day that the barons came together and said one to another that a partition should be made of the spoil So was it divided— save only the coarser silver which was there to wit, the silver ewers that the ladies of the city carried to the baths And a portion thereof was given to each knight, each serjeant of horse, and to all the other common people of the host, to women, and to children—to every one

But Aleaume of Clari, the clerk (of whom I have spoken to you before, who was so valiant of his body and wrought such deeds of arms, as we have said before this), said that he wished to have his share as a knight And some said that it was not right that he should share as a knight, but he said that it was right, for that he also had horse and hauberk, like a knight, and that he had wrought deeds of arms there, yea, more than many a knight had done had he himself wrought And at last the Count of Saint-Pol adjudged that he should share as a knight, since he had wrought there more deeds of arms and of prowess For the Count of Saint-Pol bare him witness that the knights, albeit there were three hundred of them, had not wrought such deeds as he, and rightly therefore should he share as a knight Thereby did this clerk cause it to be adjudged that the clerks should share even as the knights

Then was all the coarser silver apportioned, even as I have told you, and the rest of the spoil—the gold, the silken stuffs, of which there was so much that it was a fair marvel—remained to divide And this was put under the common guard of the host, in the ward of such persons as it was believed would guard it honourably

XCIX

OF THE CONQUESTS OF THE EMPEROR BALDWIN, AND HOW THE MARQUIS OF MONTFERRAT DEFIED THE EMPEROR

It befell, no very great space after this, that the emperor summoned all the high barons, and the Doge of Venice, and Count Lewis, and the Count of Saint-Pol, and all the high nobles, and told them that he desired to go forth and conquer somewhat of the land, and so was it determined that the emperor should go forth Then was it also determined which ones should remain for a guard to the city And it was determined that the Doge of Venice should tarry there, and Count Lewis, and their people with them The marquis, also, tarried there, and he married the wife of Isaac (that had been emperor), who was sister to the King of Hungary When the marquis saw that the emperor was about to make ready to go forth and conquer lands, he came and demanded of the emperor that he give him the kingdom of Salonika, a land that lay distant a fortnight's march from Constantinople But the emperor answered that this land was not his to give, for the barons of the host and the Venetians had the greater share therein Yet so much of it as appertained to himself, that would he give him right freely and willingly, but the portion that belonged to the barons of the host and to the Venetians could he in no wise give him

When the marquis saw that he could have none of it he was sorely vexed thereat Thereafter the emperor went away, whither he had purposed to go, with all his people And as he came to the castles and the cities, they that were in them yielded themselves to him without any gainsaying, and came out to meet him, bringing their keys, and the priests and clerks came forth in procession to meet him, and received him, and the Greeks all did him reverence, as to an holy emperor And the emperor set his garrisons in the castles and cities whithersoever he came, until he had fully conquered the land for a space of fifteen days' march from Constantinople and until he was come within one day's march of Salonika

In the mean time, whilst the emperor was thus conquering the land, the marquis had set forth, together with his wife and all his people, to follow after the emperor, so that he overtook the host of the emperor ere the emperor was come to Salonika And when he had overtaken the host he went and pitched his camp about a league away, and when he had encamped he took messengers and sent them to the emperor and bade him not to enter his land of Salonika, which had been given to him, for let the emperor know well that if he went thither, then would the marquis go no further with him, nor would he any longer cleave to him, but, rather, would turn back again to Constantinople and do the best that he could for himself

C

HOW THE BARONS RECEIVED THE DEFIANCE OF THE MARQUIS

When the barons of the emperor's company heard the word that the marquis had sent him, then were they very bitter and sore displeased, and they sent word back again to the marquis that neither for him nor for his behest would they forbear to go on, holding both of no account, for the land was not his

CI

OF THE REVOLT OF THE MARQUIS OF MONTFERRAT

When the marquis heard this he turned back, and he went until he came to a city wherein the emperor had put certain of his people to guard the city   This city he took by treachery   When he had taken this city he put therein guards of his own people, and then, when he had done this, he passed on to another city, which was called Adrianople, wherein the emperor had posted certain of his people   And he laid siege to it and set up his petraries and his mangonels to attack the city, but they of the city held out strongly against him   And when he saw that he would not be able to take them by force, he spake to them that were upon the walls and said to them ·

"Bah, sirs ! And have ye not perceived that here is the wife of Isaac, the emperor ?"

Then did he bring forward his wife, and his wife said

"Bah ! Have ye not recognized me, that I am the empress ? And have ye not recognized my two children, that I had by Isaac, the emperor ?"

Then did she bring forward her children   And then a certain wise man of the city made answer

"Yea !" quoth this man "We have perceived clearly that this was the wife of Isaac and that these were his children "

"Bah !" quoth the marquis "Wherefore, then, have ye not recognized one of these children as your lord ?"

"I will tell you," quoth the man "Get you hence to Constantinople and cause him to be crowned, and when he shall have sat down on Constantine's throne and we shall have learned thereof, then will we do in the matter that which we ought to do "

CII

HOW THE EMPEROR BALDWIN TOOK SALONIKA

In the mean time, whilst the marquis was proceeding in this sort, the emperor went to Salonika and laid siege to it   And after he had laid siege thereto, the host was so poor that there was not bread there to feed more than an hundred men, but of flesh and wine had they a plenty   And the emperor had not long besieged the city until it yielded to him, and when the city had yielded, then was there an abundance of all that was needful—both bread and wine and flesh   And then the emperor set his guards there, and since he had no thought to go further, he turned about to go back thence to Constantinople

CIII

OF THE DEATH OF MY LORD PETER OF AMIENS, AND HOW THE MARQUIS LAID SIEGE TO ADRIANOPLE

But then befell a very great loss and there was very great dole in the host, for my Lord Peter of Amiens, the fair, the valiant, died as they were returning, at a city which was called the White City and lay very nigh to Philippi, where Alexander was born, likewise, there died full fifty knights on this march And as the emperor was returning he heard tidings that the marquis had taken one of his cities by treachery, and that he had put therein guards of his own people, and that he had laid siege to Adrianople

CIV

OF CERTAIN DISSENSIONS THAT AROSE AMONGST THE MEN OF THE CROSS

When the emperor and the barons of the host heard this, they were sore vexed and troubled exceedingly, and they threatened the marquis and his people, saying that if they overtook them they would cut them all in pieces, nor would they leave him a living man When the marquis knew that the emperor was returning, then was he greatly afeared, even as one that had done great naughtiness, so that he scarce knew what counsel to take But at last he sent word to Constantinople—to the Doge of Venice, to Count Lewis, and to the other barons who had remained there—saying that he would put himself in their ward, and that he would make amends through them for the mischief that he had wrought. And when the Doge and the count and the other barons heard that the marquis was willing to make amends, through them, for the mischief which he had wrought and that which he had essayed, then did they despatch four messengers to the emperor, sending him word that the marquis had given them this promise and that the emperor should do no harm either to him or to his people

CV

HOW THE KNIGHTS AND YOUNG BACHELORS RECEIVED NEWS OF THE UNJUST DIVISION OF THE SPOIL, AND OF THEIR WRATH THEREAT

When the barons and knights of the host heard this, they answered that all this would not avail one whit to keep them from putting the marquis and his people to shame, or from cutting them all in pieces if they could overtake them And only with great difficulty were they appeased, nevertheless, they granted a truce to the marquis

Thereafter the barons asked of the messengers tidings of Constantinople, and what was befalling there And the messengers answered that all was well, and that they had divided the spoil which remained, and likewise the city

"What!" cried the knights and the young bachelors of the host "Our spoil have ye divided—for which we suffered great pains and travails, hungerings and thirstings, cold and heat? And this have ye divided without us? Take this!" cried they to the messengers "Here! Take my gage! For I shall prove you all to be traitors!"

Forth sprang another, and spake likewise, and another also, for so sorely were they angered that they would have hewn the messengers all in pieces, and it lacked but little that they would have slain them, until the emperor and the nobles of the host brought them to reason and wrought the best concord that they could And they returned together to Constantinople

And when they were returned, then was there never one of them was able to come back to his former lodging, for the lodgings which they had left behind no longer remained for them, since the nobles had divided the city and their retinues had taken their lodging elsewhere in the city, so that they of the host must needs seek for themselves habitations distant a league or two leagues from those that they had left

---

CVI

OF AN ADVENTURE WHICH BEFELL MY LORD PETER OF BRACHEUX

Now we had forgotten to recount an adventure which befell my Lord Peter of Bracheux It chanced that the Emperor Henry[92] was with the host, and John the Wallach and the Comans had made an incursion into the emperor's land And they had encamped some two leagues or less away from the host of the emperor And much had they heard told concerning my Lord Peter of Bracheux and his excellent knighthood And at last they sent word one day to my Lord Peter of Bracheux, by messengers, that they would be very fain to speak with him one day under safe-conduct, and my Lord Peter answered that if he had safe-conduct he would gladly go thither to speak with them So the Wallachians and the Comans sent good hostages to the emperor's host, until my Lord Peter should return Then went my Lord Peter, and three other knights with him, and he rode upon a great horse And as he drew near to the host of the Wallachs and John the Wallach beheld him coming, then did John go forth to meet him, along with certain noblemen of Wallachia And they saluted him and welcomed him, but they looked up to him with very great difficulty, for he was an exceeding tall man And they spake to him of this thing and of that, and at length they said to him

"Sir, we marvel much at your excellent knighthood, and we wonder much what ye are seeking in this country—ye who are from such far countries and are come hither to conquer lands For have ye not," asked they, "lands in your own countries wherewith ye could maintain yourselves?"

And my Lord Peter made answer

"Bah!" (quoth he) "And have ye never heard, then, how Troy the Great was destroyed, or by what strategem?"

---

[92]This reference to Henry as emperor makes it appear that the incident here related occurred at a later date than the events described in the preceding chapters or in those immediately following

"Bah!" answered the Wallachs and the Comans "Verily have we heard tell of these things, but most likely all this never was!"

"Bah!" quoth my Lord Peter "Troy belonged to our ancestors, and they who escaped thence came to dwell in that place from whence we are come, and because it belonged to our ancestors are we come hither to conquer lands!"

Thereupon did he take his leave of them and went back

CVII

HOW FIEFS WERE ESTABLISHED IN THE EAST

When the emperor had returned, and the barons who went with him, having conquered a good part of the land and full three score cities, beside castles and towns, then was the city of Constantinople so divided that the emperor had the fourth part thereof in freehold, and the three other parts were so divided that the Venetians had the one-half of these three parts and the pilgrims the other half Thereafter was it determined to divide the lands that had been conquered, and first, division was made amongst the counts, and afterward, among the other men of high rank And it was taken into account who was the richest man and highest in rank, and who had had the most people in his following in the host, and to him was the most land given There were some to whom were given two hundred knights' fiefs, and to some were given one hundred, to some three score and ten, to some three score, to some forty, to some twenty, to some ten, and they who received least had seven or six And the value of the fief was three hundred pounds Angevin And to each of the noblemen they said

"Ye shall have so many fiefs, and ye, so many, and ye, so many, and therewith shall ye enfeoff your men and those who shall desire to hold in fee from you And ye shall have this city, and ye, that one, and ye, this other" (and the seigniories that appertained thereto)

When, in this manner, his portion had been given to each one, then did the counts and the other noblemen go forth to view their lands and their cities, and they established there their bailiffs and other guards

CVIII

HOW MOURZUPHLES THE TRAITOR WAS TAKEN CAPTIVE

At last it came to pass one day that my Lord Thierri, brother to the Count of Loos, set forth to view his lands, and as he was going he met one day by chance, in a narrow pass, Mourzuphles the traitor, who was going I know not whither And he had in his company ladies and damsels and other folk a many, and he rode in pomp and circumstance, like an emperor, with as many folk as was possible And what did my Lord Thierri do but charge straight on him, and he contrived, he and his people, to seize this emperor by force And when he had thus taken him, he brought him to Constantinople and gave him over to the Emperor Baldwin And when the emperor had seen him, he cast him into prison and had him well guarded

CIX

HOW MOURZUPHLES THE TRAITOR WAS PUT TO DEATH

When Mourzuphles was in prison, the Emperor Baldwin sent one day for all his barons and all the noblest men who were in the land of Constantinople to come to the palace—the Doge of Venice, Count Lewis, the Count of Saint-Pol, and all the others—and they came thither And when they were come, then did the Emperor Baldwin tell them how he had Mourzuphles in prison, and he asked them what they advised him to do with him Then some said that he should be hanged, others, that he should be drawn and quartered, but at last the Doge of Venice said that he was a man of too high birth to be hanged

"But to such a man of high birth," quoth the Doge, "I will tell you what manner of high justice[93] shall be done There are in this city two high pillars, nor is either less than sixty or fifty fathoms high So let him be made to mount to the top of one of these, and then let him be hurled headlong to the ground!"

Now this was one of those two pillars whereon the hermits dwelt and whereon the fortunes of Constantinople were written, even as I have told you heretofore And to what the Doge said the barons agreed So was Mourzuphles taken and led to one of these pillars and made to mount the steps which were on the inside thereof And when Mourzuphles stood at the top, then they pushed him, so that he fell to the ground and was dashed all in pieces Such was the vengeance that they took on Mourzuphles the traitor

CX

HOW PEACE WAS MADE BETWEEN THE MARQUIS AND THE EMPEROR

After the lands had been so apportioned as I have told you, it came about that peace was made between the marquis and the emperor And the emperor was blamed for this, because he did not call thither all the high barons None the less did the marquis demand the kingdom of Salonika, and none the less did he have it, for the emperor gave it to him And when the kingdom was bestowed upon him, then did the marquis depart thither, with his wife and all his people; and when he was come thither he took over the garrisons of that country and was lord and king thereof

CXI

OF THE DIVISION OF THE CONQUESTS

Afterward, my Lord Henry, the emperor's brother, demanded the kingdom of Adramyttium, which lay beyond the Strait of Saint George, if he could conquer it, and it was given to him Then thither went my Lord Henry, with all his people, and conquered a good part of the land And after that, Count Lewis de-

[93]"*De haut home   haute justiche   *" The Doge's grim humour is playing on the different significations of *haut* Mourzuphles is a "high man" (see Chap XIII, footnote), the right of administering "high justice" included authority to pronounce the death sentence, and the place of execution is one of the highest points in the city

manded another kingdom, and it was given to him, and the Count of Saint-Pol demanded yet another, and it was given to him Next, my Lord Peter of Bracheux asked another kingdom, which lay in the land of the Saracens, toward Konieh, if he could conquer it, and this was granted to him And my Lord Peter went thither with all his people and conquered this kingdom very easily and became lord thereof

In this wise did the rich men demand their kingdoms, which had not yet been conquered, and the Doge of Venice and the Venetians had the island of Crete and the Isle of Corfu and the Isle of Modon,[94] and yet others a plenty which they had already coveted

But a very great loss befell the host, in that the Count of Saint-Pol died but a short time thereafter

CXII

OF THE VERY GRIEVOUS BATTLE OF ADRIANOPLE, OF THE LOSS OF THE EMPEROR BALDWIN AND OF MANY OTHER MEN OF HIGH ESTATE, AND HOW THESE THINGS WERE BUT GOD'S VENGEANCE FOR THE PRIDE AND THE BAD FAITH THAT THEY HAD SHEWN TOWARD THE POOR MEN OF THE HOST

Then it befell after this that a certain city which the emperor had conquered revolted against him, and the name of this city was Adrianople When the emperor learned thereof he sent for the Doge of Venice and Count Lewis and the other barons, and he told them that he wished to go and lay siege to Adrianople, which had revolted against him, and desired them to help him conquer this city And the barons answered that they would be very fain to do this So the emperor made ready, and the barons likewise, to go to this city

When they were come to this city they laid siege to it, and as they were sitting down before it, lo and behold, one day came John the Wallach, both he and the Comans, with a great multitude of folk, into the lands of Constantinople, even as they had done aforetime And they found the emperor and all his host sitting down before Adrianople And when they of the host saw the Comans all clad in skins, they suspected them not nor regarded them any more than they would have regarded a band of children But the Comans and their people came on at full speed and rushed upon the Franks and slew many of them and routed them all in this battle So was the emperor lost, so that none ever knew what became of him,[95] likewise Count Lewis and many another of the noblemen, the number of whom we know not, but of a certainty there were lost there full three hundred knights

---

[94]Near the southwestern coast of the Peloponnesus

[95]"The fate of the Frank emperor is one of those historical mysteries which research has failed to solve It is known that he was imprisoned, and a ruined castle on the ramparts of Trnovo retains the name of 'Baldwin's Tower' to this day According to one version, Kalojan is said to have treated his prisoner with kindness, though he refused to release him even at the request of the Pope According to another, he cut off his hands and feet and then had him thrown into a ditch to die, while a third account ascribes his end to the injured feelings of Kalojan's Kumanian wife, who had in vain endeavoured to attract the comely Frank" William Miller, *The Balkans,* p 173

And whosoever was able to escape came fleeing to Constantinople, so came the Doge of Venice fleeing thence, and much people with him And they left behind their tents and their harness, even as they had been sitting before the city, for never durst they turn again in that direction And great was their discomfiture

Even in this manner did the Lord God take vengeance on them for their pride and their bad faith which they had shewn toward the poor folk of the host, and for the horrible sins that they had committed in the city after they had taken it

CXIII

HOW THEY SENT FOR MY LORD HENRY, THE EMPEROR'S BROTHER

When the emperor was lost through this misadventure, the barons departed, and they remained exceeding sorrowful Thereafter they came together one day for to choose another emperor And they sent for my Lord Henry, brother to the Emperor Baldwin that was, to make him emperor, for he was in his own country which he had conquered beyond the Strait of Saint George

CXIV

HOW MY LORD HENRY WAS MADE EMPEROR

When the Doge of Venice and the Venetians saw that the Franks desired to make my Lord Henry emperor, then were they all against it, nor would they suffer it to be unless they should have a certain likeness of Our Lady, which was painted upon a tablet Now this picture was exceeding rich and was all set with rich and precious stones And the Greeks said that this was the first likeness of Our Lady that ever was painted or portrayed And in this likeness had the Greeks so great trust that they adored it above every other thing, and they carried it in procession on every Tuesday, then did the Greeks adore it and give it great gifts Now the Venetians would on no account suffer my Lord Henry to be made emperor unless first they had this picture, so at last the picture was given to them Then was my Lord Henry crowned emperor

CXV

HOW THE EMPEROR HENRY MARRIED THE DAUGHTER OF THE MARQUIS, AND OF HER DEATH

When my Lord Henry was become emperor, then he and the marquis (who was king of Salonika) spake together, and the marquis gave him his daughter, and the emperor married her, however, the empress lived not very long thereafter, but died

CXVI

HOW THE EMPEROR HENRY SOUGHT THE DAUGHTER OF THE KING OF WALLACHIA IN MARRIAGE

Now it came to pass no very long time after this that John the Wallach and the Comans overran the marquis' land of Salonika And the marquis was in his land and fought against these Wallachs and Comans, and he was slain in that battle, and his people all routed So goeth John the Wallach, and the Comans, and he layeth siege to Salonika And they set up their engines to assail the city And the marquis' wife had remained in the city, and knights and other folk with her who were defending the city Now there lay within the city the body of my Lord Saint Demetrius, who would never suffer the city to be taken by violence, and there flowed so great an abundance of oil from this holy body that it was a fair marvel And it came to pass, as John the Wallach was lying one morning in his tent, that my Lord Saint Demetrius came and thrust him through the middle of his body with a lance and slew him [96] When his own people and the Comans knew that he was dead, they brake camp and returned to their own land And after this the kingdom of Wallachia escheated to a nephew of John, Borislas[97] by name This Borislas became thereafter king of Wallachia, and he had a fair daughter And afterward it came to pass that Henry, who was a right good emperor, took counsel with his barons, what he might do with these Wallachs and Comans, who were ever making war on the empire of Constantinople and had killed Baldwin, his brother And the barons advised that he should send to this Borislas, who was king of Wallachia, and demand of him that he give him his daughter to wife But the emperor answered that a wife of so low lineage would he never take And the barons said

"Sire, this shall ye do! We advise you well that ye come to an agreement with them, for they are the strongest people and the most redoubtable of the empire and of the whole earth!"

And thus spake the barons, until the emperor sent thither two knights of high birth, and caused them to be richly accoutred, but these messengers went very fearfully into that wild land Nevertheless, the messengers spake to this Borislas, until he made answer to them that he would gladly send his daughter to the emperor

CXVII

IN WHAT FASHION THE KING OF WALLACHIA SENT HIS DAUGHTER TO THE EMPEROR

Then did King Borislas cause his daughter to be very richly decked and magnificently adorned, and a multitude of people with her, and sent her to the em-

---

[96] John was stabbed with a lance, at the instigation of his wife, by one of his own generals When accused of the crime, the assassin declared that it was not he himself, but his double, who had attacked the king, hence the origin of the Demetrius legend

[97] Or Boril "Boril has been described by his contemporary, King Stephen of Servia, as a man 'whose soul found a sweet pleasure in shedding the blood of his countrymen'" William Miller, *The Balkans*, p 174

peror And he bestowed on her sixty sumpter-horses, all laden with wealth of gold and silver and silken cloth and rich jewels, nor was there an horse that was not caparisoned with cloth of crimson samite, which was so long that it trailed full seven feet or eight behind each one, and notwithstanding they passed through mire and over grievous roads, yet never one of the samite cloths was frayed, because of their elegance and excellence

CXVIII

OF THE MARRIAGE OF THE EMPEROR HENRY AND THE DAUGHTER OF THE KING OF WALLACHIA

When the emperor knew that the damsel was coming he went forth to meet her, and the barons with him, and made great rejoicing over her and her people. And shortly thereafter the emperor married her

CXIX

OF THE DEATH OF THE EMPEROR HENRY

And no great space after this the emperor was summoned to Salonika for to crown the marquis' son as king, and thither the emperor went And when he had crowned him (the marquis' son) he fell sick there, and there he died, which was a very great loss and a very great pity

CXX

OF THE TRUTH OF ALL THAT HATH BEEN RELATED IN THIS HISTORY

Now have ye heard the truth, in what manner Constantinople was conquered, and in what way Count Baldwin of Flanders became emperor thereof, and my Lord Henry his brother after him, for he who was there and who saw these things and who heard the testimony thereof, ROBERT OF CLARI, Knight, hath also caused the truth to be put down in writing, how the city was conquered, and albeit he may not have recounted the conquest in as fair a fashion as many a good chronicler would have recounted it, yet hath he at all times recounted the strict truth, and many true things hath he left untold, because, in sooth, he cannot remember them all

EXPLICIT

THE CHRONICLE OF REIMS

(La Chronique de Rains)

WHEREIN IS CONTAINED THE HISTORY OF THE EMPERORS AND KINGS

COUNTS AND BARONS, POPES AND BISHOPS

WHO LIVED IN FRANCE, FLANDERS, ENGLAND, GERMANY, ITALY

AND THE LANDS BEYOND THE SEA

FROM THE DAYS OF LEWIS THE FAT TO THOSE OF LEWIS THE SAINT

Written by an unknown Minstrel of Reims
in the year 1260

Done into English

by

EDWARD NOBLE STONE

1937

FOREWORD

"A certain minstrel, a native of the diocese if not of the city of Reims, composed in the year 1260 a remarkable little work which has been published in our times under the titles *Chronique de Rains, Chronique de Flandres et des Croisades,* and *Récits d'un ménestrel de Reims* It is a sort of universal chronicle, wherein are portrayed the pope, the emperor, France, the lands beyond the sea, England, Flanders, Spain—but, especially, France and the Crusades The intention of the writer was not to record history in an impartial, orderly, and serious fashion, but to relate historical narratives, interesting and entertaining, for the edification of his wealthy burghers and his nobles Other minstrels had their repertoires of purely fictitious anecdotes, our author preferred instead, in his readings or recitations, to relate the gossip and the tradition that attached to the great events and the great personages of the past "[1]

Suetonius followed the same method in his *Lives of the Twelve Caesars;* yet Suetonius is classed as an historian, while our unfortunate Minstrel has become the target of much bitter criticism on account of the historical inaccuracies with which "he deceives his auditors without scruple "[2] But were his hearers actually "deceived" to any greater degree than are the readers of modern historical fiction? For our Minstrel was, perhaps, the first of the writers of historical romance, and the liberties he takes with real personages, like Richard Cœur de Lion, are no greater than those we encounter in Scott's *Ivanhoe, The Betrothed,* or *The Talisman,* or in Maurice Hewlett's *Life and Death of Richard Yea-and-Nay* The truth is that the average reader prefers the historical novel to the historical textbook, because he finds it more entertaining Sometimes, too, the novel leaves in his mind a clearer and juster picture of a given time, or place, or person, than does the history

History is a photographing of events, romance is painting them The historian is satisfied with informing us that "Louis VII repudiated his wife Eleanor for alleged misconduct"[3] in the Holy Land There is little in this statement to furnish the basis of a suit for slander or libel, nor does it make particularly interesting reading But our Minstrel gives us the whole story He describes the violent passion of the queen for Saladin, whom she has never seen; her letter to Saladin, wherein she offers herself to him and promises to abjure the Christian faith; the coming of Saladin's galley at midnight; the secret entry of the messenger into the queen's chamber, the suddenly roused suspicions of the faithful maid; her awakening of the king, his elaborate preparations for pursuit, his discovery of the queen "with one foot already on the galley", his taking her by the hand, leading her back to the palace, and mildly enquiring of her "wherefore she hath done this

[1]Petit de Julleville, *Histoire de la langue et de la littérature françaises,* II. 300
[2]Bédier et Hazard, *Histoire de la littérature française*
[3]Masson, *Mediaeval France,* 61

thing " But when she informs her husband that he is "not worth one rotten pear," and when his barons declare her to be "a very devil," the king makes up his mind to be rid of her

After all this, why should we be concerned with the fact that Saladin was at this time barely thirteen years of age?

It should by no means be assumed that the whole of the Minstrel's work is unworthy to be classed as authentic history The first part of his account of the battle of Bouvines, for example, is quoted verbatim in Masson's *Mediaeval France* And even Natalis de Wailly (from whose scholarly edition of the chronicle[4] the present translation is made), who prefaces his text with a lengthy "critical summary" correcting the inaccuracies, anachronisms, and other errors in the Minstrel's narrative, admits that many of the chapters are practically free from serious misstatement of facts

And even his severest critics acknowledge the charm of the Minstrel's style, his mastery of the art of narration, and the ever fresh variety and vividness of his pictures of life in the middle of the thirteenth century The *Chronique de Rains*, says Petit de Julleville, is "one of the most delightful books that the Middle Ages have left us, if one will but read it as it should be read, without seeking in it the knowledge and the accuracy which are not there "

Most readers will doubtless be content to follow the advice of this eminent literary historian, however, those who, dreading the contagion of historical error, refuse to do this, may use the appendix to this translation (an abridgement of De Wailly's *sommaire critique*) as a sort of mental antiseptic

E N S

---

[4]Natalis de Wailly, *Récits d'un ménestral de Reims au treizième siècle,* Paris, Libraire de la Société de l'Histoire de France, 1876

CONTENTS

CONTENTS—(Continued)

CHRONICLE OF REIMS

Book III, of

Three Old French Chronicles of the Crusades

CHRONICLE OF REIMS

I

OF THAT WHICH BEFELL BEYOND THE SEA AND IN FRANCE AFTER THE DAYS OF GODFREY OF BOUILLON

After that time when Godfrey of Bouillon and the baronry of France had conquered Antioch and Jerusalem and had again set up therein the Christianity which had for a long season been thrust out from thence, the Christians won no victory over the Saracens in the land of Syria save only that of Acre, which was conquered again in the time of Saladin and in the time of King Philip (of whom ye shall hear tell hereafter), and that of Constantinople, which the Doge of Venice conquered, who was a blind man[5]

Now there came a time after the death of King Godfrey and of King Baldwin his brother, who were kings of Jerusalem the one after the other, that there was a king in France who was called Ralph the Justicer[6] And for this reason was he called the Justicer for that he kept justice right fairly, nor hanged evildoers with his own girdle, as do in these days the wicked princes who seek to stir up riotings and brawlings for to fill their own purses Ill do they call to mind the scripture which saith, through the mouth of the prophet David "Do justice and judgment at all times"[7]

And this king had by his wife two sons, of whom the elder was called Robert and the younger Lewis Robert had but little wit, nor did he know aught, but Lewis was wiser and more understanding And it came to pass that the king their father died, and must needs pay the debt which we all shall pay Then came together the peers and the barons of France for to make the elder brother king, but there was one of the peers that was very wise and worthy of trust, who said

"Fair sirs, an ye will heed me, we will make Lewis king, who is both wise and understanding, whereas ye clearly perceive that Robert knoweth nought, and if ye make him king the kingdom may lightly go to wrack thereby, and amongst us may great discord arise For it is most needful both for us and for the people that there be in France a king who will govern the realm, and ye know how it is with my Lord Robert And, God wot, I say this not save with all good intent, for the elder is as dear to me as the younger Do ye, then, in this matter that which God shall shew you to be good"

"I' faith!" cried the barons and the peers, "it seemeth us that ye say well, and ye have shewn us good reason therefor"

---

[5]Antioch was taken by the crusaders in 1098, Jerusalem in 1099, Acre was retaken in 1191, Constantinople was captured in 1204 by the French under Boniface, Marquis of Montferrat, and the Venetians under their doge, Henry Dandolo, who was ninety years old and blind

[6]Louis VI, surnamed the Fat *"Raoul li Joustcieres"* may have been another of the nicknames bestowed by his subjects on this popular monarch

[7]Apparently quoted from Ezekiel (xlv, 9), rather than from the Psalms

So did they all agree upon the younger, and he was consecrated king at Reims and anointed from the holy ampulla which God sent down from heaven to Saint Remigius [8]

As for my Lord Robert, they made him Count of Dreux, who held himself well recompensed, for he wist not what all this signified And from this Robert issued the Robertois, and even yet do these say that they are defrauded of the kingship, for that he was the eldest born

II

OF LEWIS THE YOUNG AND OF THE DUCHESS ELEANOR

Now return we to our matter The barons agreed that the king should marry, and they gave him the Duchess Eleanor,[9] who was a very evil woman And she held in fief Maine and Anjou and Poitou and Limoges and Touraine—yea, thrice so much land as the king held

Now it came to pass that the king had a mind to go oversea, and fain would he go about to deliver the Holy Land out of the hands of the Saracens So he took the cross, and he took much people with him and made ready for his departure And they put to sea on a Saint John's Day,[10] and they sailed over the sea and for a month were they thrall to the winds, until they landed at Tyre, for no other land did the Christians then hold in all the country of Syria And he was there all that winter that followed, and he abode in Tyre, nor did he there aught else than waste his substance

When Saladin was ware of the king's impuissance and of his simplicity, then did he challenge him many a time to battle, but the king would never have aught to do with him And when Queen Eleanor perceived how the king had failed her, and when she had heard tell of the goodness and the prowess and the understanding and the bounty of Saladin, she was desperately enamoured of him in her heart And she sent greeting to him by one of her dragomans, and bade him know of a surety that if he could contrive to carry her away she would take him to be her lord and would forswear her own religion

When Saladin knew this, through the letter which the dragoman had delivered to him, he was much rejoiced thereat, for well did he know that she was the best-born lady in all Christendom, and the richest So did he cause a galley to be manned and to set forth from Ascalon, where he was, and go to Tyre with the dragoman, and they landed at Tyre a little before midnight

And the dragoman went up by a secret postern door into the chamber of the queen, who was awaiting him When she saw him, "What news?" cried she

---

[8]Remigius was Archbishop of Reims about 457-530 He baptized Clovis there in 496

"The famous ampulla formerly used in France, kept at Rheims and reputed to have been brought from heaven by a dove for the baptism of Clovis I, was broken at the Revolution" *Century Dictionary*

"Amongst the other reliques the Monkes shew'd us the Holy Ampoule, the same with that which sacres their Kings at Rheims, this being the one that anointed Hen IV" Evelyn, *Diary,* June 6, 1664

[9]Eleanor of Guienne, Duchess of Aquitaine

[10]24th June

"Lady," quoth he, "lo, here is the galley all ready and waiting for you Haste you now, that we be not perceived "

"I' faith," quoth the queen, " 'tis well done !"

Straightway she took two of her damsels and two coffers filled full with gold and with silver And these would she fain bear away to the galley, when one of the damsels perceived it and gat herself away so softly as she could and came to the bedside of the king, who was asleep Him she woke, and said to him.

"Sire ! Ill goeth it ! My Lady will needs go unto Ascalon, to Saladin; and the galley is even now waiting in the haven. In God's name, Sire, make haste !"

When the king heareth this, up leapeth he, and doth clothe and array himself, and biddeth his household arm themselves, and off he goeth to the haven And there he found the queen, who was standing with one foot upon the galley. And he taketh her by the hand and leadeth her back to her chamber And they of the king's household held fast to the galley and to those that were within it, for these were so dumfounded that they had not the power to defend themselves

And the king enquired of the queen wherefore she would do this thing

"In God's name," quoth the queen, "because of your own naughtiness ! For ye are not worth one rotten pear ! And I have heard tell so much good of Saladin that I love him better than you, and know ye of a truth that henceforth shall ye have no joy of keeping me !"

Thereupon did the king leave her, and he had her well guarded, and he determined in his mind that he would go back to France, for his moneys were fast failing him and he was earning there naught but shame So did he again put forth to sea, with the queen, and came back to France And he took counsel of all his barons what he should do with the queen, and he told them how she had demeaned herself

"I' faith," said the barons, "the best counsel that we can give you is that ye let her go, for she is a very devil, and if ye keep her long we fear that she will cause you to be murdered Furthermore, and above all else, ye have no child by her "

To this counsel did the king cleave, and therein did he act as a fool Far better had it served him to have immured her, then had her vast lands remained to him during her lifetime, nor had those evils come to pass that did befall, even as ye shall hear related hereafter

Thus did the king send Queen Eleanor back to her own land, and straightway she sent for King Henry of England—him who caused Saint Thomas of Canterbury to be put to death And he came gladly, and he married her, and he did homage to the king for the land that he received, which was very great and rich And he carried the queen away to England, and he kept her until he had by her three sons, of whom the eldest was called Henry Courtmantel, who was a valiant man and a good knight, but lived only a short time, and the second was called Richard, who was bold and valiant and bounteous and knightly, and the third was called John, who was wicked and faithless and believed not in God

III

OF THE MARRIAGE OF LEWIS THE YOUNG WITH ALICE OF CHAMPAGNE

Now will we let be to speak to you of King Henry and his children, and we will tell you of King Lewis, who was now wifeless The barons had told him that Henry, Count of Champagne, who was so bountiful, had a fair and lovely daughter who was called Alice and was own sister to Archbishop William White-hands, who was so powerful in those days and once more established the Échevins[11] at Reims

"Sire," said the barons, "we counsel you to take her to wife, for we see not where you could do better "

The king believed them and sent word to Count Henry to send his daughter to him, and he would take her to wife The count sent her willingly and the king married her, and they remained together until the king had by her a son and a daughter The son was christened Philip and became very powerful, and the damsel, Agnes And the son grew and prospered until he reached the age of sixteen years

The king his father saw that the child was wise and upright, and he knew that he himself was simple and old and lightly esteemed in his realm and little feared of his enemies So he desired (and in this did he act wisely) that his son be crowned at Reims, and he caused all things to be made ready which were fitting for a king at his crowning So was he crowned at Reims, at Allhallow-tide, in the year of the Incarnation of Our Lord eleven hundred four score and one, by the archbishop, William Whitehands, who was his uncle, and at his dinner, King Henry of England served him, kneeling, and carved before him

Now it came to pass a short time thereafter that King Lewis his father (whom they called God's Paw[12]) laid himself down upon his deathbed and must needs depart out of this world And he died and was buried magnificently beside his father at Saint-Denis in France, even at the side of Ralph the Justicer. And King Philip began to hold land in fee and to increase daily from better to better, and right needful for him was this, for he had not of his own land more than three score thousand shillings' revenue

IV

OF THE TREACHERY OF KING HENRY OF ENGLAND AND OF HIS DEATH

Now will we tell you of Henry Courtmantel, the eldest son of King Henry of England, who had heard tell that King Philip had a sister, fair and lovely And he besought his father that he send word to King Philip to send him his sister for himself, and he would take her to wife and she should be queen of England if he outlived his father The king made answer that he would do this right willingly, and he sent his letter with ten knights, valiant men and wise And they crossed

---

[11]Aldermen, or communal magistrates
[12]*Poe Dieu*

over the sea and found King Philip at Laon, and they greeted him in King Henry's name and delivered to him the letter

And the king caused it to be read, and well did he understand what King Henry demanded of him And he said to the messengers that this would he do right willingly And he caused the maid to be richly arrayed, like the daughter of a king and a king's sister, and he bestowed on her gold and silver and a goodly company of knights and maids of honour And they took their leave of the king and passed over the sea and came to London And there found they King Henry, who made marvellous great rejoicing over the damsel's coming But Henry his son, Courtmantel, was not at that time in England, nay, he was in Scotland, where he had a weighty business to do

But in this interval, the faithless King Henry gat such advantage of the damsel that he lay with her carnally But when Henry Courtmantel was come back again and knew the truth of the happening, then waxed he so exceeding wroth thereat that he took to his deathbed, and he died of this cause And the damsel was sent back again to this side of the sea, and she landed in the county of Ponthieu, and there did she sojourn for a long season, for she durst not shew herself to her brother, King Philip, because of her misdoing

Now it chanced that the Count of Ponthieu was dead, and he had a son, a fair bachelor, who was a clerk, to whom the land of Ponthieu escheated And this son heard tell of this lady who was sojourning in his land, and he brought it to pass that he held converse with her and became acquainted with her, and at last he told her that he would take her to wife if she were willing and if the king her brother would consent thereto Thus far had there been but words, but the count left not the pullet[13] on the fire, but he came to King Philip and said to him

"Sire, an it be your pleasure, I would fain take your sister to wife, and she shall be countess of Ponthieu "

When the king had heard him speak he bethought himself for a little, then said he

"By the lance of Saint James ! Verily do I desire that ye take her !"

The count departed straightway and held himself well paid with the king's answer And he came to the lady and told her that the king had indeed granted his request This greatly pleased the lady, and she married the count and was a right good wife and a prudent And she and the count loved each the other, and they had a daughter, fair and winsome, who was given in marriage to Count Renaud of Boulogne and bare him three daughters, of whom one became Queen of Spain, the second Countess of Guelders, and the third Countess of Rouci

And here will we leave off to tell you of the Count of Ponthieu, and of the countess, and we will come back to Philip, who was now at the age of twenty years nor had forgotten the very great shame which King Henry had put upon him through his sister He was one day at Beauvais, and King Henry was at

---

[13]De Wailly's text has *poire,* "pear," but one of the manuscripts reads *poile* (dialectic form of *poule*), "chicken " Evidently, this is a proverbial expression, referring either to the ripening of fruit or the turning of a spitted fowl in the fireplace, and similar to our "not letting the grass grow under one's feet "

Gerberoi, an abbey of the Black Monks some four leagues from Beauvais. When King Philip knew this he was marvellous glad thereat, for he thought to himself that he would avenge his shame if he were able So he had his knights to supper, and all his folk of high degree, and he caused oats to be given to the horses, and when the evening was come, he bade his folk arm themselves, but never once did he let them know what he had in mind to do And they rode until they came to Gerberoi, whither King Henry was come to be let blood But or ever he was laid upon his back, King Philip entered the hall, where King Henry was leaning upon his elbow, on a couch

When King Philip saw him he drew his sword and attacked him openly, and thought to cleave him through the middle of his head But a knight sprang betwixt them and turned aside the blow And King Henry leapt up, all distraught, and fled into a chamber, and the door was fast shut And when King Philip saw that he had missed his stroke he was marvellous grieved thereat, and he came back to Beauvais, for he found it not good to tarry there

When King Henry knew that it was King Philip that sought to slay him, he cried

"Faugh! Now have I lived too long, when this lad of France, son of the evil king, hath come to slay me!"

Then hasted King Henry forth and gat a bridle, and he passed out of the stately chambers, being utterly beside himself and possessed of a devil, and strangled himself with the reins of the bridle

When they of his household perceived that the king was not amongst them, they sought him everywhere until they found him, strangled, the bridle reins about his neck Then were they marvellous sore troubled, and they took him, and raised him up, and laid him on his bed, and they gave the people to understand that he had died suddenly But not often doth it chance that such an happening befalleth such a man an folk know it not, for what a man's household knoweth, not often doth that remain hid

The king's corse was made ready for sepulture and carried to Rouen, in Normandy, and buried in the mother church And now will I leave off telling of King Henry and will tell you of King Richard his son, who came into this land And he was a valiant man, and bold and courteous and bountiful, and a courtly knight, and he came a-jousting on the marches of France and of Poitou, and he so demeaned himself for a long season that folk all spake well of him

V

HOW GUY OF LUSIGNAN KEPT THE CROWN OF JERUSALEM

Now will we have done for a while with King Richard, and we will tell of King Amaury of Jerusalem, who died about this time, leaving no heir of his body And the kingdom escheated to a sister that he had, who was in the land of Jerusalem and was married to my Lord Guy of Lusignan, who was a worthy man but was in no wise of so high lineage as were befitting a king This Guy of whom I am speaking to you was king in his wife's name, to whom the kingdom had escheated, and for a season he reigned, like the honourable man that he was; and the queen was an honourable woman

And it came to pass that the barons of the land—to wit, the Marquis of Montferrat,[14] the Count of Tripoli,[15] the Seignior of Beirut, and the Seignior of Sayette[16]—were exceeding envious of my Lord Guy, and they procured of the Patriarch of Jerusalem that he would make King Guy to give up the kingship, for that he was by no means worthy (so said they) to be king Nor did they this in good faith, but because every one of them wished himself to be king of Jerusalem The Patriarch consented thereto, and he came to the queen and said to her

"Lady, it behooveth you to leave your lord, for he is not a man that is wise enough to hold and to govern the kingdom of Jerusalem "

When the queen heard the Patriarch she marveled greatly, and she said to him

"Sir, how shall it come to pass that I leave my lord, to whom I am lawfully wedded, and who is an honourable man ?"

"Lady," quoth he, "ye can lightly do this; for if ye were not to do it, the kingdom might well be lost and fall into the hands of the Saracens And, lo, here cometh Saladin, who is most wise and puissant and waiteth for nought else but a falling-out betwixt you and your barons "

"I' faith," quoth the queen, "ye have the cure of my soul and ye are in the Pope's stead on this side of the sea, advise me, then, in this matter, so that I may do no wrong either toward God or toward my lord "

"Lady," quoth the Patriarch, "ye say well, and we will see in what manner this can be done and who will be the best man for yourself "

Then was it determined by the council of the barons that the queen should be on a certain day within the Church of the Holy Cross, which is the cathedral church of Acre, and should hold the royal crown in her hand, and all the barons should be round about her, and on whosesoever head she should set the crown, he should be king And in sooth the day was set, and the queen was there, the crown in her hand, and the king, who was her lord, was there also, and all the barons of the realm were around and about her on every side And the queen stood in the midst of them all, and she looked at them and said

"My Lord Patriarch, and ye, my lords barons all ye have resolved that he on whose head I shall set the crown that I hold in my hand shall be king "

And they all made answer that this was the truth

"Now, then, I desire that ye all swear to this on the precious body of Our Lord, and do ye, my Lord Patriarch, swear that ye will never constrain me to take any other man as my lord "

The Patriarch and all the barons sware to this, even as the queen had enjoined them The queen sained herself with her right hand and commended her-

[14]Conrad of Montferrat, brother of Boniface of Montferrat who led the Franks in the Fourth Crusade
[15]Raymond II
[16]The ancient Sidon

self to God, and straight went she yonder, where she saw her lord, King Guy, and on his head she set the crown, and she said to him:

"Lord, I see no man hereabout more honourable or more loyal than you; or any man more worthy to be king of Jerusalem, than you, and I give and bestow upon you this crown, and the kingdom, and myself, and my love"

VI

HOW THE BARONS BETRAYED GUY OF LUSIGNAN

When the Patriarch and the barons who were there present saw what the queen had done, they marveled greatly, for each one of them trusted, in sooth, himself to have had the crown And straightway they departed thence, and they all went apart and devised a counsel of deadly treachery And they sent word to King Saladin, who was within one day's journey of them, to come to a place whither they summoned him, privily, to his own great advantage And Saladin went thither, who was a wise man and bountiful, and he said to them

"Fair lords, ye have summoned me hither, tell me, now, what is your pleasure"

"Sire," answered the Count of Tripoli, "we will tell you Ye know well that King Amaury is dead And the kingdom hath escheated to his sister and to her husband, who is not such a man as should maintain such a kingdom Nor will the queen hearken to our counsel, nor to the counsel of the Patriarch So, an ye will, for a portion of that which is yours would we give the land over to you For the king is foolish and wicked"

When Saladin heard these words he was marvellous glad thereof, and he said to them

"Fair sirs, if I were assured of you, I would give you so much of my treasure that ye would not dare take it all"

"Sire," quoth the Count of Tripoli, "choose what surety ye will that we shall give you for ourselves, and we are ready to give it"

"By Mahomet my god!" cried Saladin, "ye say well Ye shall all swear to me by your own religion—nay, ye shall do more, for we will all let our blood together, and each shall drink of the others' blood in token of alliance and in witness that we are all one"

Even as Saladin had devised, so was it done, and they all were let blood, and they drank each of the others' blood And betwixt them they set a certain day when Saladin should come before Acre with all his hosts (but he should not shew all his people) and should demand battle of King Guy And these traitors said that they would advise King Guy to give battle "And we will promise him that we will aid him loyally, but when we shall all be ready to join battle, then will we lower our banners and hold ourselves quiet, then can ye full lightly have your will of the king and of his people"

Thereon was ended this council of deadly treachery Saladin departed unto his own country, and the traitors went back to their own lands And Saladin sum-

3 CHRONICLE OF REIMS

moned his armies secretly and came and drew nigh unto Acre When King Guy knew this, then was he troubled in his heart, and he caused letters missive to be written and sent them to his barons and his men everywhere, and to all those that were able to bear arms And he gathered together so much people as he could, but these were as nothing to the host which Saladin had assembled, in two divisions

When the barons of the land of Syria were met together outside Acre, King Guy came to them and said

"Fair sirs, hither am I come to you, and I come to beseech you, for God's sake and for the sake of that which ye ought to do for Him, that ye devise some good and honest plan to defend and uphold the kingdom of Jerusalem For, lo, here is Saladin near at hand with a great multitude, and I am but one single man; yet am I your lord, whatsoever I be, and ye are all my men and are in fealty to me. And I have great confidence in you and greatly do I desire you to know that I will in all ways trust to your counsel"

Then answered the Count of Tripoli, who had contrived all this treason

"Sire, ye say wisely, and all we are ready to defend the kingdom, and ourselves, and you, and our own fiefs, and so much will we do that neither God nor the world can ask more of us"

When the king heard the Count of Tripoli speak on this wise he was marvellous glad thereat, and he went back to his tents and made ready his people as best he could And oft came the barons to speak with him and made great shew of love to him, and they said to him

"Sire, have no fear, for if they that lie yonder were twice so many as they are, yet would they have no power against us"

And the king took heart exceedingly because of their words, and so he waited until Saladin was come within three leagues of Acre and sought battle of the king And the king said that he would take counsel in the matter, and he sent for the Count of Tripoli, the Marquis of Montferrat, the Seignior of Beirut, the Seignior of Sayette, the Governor of Ascalon, and other barons whom I cannot now remember, and he said to them

"Fair sirs, I have called you hither, for I wish to tell you that Saladin summoneth me to battle on the day of the Decollation of Saint John [17] And I would fain take counsel of you what we shall do in the matter, for I would not do aught save through you For God's sake, then, counsel me in all good faith betwixt me and you, for the matter concerneth you even as it doth me, and I have very great trust in you"

Then answered the Count of Tripoli, who was the greatest lord of them all and the best skilled in speaking

"Sire," quoth he, "it is my rede that ye give him battle, nor do I in any wise doubt that we shall have the victory, for we are right, and they are wrong, and we have God for our helper, and they have Him not"

[17] 29th August

When the Count of Tripoli had thus spoken, then all the other traitors answered and said

"Sire, the Count of Tripoli giveth you good counsel, and we are all agreed thereto"

"I' faith," quoth the king, "since ye are all in accord in this, I will not disaccord therefrom"

Then were summoned the messengers that Saladin had sent, and it was declared and affirmed to them that they should have battle on the day that they had asked Straightway departed the messengers and came to Saladin and told him, in King Guy's name and in the name of the barons of Syria, that he should have battle assuredly

And the day came when the battle should be fought, and the hosts drew nigh the one to the other until they were joined And the archers began to shoot one at another, until many were they that were hurt and wounded, and Saladin's archers fell back

When Saladin saw this, he cried to his people and bade his horns and trumpets sound And the Turks moved forward, shouting and howling, and charged the Christians But the king and his household received them well and valiantly, and many were the Saracens that were slain, or maimed and wounded and overthrown When Saladin saw that his first battalion was discomfited, he was exceeding wroth and sent word to his ambushment which he had left in hiding, and they all charged at once against the Christians and compassed them about on every side, so that never one of them was able to move from his place

When King Guy saw himself thus hemmed in, then, an he was afeared, 'twas no great wonder But he took heart and cried "Holy Sepulchre!" and charged the Saracens, and so many of them did he slay or overthrow that all they that saw him gave him laud and praise Then cried Saladin, saying "O Count of Tripoli! Count of Tripoli! Keep your covenant!"

When the Count of Tripoli heard Saladin, he lowered his banner, and all the other barons did likewise, nor ever thereafter was there one that moved And when King Guy perceived the treachery of his barons, then had he exceeding great anguish in his heart and said

"Ah, fair Lord God! I am Thy servant, and 'tis about Thy business I am here, and for to defend Christendom Lord, help us, even as Thou knowest that we have need thereof, for well do I know that all my barons have betrayed me"

Straightway he charged the foe, and wondrous deeds of arms did he perform, both he and his company, but all this availed him nought, for too many were the Saracens, and his barons had failed him And taken was the king, by main force, likewise all his company, and he was led away to prison in Babylon [18]

But the traitors departed unto their own lands, and Saladin sent them gold and silver in great abundance

So Saladin went on to Acre, and there was none there to defend it, for all the defenders were taken or slain And the queen was at Tyre, and the governor

---

[18]Cairo was called Babylon by the crusaders, from the name of its citadel

of Tyre was guarding the city, nor had the queen any power there And of a truth did Saladin conquer all the land which the Christians were holding, save only Tyre, but Tyre could he never take

VII

HOW SALADIN GAVE GUY OF LUSIGNAN HIS FREEDOM

Here will we let be King Guy, who was in prison at Babylon, in great distress, and we will speak of Saladin, for never did better Saracen set foot in stirrup. He was one day in Babylon and sent for King Guy to be brought before him, and he said to him

"King, I have you, and I will have your head cut off "

"Surely," answered the king, "it is your good right, and well have I deserved it, for through me is lost the land beyond the sea, and Christendom dishonoured "

"By Mahomet!" quoth Saladin "Not so! For it is through your barons, who have betrayed you and have taken my gold and my silver And well know I that ye are an honourable man and a good knight, and I will shew you a great kindness For I will set you free, and a score of other knights with you, with both horses and arms and victuals, then do ye shift for yourselves as best ye can "

Straightway did Saladin cause all the prisoners to come before him, and he said to the king

"Now take a score of these, whichsoever ones ye will "

And the king chose a score of the knights, the best and the most loyal, and Saladin caused arms to be bestowed on them, and horses, and victuals, and they were conducted even to the walls of Tyre

The king sent word to the governor of Tyre to open the gates to him and let him enter therein, but the governor sent back word that he should not set foot therein, nor did he hold the king to be his lord When the king knew that he could not enter, he caused his tent to be pitched and abode there for a season, having no power to accomplish aught

But when his lady knew that her lord was lodged in the fields and could not enter within the city, she was sore distressed, and she came to the governor of Tyre and said to him

"How, sir! How is it that ye suffer not the king, our lord, to come in, as ye ought to do?"

"Be still!" quoth the governor "I would do nought of the sort for you, and if ye speak again thereof, I will cause you great annoy "

Thereon did the queen hold her peace, and she went away to her own chamber and considered what she could do, for well did she perceive that she had no power there And she thought in her heart that she would have herself let down at night by a cord, from the battlements, by her damsels And she contrived to get a cord, goodly and stout, that reached even to the ground And she caused herself to be let down, and one of the damsels with her, and came in due season unto the tent of the king, who was asleep, and she awoke him And when the king saw her, then was he marvellous glad thereof, and great joy had they together, even as honest man and honest woman ought

And on the morrow, when it became known that the queen had done this, greatly was she praised for her deed And the king, and the queen also, abode there with all the people that they had, before Tyre Much had he to suffer there, for he could accomplish no great thing, nevertheless, Saladin sent him bread and wine and other victuals, even as he had promised him

VIII

HOW PHILIP AUGUSTUS AND RICHARD LION-HEART WENT TO THE HOLY LAND

Here will we, for a season, leave King Guy and the queen (God keep her!), who had much to suffer, and we will tell you of Lucius, who was then Pope, who had received letters from the Patriarch saying that the land beyond the sea was all lost, except Tyre alone And he was sore troubled thereat, and he sent one legate to France, and one to England, and one to Germany, and to all the lands that were under the holy law of Rome, for to preach the taking of the cross These legates were worthy men and good clerks, and well did they expound God's business, and the people dedicated themselves and took the cross in great numbers

King Philip took the cross, and King Richard also, and Count Philip of Flanders, Count Henry of Champagne, the Count of Blois, and many another baron who is unnamed in my chronicle And they accoutred themselves richly and well and set out to sea with fifty-four ships, and they sailed without stop until they came to Tyre, of a Wednesday morning And they went on land, and caused their lodges and their tents and their pavilions to be set up, and laid siege to the city by land and by sea

When the governor saw that this was so, and that so great lords were coming to besiege him, he sent them word that he would yield up Tyre if his own life were safeguarded And King Philip and the other princes sent word back to him that they would do nothing of the sort, and that if he held out more than three days he would not escape thence save by way of the halter When the governor heard these words he was mightily afeared, and he sent word that he would yield the city and would put himself in the king's hands Thus was he received and the city yielded up, and he was doomed to perpetual prisonment

Then did all the barons take counsel together, and they agreed amongst themselves that they would go and lay siege to Acre And they sware an oath that they would not depart thence until the city were taken And they struck their tents and took down their lodges and all their engines, and ceased not to go on until they were come before Acre And they pitched their tents and their pavilions, but King Richard would have the best place, and that had he, for he was the richest man there and he who spent the most, and he had more sterlings[19] to spend than the King of France had coins of Paris

---

[19]The English silver "sterling" was first struck during Richard's reign The *parisis* was of about the same value as the present British shilling

And many a time did they assail the walls of the city and let play their petraries and their mangonels,[20] but nought did it avail them, for the Saracens burned with Greek fire both the petraries and the mangonels And be it known to you that King Philip assailed not the city So were they there all that winter, nor did they accomplish any thing And King Richard went away to disport himself amongst the isles and to visit the ladies But King Philip did otherwise, for he caused engines to be builded in great numbers on this side the sea And these were brought by the fleet before Acre and were speedily set up And they were all covered with lead, against the Greek fire And these began to cast great roaring stones, which destroyed utterly whatsoever they hit

Then were the Saracens sore afraid, and the governor of Acre, who was in Saladin's stead, sent up to the battlements a man of great age, who was very wise And the man had beside him an interpreter, a spy, who shewed him the tents and the pavilions and told him the names of the high barons, and he said to him

"Sir, behold yonder the tent of King Richard, and yonder behold the tent of Count Philip of Flanders, and the tent of Count Henry of Champagne, and all the tents of the other barons"

Then the Saracen looked and saw all the engines of King Philip, and he enquired

"Who is he to whom those engines belong?"

Then answered the interpreter and said

"Those be the engines of King Philip of France"

Then said the Saracen

"By Mahomet! Through him shall we lose Acre!"

And on the morrow morn King Philip caused an assault to be made with might and main, and "Evil Neighbour," the mightiest petrary that he had, to hurl her stones, and with each stone that she hurled she brake down full a fathom's length of the wall And all the other barons did likewise, save King Richard who was on the isle of Cyprus And so long did they continue the assault that they who were within the walls could no more endure And the Christians entered in from every side, and the city was taken

And many lay there dead, of the Saracens, and cut in pieces, and many found they along the streets who had died of disease and rotted there.

Then did King Philip cause it to be cried about that the city should be cleansed of the bodies of the Saracens, and this was done, even as the king had commanded And into Acre entered whosoever would, and King Guy was put back again, with his queen, into his seigniory, as king and lord

---

[20]The petrary and the mangonel were huge ballistic engines, both were used for hurling stones, and the mangonel also employed other missiles

IX

OF THE TREACHERY OF KING RICHARD

Now will we tell you of King Richard, who was in Cyprus and who had letters from Acre telling that it was taken, and he was so exceeding wroth thereat that he well-nigh went mad And he came to Acre so swiftly as he could, and in his heart was bitter envy and fierce anger, for well he wist that it was through King Philip that Acre had been taken

And it befell one day that my Lord William of Barres was riding through the midst of Acre, and King Richard also, and they met And King Richard was holding the truncheon of a great lance, and he charged the Barrois[21] and thought to have borne him out of the saddle

The Barrois held himself fast, for he was a proved knight, and on the passade which the English king thought to make, he seized him by the neck Then doth he spur his horse and drag the king by force of his arms out of the saddle, then looseth he his arms Down falleth the king upon the pavement, so grievously that his heart came nigh to bursting, and there lay he for a long time aswoon, so that they could perceive neither pulse nor breath in him Straightway departed the Barrois and went on to King Philip's lodging and told him how it was When the king heard this he was sore distressed, and he bade his folk arm themselves, for much did he mistrust King Richard

Now it happened that King Richard was recovered of his swoon, and he bade his English arm themselves, and came on to assault the lodging of King Philip But him found he neither dismayed nor unprepared, nay, the king's people defended themselves well and vigorously, and other barons a plenty with them So they appointed a three days' truce, and within that time was the matter accommodated

King Richard's heart was all swollen with rage because of King Philip, who held the fief of Acre And he began to hate him bitterly, and chiefly, also, because of the death of his own father And by means of gifts he brought it about that the king was poisoned, but—thank God!—his poisoning was not unto death When King Richard saw that he had failed, then did he betake himself to the Count of Flanders, and to the Count of Champagne, and to the Count of Blois And he gave them of his sterlings until they sware the king's death, and they had contrived how he should receive his death But God, who forgetteth not his own, sent a sickness upon Count Philip, whereof he died And when he felt himself stricken, he sent for King Philip, his godson, and said to him

"Fair godson, bid a cord be fetched, and bid it be laid about my neck, and bid me be haled through all the streets of Acre, for well have I merited this!"

When the king heard him speak thus, he was amazed, and he thought that he was not in his right mind, and he said to him

"Fair godfather, what is this that ye say?"

"In God's name, well do I know what I am saying! Know ye of a truth,

---

[21]Surname of Guillaume des Barres

fair godson, that I have sworn your death—both I, and Count Henry your nephew, and the Count of Blois And know ye well that unless ye get you hence right speedily, ye are already betrayed and dead "

"Ha !" quoth the king "Fair godfather, wherefore did ye agree to this ?"

"In God's name, fair godson, they had slain me else !"

Straightway the king left the count, in great heaviness of heart; and all that night he meditated what he should do And he resolved that he would cause it to be cried about that all the knights should come to dine at his court the third day thereafter And he caused meats to be prepared in great abundance, as becometh a king's court, nevertheless he was not unmindful of that which Count Philip had told him So he had his ships made ready in secret and caused all things needful to be put therein, and on the morrow, before the day brake, he put forth to sea with his priviest friends

When Count Henry knew that the king was departing, he gat himself into a barge and set out after him, and he overtook him, for he was not yet far on his way And he said to him·

"Fair sire, fair cousin, will ye leave me on this side the sea, in this strange country ?"

And the king answered and said

"Yea, by the lance of Saint James, thou foul traitor ! Nor ever hereafter shalt thou enter Champagne, neither thou nor thine heirs !"

Straightway did Count Henry turn back to Acre, and he came to King Richard and said to him

"Sire, we are shamed and undone, for the king goeth away to France, and well knoweth he through Count Philip what we have contrived, and know ye well that he will destroy us all "

Then was summoned the Count of Blois, and they took counsel together and determined that they would go and speak to Count Philip But while they were yet speaking, word was brought to them that the count was dead, and they were utterly dumfounded But the count's body was prepared and borne to the church, and he had such obsequies as befitted so great a lord, and he was buried in the parvis of Saint Nicholas'

Then back came the king and Count Henry and the Count of Blois and entered into a chamber and took counsel what they should do

"By my head !" quoth the English king, "back to England will I go, and so soon as I am come thither I will make war upon the king !"

"In God's name !" quoth the Count of Blois, "I will set off to France and will cry the king mercy "

"I' faith !" quoth Count Henry, "I will abide in this land, for I know of a surety that I am disinherited "

Then did King Richard bid his ships be made ready, and he put out to sea and steered his course as best he could toward Germany and came into harbour Thence went he by land, with a privy retinue, and journeyed until he came into Austria And he was spied upon and recognized When he perceived this, he took the dress of a kitchen-knave and gat himself into the kitchen to turn capons on the spit But a spy went and told the duke,[22] and when the duke knew it he sent so many of his knights and retainers that they perforce outmanned him So the king was taken captive and sent away to a strong castle, nor had any one cognizance of him—not they even that were guarding him—save the duke alone

X

OF THE DEATHS OF THE COUNT OF BLOIS, THE COUNT OF CHAMPAGNE, KING GUY, AND HIS WIFE

Here will we, for a space, leave King Richard, who is imprisoned, and will tell you of the Count of Blois, who put out to sea and came even to Marseilles, with the cross upon his sails And a great storm overtook him, so great that it seemed that the ship was mounting to the clouds, then she went so deep down that she seemed to be entering the abyss, and this was nigh unto the land When the Count of Blois beheld these marvels, he caused the ship's boat to be launched and entered into it, and three of his retainers with him But scarce were they afloat, ere the tempest bore them against a rock and brake the boat all in pieces So was the count drowned, and all they that were with him, but the storm grew calm and the ship came into an haven of safety

Now will we tell you of Count Henry, who had remained in Acre To him came tidings that the King of Cyprus was dead, and there remained after him none save one only daughter Her did the count seek as wife, and she was given him willingly because of his gentle birth And he became king of Cyprus, and had by her two daughters, of whom the elder was left queen of Cyprus And the other daughter did my Lord Érard of Rameru[23] take, and he thought through her to have held the countship of Champagne—but much remaineth unfulfilled of that which a fool thinketh

Now it chanced that the King of Cyprus came to Acre and desired to borrow moneys of a certain burgess of the place, and the man drew him apart, privily, to a window which was both door and window and opened outward; and it was closed but was not fastened And when the king leaned against this door, it opened, and he fell and brake his neck And his knights and his retainers ran down and raised him up, and they found that his neck was broken, and they all made great lamentation The king's body was carried to Cyprus, and there was it buried

Now will we leave King Henry of Cyprus and will come back again to King Guy, and to his wife the good queen, who abode in the land of Syria but had, of all the kingdom of Jerusalem, only Tyre and Acre and Beirut, nor lost nor won aught else thereafter And they lived fourteen years in this case, and King Guy died, and the queen a short space thereafter, without heirs of their bodies And

---

[22]"Leopold of Austria, whose banner he had outraged at Ptolemais Leopold turned him over to Henry VI, the Emperor" Kitchin, *History of France*, i, 291

[23]Erard de Brienne, seignior of Rameru

the barons of the realm assembled and made a king by election, and this king[24] held the kingdom in such state as King Guy was holding it on the day that he died And of him issued one daughter, who afterward wedded King John, as ye shall hear hereinafter

XI

OF THE COMING BACK OF PHILIP AUGUSTUS AND OF HIS MARRIAGE WITH THE SISTER OF THE COUNT OF FLANDERS

Now at this point will we come back to King Philip, who hath passed through the perils of the sea And even where he was in the greatest peril, and when he thought to suffer shipwreck from moment to moment and from hour to hour, and when the waves of the sea bare his ship, as it were, up to the very clouds and dropped it down again even unto the abyss (and at that season was darkest night), then the king, firm in faith and fully trusting in God, enquired of the sailors what hour it was And they answered him that it was about midnight Then said the king

"Be assured that we need have no care, for my friends of the Order of Cîteaux[25] have now risen to sing matins and to pray for us"

Then the storm was quieted, and the sea was calm and still

But the king was not on his guard against the draught which the traitors had made him to drink, nevertheless, thanks be to God, this poisoning was not unto death But the nails dropped from his feet and from his hands and all his hair fell out, and he lay sick for a whole year, then was he made whole again, and was hale and hearty and merry

And the barons of France came to him and said

"Sire, it were high time for you to wed"

"Certes!" quoth the king "That is my will and my desire; and truly do I wish to act in the matter through your counsel"

"I' faith," quoth Archbishop William, who was his uncle, "Count Philip of Flanders is dead and his land hath escheated to his brother Baldwin, neither know I in France a man of gentler birth nor richer than he And he hath a sister, fair and lovely and wise, and I would counsel you to take her to wife"

"Sire," quoth the other barons, "your uncle giveth you good counsel"

"I' faith!" quoth the king "I also agree thereto!"

Then were chosen two of their number, and these went to Count Baldwin And they found him at Lille, in Flanders, where he was holding a great parliament of his barons Straightway the king's messengers dismounted and entered into the hall, and they greeted the count and delivered unto him the king's letter The count took the letter and gave it to the Bishop of Arras, who stood beside him The bishop read the letter, and expounded it to the count privily The count called his men and went into a chamber with them, and he said to them

[24]Conrad of Montferrat
[25]The Cistercians

"Fair sirs, the King of France seeketh of me my sister to wife, and in this matter would I fain act through your counsel"

"Sire," said his men, "the King of France doeth you very great honour, we all counsel you to give her to him, together with so much land as he requireth of you"

The count made answer to his men that so would he do Straightway came he forth of the chamber and said to the king's messengers

"Fair sirs, I have resolved that I will do gladly that which my lord the king demandeth of me"

"Sire," quoth the messengers, "ye speak as a wise man Now will we tell you what the king demandeth of you The king demandeth of you, together with your sister, the county of Artois to wit, Arras, and Peronne, Bapaume, Saint-Omer, Hesdin, and all the county even as it now standeth"

The count answered and said unto them that he would give these gladly, and yet more, an the king so desired Straightway the messengers departed from the count, taking their leave of him, and they journeyed day by day until they were come to Paris, where the king was in council The messengers greeted the king in the name of Count Baldwin of Flanders, and they said to him

"Sire, the count received us willingly and gladly, and did us very great honour on your account, and we delivered to him your letter, and when he had taken counsel of his men who were there he spake to us and said 'Fair sirs, much do I thank the king for the honour which he hath shewn me, and it is my will and my behest that my lord the king shall have my sister and the county of Artois, and yet more, an he so will'"

Then Archbishop William answered and said to the king "Sire, now remaineth only to speed this business"

Straightway the king caused a letter to be written, and sent word to the count that he would wed his sister in three weeks' time, at Amiens, and that the count should bring her thither on that day And so was done as the king commanded, and the damsel was conducted thither magnificently and with a great company, and marvellous rich house did Count Baldwin keep Presently came the king to Amiens and wedded the damsel, whose name was Isabel, and there was great rejoicing throughout all Amiens And the king abode in the city three days, then he departed and went into France, and had the queen brought to Paris, and there was she received with great pomp

And she and the king loved each the other exceedingly, and they had a son, who was called Lewis in baptism This Lewis was prudent and bold and a valiant warrior, and he had the heart of a lion, but so long as he lived he was never without pain and suffering

XII

HOW BLONDEL DELIVERED KING RICHARD

Henceforth will we tell you of King Richard, whom the Duke of Austria was holding in prison, nor had any one cognizance of him save only the duke and his council

Now it chanced that the king had brought up from childhood a certain minstrel, Blondel by name This man bethought himself that he would go seeking through all the lands until he should hear tidings of him, and he set forth upon his way, and he went so far through strange countries that he had spent already a year and a half, nor yet could he hear any true tidings of the king And so did he wander on until he was come into Germany, even as his wanderings led him; and he came straight to the castle where the king lay prisoner

And he found lodging with a widow woman, and he asked her whose was this castle which was so fair and strong and well situate His hostess answered and said to him that it belonged to the Duke of Austria

"Fair hostess," quoth Blondel, "is there now any prisoner within the castle?"

"Certes," said the good woman, "yea, one, for these four years past But we cannot discover who he is, and I tell you of a surety that they guard him well and carefully, and verily do we believe that he is a man of gentle birth and a great lord."

When Blondel heard these words he was marvellous glad, and him seemed in his heart that he had found that which he sought, but never an inkling thereof did he give to his hostess That night was he blithe in heart and slept until the day And when he heard the watchman sound his horn, he arose and went to the church to pray God to help him Then came he to the castle and made himself known to the castellan of the place and told him that he was a minstrel and would be very fain to abide with him, an he were willing The castellan was a young knight and a merry, and he said that he would keep him gladly

Then was Blondel right glad, and he went and fetched his viol and his other instruments And he continued to serve the castellan and pleased him well And he was on good terms with them of the castle and with all the household So Blondel abode there all that winter; yet never could he find out who the prisoner was, until one day in Eastertide he went all alone into a garden that adjoined the tower And he looked about him and bethought himself if by any chance he might see the prisoner And while he was yet thinking of this, the king looked out through a loophole and espied Blondel And he took thought how he might make himself known to him Then did he bethink himself of a song that the two of them had made betwixt them, which none other knew save they two So began he to sing the first words thereof, loud and clear (for he sang passing well), and when Blondel heard him, then knew he of a surety that this was his lord And he had in his heart the greatest joy that ever yet he had had in all his days Straightway he left the garden and went into his own chamber, where he slept, and he took his viol and began to play a strain, and as he played he rejoiced over his lord whom he had found

So Blondel abode there even until Pentecost, and so well did he cover himself that none of those that were in the castle had inkling of his doings   Then came Blondel to the castellan and said to him

"Sir, and it be your pleasure, I would fain go unto my own country, for long indeed is it now since I have been there "

"Blondel! Fair brother! That shalt thou not do, if thou wilt heed me   Nay, rather, abide thou here yet longer, and I will entreat thee right well "

"In sooth, sir," quoth Blondel "I would in no wise tarry here any longer "

When the castellan saw that he could not keep him, he gave him his discharge and bestowed on him a sumpter horse and a new robe   Straightway Blondel left the castellan and journeyed day by day until he was come into England   And he told the king's friends and the barons that he had found the king, and where he was   When they heard these tidings, then were they all passing glad, for the king was the most bountiful man that ever buckled spur

And they took counsel together, whom they should send to Austria, to the duke, for to redeem the king, and they chose two knights to go thither, of their most valiant and wisest men   And so these journeyed day by day until they were come into Austria, where they found the duke in one of his castles   And they greeted him in the name of the barons of England and said to him

"Sir, we are sent hither on behalf of the barons of England, and we have learned that ye are holding King Richard prisoner   Sir, they ask and pray you that ye accept ransom for him, and they will give you so much as shall seem you good "

The duke answered them that he would take counsel in the matter, and when he had so done, he said to them

"Fair sirs, if ye desire to have him, ye must needs redeem him with two hundred thousand marks in sterlings   And say no more in this matter, for that were but pains wasted "

Straightway did the messengers take their leave, and they said that they would take back this word to the barons and these would deliberate the matter. So back came they to England and told the barons what the duke had said, and these declared that never, on this account, should he remain in durance longer   Then they raised the ransom and caused it to be carried to the duke   And the duke delivered the king unto them, but first he made them give good surety in the king's behalf that never would he cause the duke any annoy

XIII

HOW KING RICHARD ATTACKED KING PHILIP AUGUSTUS

Thus did it come about that King Richard was redeemed and was received in England with great honour, but grievously was his land burdened thereby, and the churches of his realm, for these must needs give up their chalices for the ransom, and for a long time thereafter mass was said with chalices of pewter or of wood

Now it chanced that King Richard was lying one night upon his bed, but he could not sleep And within him rose a thought that was very evil and very cruel. For he thought of his father, King Henry, who strangled himself with the reins of his horse's bridle for the spite that he had of King Philip, who rushed upon him with sword drawn, at Gerberoi And he remembered his captivity, and the ransom which the Duke of Austria had put upon him by the command and through the prayers of that King Philip, and so great bitterness and so great anger had he in his heart because of this, that he declared and affirmed to himself that never once would his heart be at ease or in peace until he should have avenged himself Then brake the day, and he went and heard mass after he had arisen; then sent he for his barons and his council and told them what he thought

And the barons and his council told him that this was a very great shame and a most grievous wrong, and well did it deserve redress And let him know of a certainty that they all were ready to aid him both with their bodies and with their substance, and that easily had he the better of King Philip both in friends and in land And so indeed had he

When King Richard perceived that he had the hearts of his barons, then was he marvellous glad in his own heart And he caused a letter of defiance, bearing his seal, to be written to King Philip, and he let him know through this letter that he held him neither his lord nor his friend And let him know of a surety that he would come to see him, within a very few days, in the very midst of his own land nor would Philip be man enough to dare meet him or await him

Straightway he chose a knight, a wise man, and charged him with the letter The knight received it from the king's hand, and he journeyed by sea and by land until he was come unto Orleans, where King Philip was And he reached him the letter without saluting him, and he said to him

"Sire, King Richard of England sendeth you this letter, let me know, an it please you, what is to do in the matter, for I care not to tarry here long"

The king bade the Bishop of Orleans, who stood beside him, unseal the letter The bishop read it, and after he had read it he said to the king

"Sire, King Richard sendeth you his defiance, and he saith that he will come to see you, within a few days, in the midst of your land, nor will ye be man enough to find yourself there"

When the king heard the word that King Richard had sent him, he took thought for a little, then said he

"God, Our Lord, who is all powerful, is well able to help us And know ye this if your lord cometh into our land for to do mischief, we will withstand him with so much people as we can gather"

Then the knight departed without taking leave, and passed again over the sea, and he found King Richard in London together with very many of his knighthood, and he said to him

"Sire, I have been in France, and I found Philip at Orleans, and I delivered him your cartel And he caused it to be read, and said to me that if ye enter into his land to do any mischief he will meet you with so much people as he shall be able to raise"

And therewith was an end of parleying.

King Richard caused ships to be built, and tents and pavilions to be made in great plenty, for well was he able to do this, and he made ready for his departure with great speed, for he was but awaiting the spring season. And King Philip forgat not the fowl over the fire,[26] but he strengthened his castles and fortified his marches, and caused wines and victuals to be fetched, and men to be mustered for to defend his land, for greatly did he mistrust King Richard because of his prowess and his boldness

Presently came the spring, when the May month was come in, and King Richard put forth to sea with a great multitude of his knighthood And they had favouring winds and fair weather, and landed at Dieppe, an harbour in Normandy which belonged to him Forth came they then from the ships and went to Rouen, his city, which lay fourteen leagues distant from the harbour, and there they tarried a month, for to refresh themselves and make their preparations

Then did King Richard command the host to go straight on to Gisors, one of his castles, which is strong and marvellous well situate and lieth some seven leagues distant from Beauvais And when they were come thither they sojourned there for two days, and on the third day he commanded his vanguard to march, and the foragers sped forth

Ah! then had ye seen sutlers and grooms, on foot and on horse, scattered abroad through the Beauvais country-side, taking oxen, and kine, and swine, and sheep, and geese, and capons, and hens, and plough horses, and churls, and bringing them back to the host round about Gisors, where they were encamped And they wrought all the mischief that they could throughout the land and the country-side Thus did they a long time, working their will outside the strong holds, nor did any molest them

But it so chanced that rumour, which flieth everywhere, came even to King Philip And it was reported to him that King Richard was at Gisors with a great multitude of people, and that he was burning and plundering all the land about Beauvais And when the king heard these tidings he was exceeding wroth, and he sent for the Count of Chartres, the Count of Vendôme, the Count of Nevers, the Count of Sancerre (who was a valiant man), the Vidame of Châteaudun, my Lord William of Barres, my Lord Alain of Rouci, and many other valiant men who are not named here, and he shewed them the mischief wrought by King Richard, who ought to be his man, and besought their counsel, how he should act in the matter

"Sire," quoth the Count of Sancerre, "an it please you, we who are here will betake ourselves thither, and we will go even to Beauvais and will see what can be done, and if it please God, that Englishman shall not utterly strip us of our heritage"

Then did the king bid them make themselves ready so soon as they could, and caused moneys to be delivered to them by cart-loads And when they were equipped with both arms and horses, they went their ways straight to Beauvais

---

[26]See p 261, note

and awaited one another there And they formed a vanguard and a rearward and rode on towards Gisors, and they of Gisors came out to meet them And they skirmished sharply, the one side with the other, and much was lost there and much gained, and at last they withdrew for this time, but each day they fought in the same manner

Now, as it befell, King Richard sent word to the Count of Sancerre and to the Barrois that they were eating the king's bread for nought, but if they were so bold that they durst come so far as the elm tree before Gisors, then would he acknowledge them to be valiant and bold And the king's men sent back word that they would come on the morrow, before the third hour, and would cut down the tree in his despite When the English king heard that they were coming to cut down the elm, he caused the trunk of the elm to be ironed with bands of iron, to a breadth of full five fathoms

On the morrow, early in the morning, the king's men armed themselves and drew up their people in five battalions, whereof the Count of Sancerre led one, the Count of Chartres the second, and Count of Vendôme the third, the Count of Nevers the fourth, and my Lord William of Barres and my Lord Alain of Rouci the fifth And they rode so far as the elm of Gisors, the crossbowmen and the carpenters in the front with axes good and sharp, and with goodly pickaxes to tear away the bands wherewith the elm was bound And they halted by the elm, and tare away the bands by force, and cut down the elm—let this irk whomso it might

But King Richard was not sleeping in the mean time, but he too had drawn up five battalions, and he charged right featly into the midst of them, like the bold warrior that he was And well and boldly was he received by the king's men, and they brake their lances, and many there were wounded and overthrown Then drew they their swords and intermingled, the one company with the other, and many on both sides were laid low And marvellous many fair deeds of knighthood did King Richard perform there, and overthrew both knights and horses, tearing helms from heads and shields from necks, and so many feats of arms wrought he that the king's men were dumfounded thereat And on the other side did the Barrois maintain himself so vigorously that he met no knight whom he laid not on the ground, and so were they abashed before him that none of them durst await him, but all made way for him

But whilst he thus valorously deported himself, King Richard was beholding him and had great envy of him, for he hated him of old So he took up a great lance and cried out to him ·

"Barrois, too far hast thou ridden !"

When the Barrois heard him he recognized him, and he took a great lance strong and tough, from the hand of a squire, and pricked his steed to meet the king, and the king came on to meet him And they shock so violently, breast to breast and horse to horse, that they make the very earth to leap up, and so grievously hard smite they each the other's blazoned shield that they burst poitrels[27] and

---

[27] A piece of armour protecting the horse's breast

saddle-girths and bear each other to the ground over their horses' croups, their saddles betwixt their thighs Up leap they again and draw sword from scabbard, and rush the one upon the other, and strike mighty blows against the middle of their helmets and on their shields Nor could it fail to come about that the one or the other of them were undone, had the battle long endured But presently they sprang apart, to the one side and to the other, and mounted again each his own steed, and withdrew immediately each from the other, and went back each to his own lodging, for night was drawing nigh

So was there respite from that hour until the morrow, when King Richard had heard mass Then, lo, came a messenger post-haste, who dismounted at the stairs of the hall and came up and called for the king, and they shewed him where the king was And to the king he went, and saluted him, and said

"Sire, the Count of Gloucester, to whom ye left England in ward, is dead; and they of your country are sore troubled, for the King of Scotland and the King of Ireland and the King of Wales are entered into your land and are working you much mischief there For God's sake, sire, devise some counsel for this case, even as ye ought, as lord and king that ye are"

When the king had heard the messenger, it lacked but little that he had gone utterly mad But he called his council, and of his barons the most valiant and the wisest, and sought counsel of them And they made answer that there was none other counsel to give save that he go in all haste to England and take with him of his men whatsoever ones he would and those that would be most profitable to him, and that the remnant should abide here and guard the castle and harass the king's men "And in sooth will we make them to spend the king's moneys!"

"I' faith," quoth the king, "ye say well"

Immediately the king left his council, and on the morrow he bade make ready for his journey And he chose the best of his barons and went away to England; and he found his land in sorry case and his people sore distressed, as folk that were without a lord

XIV

HOW THE WAR BETWIXT THE TWO KINGS CONTINUED

Here let us leave King Richard, and we will tell of King Philip, who had letters from the Count of Sancerre (he was captain of the host) saying that King Richard had gone away to England with the best of his barons So thought the king that now was the hour And he caused letters missive to be written and to be sent to all his vassals, and commanded them all to be at Beauvais within one month, armed as it behooved them to be So were they there within the month, nor was there one belated, and they found the king, who was already come thither

And he formed a vanguard and a rearward of valiant knights and crossbow-men to conduct the host And they came of a morning before Gisors and pitched their tents and their pavilions all around about the castle, a crossbowshot away And they that were within came forth and wrought them what annoy they could;

but it availed them nought, for they were very few to the king's men, nor any longer was he there who had been their stay

So were the French lodged, and on the morrow morn the king commanded the engines to be set up, and trebuchets,[28] petraries, cats,[29] and mangonels a many to play upon the place Thus was done, and after a little they that were within were so tormented, both by night and by day, that they knew not whither to turn or what to do, for so many of them had been slain that scarce the third part of their number remained sound and whole

And when the captain of Gisors saw that they were all doomed to death, he sent word to King Philip, by advice of his people, saying that he would yield him the castle in a month's time if he had no succour from King Richard The king granted him a respite, but on condition that he hold the castellan's son as hostage Now in the mean time the messenger that the castellan had sent to England had returned, and the castellan had heard his lord's answer to the letter that he had sent him And well he wist that never would he have succour of his lord, so he yielded up the castle of Gisors to King Philip, stately and strong though it be, and the king caused it to be garrisoned with good men and stocked with whatsoever things were needful for them Then King Philip departed thence and passed through the country of Normandy, and there he wrought his will in full, outside the strong holds, until King Richard had ended his war with his enemies and had made peace with them

And King Richard came to Normandy so speedily and with so great numbers as he could And he landed at Dieppe of an evening, and on the morrow, before daybreak, he bade his folk arm themselves and march toward the place where King Philip was

And at that hour the king was riding with a privy retinue, nor aught recked he of being on his guard, for he thought that King Richard was in England, but the churl saith in his proverb "In an hogshead of thinking is not a potful of wisdom" And albeit King Philip was the wisest prince in the world, yet ofttimes it befalleth that a wise man committeth great folly And at this time was the Barrois not with him, but Alain of Rouci was there, who grievously hated the Barrois, even as the Barrois hated him

And my Lord Alain looked before him, and he saw, less than two leagues away, a great multitude of baronry scattered along the land to the right and to the left And he came to the king and said to him

"Sire, I see banners in great number, and we are in a war-torn land, therefore should we arm ourselves, an ye will listen to me, for King Richard is a very perfect knight and most cunning in war"

"By the lance of Saint James!" quoth the king "Alain, never yet have I seen thee a coward ere this hour!"

---

[28] A ballistic engine somewhat resembling the petrary and the mangonel

[29] The "cats" were heavy timber frames, with projecting teeth, to be hoisted up and dropped on assailants or defenders The same name was applied to a kind of shed, somewhat like the Roman *vinea*, mounted on wheels or rollers and used by the besiegers in attacking the walls

"By my head!" quoth my Lord Alain "Now am I one that straightway hold eth his peace!"

Then did the king look before him, and he saw that the banners were drawing near to him and that the land was fair peopled with warriors So called he my Lord Alain and said to him

"Alain, an thou so redest, it were well that our people be armed"

And my Lord Alain made answer to the king

"A fitting time to glean bare ground [180] Sire, know now of a truth that it is King Richard without any fail, and I tell you soothly that presently shall we all be taken But do your endeavour! Mount the swiftest steed that ye have and get you away to Gisors, which lieth hard by, and put yourself in safety there, and I will abide here and will don your armour, and we will do the best that we can"

Then did the king mount a steed that was both strong and fleet, and away he galloppeth toward Gisors And he was espied of the vanguard, and after him ran more than two hundred of these, but they were armed, while he was without armour and better mounted than all they And on went he, by the aid of his horse, even to Gisors, and he was received therein with all haste But my Lord Alain of Rouci abode behind, and took the king's armour, and he made two battalions of such folk as he had, and set them in order

Then, lo, on cometh King Richard, and his people, and they charge into the midst of them The king's men received them vigorously with all the force that they had and defended themselves marvellous well, but all their prowess availed them nought, for few were they against the English, and King Richard was a right good knight of his hands And in the end the king's men were discomfited, and he took captive of them such as he would, so was my Lord Alain taken, armed with the armour of the king When King Richard saw him, he cried

"In God's name, King, now have I thee!"

"Nay, verily," quoth my Lord Alain, "that do ye not, but ye have Alain of Rouci, a poor vavasour"[81]

"How?" quoth the king "Thou devil! Art thou that Alain! I thought—by Saint Thomas!—to have held the king's own person Ah, God!" (quoth the king) "Since we have failed of the king, have we the Barrois?"

"Nay, indeed!" answered my Lord Alain, "for an he had been here, ye had all been taken or slain"

And this saying was reported to the Barrois, who hated him bitterly, and because of this saying they became reconciled the one to the other

Straightway King Richard departed thence with his prisoners and went on to Vernon, a castle that he held, which is very fair and goodly and well situate on the Seine And he caused his prisoners to be distributed among his castles, but my

---

[30]"*A bele eure vial tondre!*" Literally "clip a calf" A proverbial expression of doubtful meaning, possibly something like our "locking the stable after the horse is stolen" *Vial* is sometimes used of a barren spot in a field of grain, and *tondre*, in the sense of "mow" or "glean" My translation is only tentative

[31]Vassal's vassal

Lord Alain he kept with himself and took him to Rouen, and there did he sojourn for a season

And now will we tell you of King Philip, who was at Gisors and had summoned his men and rallied them together And he came back into France and sojourned there for a season And King Richard, who was at Rouen, was sore grieved because of Gisors and Niort, which he had lost, so he took a part of his people and sent them to the marches for to harry and to lay waste the country And the other part he led against one of King Philip's castles, which was on the marches, and laid siege to it And he lay for a long time before the place, ere he took it, but so well kept he the roads guarded that not a messenger was able to get himself out of the castle And he lay before the castle until, at last, he took it by storm And as for each of the crossbowmen, he caused one of his hands to be cut off, and for each of the serjeants, one eye to be put out, but the knights he held for ransom, and let them go for such or such a sum And when King Philip knew this, it irked him sore; but nought could he do concerning it at this time, for a grievous sickness laid hold on him for a year and a half, so that he was able to take no measures in the matter

XV

OF THE WAR THAT KING RICHARD MADE ON THE KING OF SPAIN AND OF THE DEATH OF KING RICHARD

Now will we come back to King Richard, who kept his bears a-dancing,[82] nor was there any to say him nay, but he did whatsoever him listed, outside the strong holds And he seized booty and he seized churls, and he so harried the land that there was no sowing and no tilling so far as the border country runneth, and yet farther But the strong holds of the French king were so filled with good men and with wines and victual and whatsoever things were needful, that they were not careful for King Richard, none the less he kept them so close that not one of them had power to remove from his own place

Now it so befell that word was brought to him that the King of Spain had laid siege to Réole and Bergerac, two good towns that were his And when he heard these tidings he shook his head, and he said that, by the soul of his father, the thing pleased him well nor would he longer tarry thus, for now had the King of Spain awaked the sleeping cat, and the proverb runneth of yore "The she-goat paweth so long that she getteth her an hard bed" Then King Richard bade summon his vassals and gathered together a great host, and they put forth to sea and sailed until they were come to Bayonne, one of his cities, which lieth in Gascony beside the sea And there were they eight days, and on the ninth day the English king commanded the host to march and so quickly as it could to enter into the lands of the King of Spain And they put all the country-side to the fire and to the flame, and they wasted cornfields and vineyards and gardens and destroyed whatsoever they touched And so a fortnight passed or ever the King of Spain knew

[82]*Faisoit ses ours tumber,* a proverbial expression

this But then a certain spy gat him away from the host and came straight to
Réole, where the King of Spain had his own host, and he said to the king

"Sire, ill goeth it ! King Richard hath landed at Bayonne with much people
And know ye that he hath already wrought you much mischief, for he burneth
and destroyeth all that which he toucheth, outside the strong holds, nor is there
any to say him nay "

When the king heard these words, they pleased him not one whit, and verily
in his heart he weened that he might have encounter, for well he wist that King
Richard was bold and courageous and would leave him nought of that which was
his own Howbeit, he thought that King Philip would so have busied him that
he would have none occasion to come, but it hath oft been said that "hope and
expectation are two ninnies " Straightway King Ferdinand of Spain gat him to a
place apart, and called his council, and said to them

"Fair sirs, counsel me now, for I have sore need thereof Lo, here is King
Richard, who hath entered into my land, and well know I that he is right overweening and that an he could have his will of me I should not come thence with
my life, or at the least I should be cast into prison "

"By our faith," quoth his barons and his council all, "never shall ye find one
of us that would so rede you ! But bid your arrière-ban[88] be called, whereof there
is a great force, and summon succour, and on pain of losing goods and fief let
none tarry behind, or if he tarry he shall tarry on a gibbet And know of a truth
that ye will have yet twice again so many people as ye have here, moreover, ye
will be in your own country and every day will the number of your men increase "

To this counsel did they all agree, and the king caused his letters to be written and to be sent in all haste throughout his land And they came on the day that
they were bidden, and King Richard drew nigh to them, even within four leagues,
and sent word to King Ferdinand, asking battle on the third day, and King Ferdinand sent back word to him that right freely should he have it and that himself desired it greatly

Then had ye seen, on the one side and on the other, hauberks rolled, lances
pointed, pourpoints and plastrons and shields put in order, saddles, housings and
poitrels made ready, and horses shod—then had ye seen how every one saw straitly
to it that him was nothing lacking ! And when came the third day, then all arose,
and each of the two kings caused his own men to be drawn up in ten battalions
and so ranged and ordered as seemed him best, and in each battalion was a constable, a valiant and a gentle man, who should direct it

Immediately the hosts drew nigh the one to the other and joined battle, the
first battalion with the first, and many of them were overthrown and wounded,
and the English had the worse thereof But the second battalion succoured them
vigorously and bare hard upon their adversaries When the second battalion of
the Spaniards saw their own side going under, then they charged straight into
the midst of the English and slew or overthrew many of them Then charged the
third battalion—of the one side and of the other—and the fourth, and the fifth,

---

[88]The body of vassals subject to summons from their sovereign for three months' service

and all the others, and they were all commingled And there were overthrown so many knights and so many a steed astrayed that no man could tell you the number thereof

Then, lo, King Richard, lance in rest, cometh crying

"King Ferdinand of Spain! Whither have ye gone? Behold here King Richard, who cometh to forbid you Réole and Bergerac and all the land of Gascony, wherein ye have no right, and thereby are ye proved an evil man and a disloyal But ye thought that the French King would have given me so much to do that I could not come hither"

Then forth from his mouth came a word of great arrogance

"Certes," quoth he, "battle a plenty will I give both him and you so long as I shall live!"

Ah, God! He thought to have lived far longer than his life did last!

When the King of Spain heard himself called traitor, it liked him not at all And he struck spurs to his horse and went to the place where King Richard was, and he hanged fast about his neck his shield, which was painted vert with three castles or, signifying that he was King of Castile And he couched his lance and moved against King Richard, and King Richard against him And King Richard was armed in vermilion armour, and couching his lance, he moved against the King of Spain And they came together with so great violence that neither saddle-girth nor poitrel could save them from falling to earth, each with his saddle betwixt his feet

But up they sprang so soon as they were able, and drew their naked swords from their scabbards, and dealt each the other mighty blows upon the neck Nor could it fail to come to pass that the one or the other of them should suffer sore mischief, for they were both good knights, but the people of each one succoured their own lord, and by main force were they gotten to horse again And the battle endured until mid-afternoon, but the Spaniards had the worse thereof, for they were but ill armed neither knew they so much of warfare as did the English Likewise did these take heart of King Richard their lord, who wrought such deeds of arms that all they that saw him marveled greatly thereat--yea, even the King of Spain himself, nor ever thereafter durst he meet King Richard, so well had he proved him

When King Ferdinand and his people saw that they could not endure the battle, then turned they their backs And the English followed hard upon their heels, and the chase endured until the darkness of night when one man could not see another Then the English went back to the tents of King Ferdinand and lay there the night, and there found they whatsoever things they needed and they gat great treasure there And on the morrow morn back went they to Bayonne, and they put forth to sea, glad and joyous and light of heart Twelve days they journeyed by sea, then came they to land at Dover, one of the king's castles, and great joy had the English of their lord's victory

And after the king had supped he gat him to bed, howbeit, he could not sleep, but he called to mind Gisors and Niort which he had lost, and he thought that he would go and lay siege to Gisors and take it by force, for King Philip was sick, and King Richard had the more part of his own people with him and his fleet was in readiness And on the morrow he bade his folk make themselves ready and put forth to sea, and they went gladly, for his palms were fair pierced with largess.

So on they went until they came into port at Dieppe, which belonged to him, and thence came they to Rouen, which he greatly loved, and there they took whatsoever was needful for them And he caused his host to march even to a certain castle which belonged to King Philip, which was called Loche and was very strong and well situate and well stored, and it was a sore grievance to King Richard And he betook him thither and laid siege to it, and he sware that he would not depart thence until he should have taken it by force So he caused it to be assaulted both day and night, but they that were within it defended themselves right vigorously, for they were many and were well supplied

And it befell one day that King Richard was going about to survey the castle, having a targe before him; and he was shot through by an arbalester who stood in a turret on an angle of the wall, which thrust forth beyond the other turrets. For the arbalester set a quarrel in his arbalest and discharged it right at the king, and it hit him in the bend of the right shoulder, which was uncovered, and wounded him sore And when the king perceived that he was wounded he gat himself back and came unto his tent And the leeches were summoned, and they drew forth the bolt from his shoulder, all whole, and they searched the wound and said that he need have no concern an he would but take good heed to himself Howbeit, the king, who was bold of heart, took no note of the wound or of the counsel of his physicians, but he ate and drank whatsoever him listed and lay with women And the wound began to wax angry and to burn as with a fire, and in a very little time his side and his arm were all inflamed thereby

And when the king saw that he was all a-burning and that die he must perforce, then began he to make lamentation for himself and to utter his plaint, and thus he spake

"Ah, King Richard! Shalt thou then die? Ah, Death, how bold art thou, who hast dared assail King Richard, the most perfect knight and the most courteous and the most bounteous in all the world! Ah, Chivalry, how wilt thou wane away! Alas, poor knights, poor ladies! What will become of you? Ah, God! Who will henceforth uphold chivalry, largess, and courtesy?"

Thus did the king make his plaint, and when he saw that he must surely die he commanded that his heart be buried at Rouen, for the love that he had of that city, and that his body be borne to London and buried there in the mother church Presently he passed, and gave up the ghost, and then began his people to make the greatest lamentation that ever yet was made of men And the host departed thence and went their ways to Rouen And there was buried the heart of King Richard, but his body was borne to London, where was made the greatest lamentation that ever was made for any soul, and the body was buried in the great church with great honour, and there was a tomb reared, fair and rich and such as befitteth a king

XVI

HOW JOHN OF BRIENNE BECAME KING OF JERUSALEM

Now will we leave King Richard, who died without heirs of his body, and we will tell of the King of Jerusalem, who was made king by election and reigned eight years And he died, both he and the queen his wife, and there remained after them one daughter, and the kingdom was in the hands of the barons, and they had the ward of the damosel and she was in ward to them until she was of age to marry

Next will we tell you of John of Brienne, who was son to Count Walter of Brienne, the aged, who had divers children that were older than John Now the count would have his son John be made a clerk, but a clerk he would not be, so he ran away to Clairvaux, where he had an uncle, his mother's brother, who caused to be given him whatsoever he needed And he took in good part whatsoever was done with him, for he was a lad of but fourteen years

Now it befell one day that certain knights of his lineage were going to a tournament and were passing before the gate of Clairvaux, and they saw the boy John standing in the gate and perceived that he was a well-favoured lad and lusty, and soothly seemed he gentle-born So they halted at the gate and enquired who the lad was And it was told them that he was son to Count Walter of Brienne, and that he had fled away to his uncle at Clairvaux because he would not become a clerk And the knights said that he had done well and had acted from a good and a gentle heart And they caused him to be brought by a squire and set upon a sumpter beast, and they took him with them to a tourney where they procured him an horse And they took him from march to march, and the lad grew and waxed in wisdom until he could featly serve and aid his friend in the greatest press of the tournament And so served he until he was eight and twenty years old, but when the Lord of Châteauvillain saw and recognized his good sense and his prowess he would have made him a knight And he was a worthy and a knightly man and kept the youth in his own household

Then his friends took counsel together and they requested Count Walter, his father, that he give him land, for it seemed to them that land would thus be well employed But the count sware to them that never, in death or in life, should his son have a pennyworth of his land, and from that day forth bare he the name of John Lackland But for all that ceased he not to go to tournaments and to combats of war and to all the marches whither other knights went for to gain glory, for his friends gave him whatsoever he needed, because of his prowess

So for a long time did he fare, and exceeding great praise did he win and glory of chivalry, and so great fame of him spread abroad throughout all lands that he was known even in the land of Syria And the barons thereof came together and agreed that they would send to seek him for the damosel and make him king And even as it had been determined, so was it done, and he was summoned by the barons through letters And when he received these tidings, then gave he thanks to Our Lord, and he made known the matter to the Seignior of Châteauvillain and to

the Seignior, of Joinville and to his other friends, who were right glad thereof
And they bestowed on him that which was needful—money and raiment, horses
and suits of armour, and knights of his own lineage for to bear him company and
for his honour's sake

Straightway John gat him clean away from his friends and from his country and took leave of them all, and he journeyed day by day till, after a fortnight,
he was come to Marseilles And there his company found the ship made ready
and they put therein that which was needful for them, and they put forth to sea
on a Tuesday morning And God gave them so favourable a wind that they accomplished their passage in one and twenty days, and they landed at Acre on a
Monday at nones, and John rested fifteen days in Acre because of great weariness
of the sea

Then came the barons to him, saying "Sire, we have sent for you for your
own good and for your own honour's sake, and well know we that ye are gentle-
born, and a valiant man, and full of chivalry, and loyal, neither see we where the
kingdom could better be bestowed than on you And we give you the queen and
the land, and God grant that we have bestowed them well!"

"I' faith, God give it!" quoth John Lackland

And he received the damosel and wedded her in the church of the Holy
Cross, which is the bishop's church, and there was made a very great and goodly
marriage feast, which endured eight full days At the end of these eight days
were they taken to Beirut, and there were they crowned, for this is now the seat
where are crowned the kings of Jerusalem, because Jerusalem itself is in the
hands of the Saracens

Thus, even as I have told you, was John Lackland made King of Jerusalem,
and he lost the name of John Lackland, and ever thereafter was he called Good
King John And he maintained the kingdom well and justly, and he was a good
justicer and reigned for a long time as a good king And he had by the queen one
daughter, who was afterward wife to the Emperor Frederick,[34] and of her issued
a son, who took to wife the daughter of the Duke of Bavaria, and of this son is
there also a son, who ought to be King of Jerusalem

Now it came to pass that the Queen of Jerusalem died, who was a very noble
woman and an holy, and she was buried in the church of the Holy Cross And it
also came to pass that a little time thereafter the king took to wife the daughter of
the King of Armenia, and he had by her a son who was christened John, after
his father who was also called John, and the child lived only seven years, and he
died

XVII

HOW THE MEN OF THE CROSS LAID SIEGE TO DAMIETTA

Now falleth silent the tale of King John, yet shall we come back to it again
when time and place are fitting And now will we tell you of Pope Innocent, who had
heard that the land beyond the sea was in the hands of the Saracens and that they

---

[34]Frederick II of Germany

grievously entreated it, nor was the service of Our Lord celebrated at all therein And he was moved to exceeding pity and caused a council general to be assembled, of all the orders that were under the law of Rome

And on the day set were they at Rome, and there were decreed many rules that were necessary for Holy Church There was it decreed that a little bell should be borne with the *Corpus Domini,* for as yet was none carried with it Likewise was it decreed that the priests who wore copes with sleeves should have these round And there were many other things decreed there which are in no wise well observed or kept

Then began they to speak of the land beyond the sea, which was in the hands of the Saracens, for which cause Christendom ought to be exceeding wroth And then was it agreed by all the prelates that the cross[35] should be preached And the legate of France was called Master Robert of Courson, and he was an Englishman and drank lustily (and even so do many worthy men), and he bestowed the cross on many folk

And these departed in two companies The first company landed at Acre on Michaelmas, and there was a great multitude of them And they held council with the King of Jerusalem to the end that they should go and lay siege to Damietta, and in the mean time their number waxed greater And with this counsel were all the high barons in accord, and they made ready their fleet and put forth to sea And they came to Damietta and sought haven there And they pitched their tents and their pavilions and lodged themselves as best they could

And when the Saracens perceived them, then had they great fear of them, and they shut their gates and fortified their towers and made marvellous preparation for to defend themselves, and they sent word to Saphadin,[36] Soldan of Babylon, who was the Seignior of Damietta, asking that he send them succour, for that King John and all the Christendom of France had laid siege to them And when Saphadin had heard these tidings he was no whit glad thereof And he caused his letters to be written and sent throughout all Heathendom, and he bade them come and succour him "For King John" (quoth he) "and all the Christendom of France and of Lombardy and of Tuscany and of Germany have laid siege to Damietta, and well know they that it is the key to all Heathendom"

Then came together all their high barons to Bagdad, and there took they counsel what they should do There was the Soldan of Damascus, who was named Coradin and was own brother to Saphadin, Soldan of Babylon And there was the Soldan of Iconium, and he of La Chamelle, and he of Aleppo (where are all the good knights of Heathendom), and many another soldan and admiral [37] And they were all agreed that they would go, and they sent word to the Soldan of Babylon that they would be with him on a day which they appointed, then went they back each of them to his own country

---

[35]I e, Crusade

[36]Malek-el-Kameel, Saphadin's son, instead of Saphadin himself, was at this time Sultan of Egypt (Babylon)

[37]Emir

And they gat together so much people as they could move and came to Baby-lon on the day that had been set, and they took counsel how they should proceed. And for a long time they continued in such sort that neither of the two armies wrought any mischief to the other that were worth the telling, nevertheless the Christians fortified themselves and digged them good trenches and builded good barriers over against the heath And they made a bridge of boats athwart the stream, which is very wide and deep, for to shut off them of Damietta from their harbour, for by this harbour came all their merchandise to them And they made of their army two hosts, the one at this end of the bridge and the other at the other end thereof, and this it was that gave them most annoy

Now here for a little season will we leave King John and his host, and we will tell you of the other company of the Christians, which was left behind to wit, of Milo, Bishop elect of Beauvais, who was brother to my Lord Gaucher of Nan-teuil, and my Lord Andrew, his brother, and my Lord John of Arcis, and the Count of Pingin,[88] and the Seignior of Loupines, who was a worthy man, and my Lord John Fuinon, and many other valiant men, whom I will not name to you, for it were a weariness to name so many folk

And the bishop elect received the tithe of the clerks at the hand of the Pope, and they prepared to depart about the feast of Saint John, and they made ready their ships and put out to sea And they sailed on without any hinderance until they were come to Acre, and there they enquired where the king was, and it was told them that he lay before Damietta, to which he had laid siege, and that he had been there a year When the bishop elect heard this he caused his ships to be made ready, and on the morrow they put forth again to sea, and they were six days in coming to Damietta, and there sought they harbour and lodged themselves with the others, who were right glad of their coming Howbeit, nought but ill befell them there, as ye shall hear tell hereafter

XVIII

HOW THE MEN OF THE CROSS WERE DEFEATED, YET QUIT NOT THE SIEGE

Now will we tell you of Saphadin, the Soldan of Babylon, who was encamped some two leagues away from the host, and whensoever the Christians assaulted Damietta, the Saracens assaulted the Christians for to help them of Damietta, for they could not enter into Damietta save through the host of the Christians So they harassed them for a season, until one day the legate and King John and the Bishop elect of Beauvais and all the other barons held a parliament together, and they said that it were best that they go and assault the Saracens, and if it so pleased God they would have the victory, but some said that it were well first to challenge them

"I' faith," quoth King John, "it booteth not to challenge them so far away, for all day long shall we have them at the barriers an so listeth us!"

---

[88]Unidentified

"Sooth, Sire," quoth the Bishop elect of Beauvais, "would ye now have us tarry for ever in this country?"

"Certes," quoth the king, "that would I not! Rather do I believe that your going were more profitable than your staying Nevertheless, I will do what the rest desire, let befall what will "

Upon this they agreed, nevertheless, that they would send gage of battle to the Soldan of Babylon, and the soldan granted them battle for the day of the Decollation of Saint John[39] And know ye of a truth that never on that day did Christians combat Saracens but they themselves were beaten The Christians made them ready as best they could, and the Saracens did likewise, and they caused their battalions to be ranged and set in order But the Christians, who were too confident, perceived not what the end of their undertaking might be, and they sought the enemy two leagues away in the midst of the hot and burning sand-waste, and their horses, step by step, struck knee-deep into the sand, and the footfolk also

And when they drew nigh to the Saracens the folk on foot were so forspent that they lost both heart and breath, and by their own selves were they discomfited and they turned and fled toward the barriers And when the Saracens perceived this, they ran after them and slew so many of them as they would And all the footfolk had died but for the horsemen who were in the rear ward and withstood the rout of Saracens that pressed them sore But so greatly did the Christians suffer that no longer could they endure, for the day was hot, and they were heavy-armed and had come a long way But the Saracens were fresh and lightly armed, and they were able to suffer the heat and had their will of the Christians

And there was taken prisoner the Bishop elect of Beauvais, and my Lord Andrew of Nanteuil, his brother, and my Lord John of Arcis, and the Seignior of Loupines, and my Lord John Fumon, and many another valiant man, who were all led away to Cairo, to a castle that standeth outside Babylon, which is the soldan's, and there were they cast into prison and into durance vile And when King John knew this—and the legate and the other barons—then were they sore grieved, and they stood in greater dread of the Saracens and guarded against them more straitly And for this reason it was not long until they held their host even as it had been afore, and they so distrained them of Damietta that none could either enter in there or come forth of the city

Thus remained they for a long season ere Saphadin and the other soldans moved themselves And they of Damietta were in sore distress and they suffered a grievous disease of the mouth which kept them from drinking and from eating and they died of this pestilence And so horrible in Damietta was the stench of the bodies of them that had died that none could endure it, nay, well-nigh all the people died, either of the stench or of the sickness, and they were so afflicted that they could not suffer more

And they took a carrier-pigeon that had been bred in Babylon, and they caused a letter to be written wherein were described their misease and their mortality And,

---

[39] 29 August

by Mahomet (said they), let their friends send them succour, for great was the need thereof, and let it be known to them that they no longer had any captain, for he had died in the common sickness And they desired that there be sent to them as captain some man of gentle birth, valiant and wise, who might have the knowledge and the power to govern the city And they made fast the letter to the pigeon, underneath her right wing

Straightway they let the pigeon go, and she lifted herself into the air and sought out her path and addressed herself straight toward Babylon And she flew until she came to the dovecote wherein she had been bred And when the keeper of the pigeons, who watched the dovecote, perceived her, he went and told the soldan, and he said to him "Sire, here is come a new messenger"

And the soldan said that the bird should be brought to him, and so it was done And he took the bird and he drew the letter from under her right wing and caused it to be read, and he knew how it was with them of Damietta And when he knew this he was sore distressed thereat—and very justly, for this city was the key to his land And he advised himself how he should proceed, and counsel was given him that he take some man of gentle birth, both wise and vigorous, and send him to Damietta for to be captain there And so did he, and he caused an ox-hide to be folded four times, in the shape of an egg, and the man was put within it, along with the soldan's letter And this vessel was well sewn and well daubed with pitch, and it was upheld with cork in such sort that it could not be overturned or sunk, and it was all in the water save that about a foot of it appeared, and it had an hole in its top whereby the man might get him air to breathe So was he set in the river by night, and the vessel floated until it came to the bridge which the Christians had builded athwart the stream

And the Christians had stretched a net from end to end of the bridge, for whatsoever things might chance to come, and when midnight was at hand the vessel rested at the bridge because of the net which held it fast, and there it remained until daylight, when they saw the top thereof which appeared above the water And they went thither in boats, and the vessel was drawn out with hooks, and they carried it to the king's tent And there was the vessel cut in pieces, and forth they drew the Saracen along with the letter And the king bade the letter be read, and he knew by the letter that this was the soldan's nephew and that the soldan was sending him to Damietta for to be captain there, and he knew all the state of them that were within the city And the king caused him to be put in irons and to be guarded right carefully, until one night when it chanced that the guards all gat themselves drunk and slept so sound that the prisoner escaped and fled away behind the tents

Straightway the guards awaked who were guarding him, and they cried "Hoy! Hoy!" and went seeking him throughout the host, but the prisoner had already gotten himself so far away that he was amongst the hindermost tents And surely had he escaped had it not been for certain bakers who had risen up for to knead their dough and heard the rattling of his irons and men crying after him "Seize the prisoner! Seize the prisoner!" And one of them was holding a rolling-pin, and therewith smote he the man so violently upon his pate that he killed him, whereat the king was sore grieved when he knew it, for he would have gotten rich ransom for the man, or exchange of some Christian of gentle birth

XIX

HOW DAMIETTA WAS TAKEN

Henceforth will we tell you of Saphadin, King of Babylon, who was sore oppressed in his heart for the sake of Damietta, which he thought to lose And he assembled all the high princes of his host and said to them

"Sirs, an we lose Damietta, then have we lost all, for it is the key to our land, and through it cometh all our merchandise, our corn, and other things And very great pain of our bodies should we be fain to suffer or ever we get it back again, for, by Mahomet, if the city is lost now, much do I fear me that it is lost beyond all recovery ! And I have bethought me of a thing, so ye approve it that we send word to the king and to the legate that we will restore all the prisoners that we hold, both the old and those newly taken, and all the land which King Amaury held, save only Kerak and Montreal[40] which are held by men over whom we have no authority, and that we will pay them each year whatsoever the two castles are worth And they shall have a truce for twenty years, with the understanding that they raise the siege of Damietta "

To this counsel did they all agree, and they caused the prisoners to come before them and told them these words, which pleased them right well And the prisoners chose two of their own number for to carry the message, of whom the one was my Lord Andrew of Nanteuil and the other was John of Arcis, and the rest stood surety for these, under pain of having their heads cut off And these twain came to the host, even unto the king's tent, and the legate was summoned and all the barons, then my Lord Andrew spake thus to them

"Fair sirs, hither are we sent by the baronry of Heathendom, who send you the fairest peace that ever was offered to Christians For they will restore to you all the prisoners whom they hold, both old and new, and all the land which King Amaury held, save Kerak and Montreal, for these two castles can they not restore to you, since they are in the hands of those over whom they have no authority, howbeit, they will render you yearly for them so much as they are worth Moreover, ye shall have a truce even for twenty years, but this shall ye only so ye raise the siege of Damietta and go back to your own country "

The king and the legate and the barons said that they would take counsel in the matter, and for a long time were they in council, and many were the words that were uttered by the one party against the other And in sooth some would accept the peace for the sake of their friends who were in captivity, others said that this were not a good thing to do, for they had tarried here well-nigh two whole years, and had suffered cold and heat and all manner of misease, and had expended their substance, and now were they at the point to take the city, nor would they ever agree thereto

---

[40]Two fortresses near the southern end of the Dead Sea

But in truth were these possessed by their own pride and by the pride of the Bishop elect of Beauvais, who had more pride than had even Nebuchadnezzar—and he had thereof a plenty! To their counsel did the more part incline; and back went the messengers all weeping, and what they had heard from the king and the barons told they again to the other prisoners, who made great dole thereover And then told they these things to the soldan, who was sore displeased thereat, for he had more at stake than all the others

Now leave we here the prisoners, who are in durance vile and sore misease in their prison at Cairo, making great dole among themselves nor having any hope that ever will they be delivered, and we will tell you of the king, who was maintaining his siege before Damietta It befell one night that the guards drew nigh to the walls of the city and listened, nor heard they aught anywhere—neither on the walls, nor by the gates, nor in the towers And they came to the king and said to him

"Sire, us seemeth that in Damietta is no man, either are they dead, or they are fled"

"I' faith," quoth the king, "now is nought else to do but to make the assault! Now to the ladders! And whoso shall be the first to enter there, he shall have a thousand bezants"

Then were ladders raised and made fast to the walls, and up went they, every man for himself, and entered into the city Nor was there any to gainsay them, for well-nigh all the folk were dead or sick And they came to the gates and cut the bars thereof, and into the city entered all the men of the host And they found so great mortality of Saracens that scarce could they abide there for the stench; but the King commanded that the bodies should be carried out into the fields and burned So was it done as the king had commanded, and the city was cleansed, and there entered therein the king and the legate and all the others, and they found the town well supplied with corn and with wine, with arms, and gold, and silver, and whatsoever belongeth to a good city

So abode they in Damietta until a day when the barons and men of high estate spake together saying

"What is to be? Shall we remain yet all this year shut up in this city and do nothing more? Come, let us conquer Heathendom, for the Saracens are scattered, nor will ever be gathered together again And, lo, here is a castle which is called Tanis, lying but four leagues away, which we will take at the first blow, and if we shall have taken it, then lightly shall we have Babylon"

To this counsel did they all agree, then away went they to the king and to the legate and said these selfsame words to them And the legate said that this was a good thing to do But the king answered that the legate was but uttering his own desire nor did he know aught of what this undertaking signified "The Saracens" (quoth he) "are very wise, moreover they are on their own ground, and well do they discern their advantage when time and place offer And now are they exceeding wroth because of Damietta, which they have lost, and for mine own part would I advise that we wait until the flooding of the river is past"

"Nay verily," quoth the legate, "it seemeth to me that going were far better than remaining here"

"Nay verily," quoth the king, "I think that it will be far worse Nevertheless, through me shall there be no hinderance, nor will I that any man lay the blame thereof on me"

"I' faith," quoth the legate, "remaineth then nought else to do save to move ourselves and go to Tanis, and so soon as we are come thither we will assault it and take it"

But the event was far otherwise

And they caused the host to move and came to Tanis, which hath a marvellous fair situation, for it sitteth in an angle of the river, which there is divided, and the one arm runneth to the right and the other to the left And there lieth a champaign between the two arms of the river, where the soil can be ploughed and tilled, and thither did the Christians have their tents carried with the fleet, and they pitched their tents there and laid siege to the castle

But they remained there no great time When Saphadin knew of their coming, who was a very wise Saracen, he caused the river to be dammed and to be forced backward and to go forth of its bed and to overflow the isle where the legate and King John and the Christians were encamped. And ere midnight was come they all found themselves floating in the water, and all had been drowned had the soldan so willed But he was exceedingly wise, and he knew that through them that were here would he have Damietta again, whereas, an he had drowned them, then had he not gained much, for Damietta remained garrisoned with good men. Therefore did he keep them in such constraint, and he made known to them that if they would not render up Damietta, then would he drown them all

When the king and the legate and the other barons saw what their case was, then did they esteem themselves fools, and they said that better had it been for them an they had followed the king's rede But now was it too late So made they such a peace as they were able to obtain, altogether after the soldan's will And the soldan delivered unto them the prisoners, all that he held, both old and new, nor did he require aught of that which was theirs save Damietta, such as it should be found, with all its provision And this was accepted by the king and by the Christians, but the soldan would never take surety of the Templars, or of the Hospitalers, or of any man living save the king himself So must the king himself perforce remain as an hostage until Damietta should be restored to the soldan's command And it hath been said of old "Thus doeth he who cannot do better"[41]

XX

OF BISHOP MILO OF BEAUVAIS

So was the city yielded up and the king and the barons delivered And they put out to sea, and they came to Acre, and there went they to land and tarried there for a season And it came to pass that Milo, Bishop elect of Beauvais, who was chief of them all, desired to go back to France, and so did all they that had

---

[41]Cf "Hobson's choice"

come with him So they put to sea again and came to Saint Nicholas of Bari,[42] and thence went they by land even to Rome And they came to the Pope, and the bishop elect desired the Pope that he would sacre him And the Pope answered him that he would sacre him gladly, and he sacred him and anointed him bishop And he caused him to be shod with shoes which the clerks call sandals, which signify that he must take no step idly Then they put upon him the rochet, which is white and signifieth chastity Thereafter passed they the amice over his head, which signifieth humility, and after that the alb, which is pure white and signifieth virginity And next laid they the fanon[43] on his left arm, which signifieth abstinence, for the left arm, being bound, should withhold, and the right arm, being unbound, should give And thereafter took they the stole and laid it about his neck, which signifieth obedience And next they clothed him with the tunic, which must be green, wherein one readeth the epistle, which signifieth suffering, and thereafter with the dalmatic, wherein one readeth the gospel, which must be white and signifieth righteousness And over all the other vestments they laid on him the chasuble, which must be of vermillion purple and signifieth charity And then they placed the crook in his left hand, which is bent above and sharp below and signifieth mercy and vengeance, for the prelate ought to draw sinners unto him by his preaching and by his good example, and he ought to have mercy and to lighten a portion of their penance For the sinner might be so terrified by his own sins that he would fall into despair, and this is one of the sins that God most hateth And for this reason is the crook bent above And know ye wherefore it is so sharp below? Because the prelate ought to lay penance on the sinner, pricking him even as the point of the crook pricketh, and because he ought not on any account to relieve the sinner altogether of his penance, for if he should relieve him altogether, then would he the more lightly fall again into sin And after this they put the ring upon his finger, which signifieth marriage, for he is the spouse of Holy Church Then set they on his head the mitre, which must be white and hath two horns, whereof the one signifieth confession and the other satisfaction

Now have we told you how the Bishop elect of Beauvais was sacred, and the Pope gave him to hold the Vales of Alise,[44] and these held he for a long time, nor did he aught but evil But he must perforce depart thence through Chanteleu,[45] for he might have tarried there too long And he came back to France, and at that season was the Cardinal Romain there, preaching the cross[46] But the bishop preached of other matters, for he brought it to pass through his power that not one of the archbishops or of the bishops of the realm made answer before the king And ofttimes held they their parliament in the matter at Saint-Quentin, and at that time was Henry of Braîne archbishop, who was in accord with him, as were many of the other bishops But at the last the queen knew of this through a certain bishop who would not accord with him

---

[42]Bari in Apulia

[43]Probably used here for the maniple

[44]A name given to the Marches of Ancona and the Duchy of Spoleto

[45]Literally, "Wolf-howl" "By the name Chanteleu we are to understand some region whence one is in haste to escape, because he hears the wolves howling" Natalis de Wailly

[46]I e, crusade

And yet worse did he, for he brought accusation against the queen that she was with child by Cardinal Romain, wherein he lied But the queen took no note of this, rather, she kept the matter in her heart and thought that she would set the thing to rights at a fitting time and place So did Queen Blanche suffer it to lie until a certain day when the people of Beauvais came to complain to her of their bishop, who excommunicated them wrongfully and without reason, and they said to her

"Lady, our bishop excommunicateth us wrongfully and without reason Lady, for God's sake, cause us to be assoiled! For we are ready to do right, whithersoever the right shall lead us"

When the queen heard this, then was she right glad, for now wist she well that the thing would be put to rights which he had said of her And she bade him assoil the townsfolk and entreat them justly But the bishop sent back word to her that for her would he do nothing whatsoever in matters of his own jurisdiction And when the queen heard his message she summoned him to her presence for a certain day, but he defaulted, for he came not himself nor sent any one Then did the queen cause all her liege barons and prelates to be summoned, likewise the Bishop of Beauvais, and they all came to the parliament

And the good and wise queen bethought herself prudently, nor had she forgotten the villainy which the Bishop of Beauvais had uttered concerning her For she stripped herself, even to her shirt, and wrapped her in a mantle, and thus came she forth of her chamber And she came out into the hall where the princes and the prelates were and through the ushers she caused a silence to be made And when the noise was abated, she gat her up on a table that was set on two legs, and she said, in the hearing of the Bishop of Beauvais who was there present

"Sirs, look ye all upon me A certain man hath said that I am with child"

And she let fall her mantle upon the table, and she turned herself about, before and behind, until all had seen her, and it was very evident that she had no child in her womb

When the barons saw their lady standing there naked, they leaped forward and happed her in her mantle and led her back into her own chamber and caused her to clothe herself Then came she back to the parliament, and much was there spoken of one matter and another And in the end were summoned the burghers of Beauvais, and they made complaint of their bishop who was excommunicating them And the queen bade the bishop be called and asked him for what reason he excommunicated the king's burghers And the bishop said that to her was he not bound to make answer

"How!" quoth the queen "Are ye not yourself the king's man, and will ye not do right before us, who hold the rule of France in ward?"

"By Saint Peter!" quoth the bishop "I will that all now present know that I have no lord in the whole world save the Pope alone, under whose protection I am, nor before any other lord will I make answer"

When the queen heard the bishop speak thus, she was well pleased, for well knew she that he erred Then said she, in the audience of them all

"Sirs, ye hear clearly what the bishop saith, I will that ye be mindful thereof at the fitting time and place And I will take counsel touching that which hath been said "

Straightway departed the parliament, every one to his own land Then the queen assembled her council and asked them what was to do with the Bishop of Beauvais, who had wrought thus against the crown of France And her council said that inasmuch as he refused homage to the king she could rightfully seize herself of the fief which he held of the king And immediately the queen caused a letter to be written and to be sent to the bailiff of Beauvais And when the bishop knew this he was sore dumfounded, but never for that would he humble himself or cry the queen mercy, for the very great pride of his heart suffered him not to do this; rather, it put out the eyes of his heart, so that he saw not at all And this is of all the vices in the world the one that most destroyeth reason in a man, and righteousness

When the bishop saw that the thing was certain to befall, then made he preparation for a journey and gat him a retinue (for he had money and horses in abundance) and departed with a great company from Beauvais—nevermore to return thither So went he on day by day until he was come to Turin, a city of Lombardy, and there he rested, and he had right good lodging there And on the morrow morn he arose and heard mass and went on his way, nor had he journeyed far until he found a man digging in a vineyard, who had a great tonsure and wore a golden ring upon his finger And he stopped, and greeted him, and said to him

"Fair sir, who are ye, who dig in this vineyard?"

"In sooth, sir," answered the good man, "I am the Bishop of Turin, who here gain my bread "

"How !" quoth the Bishop of Beauvais "It is not seemly for a bishop to be a digger in a vineyard "

"In God's name," quoth the Bishop of Turin, "my bishopric is so poor that it sufficeth not for my living, so me behooveth to do the best that I can "

Then said the Bishop of Beauvais "Sir, for God's sake, pray for me, for great need have I thereof "

And the bishop answered him that so would he do right willingly, and, an it so pleased him, the other bishop should pray for him And he bade him tell him his name And he told him that his name was Milo and that he was Bishop of Beauvais Then he left him, and his household followed with eighteen sumpter beasts And the bishop that digged amongst the vines asked them whose folk they were, and they answered him that they were the Bishop of Beauvais' men And when the good man heard this he threw down his spade and ran after the Bishop of Beauvais, crying after him "Lord, hear me! Hear me !" So the bishop stood still and asked him what he desired And the good man said to him

"Sir, ye had promised me that ye would pray for me Dear, fair lord, I release you thereof "

"God-a-mercy !" quoth the Bishop of Beauvais "What mean ye thereby?"

"In God's name," quoth the Bishop of Turin, "I will tell you! Me seemeth that ye are sore cumbered with business and have so much to do with your own businesses that ye could not attend to mine"

Straightway they departed the one from the other, and the bishop journeyed day by day until he was come to Assisi, where Saint Francis was born and where his body now resteth There was he seized of a strange sickness, for a swelling arose in the middle of his back, within his body, and it waxed so great that it divided his backbone from the rump clean to the shoulders, and it gaped, as he had been laid open with a cleaver Thus lived he for four days in so great anguish, then he died And he was buried, as a bishop, in the mother church, and his household made havoc of all that he possessed Even so fareth it with those clerks that take not heed to their calling And the bishop's household went back to their own country

XXI

OF THE ADVENTURES OF SALADIN, AS THEY WERE RELATED BY A CAPTIVE

Here will we leave Bishop Milo of Beauvais, who died even as ye have heard tell—and he died to the great contentment of his neighbours—and we will tell you of the king, John of Acre, who remained in Syria and demeaned himself ever as a valiant man And there was a truce established betwixt Christians and Saracens for twenty years

Now it befell one day that the king was in Acre and it was told him that there was a noble Saracen in prison there; and the king commanded that he should be brought to him immediately, and the Saracen was brought before the king When the king saw him he was well pleased in him, and he asked him who he was And the man made known to him through interpreters that he was uncle to Saladin, who was so valiant And the king regarded him straitly, and considered his face, and he saw that he was tall and straight and well shapen and sturdy of all his members And he was of a ruddy countenance and had a great white beard that came to the middle of his breast, and he ware his hair in a braid both thick and long, which reached even to his hips; and in sooth he seemed a valiant man And when the king had so long looked upon him, he commanded him to sit down And then, through an interpreter, he caused inquiry to be made of him concerning the deeds and adventures of Saladin, and the man answered and said that he would tell him many of these, and true ones

Then said he to the king "I saw my nephew Saladin, who was King of Babylon and had thirty kings to govern under him, how he caused one of his retainers, a wise man and a prudent, to mount and to ride abroad through all his good cities And he bare three ells of cloth fastened to a lance, and he cried at every crossing of the streets 'Nothing more shall Saladin carry away with him, of all his kingdom and of all his great treasure, than these three ells of cloth for his winding sheet'

"Thereafter wrought he a great marvel He had heard tell of the great charity of the Hospital of Saint John of Acre, and it was said that no person that was in misery was refused there, but there was given him whatsoever he asked, if it could be had And Saladin bethought him that he would try whether this were true or not So took he unto him staff, wallet, and pilgrim's cloak, and disguised himself as best he could, and came straight unto Acre, and there he played the sick man and the miserable and went to the Hospital of Saint John and sought lodging there, saying that he had sore need thereof

"When the master of the hospital beheld him, who received sick folk, he received him also because of the need that he seemed to have And immediately he had him to bed and eased him what he could And he asked him what he desired to eat 'Nay, for God's sake' (said he), 'let me take my rest, for I have great need thereof, and long have I desired to die amongst the poor people that are in this place'

"Then left they him in peace, and he fell asleep, and he slept all that day and all that night And on the morrow the master of the sick asked him if he would eat, and he said that for food had he no care 'I' faith,' quoth the master, 'an ye eat not ye cannot live for long' So did Saladin fast for three days and three nights, without eating or drinking The master came again to him and said unto him 'Fair friend, it behooveth you to take something for your sustainment, for greatly should we be blamed an ye were thus to die here by default' 'Know ye this, master,' quoth Saladin, 'never more in my life will I eat, an I have not to eat of a thing which I desire mortally, and well know I that never could I have it, and it is madness to think thereon or to desire it' 'Ah, fair friend! Have no fear to ask any thing, for this hospital is of so great charity that never any sick man that hath lain herein hath come short of his desire, so be it the thing could be gotten for gold or for silver So ask boldly, for ye shall in no wise fail of your wish'

"When Saladin heard the master so affirm, he said that he would make known his request 'I desire,' quoth he, 'the right fore foot of Morel, the good steed of the Grand Master of this place, and I will that I may see it cut off before mine eyes and in mine own presence, else will I never eat thereof Now have ye heard,' quoth Saladin, 'my folly, but in God's name I pray you, pay no heed thereto, better is it that I die, who am but a poor man, than such a beast, which is so much worth, for it is said of a truth that the Grand Master would not take for the horse a thousand bezants'

"Incontinent the master left him and went to the Grand Master and told him the sick man's request When the Grand Master heard it he pondered a little, and he marveled much whence came such a wish to the sick man, but to the master of the sick he said 'Go, take the beast and fulfill the man's desire Better is it that mine horse die, than a man, and otherwise would the thing ever more be held in reproach against us'

"Straightway was the horse led before Saladin's bed and was bound and cast to the ground And a knave stood ready, a great axe in his one hand and a block in the other, and he said 'Which foot is it that the sick man demandeth?' And they said to him 'The right fore foot' So he took the block and laid it underneath the foot and would deal so hard a blow as he could strike, when Saladin cried unto him 'Hold! My wish is fulfilled and my desire turned toward other flesh, now do I crave mutton to eat' Then was the horse unbound and led back to his stall

"And when the Grand Master knew this he was right glad thereof, likewise the other brethren of the place And to the sick man gave they that which he had asked, and he ate well and drank, for three whole days had he fasted And yet four days abode he there, and there was done for him whatsoever him listed Then called he for his robe and his staff and his cloak, and he took his leave of the master and thanked him much for the good things that he had done to him and the honour that he had shewn him Back went he then to his own land, but he had not forgotten the good things that were done unto him in the hospital, and he caused a charter to be drawn up and to be sealed with his seal, and in the charter stood written

" 'Know all men, both they that now are and they that are yet to be, that I, Saladin, King of Babylon, do leave in perpetuity and for ever unto Saint John of the Hospital of Acre a thousand bezants of gold for sheets and for coverings for to cover the sick folk that are therein, and I appoint these to be taken every year, on the day of my Lord Saint John, out of my revenues of Babylon, and in such sort that despite any war which may arise betwixt us and the Christians these moneys shall not cease to be paid And be it known to the masters of the hospital that I do this because of the very great charity which is in that house and because they lodged me there Nor knew they a word thereof, insomuch that I asked for the right fore foot of the Grand Master's horse, and they would have cut it off in my presence, but I would not suffer it'

"And the charter was sent unto the Hospital of Saint John and delivered unto the Grand Master and the brethren, who made great joy over it, for they knew concerning Saladin that never for any cause would he lie And from that day forth were the thousand bezants paid every year on Saint John's Day, and are yet paid

"Moreover," quoth the Saracen, "yet another thing did he For the Marquis of Caesarea, who was then holding that city of the King of Jerusalem, was well supplied with horsemen and with serjeants and with arbalesters, but, because of his very great covetousness, every fortnight he discharged some of the garrison of the place and put the gold and silver of their pay into his own coffers And he thought that Saladin gave no heed thereto, but that did he And in sooth men told the marquis that he did very ill in that he diminished the garrison, for thereby would the city be lost For he was very far away from the other Christians and too late would succour come to them an need arose, moreover, Saladin was wise and warlike, and well understood he his hinderances and his vantage 'Hold your peace!' quoth the marquis 'I shall, when I so will, cause a thousand horsemen to sally from my coffers'

"Now this speech was reported to Saladin by a spy who told him all the counsels of the marquis and of the men of the city, and in sooth was it told him that the garrison was so decreased that there remained but a little part thereof, or less than nothing When Saladin knew this, then was he right glad, and he summoned his men privily to a place three leagues distant from Caesarea, and they were all gathered there on a Saturday evening And they marched three leagues before daybreak, and came at dawn to Caesarea and assailed it on every side, and they raised their ladders against the walls And they that were within the city heard the noise of the Saracens and ran to the walls for to defend the town, but little did this avail them, for they were very few and ill equipped and they had been taken unawares

"And the Saracens entered the city by force and the marquis was taken prisoner with his wife, and he was led away, his hands bound behind his back, into the presence of Saladin, who greatly desired to see him And when he saw him, he said to him 'O Marquis! Marquis! Where are the thousand horsemen that ye were to cause to come forth of your coffers? By Mahomet, your own covetousness hath betrayed you! Never yet have ye your fill of gold or of silver, but I will give you your fill thereof this day! Then did Saladin bid them fetch gold and silver and melt it in an iron pot and pour it, all boiling, down his throat, and he died forsooth incontinent But Saladin of his courtesy had the lady, the tithe of the Christians, and ten damosels sent back to Acre, and there the marchioness found safety

"Much could I tell you," quoth the Saracen, "of the deeds of Saladin, but one thing did he at his death which sorely vexed us For when he was so forspent that he perceived clearly that he must die, he called for a basin filled with water And immediately a servant ran and fetched a silver basin and set it at his right hand And Saladin caused himself to be raised up until he was sitting, and with his right hand he made the sign of the cross over the water, touching the basin in four places and saying 'So far is it from this place unto this as from this unto this' This said he that it might not be perceived what he was doing And then he poured the water upon his head and upon his body, uttering therewithal three words in French, which we understood not, but verily it seemed, inasmuch as I could see, that he baptized himself

"Then departed Saladin, the best prince that ever was in Paynimry, and he was buried at the head of the cemetery of my Lord Saint Nicholas at Acre, beside his mother, who was buried there most magnificently And over them standeth a tower, fair and tall, wherein burneth both day and night a lamp filled with olive oil, and this is kept and lighted by the brethren of Saint John of the Hospital of Acre, who receive thence rich revenues which Saladin and his mother left to them"

XXII

HOW THE POPE CALLED ON THE EMPEROR TO HELP HIM
AGAINST THEM OF MILAN

Henceforth will we tell you of the Childe of Apulia,[47] who was called Frederick at his christening and held three kingdoms as his heritage to wit, the kingdom of Apulia, and that of Sicily, and that of Calabria And it came to pass that he was chosen of the barons of Germany for to be King of Germany, by the grace of the Pope, who had removed the Emperor Otto,[48] from his seat because of his misdoing And he was consecrated king at Aix-la-Chapelle at the hand of the Archbishop of Trèves, and then was he presented by the barons of Germany to the Pope for to sacre him emperor And they were a long time together in amity —he and the Pope—and he was very obedient to the Church of Rome, and he was a good justicer, and so wrought he that he was feared and held in awe throughout all the lands and that a man could carry a purse full of money hanging at his neck from his pilgrim's staff nor take any thought thereto

And so for a long time did the emperor demean himself that all the world spake well of him, until one day the people of Milan fell out with their bishop and he excommunicated them The burghers craved absolution of him and besought him to deal with them justly and in order, but the bishop made answer to them that assoiled should they never be an they did not his will in every way When the citizens saw that the bishop would not do otherwise for them they thrust him forth of the city, nor was he able to make use of aught that he possessed Then went the bishop straight to the Pope and made his complaint, concerning every thing whereof he could make it, against them of Milan who had driven him out of the town and disinherited him of all his possessions The Pope was much moved thereat, and he sent a cardinal to look into these matters And the cardinal came to Milan and called before him the chief magistrate and the councillors of the city, and he asked them for what cause they had thrust out their bishop and seized them of all his goods, wherein they had sorely sinned against God and against the Pope and against the bishop And the burghers made answer that if they had sinned in aught, then were they ready to make atonement, but, in God's name, let him assoil them, then were they ready to follow his counsel

"By Saint Peter," quoth the cardinal, "assoiled shall ye never be until such time as ye shall have made amends to me for your offense and shall have done the bishop's will in every thing !"

"I' faith, lord," answered the townsfolk, "we have no thought so to do, but an ye are willing to take the matter up with us justly and in due order, we shall both ourselves receive that which is just and do that which is just toward you But in God's name, lord, see to it that worse befall not in this matter !"

"Verily," quoth the cardinal, "I know not what will befall, but justice will never be done you therein, rather shall all go according to his will "

---

[47]The Emperor Frederick II
[48]Otto IV

"I' faith," quoth the burghers, "this is not the word of an honourable man, nor of such a man as ye ought to be!"

Straightway the burghers departed from the cardinal, who promised to work them much evil, and he made heavier the bishop's sentence in so far as he could and caused all the clergy to be withdrawn from the city and himself departed from the town, threatening the townsmen

Now it befell that the chief magistrate and the count were privily met in council, and they were sore dismayed because of the words which the cardinal had spoken to them And they resolved together to send to the Pope, asking him that he himself give heed to the matter But presently was another ply given to the case, for the common people of the city and the idle folk held a parliament by themselves, and they said it were well if they should go after the cardinal and bring him back by force, and they said that they would hold him until they were assoiled by him and by their bishop, and until these should give them letters to the intent that never more would they be excommunicate So they chose of their number an hundred men to go forth, and these went after the cardinal and they overtook him a league beyond the city And they stopped him and said unto him "Pardi, Lord Cardinal! Back to the city behooveth you to turn, for—will ye, nil ye—assoil us ye shall"

When the cardinal heard them speak thus he said unto them "Verily, ye stinking rabble, never will I turn back! Rather will I bring ruin on you all, and I will cause Milan to be rased to the ground, in such sort that there shall not remain therein one stone upon another!"

Then, lo, a certain foolish fellow took the cardinal's horse by the bridle and would have turned him back, but the cardinal cried to them of his household. "Up and at the villains!" And one of his servants drew his sword and smote him that held the cardinal and laid him dead at his feet And when they of Milan saw their companion lying dead they all went mad and cried "Put them to death! Put them to death!"

Very fain had the cardinal fled away, but he could not, for now was he hemmed about utterly on every side And they would have taken him and brought him to Milan, but a certain butcher sprang forth and smote him with an axe and slew him And they took the man that had slain their companion, and they bound him to the tail of his own horse and brought him to Milan and dragged him through all the streets of the city When the chief magistrate and the count knew this they were sore grieved, for well wist they what this cost the ell [49] And they thought to send word to the Pope for to cry him mercy, but no man of them was so bold that he durst go that errand, for fear of his own life

So the matter rested until the Pope knew of it, and then so wroth waxed he that none might appease him And he took counsel of the brethren and they determined to summon the emperor And the emperor was summoned and came forthwith, and the Pope told him how they of Milan had behaved themselves

---

[49] *Combien c'estoit l'aune* A proverbial expression, meaning "what the upshot of the matter would be"

"Verily," quoth the emperor, 'this thing grieveth me "

"In God's name," quoth the Pope, "I desire that the city be destroyed and that they all be put to the sword!'"

"I' faith," answered the emperor, "that may not be done without sore travail and great cost, for well know I that they of Milan are great folk and rich and powerful, and many good horsemen are there amongst them and much know they of warfare "

"In God's name," quoth the Pope, "I myself will aid you, and I deliver and grant unto you all the things that they possess "

"Now know ye this," said the emperor, "I will not go unless ye give me your letters, for so well do I know you that if they of Milan should make their peace with you, then should I lose all that I have put into the venture "

"By Saint Peter!" quoth the Pope "Letters shall ye have right gladly, and I swear to you by the saints—by Saint Peter and by Saint Paul—that never shall peace be made save by you alone "

So was the covenant ratified and sealed, with the assent of all the brethren, and the emperor departed unto his own land and gathered together much people there and led them before Milan, and he laid siege thereto And right often did the one party harass the other, and they that were without made little gain, for they that were within the town were well supplied and but lightly regarded them that were without Thus did the Emperor Frederick maintain his siege for a year and an half, and little gained he thereby save only that none was able to enter there or to come out, and thereby were they that were within the city sore distressed

Now it chanced one day that the chief magistrate and the Count of Milan were met with the council, and one of them said "Fair lords, we are in an evil case, for we are under the ban, and we are at war with the Pope and with the emperor, who are the two men in the world who have the most power And in good faith do I rede you that we make our peace with them, else shall we all be destroyed, for we are losing all our gains and our merchandises and our living waxeth dearer every day And if the war endure yet a long time, we shall be utterly undone, and even if our case should remain thus for twenty years, yet in the end must we perforce make peace, and very great were the cost thereof Better, then, were it for us to put our trust in making peace than in waging war "

"I' faith," said the other councillors, "ye speak sooth Now let us consider how we shall go about the thing in a fitting manner, for greatly doth it behoove us so to do "

"In God's name," quoth that wise man, "it were well that we treat for peace with the emperor "

So they chose two wise men from amongst them, whom they sent to the emperor, and these sent him word that they desired to speak with him under safe-conduct, going and coming And this the emperor granted them willingly And they came to the emperor's tents and gat them off their horses, and they conversed long time with him privily But no peace could they obtain that would not be to their own destruction and dishonour So back they came to the city, and they told their fellows what they had heard from the emperor

"I' faith," quoth the wise man, "since we cannot have peace with the emperor without destroying ourselves, I, for my part, counsel that we send to the Pope and offer him so great treasure that we shall utterly blind him therewith And so well know I the custom of the Lombards and how covetous they are by nature of getting gain, that we shall have peace on our own terms "

To this counsel did they all agree, and they sent to the Pope a burgher of Piacenza to seek surety for their going and speaking to the Pope concerning peace And the Pope granted their request and gave the man letters of safe-conduct, both going and coming, and back came he to Milan and delivered unto them the Pope's letters And straightway chose they two of their wisest men and committed to them the letter of the city, unsealed and speaking clearly, which said that they of Milan would confirm whatsoever these twain should do And on the morrow they made an assault at daybreak on the folk that were without, who were not keeping good watch, and they fought against them and caused them great shame and loss and took ten of them captive and led them into the city And whilst they were harrying them that were without, the two messengers were able to go their ways and to get themselves so far from the host that none perceived them

Here the tale telleth how the two messengers hasted on their way until they were come to Rome And when they of the court perceived them they looked askance upon them, and they were eight days at the court, nor ever could they get them an hearing But at the last they were called and it was asked them what they sought "I' faith," said they to the Pope, "we are come hither for to seek your grace, and in God's name have mercy upon us !"

"Ah, evil folk ! Faithless heretics !" cried the Pope "Ye have deserved to lose both body and goods !"

"Ah, lord !" answered the burghers "God's mercy ! Surely ye have not heard the truth in this matter, but they have told you altogether the contrary For God's sake, lord, acquaint yourself with the truth and make your dealings accordingly, and they of Milan will aid you with thirty thousand marks of silver "

When the Pope and the brethren heard them name this great sum, they curbed themselves and humbled themselves before them and asked them how this sum would be assured And the wise men made answer right featly "We will remain with you, and ye shall command the children of the twenty richest men of Milan to be sent to us, and ye shall keep them with you and hold them as hostages, even until all your pleasure is performed "

To this the Pope and the brethren agreed, and the children were sent and put in the Pope's keeping, and he caused them to be well guarded

XXIII

OF THE QUARREL THAT AROSE BETWIXT THE POPE AND THE EMPEROR

Thus were they of Milan reconciled with the Pope, and he absolved them and held them to be good Christians and sent word to the emperor that he should leave them and return, for he had made thorough enquiry and had found that the bishop had been in the wrong and that the cardinal had died because of his own frowardness When the emperor had heard these tidings, then was he utterly dumfounded, for he had spent much money before Milan And he sent back word to the Pope that he would not remove himself thence until he should have recovered his costs at the least, and that the Pope had wrought very ill in that he had made this covenant And yet again the Pope sent him word that unless he raised the siege he would excommunicate both him and his helpers When the emperor saw how the matter lay he raised the siege and went back to Apulia and abode there for a season

And there came men to him, saying "Sire, it is indeed fitting that ye marry to your own advantage Now King John of Acre hath a daughter by his wife, through whom the kingdom of Jerusalem escheateth, and we rede you that ye send after her and espouse her, for we see not how ye could do better"

The emperor agreed thereto and sent to ask for her by the mouth of ten knights and by his own letter King John sent her to him willingly, and the emperor wedded her And he had by her a son, who was called Conrad and was wedded to the daughter of the Duke of Bavaria, and by her he had a son, who yet liveth and ought to have the kingdom of Jerusalem

The Emperor Frederick determined that he would go to the Pope and would demand of him the ransom which he had taken from them of Milan, for the Pope had given him by his letter all that which they of Milan possessed, and yet more; for he had sworn to him by Saint Peter and Saint Paul that he would not make peace save through the emperor, yet had he received of them thirty thousand marks of silver and he had kept a part of the children of the burghers of Milan, whom he had now restored, for their ransom had been paid to him Then went the emperor to Rome, and he found there the Pope and the brethren, and he demanded of them this thing which ye have heard The Pope said that this thing was not befitting his Christianity, and the emperor said that the Pope had not gotten the ransom through his Christianity "but through mine own force, nor ever will I raise the siege until I have taken them by force!"

In such sort stood the matter betwixt the emperor and the Pope that the emperor could get neither all nor a part, nor aught of that which he had expended So he departed, full of bitterness and defiance, and he entered into the lands of the Pope and took of his possessions whatsoever he could get So waxed the discord, even as ye have heard, betwixt the emperor and the Pope, and when the Pope knew that the emperor was making war upon him and taking of his possessions, he caused him to be excommunicated throughout the bounds of Christendom And so long time did the war endure that no clerk could go to Rome but he was taken captive and robbed

And it came to pass that the Pope died, and another was made pope by the cardinals, who was called Sennebaud,[50] but his name was changed to Innocent IV,[51] and he confirmed the sentence against the emperor which the other pope had laid upon him And yet did the war endure, until one day there was held a council at Rome, and thither were summoned many prelates of France—with the others, the Archbishop of Rouen, who was named Peter of Colmieu And he caused to be made ready four galleys, goodly and strong, for to go thither by sea (since he durst not go by land), and he put forth to sea so privily as he might But not one whit did this avail him, for the emperor was causing all roads, by land and by sea, to be guarded, and the bishop was taken with three others, together with great treasure And the emperor kept them in prison until he received from them great ransom, and the galleys remained in the harbour of Naples, nor ever again was use made of them When the Pope saw how the matter stood, then was he exceeding wroth, and he perceived that his court was lost and that none would go thither from this side the mountains

So they agreed together—he and the brethren—that they would come to Lyons on the Rhone, and thither came they right warily, in the year of the Incarnation of Our Lord one thousand two hundred and forty and three And they were a long time there, until a certain day when the pontiff caused a great council to be assembled for to condemn the emperor And there were gathered many prelates, and the emperor sent thither Master Peter of Vinea, who was a very great clerk, and he demanded of the Pope that the emperor be dealt with according to the law, and he was ready to lay the matter before the King of France, who was an honourable man, and he would abide altogether by that which the king should ordain in the matter But the Pope made answer that he would do nothing of the sort, rather, he condemned the emperor to lose his land, and from that day he was no more called Emperor, but Frederick So was he condemned; and Master Peter of Vinea came back from Lyons and told the emperor how he was condemned to lose his land by sentence definitive, nor aught that he might purpose to do would avail him any whit, nor justice could he have Thereat was the emperor more grieved than ever yet he had been, and the more did he fear treachery, and he fell into a state of sore misdoubt, so that he put his trust in no man And he caused many of them of his own household to be put to death—whether wrongly or rightly, I know not

And it came about that he was advised that my Lord Peter of Vinea had betrayed him to the Pope, this learned he through certain letters that were found in his coffers And he caused Peter's eyes to be put out, and he had him led about after him on an ass in all the good cities whither he went, and raised up at the corners of the streets, and a knave who led him cried "Lo, this is my Lord Peter of Vinea, the master counsellor of the emperor, who was in every way his lord, who sought to betray him to the Pope for a guerdon Behold what he hath gained thereby! Well may he say 'From place so high so low brought down!'"

---

[50]Senibaldi di Fieschi

[51]Evidently a slip on the part of the minstrel for Gregory IX, since he names Innocent IV a little later as succeeding this pope

Thus did the emperor demean himself, and he had builded a city of Saracens, which was called Nocera, and he put more trust in the Saracens than he put in the Christians, and he wrought much evil against all' clerks and all that were in orders, and he subjected them to ransom every month And he kept three score women or more in concubinage, and he stabled his beasts in the minsters and in the churches, nor did he behave himself in any wise as a good Christian And greatly did he impoverish his land, for he spent his substance most foolishly

Now come we back to the Pope, who was at Lyons and had tarried there for a long season And it irked him to abide there, and he and the brethren determined that they would go to Rome, and thither returned they under the safe-conduct of the Count of Savoy, who conducted them Nor had the Pope been long time in Rome when he died, and in his room was Innocent IV chosen pope, and straightway they confirmed the sentence against Frederick

And it came to pass that the Emperor Frederick sent word to King John of Acre that he desired to enjoy the kingdom of Jerusalem, and King John was fain to bestow it upon him, and the emperor held it even until his death Nor was it any great while ere he died, yet excommunicate, and a bastard son of his[52] seized the land and held it And King John went away to Constantinople unto his daughter, who had great power in the land And he was the emperor's regent so long as he lived, because of the youth of his son-in-law, who was young and childish and had many dealings with the Greeks

XXIV

HOW KING JOHN OF ENGLAND LOST NORMANDY

At this point will we leave off to speak of the good King John of Acre and we will tell of that King John who was brother to King Richard of England, to whom the kingdom escheated after the death of King Richard his brother And he was consecrated king, and he was the worst king that ever was—worse than King Herod, who caused the babes to be slaughtered, for King John, of whom I am telling you, was an evil knight and a niggard and a traitor, even as I will shew you For he had a certain nephew,[53] son to his uncle the Count of Brittany, nor were there any other heirs And the king, who was fell and cruel, caused a ship to be made ready for to go to one of his castles, and he went on board with a privy retinue, taking Arthur his nephew with him And when he was come far out to sea, he cast him overboard to the mackerel that he might have his land and the countship of Brittany, which Arthur should have held, and when he had done this he went back to London

Here will we leave him for a little space, and we will return to King Philip, to whom tidings were come that King Richard was dead And he had great joy thereof, for very greatly did he fear Richard because of his hardihood and be-

---

[52]Manfred (1231-1256), King of Sicily, killed at the battle of Benevento by Charles of Anjou

[53]I e, "cousin", cf Shakespeare "his *nephew* Richard," Henry VI, II, 5

cause of his largess, for by his largess did he make of his enemies his friends; and of them that were against him, his secret friends So thought King Philip, who was very wise, that now was the time to conquer Normandy; and he determined to summon King John through his peers, because he had not taken the land this side the sea that he ought to hold of him and whereof he ought to do him homage And straightway the king sent to him the Bishop of Beauvais and the Bishop of Laon, who were of the twelve peers, and these bare the king's letter of credence, and they put out to sea from Calais and landed at Dover and asked for King John And it was told them that he was at Lincoln, a city of his that lieth twelve leagues from Canterbury where Saint Thomas the martyr resteth And thither came they of a morning and there found they the king, and they said to him "Sire, hither are we sent from King Philip, here have ye his letter, cause it to be read"

The king took the letter and brake the seal and read it, and he found in the king's letter, that King Philip sent him word confirming and establishing whatsoever the two bishops should say

"Now tell me," quoth King John, "what is your pleasure"

"I' faith, Sire," quoth the Bishop of Beauvais, "my lord the king summoneth you and biddeth you appear at Paris, his city, within forty days from this day, for to do there your devoirs and to receive your rights through your peers, in those things that he shall see fit to require of you as of a liege vassal And we, who are peers of France, do summon you thither and bid you appear"

When King John heard such words he changed colour, and he said "My Lord Bishop, in sooth have I listened to your words, and verily will I perform toward your lord that which I ought"

Straightway departed the two bishops, and they passed over the sea and came to Pontoise, where they found the king, and they told him that which they had learned and said that they had performed his commandments in every way, even as he had commanded

King Philip waited the forty days, then the peers and their council were assembled And, lo, there came a knight, whom King John was sending to the king; and he came before the king and said unto him "Sire, King John sendeth me hither on this his appointed day whereon ye have bidden him be called, and here are his letters of credence"

The letter was read "Now say," quoth the king, "what ye desire"

"Sire," answered the knight, "my lord craveth a deferment"

"Certes," quoth the king, "that is but seemly, that shall he have for forty days from this day"

Straightway departed the knight, and he told the thing to his lord, and when the appointed day was come, he asked yet another deferment of forty days But on this day he defaulted altogether And when the King of France saw that he had defaulted altogether, then he demanded of the peers of France justice and judgment The peers took counsel together and determined that the king should cause him to be summoned yet again before him, for to hear judgment, even as one that had defaulted And the king sent yet another twain of their number, and John was yet again summoned to appear within forty days But he came not, neither sent he any. Then did the king demand judgment of the peers The peers were wise men, and they determined by judgment and by right that King Philip could and should seize the fief which King John ought to have held of him

Forthwith the council departed, and King Philip caused letters missive to be written and sent them to all that held fiefs of him and bade them all be present, within forty days, at Gisors, under arms Then had ye seen barons and knights making them ready with horse and armour, with tents and pavilions, and with whatsoever things were needful And they were all present at Gisors on the day which the king had set

And when the king saw so many good folk gathered for his sake, then was he right glad, and he bade my Lord Alain of Rouci form the vanguard—who had but newly been enlarged from his captivity in exchange for another knight— and the rear ward bade he be formed by my Lord William of Barres And they entered into Normandy and put the country to pillage, and the spoilers set fire everywhere, and they took spoils and churls, nor was there any to hinder them, save for the strong holds, which were well manned with country-folk who had driven thither their oxen and kine and sheep and whatsoever they had

Then the king determined that he would go to Mantes, and he laid siege to it and let his engines play against it furiously And when they that were within the town perceived the might of the king, they resolved that they would yield the castle, so was it yielded to him, and immediately the king put his own garrison within it And he sent to Pacy, which lay hard by, and commanded the people of the town to yield him the castle, saying that unless they yielded it within three days he would have them all hanged When they of Pacy had heard the king's messengers, then said they that they would be very fain to yield it And they brought him the keys of the castle, and the king caused it to be garrisoned

And when they of Vernon and they of Pont de l'Arche and they of Vaudreuil and of Gournay and of Louviers and of Gaillon and of Rouen and of all the country saw how King Philip was thus conquering Normandy, they took counsel together and resolved to send to King John, their lord, in England, saying that since their case was such, for God's sake let him now take thought thereto, else would he lose all Normandy

So was it done, and they sent to King John, and when he knew this thing he was marvellous dumfounded and sore cast down And he said to their messengers that he would succour them ere the feast of Saint John (and it was now September), and he caused a letter to be written and delivered it to the messengers And back went they to Rouen, where they were awaited, and the letter was read And when the captains of the castles had heard it, then were they all confounded, but they determined that they would hold out until the day that the king had appointed them So went the captains their ways and proceeded every man to his own place, and they fortified themselves as best they could

And King Philip caused his host to be led straight against Vernon, which is a very goodly castle and strong and well situate, and he bade pitch his tents and his pavilions in the meadow land along the Seine, and all the other barons did likewise   And the king caused his engines to play most violently, but little mischief wrought they, for they that were within the castle were well fortified and the castle was exceeding strong   When the king saw that the case was thus, then bade he leave off the assaulting, but he sware that he would maintain the siege for seven years, this did he in the hearing of them of Vernon, who were sore distressed thereat, for they knew right truly that the king would not remove thence until he had taken the place by force   And the king remained there all that winter and all the time until the feast of Saint John Baptist, when King John should succour them, but King John came not, neither sent he any one thither

When the captain of Vernon saw that he would get no succour from their lord, and when he perceived his baseness, and when he beheld the might and wisdom and riches of King Philip, then did he ask safe conduct for to go and speak with him, and the king granted it   Then came the captain forth of Vernon, with nine other knights, and he proceeded to the king's tent and greeted him and said unto him   "Sire, hither am I come for to speak with you   Ye have laid siege to Vernon, whereof I am captain and warden in behalf of King John   Sire, greatly do I desire that ye know that we have besought succour of him and sought it yet again, but neither succour nor aid find we in him   And, lo, here are the keys of the castle, which I bring to you for to do your pleasure   Take the castle, I yield it up to you"

The king received it gladly and entered therein, and he supplied it well with whatsoever things were needful   Then went the king forth of Vernon and went against the other castles, and so soon as he was come, the keys thereof were yielded to him   And he went his way until he was come to Rouen; and he would have laid siege to the city, but they of Rouen came forth to meet him and delivered the keys unto him

XXV

OF THE SIEGE OF CASTLE GAILLARD

So did the king possess all Normandy, save Gaillard alone, which is very strong and lieth in a valley amongst three mountains, nor can siege be laid thereto save from the one side, and it is all compassed about by the Seine, nor can it be reached with petrary or mangonel   When the king had looked upon the castle and upon the situation of the castle, which is so strong and defensible, then said he   "By the lance of Saint James, never yet have I seen castle so strong or so well situate as is this, and well do I perceive that I could spend here all my substance or ever it should be taken by force   All the land and the country-side is now conquered, save only this castle, I will establish my garrisons round about and will keep them so close that none shall be able to come hither or to enter the castle, and it must perforce come to pass that the place will be taken by famine"

Even as the king had said, so did he, and he set goodly and strong garrisons all round about the castle, and so guarded they the goings in and the comings out of the castle for a year and three months And they that were within were brought to such dearth of victuals that they had but twelve beans each day as their ration. And when they of the castle saw that they could not longer endure and that die they must of hunger, then came they to the castellan[54] of Gaillard and said to him· "Sir, we have nothing more to eat, neither in any wise can victual come to us, nor shall we receive any succour from our evil King John, nor are King Philip's garrisons diminishing Rather, every day they wax stronger and increase, for he reneweth and strengtheneth them So us seemeth that henceforth should we have no shame to yield up Gaillard "

"Surely," quoth the castellan, "ye speak idle words ! So long as I live will I not yield up Gaillard, neither will I go forth from hence save I am dragged forth by the feet !"

Straightway they held their peace before him, but they gat them to a chamber apart, and then said one of them "This castellan is mad, if we are willing to heed him, he will make us all to die an evil death Let us do better, let us send word to the garrisons that we will yield up Gaillard to them an our lives be spared "

"In God's name," cried the others, "ye say well !"

Then made they ready two of their number who should bear the message And that night, at the first hour of sleep, went they forth of the castle and came to the lodges of the garrisons, and they spake to the captain and told him even how it was with them, and how they desired the castellan to yield up the castle, but he sware that so long as he lived would he never yield up Gaillard, nor would he come forth thence save he be cast out feet foremost "And when" (said they) "we heard such words, we of the garrison gat ourselves together and resolved that we would yield Gaillard to you So cause your people to be armed, immediately will it be yielded up to you "

When the captain had heard them he said to them "See to it that ye speak truth, for by the faith that I owe King Philip, an I catch you in a lie, dearly shall ye pay therefor "

"Sir," quoth they, "fear nought "

Straightway the captain had his people armed and forth went they softly and quickly toward Gaillard And the two messengers entered within the castle and told them that had sent them how the garrisons were at the gates Immediately came they to the gates, and they brake the bars thereof without the knowledge of the castellan, and they opened the gates and let in the garrisons of the king

And when the watchman of the castle perceived this he began to shout "Betrayed ! Betrayed !" When the castellan heard him shouting he trembled greatly and was fearful of treachery, and immediately he armed both himself and his household and went thither whence the cry came And when he saw the king's men he rushed amongst them with sword drawn, and he smote to the right hand

---

[54]Roger de Lascy

and to the left and wrought such deeds of arms that it was a marvel to see them. But when the king's soldiers beheld him they fell upon him and evil entreated him, and they gave him more than thirty wounds upon his body Howbeit, he yet defended himself as best he could, but nought did it avail him , for the king's men were twenty to one, and his own men had failed him

In the end was the castellan stricken down and his horse slain, and he was taken and held prisoner In such wise was the castle taken , and the garrison of the castle departed, bearing their harness with them Howbeit, the castellan would not go forth in any manner that might be told to him, but he must perforce be dragged forth of the castle by his feet In such fashion was Gaillard taken as ye have heard, and when King Philip knew thereof, then was he right joyful And he knew how the castellan had maintained himself, and he made him again castellan and doubled his wage because of his loyalty And from that day forward the king held Normandy and all the country in peace, nor was there any to do him mischief

XXVI

OF THE TREACHERY OF THE COUNT OF BOULOGNE

Some time thereafter it came to pass that King Philip held a parliament at Laon, and there were many of his barons And it so befell that Count Gaucher of Saint-Pol[55] and Count Renaud of Boulogne,[56] who sorely hated each the other because of deeds of arms, fell out in the presence of the king, and in the end the Count of Saint-Pol smote Count Renaud in the face with his fist so that his face was all bloody And Count Renaud hurled himself upon him vigorously , but the high barons who were present threw themselves betwixt the twain, so that he could not revenge himself but departed from the court without leavetaking And when the king knew that Count Renaud had gone away, it irked him, and in sooth he said that the Count of Saint-Pol had been in the wrong, and he upbraided him bitterly. And he sent Brother Garin, Bishop of Senlis, to Dammartin, one of his castles, where Count Renaud was , and when the bishop saw him he said "Sir, the king sendeth me hither to you because of the discord which is betwixt you and the Count of Saint-Pol, which irketh him sore, and he sendeth you word that he will cause the count to make amends to you to the satisfaction of your honour "

"Brother Garin," quoth he, "I have clearly heard the word which the king sendeth me through you, and I hold you to be a faithful messenger , but this do I desire you to know, and tell ye this to the king, that if the blood that fell from my face to the ground do not of its own accord rise up again to the place whence it sprang forth, and if the blow be not annihilated, even as it had never been struck, then will accord never be made "

"Verily," answered Brother Garin, "ye demand an unreasonable thing and one that cannot be , but, rather, in God's name, accept the amend which the king offereth you "

---

[55]Gaucher de Châtillon
[56]Renaud de Dammartin

"Sir Bishop," said the count, "hold your peace incontinent concerning that, for never more would I love you an ye spake thereof"

"In sooth," quoth Brother Garin, "my peace do I hold incontinent, but know ye what will befall you because of this? For this will ye lose the king's love and the world's esteem"

Straightway departed Brother Garin from Count Renaud and came to King Philip and told him the tale, even as the count had made answer to him And when the king had heard him he sware by the lance of Saint James that this discord would be the cause of great evil So the matter rested for a long season nor was aught done concerning it, but Count Renaud went about to stir up hatred against the Count of Saint-Pol and to bring shame upon him, but he could find none occasion

And when he saw that the king was altogether upholding the Count of Saint-Pol, then did he bethink him of a great treason, and he came to Count Ferrand of Flanders, who was son to the King of Portugal and was count through the Countess Jeanne, who was daughter to Count Baldwin, and he caused him to believe that the king was disinheriting him of Arras, and of Péronne, and of Saint-Omer, and of Aire, and of Hesdin, and of Bapaume, and he made him to believe that Count Baldwin, who had made this gift to the king because of the marriage of his sister, could in no wise do so, nor could he in reason disinherit the lawful heir of his body

When Count Ferrand heard him speak thus he believed him, like the fool that he was, and he coveted the land and thought too highly of himself And they made a compact betwixt them twain that they would make an alliance with King John of England and with the Emperor Otto,[57] who declared that King Philip had given him Orleans and Étampes and Chartres against the day that he should be made emperor. And in this alliance was Hugh of Boves, and they gathered together so great a multitude that it seemed that all the earth must tremble beneath their feet And Count Ferrand bade King Philip restore to him the good cities aforesaid; an he did not this, then did the count defy him; and let him know that in a brief season they would be within the king's land

When the king heard such threats, then bade he summon his men, and he sought counsel of them regarding these words The barons made answer to him that it was a monstrous unreasonable thing which the count had demanded of him, for that he was the king's man "Nor do ye owe him one whit of recompense, but well do we know that it is Count Renaud hath stirred up this brawl because of his quarrel with the Count of Saint-Pol So do we rede you that ye proceed toward Flanders and that ye draw together to your city of Tournai so much people as ye shall be able to get"

Then did the king cause to be summoned all them that held fiefs of him and all his communes, and they were all come together on a Saturday outside Tournai with tents and with pavilions But when Ferrand and his party knew that the king was at Tournai, then was he exceeding glad, for he thought that surely he

---

[57]Otto IV

had him in his snare And he sought battle of him for the morrow When the king heard this, it misliked him, for the morrow was a Sunday And he sent to him Brother Garin to bid him wait until the Monday, but the count sent him word that this would he in no wise do, for that the king was desirous to flee away So back came Brother Garin, and Count Renaud accompanied him a little way But when Count Renaud was come back again, my Lord Hugh of Boves said to him, in the presence of the Emperor Otto and of the Count of Flanders "Ha, Count of Boulogne! What treason have ye wrought betwixt you twain, ye and Brother Garin?"

"Verily," cried the count, "now have ye lied, like the base traitor that ye are! And well becometh you to utter such words, who are of the lineage of Ganelon! And know ye well that if battle befall I shall be either slain or taken there, but as for you, ye will flee away like a foul recreant and runagate!"

XXVII

OF THE BATTLE OF BOUVINES

There the quarrel rested, and already was Brother Garin returned to the king, and he said to him "Sire, now may God help you! Tomorrow will ye have battle without fail Bid, then, your battalions be ordered, for so behooveth you to do"

Then did the king bid his battalions be ordered, and he entrusted them to the ten best men that he had And the Emperor Otto, and Count Ferrand, and Count Renaud, and Count William Longsword (who was brother to the King of England and was there in the king's stead, because the king could not be there but was in Poitou, at La Roche,[58] contending against my Lord Lewis, who harassed him sore) these great lords whom I have now named to you were already dividing France amongst them and taking it clean over, root and branch Count Ferrand would have Paris, Count Renaud would have Normandy, and the emperor would have Orleans and Chartres and Étampes, and Hugh of Boves would have Amiens, so were they taking every one his portion

> But quickly God bringeth his plans to light,
> Who laugheth at dawn may weep ere night [59]

So the case rested on the Saturday and even until the morning of the Sunday, when the king arose and caused all his people to come forth from Tournai, all armed, and his banners to be displayed, with trumpets sounding and all the squadrons ranged So marched they until they were come unto a little bridge,

---

[58]La Roche aux Moines

[59]*Mais en pou d'eure Dieus labeure,*
Teis rit au main qui au soir pleure
This proverb is of frequent occurrence in Old French literature Cf the closing lines of the fabliau *Estula*

En petit d'eure Dieus labeure,
Tels rit au main qui au soir pleure,
Et tels est au soir coroucies
Qui au main est joianz et liez

which is called the Bridge of Bouvines, and there was a chapel there, whither the king betook himself for to hear mass, for it was yet the hour of matins And the king bade mass be sung by the Bishop of Tournai, and the king heard mass all in his armour And when mass had been said the king bade bread and wine be brought and sops to be cut, and he took one of these and ate it, and then said he to them that were about him "I pray all my faithful friends that be here that they eat with me, in remembrance of the twelve apostles who drank and ate with Our Lord Jesus Christ, and if there be any that meditateth evil or treachery, let him not draw nigh"

Then forth stepped my Lord Enguerrand of Coucy and took the first sop And Count Gaucher of Saint-Pol took the second, and he said to the king "Sire, on this selfsame day shall it be seen who is tráitor to you" And he spake these words because he wist well that the king had him in suspicion through evil tongues And the Count of Sancerre took the third, and all the other barons after him, and so great was the press there that they could not come to the cup And when the king saw this he was right glad thereof, and he said to them "Sirs, ye are all my men, and I am your lord, of whatsoever sort I be, and I have loved you much, and have brought you great honour, and given you freely of my substance, nor ever have I done you wrong or injustice, but have always dealt justly with you In God's name, then, I pray you that this day ye guard my body and mine honour and your own And if ye deem that the crown might better be worn by one of yourselves than by me, I agree thereto willingly and desire it with all mine heart and all my will"

When the barons had heard him speak thus, then began they to weep for very pity, and they said "Sire, thanks be to God, we desire no king save yourself only, so ride boldly against your enemies, and we are ready to die with you"

Straightway the king mounted a war horse strong and sure, and all the barons also gat them to horse, banners unfurled, and each one with his own division

Immediately, lo, on came the Flemings in disarray and in disorder, one in front of another, and they bare cords for to bind the French withal And the king had betaken himself toward the side of the mountain, for that the sun smote him full in the face, and when the Flemings saw him turn toward the hill they said one to another that he was fleeing away So they rushed into the midst of the French, each man for himself, and the French received them vigorously, and in a little while were the first of the Flemings discomfited

For the Count of Saint-Pol passed over above the host and took the enemy in the rear, and he rushed amongst them like an hungry lion and wrought such deeds of arms with his body that it was a fair marvel And all the other barons proved themselves so well that there was not one of them did aught that could find blame And the Seneschal of Champagne, Oudard of Reson, who bare the banner of Champagne and had the first battalion of his own right, had already gone so far forward that he had fallen foul of Count Renaud, and there was marvellous fighting

And now, lo, suddenly upon them came the Count of Saint-Pol, and he recognized Count Renaud's ensign And these were the two men on earth who most hated each the other and through whom this discord was arisen When Count Renaud beheld him, then was he so glad that he had not been more fain to hold God himself by the feet And he rushed upon him, and the Count of Saint-Pol upon him And there was an hot passage betwixt them, and each had wrought the other sore hurt an they had long held together

But the king's force was ever increasing, and the Flemings were decreasing, for they were in the wrong, moreover they were in ill accord Howbeit, the hosts mingled together on every side, and great was the confusion But the Count of Saint-Pol forgat not himself, but so put forth his strength that he took Count Renaud by main force, and when he was taken all the Flemings lost heart Then the French took courage and they descended upon Ferrand's battalion, and he was taken, and the Count of Ponthieu, and my Lord William Longsword, and many other great lords of whom the tale maketh no mention

And when the Emperor Otto saw that all were undone,[60] he turned bridle and fled, along with Hugh of Boves And the emperor went away into Germany and died a while thereafter, in a lazar house, poor and in great misery And Hugh of Boves put out to sea for to go to England, to the king, but God, who punisheth all the wicked, hindered him of his purpose, and there arose a great storm upon the sea and he was drowned; and all the remnant of the host was taken and discomfited

And the king knew that Ferrand was taken, and Count Renaud, and the Count of Ponthieu, and William Longsword, and many another high baron Then said the king "How is it that we have not the emperor?" Now be it known to you that never yet had he called him emperor, but he said it now for to have a greater victory, for there is more honour in discomfiting an emperor than a vassal [61]

Then was the battle ended, and the king returned to Tournai, making great joy, together with his prisoners; and the Flemings, for their part, made great moan This discomfiture was wrought in the year of Our Lord one thousand two hundred and fourteen, in the month of June, on the second Sunday thereof, and on that day did my Lord Lewis properly discomfit King John at La Roche aux Moines in Poitou

And on the morrow the king sent to Lisle and caused it to be burned, and all the other goodly towns of Flanders did he occupy and set his own garrisons therein Back came the king to France, with his prisoners, Ferrand he caused

---

[60] *Tuit estoient tournei aus watiaus*, a phrase of doubtful meaning

[61] "The battle of Bouvines was not the victory of Philip Augustus, alone, over a coalition of foreign princes, the victory was the work of king and people, barons, knights, burghers, and peasants of Ile-de-France, of Orléanais, of Picardy, of Normandy, of Champagne, and of Burgundy And this union of different classes and different populations in a sentiment, a contest, and a triumph shared in common was a decisive step in the organization and unity of France The victory of Bouvines marked the commencement of the time at which men might speak and indeed did speak, by one single name, of *the French* The nation in France and the kingship in France on that day rose out of and above the feudal system" Guizot, *History of France,* I, xviii

to be put in the Louvre at Paris, because he had coveted Normandy, and the other prisoners did he cause to be placed whereso it pleased him From that day forth King Philip dwelt in peace, and he was feared and dreaded throughout all lands.

XXVIII

HOW THE BARONS OF ENGLAND SENT FOR AID TO PRINCE LEWIS OF FRANCE

Now will we tell you of the wicked King John of England, who shamed his barons, and lay with their wives and with their daughters by force, and took away from them their lands, and wrought so great evil that God and all the world must needs hate him And it came to pass that the barons of England took counsel together and determined that they would send to King Philip and would swear fealty to him for the kingdom of England and would place their children with him as hostages, and would help him to conquer the kingdom And they chose two of their own number, the wisest and the most valiant, and sent them to King Philip, and these told him the word that the barons of England sent to him

And the king told them that he would take counsel in the matter And the king took counsel, and he said that he had land enough, nor would he meddle with the matter But when my Lord Lewis heard that his father would not meddle in the matter he said to him "Sire, an it were pleasing to you, I would undertake this business"

"By the lance of Saint James," quoth the king, "do in this thing what seemeth thee good! But I think that thou wilt not bring the matter to fulfilment, for the English are treacherous and false, nor ever will they keep their word with thee"

"Sire," quoth my Lord Lewis, "let it be according to God's will"

Then said he to the messengers "Sirs, an ye will, I will undertake this business, and with God's help and your own I will carry it through"

"I' faith," said the messengers, "we ask nought better!"

Straightway made they their pledges one to another, and they delivered their letters pendant[62] from all the barons of England, which they had brought with them, these delivered they unto my Lord Lewis And they promised by their faith that they would send their children as hostages within one month of the day that they should be returned to England

Then did the messengers depart, and they passed over the sea and came to London, and they assembled the barons and told them how they had wrought, and the barons said that this was well done And the children of the barons of England were sent, even as they had promised, and my Lord Lewis caused them to be well kept and honourably And he caused great navies to be prepared, and whatsoever else was needful for waging war, and he gathered together great multitudes of men, for love, for money, and for kinship's sake And with him was the Count of Le Perche, and the Count of Montfort, and the Count of Chartres, and the Count of Montbéliard, and my Lord Enguerrand of Coucy, and many another great lord of whom I speak not

---

[62]I e, letters patent, with hanging seals

And they set out to sea on a Monday morning, and they came to land at Dover in the evening so speedily that they were not perceived And they pitched their tents and their pavilions along the strand And when they of the castle perceived them they marveled greatly what folk these might be, so they rushed to arms and went upon the battlements of the walls, which were very strong, and held themselves there as if to defend their own bodies and their castle And on the morrow my Lord Lewis bade the castle be assaulted and his engines to play against it, but these wrought little mischief And they were there ten days, nor did they accomplish any thing

And when my Lord Lewis and his council saw that this was so, then did he determine that he would raise the siege and would go to London and lay siege thereto So caused he his tents to be struck and his harness packed, and he bade his host be led to London, and the city was besieged on three sides And they that were within it defended themselves vigorously and guarded the gates and the walls, and they sent word to their lord in all haste that he should succour them But he sent back word to them that he had not the power to do this, for that his barons had all forsaken him and turned toward my Lord Lewis

When they of London heard these tidings they yielded up the city incontinent, and the men of the host all went in together and lodged themselves throughout the city But my Lord Lewis caused his ban to be cried that no one should work any mischief whatsoever And they sojourned thus eight days, and on the ninth day the host marched to Lincoln And the Count of Le Perche was forming the vanguard, and he rode up hard by the gates, and the garrison that was within the town came forth and attacked the vanguard, and there was great shooting of arrows and hurling of missiles, and horses slain and horsemen overthrown, and footmen dead or wounded And the Count of Le Perche was slain there by a base fellow who lifted the skirt of his hauberk and stabbed him with a knife, and the vanguard was discomfited by the count's death And when my Lord Lewis knew this, then had he the greatest dole that ever he had, for the count was his near friend and kinsman

Immediately was siege laid to Lincoln, and the city was taken by storm on the third day, and he caused it to be garrisoned with good men, and thereafter he went about England for the space of two years and an half and conquered seven cities, and boroughs and towns in great number And in this space of time King John sent to Rome, and he declared to the Pope that he would bestow on him in perpetuity four sterlings of revenue for every hearth, and he bade him, for God's sake, to give heed to the king's cause

When the pontiff and the brethren saw the great treasure which the king had sent and the great and perpetual revenue, which came to the value of a thousand marks in sterlings the year, then were the pontiff and the brethren right glad And he sent to my Lord Lewis and declared to him flatly that he desired him to return, and if he would not do this, then would he excommunicate both Lewis himself and all his helpers My Lord Lewis cared not a straw for all the word that the pontiff sent him, rather, he went on conquering lands, and the pontiff caused him to be excommunicated throughout all Christendom, and all them that helped him in any wise whatsoever

XXIX

HOW PRINCE LEWIS WAS FORSAKEN BY THE BARONS OF ENGLAND

Thereafter it befell that my Lord Lewis had spent all his substance and had lack of silver, and he sent word to his father, beseeching him for God's sake to help him and to send him moneys And the king made answer that, by the lance of Saint James, he would do nothing of the sort, nor for his sake would he ever suffer himself to be excommunicate When my Lady Blanche knew thereof she came to the king and said to him "Will ye thus suffer my lord your son to die in a strange country? Sire, in God's name, heed! He it is that is to reign after you, send him then what is needful for him—at the least the revenues of his patrimony"

"Nay!" quoth the king "I will do nought of the sort!"

"Nay? Sire"

"Nay, in sooth!" quoth the king

"In God's name, then," said my Lady Blanche, "I know well what I will do"

"What, then, will ye do?"

"By the Blessed Mother of God, I have four children by my lord, them will I set in gage, and surely shall I find one who will lend me moneys on them"

Straightway she left the king, like a woman gone mad, and when the king saw her thus depart, well weened he that she spake the truth And he bade her be called back and said to her "Blanche, I will give you of my treasure so much as ye shall desire, and do ye therewith whatso ye will and whatso seemeth you good But know ye of a surety, I myself will send him nought"

"Sire," quoth my Lady Blanche, "ye say well"

Then was the great treasure delivered to my Lady Blanche, and she sent it to her lord

And when King John saw that he was losing his land altogether he sent word to the barons and cried them mercy, and he said that he would make amend for all things according to their will, and he would put all his kingdom in their hands and all his strong holds, and, for God's sake, let them have compassion on him When the barons saw him thus abase himself, then had they pity on him, and it hath been said of yore that "true heart cannot lie," and "far better loveth one his rightful lord than a stranger" So they required an oath of him that he would amend himself according to their will and would put all his kingdom in their hands, and they were seized of the strong holds

And they came to my Lord Lewis and said unto him "Sire, know ye of a truth that no longer could we endure such damage to our own lord, for now is he willing to make amend to us And know ye now of a very surety that no longer will we be your helpers, rather will we be against you"

When my Lord Lewis heard them he waxed exceeding wroth and said· "How? Fair sirs, have ye thus betrayed me?"

And they made answer to him saying "Better doth it become us to fall short of our covenant than to let our lord be ruined and destroyed But, for God's sake, get you gone from hence, so will ye be doing wisely, for to tarry longer in this land is not to your advantage "

When my Lord Lewis saw that it could not be otherwise he caused his fleet to be made ready and came back again to France, nor could he be absolved until the hostages were returned And some time thereafter went he against Toulouse and led a great multitude of baronry thither, and therein was Count Tiebaud of Champagne, and the Count of Saint-Pol, and many another great lord And he lay for a long time before Toulouse, nor ever were the gates closed for all their number, nor aught did he accomplish there, but came back with less of substance and with more of shame.

XXX

OF THE DEATH OF PHILIP AUGUSTUS AND OF THE SACRING OF HIS SON

About this time it befell that the King of France was holding a parliament at Mantes, at the season of the feast of Saint Mary Magdalene,[63] and there were many great lords present, and of bishops and archbishops forty and eight But death, who spareth none, neither great nor small, came and laid an ambush for him And he lay upon his deathbed, and he made confession and repented of his misdeeds And he made his devises, and he left to the land beyond the sea the third part of his treasure, which was very great, and another third to the poor, and the other third to the crown of France for to govern and to defend it And his soul gave he back to Our Lord And good opinion have men of him, for he was revealed to certain worthy men to whom the Holy Spirit had made him known

The king's body was made ready for burial even as befitteth the body of so great a king and was borne of high barons and knights to Saint-Denis in France, and at every resting-place was a cross set up, whereon his likeness was figured And mass was sung for him by Archbishop William of Joinville, who with his own hands laid him away And thereafter a tomb was made for him, of fine gold and of silver, whither he was transported as a king And there are forty and eight bishops on the four sides of the tomb, standing in relief and depicted as bishops, arrayed as for to sing mass, their mitres on their heads and croziers in their hands

Here will we leave off to speak of King Philip—God rest his soul!—who passed out of this life three days after the feast of the Magdalene, in the year one thousand two hundred and three and twenty, and he reigned two score and seven years, and he was sixteen years old when he was crowned Henceforth will we tell you of my Lord Lewis and of my Lady Blanche his wife, who was daughter to the King of Spain and had four children, of whom the eldest was called Philip, and the next Lewis, and the next Robert, and the fourth Alphonse; but Philip, the eldest, died at the age of fifteen years And my lady was at this time great with a daughter, who was thereafter named Isabelle, nor ever would she marry but kept her to the state of virginity, and she wrought many good works

[63] 22 July

Now return we to our matter My Lord Lewis made ready for to be crowned, he and his wife, at Reims, and he had his men summoned for to be present at his crowning at the octaves of mid August, and to Reims came the greatest knighthood and the greatest company of folk that ever was present at any crowning Then was sacred my Lord Lewis, and my Lady Blanche his wife, and they were anointed with the holy ampulla which God sent down from heaven to my Lord Saint Remigius for to anoint Clovis, who was the first Christian king of the kingdom of France, and they were anointed by the hand of Archbishop William of Joinville, who was then Archbishop of Reims.

Then were they led to the palace, with eight trumpets sounding, and the feast was made ready—the goodliest and the richest that ever was at any king's crowning And there was the goodliest raiment of high lords that man ever saw On the morrow the court departed, the king and the queen went to France and were received with high solemnity at Paris

Archbishop William of Joinville, who must pay the expenses of the crowning, sought and demanded these of the Échevins of Reims, and he said that they ought to pay them And he brought forward false witnesses John the Clerk of Bourg, and Archdeacon Hugh of Sarcu, and Dean Peter of Lageri, and the Chanter of Reims, and they bare witness, with their seals But the Échevins of Reims to wit, Voisin le Coq, Jaques le Borgne, Cochon de Montlaurent, Gautier le Roi, Corbeau Pichet, Gérard le Coutre, Witier le Gras, Wede de Verselai, Cauchon Voisin[64]—and the other companions would not suffer this, but they went straight to the king and told him how the archbishop was seeking to do them a wrong

The king said that he did not desire that the burghers of Reims should pay for the crowning an they ought not so to do, and he sent my Lord Renaud of Beronne, who was of his council, for to enquire who had paid at the crowning of King Philip—whether the archbishop or the burghers And he came to Reims and went to the Temple, where were the archbishop and the échevins in person And my Lord Renaud of Beronne enquired of the aged men of Reims and found through diligent and honest enquiry that the archbishop had paid Then were restored to the échevins the letters of false witness which the archdeacon and the dean and the chanter had delivered to the archbishop by counsel of the chapter, and the échevins tare them in pieces in the sight of all them that were present; and from that day forth do the archbishops pay for the crowning without any gainsaying

[64]Some of these names are so comical that we might suspect the minstrel of having invented the whole list of them, were it not for the presence of many similar names in historical documents of that period

XXXI

OF THE FALSE COUNT BALDWIN

Now come we back to King Lewis, who was an honourable man and a bold, and much wrought he in his lifetime And he had (after that he was made king) a son who was named Charles and is Count of Anjou And in that year went he against La Rochelle in Poitou and took the place by force, and yet doth the king hold it

Afterward befell a marvellous adventure in Flanders, for certain great lords of Flanders contrived a great treason against the Countess Joan of Flanders And they gat hold of a certain old man and put him in an hut, as a monk, in the Forest of Mormail,[65] and there abode he a long time, and they caused him to believe that they would make him Count of Flanders

And he asked them how this could come to pass, and they made answer that they would give the people to understand that he was that Count Baldwin who had gone away to Constantinople a long time afore, who was father to the countess "And ye have escaped from your captivity at the hands of Vatace,[66] and are come to this forest for to do penance here " And they taught him how he should make answer to them that should enquire of him concerning his doings But know ye of a truth that guile cannot remain hidden at the last The old man believed them, and therein acted he as a fool, for thence came to him nought but evil, even as ye shall hear hereafter

These traitors of whom I am telling you spread the tale through all the country-side, and they gave folk to understand that this was in sooth Count Baldwin, and in a short time was it known throughout all Flanders, and there came thither so great multitudes that it was a fair marvel And they led him forth of his hermitage and brought him to Valenciennes, and they caused to be made for him a robe of scarlet lined with vair And they set him upon a great war horse and led him through all the goodly towns of Flanders, and they paid all his costs, and all Flanders held him to be their lord and rejoiced greatly over him

Thus for a long season abode he in that seigniory, until he heard tell that the countess was at Haimmon Cainori [67] And she was sitting at table, and the false count knew this and bade his people go up for to seize the countess But word thereof was brought her through certain of her friends, and so little time was left for fleeing that they must perforce set her on a sumpter beast and flee by by-paths to Mons in Hainault, and there took she refuge And when the countess saw that the thing was thus she sent word to the king, her cousin german, praying him for God's sake to give heed to her case, else would she lose her land When the king heard this he determined to send word to him who feigned himself to be Count Baldwin that he should come to him to a parliament at Péronne, with safe-conduct both coming and going, and that if he were the king's uncle, then would he be right glad thereof and would suffer him to enjoy his land And

[65]Unidentified
[66]John III Ducas Vatatzes, Emperor of Nicaea 1222-1254
[67]Not identified.

he sent a messenger with his letter, and the parliament was appointed and the man said that he would go thither And he came without default, and with much people And he was mounted on a black horse, and he wore a scarlet mantle lined with green silken stuff, and he had a bonnet on his head and held a white rod in his hand, and verily he seemed a marvellous valiant man Thus went he to the court, and he had a great rout of folk with him And he dismounted at the foot of the stairs of the hall and went up them, like a great lord, and it was announced to the king that he was come

When the king heard this, then came he forth of his chamber and went to meet him and said to him "Sir, welcome indeed be ye, an ye be mine uncle, Count Baldwin, who ought to be Emperor of Constantinople and King of Salonica and Count of Flanders and of Hainault "

"Fair nephew," quoth he, "may ye have good fortune from God and from His sweet Mother ! Truly am I he, and all that ye have said ought I to be, if only right were done me, but my daughter seeketh to disinherit me, nor will she acknowledge me for her father So pray I you, fair nephew, that ye be willing to aid me in the maintaining of my right "

"Certes," quoth the king, "for nought else am I come hither, but it behooveth me in all reason to know the truth concerning you For, as I have heard, it is now fifty[68] years since Count Baldwin, mine uncle, went away to Constantinople and was taken captive, and few are there left of them that were then living "

"Certes," quoth he, "thereto am I agreed "

"In God's name," said the king, "ye say well "

"We ask of you," said then Brother Garin, the Bishop of Senlis, " in what city ye married your wife "

When he heard this question asked, he meditated, for in this matter had he not been instructed And he knew not what to answer, so he said that he desired to get him to bed And he thought in his heart that he would enquire concerning this thing of them that were teaching him, but it went not thus, for they caused him to repose in a chamber all alone, and they kept the doors well guarded so that none might enter there

And when came the hour of rising, they asked him if he desired to answer the thing that had been enquired of him, but he feigned that he was angry and said that he desired to depart, and the king permitted this willingly Straightway the dotard departed from the king and went back to Valenciennes, whence he had come, unto the Abbey of Saint John, and that selfsame night he fled thence with two others and went into Burgundy, unto Rais, where he was born And the king returned to France, well perceiving that the man was an imposter

So passed full half a year, nor had any one news of him Then it befell that a certain squire of the Lord of Chasenai[69] saw him on a market day at Chasenai, and he pointed him out to his master and said "My Lord, I see here that man who gave himself out to be Count Baldwin of Flanders "

---

[68]This should be "twenty years "
[69]Erard de Chasenai

"Hold they peace!" quoth his lord "The Devil take thee! Thou liest—this thing cannot be!"

"Lord," quoth the squire, "hang me by the neck an this be not true!"

"In sooth," quoth my Lord Erard, "then take him! By Saint James, he will bring me good guerdon!"[70]

Then the squires took him and put him in prison, and their lord perceived that he was in truth that man And my Lord Erard caused letters to be written and sent word to the countess that he was holding the pretender When the countess knew this she was right glad thereof, and she bade letters pendant be written, wherein she promised to pay to my Lord Erard of Chasenai a thousand marks of silver at his pleasure on the surety of her own substance, if he would send the man to her And my Lord Erard sent him to her forthwith, and he kept the letters, which were thereafter of great profit to him, for the countess defaulted in her promise, and he took so much of what was hers that he was paid therewith

When the countess had this her father (who knew not how the city was called wherein he married her mother), then she asked him whence he was and by whose counsel he had done this thing And he said that he was called Bertran of Rais, and that he had done this through the counsel of certain knights and ladies and clerks And they haled him from his hermitage, wherein he thought to save his soul "I' faith," quoth the countess, "ye have acted like a fool, verily ye would be count without right thereto"

Then she bade him be stripped, and he was left in a coat of rough stuff without stripes And she caused him to be ungirt and his shoes to be taken off, and she perceived that he had no toes upon his feet And he was set upon a jade and led through all the booths of the fair of Lisle, which was held at this season And he cried before each booth "Listen to this wretch! I am" (quoth he) "Bertran of Rais in Burgundy, a poor man, who deserve not to be king, or count, or emperor, and that which I did, did I through the counsel of the knights and the ladies and the burghers of this land"

Then they made him to hold his peace And thereafter was he put upon a new pillar, which was set up in the market-place of Lisle, with two great hounds beside him, the one on his right hand and the other on his left And there was he hanged with a new chain of iron, for fear lest a cord should have broken, and he hung there a year or more Here will we leave this simple one, who wrought so foolishly, and it hath been said of old that great need, forsooth, hath he of a fool, who maketh one of himself

XXXII

OF THE DEATH OF KING LEWIS AND OF THE SACRING OF HIS SON

Now will we tell you of King Lewis, who found well-nigh no repose Tidings came to him that they of Avignon were risen up against him and had taken and slain certain of his garrisons which were on their borders And the king sent and

---

[70] *Il me rendra bon poivre*, literally, "good pepper" One MS has *bon vin*, "good wine"

commanded them to come and make amend to him, and they sent back word to the king that they would do nought of the sort for him, nor did they hold themselves subject to him

When the king heard the arrogant message which they of Avignon sent him, then was he filled with wrath, and he summoned his vassals and his friends, through homage or through love, and he gat together so great an host that it was a fair marvel And there was Guy of Saint-Pol, who was a very fair knight and valiant and loyal, and many other great lords with him And he went against Avignon and laid siege thereto, and they that were within were well supplied and little feared him And he lay before the place an half-year or more, but wrought there little loss, until the king one day desired an assault to be made on the city So were the engines set up and began fiercely to hurl great stones into the city

And the Count of Saint-Pol kept the watch that night, and they that were within were also letting their engines play upon them that were without So befell by mischance that Count Guy of Saint-Pol had gone to see them that were plying the engines, and a stone from the engines of them that were within the city fell upon his head and his brains were clean dashed out And he was borne to the tent of the king And when the king saw him dead he was so sore distressed that he was well-nigh beside himself, nor could any man living appease him, for he loved the count exceedingly And truly he had reason to be loved, for he was endowed with all good qualities

The body of the Count of Saint-Pol was stripped of his armour and was emptied and embalmed, and it was laid in a long coffin and borne to Longaut, unto a priory of nuns which he had founded, and there was it buried honourably And the assault ceased, and there was granted on the one side and on the other a truce of fifteen days And the king sware, in the eyes of them all, that if the city were not yielded up within the term of the truce and he were able to take them by force, then would he cause them all to be slain and would put them to the sword

When they of Avignon saw that the king had thus sworn, knowing the bitterness that he had because of the count who had died, they took counsel and determined that they would yield the city to the king, their lives being saved, for well wist they that in the end they could not hold it And they yielded it up, and the king caused the walls thereof to be rased, and he put a garrison therein at their cost And he departed thence so soon as he was able, for the place was full of corruption and much people died there And there died the Count of Namur, which was a sore loss, and many other rich men beside

But even as the king and the Archbishop of Reims were returning thence they were seized of a sore sickness, and they were laid in a litter and were borne even to Montpensier, a strong castle which was the king's And there the king died—God rest his soul!—and so was fulfilled the prophecy which men say that Merlin spake, for he said that the sweet lion of France would die at Montpensier And in sooth was he the sweet lion, for he was beyond measure bold nor were it fitting for a king to perform the bold deeds which he did And the king's body was embalmed with balsam and carried to Saint-Denis, where it was buried magnificently hard by his father And the archbishop lived but three days after the king, and he was carried to Clairvaux and was buried in the common churchyard

Now here will we leave the dead and will speak of the living· and we will tell you of Queen Blanche, who mourned in bitter sorrow Nor is this any wonder, for she had suffered great loss, and her children were yet small, and she was a solitary woman from a strange country And she had to do with great lords— with Count Philip Hurupel of Boulogne, with Count Robert of Dreux, with the Count of Mâcon his brother,[71] with the Seignior of Courtenai, with my Lord Enguerrand of Coucy, and with all that great lineage that then were living, and she feared them greatly And she called the princes of the kingdom in whom she put the most trust, and the most honourable men, and said to them "Fair sirs, my lord is dead, which is a great loss to me and to you, so do I seek your counsel, what I shall do, for I have great need thereof"

"I' faith," answered the barons, "lady, ye will have your son Lewis crowned at Reims, and we will all go thither armed, and he shall be crowned, whomsoever it irketh"

And the day was set for to crown the lad, who was fourteen years of age, at the season of the feast of Saint Andrew, in the year of the Incarnation of Our Lord one thousand two hundred and twenty and six And they came on that day to Reims all quietly, and the lad was crowned by the hand of Bishop James of Soissons, for then was the see vacant And homage was done to the king, and to the queen for so long as she should have ward of the king, and thereat were the barons sorely vexed And about this time was Henry of Braine chosen Archbishop of Reims, nor ever had they peace so long as he lived And he was archbishop fourteen years, and he died about Saint John's Day in the year one thousand two hundred and forty

XXXIII

HOW THE BARONS OF FRANCE REVOLTED AGAINST QUEEN BLANCHE

Now come we back to the barons, who meditated nought but evil against the Queen of France Oft held they parliaments together and saw that there was none in France could do them hurt, for they saw that the king was young, and his brethren also, and they held the mother of small account And they gat them together and gave the Count of Boulogne to understand (so it is said) that they would make him king, and he was not over-wise and believed them And they took counsel among them that they would first deal with Count Tiebaud of Champagne and would impute unto him the death of King Lewis, for that he had left him at Avignon and had departed basely, like a traitor, and if they had accomplished his death or imprisonment, then would they have had none to gainsay them in seizing the kingdom Thus was the matter arranged, and the Count of Boulogne sent a defiance to Count Tiebaud by two knights and demanded of him satisfaction for the death of his brother

[71]Jean de Braine

The count was sore dumfounded thereat, and he caused his men to be summoned and asked of them what he should do And his men answered him perfidiously, for they were all in accord with the barons When the count beheld their evil faces and heard their evil answers, then lost he heart utterly, howbeit he put a better face on the matter than he thought within him

And he commanded an arch of the Bridge of Binson to be torn down, and barbicans and other defenses to be built above the bridge, and the guarding of the passage he committed to Count Hugh of Rethel, who, forsooth, played his part none too well therein And he garrisoned Fismes and made Simon of Trelou captain thereof, and he caused Mont Aimé to be garrisoned, and this was the garrison that best proved itself in his behalf And he betook himself to Provins and bade the borough be fortified in all haste, and there he kept himself, for he knew not in whom to trust

Now, for a little, will we leave off to speak of Count Tiebaud, and we will tell you of the barons, who had assembled so great an host that it was a marvel to behold And they came straight against Fismes, and siege was laid to the place, and they lay a long time before it But in the end was it given up to them, and they caused it to be mined and set fire therein But the tower was so good that never a whit did it give way, and it yet standeth Then betook they themselves straight to the Bridge of Binson, and there could they not pass, for it was very strongly fortified

And when Count Hugh of Saint-Pol saw that they would not pass over by the bridge, he went a little way up the Marne until he was hard by Reuil, and there, himself first, both he and his people passed over But there was a little resistence on the part of ten knights of the following of the Count of Rethel, who contested their passage so long as they could, but this availed them nought, for the Count of Saint-Pol was already passed over And when the Count of Rethel saw them on this side the river he turned his back and fled, and the Monk of Mongon was wounded and taken captive there

Straightway they all passed over, for the Marne was low at that season Then went they to Épernay and brake it down, and very great spoil gained they there, and much thereof came to Reims and not a few were they that made their profit of it And then went they to Damery and occupied it And thence went they to Sesanne, and found it all empty, for Count Tiebaud had commanded it to be set on fire And know ye of a surety that they of Mont Aimé withstood them vigorously

And they went against Provins, but their victual was beginning somewhat to fail them, and they of Mont Aimé snatched whatsoever was coming to them from the side of Reims And that was the region whence came the most of their provision, for Archbishop Henry was aiding them with all his might So they burned the country-side of Champagne, and there was none to hinder

When Queen Blanche knew of a truth that they did this to no other end than that they might get the kingdom of France (and well she wist that my Lord Enguerrand of Coucy had already caused the crown to be made wherewith he should be crowned, albeit they had already given the Count of Boulogne to understand that they would make him king, but it hath been said of yore "Whom God will help, him can no evil man harm"), then the queen determined that she would help to defend the land of Champagne and of Brie, for the Count of Champagne was her kinsman and the king's man

And she caused a great host to be assembled four leagues from Troyes, and there were the king and she, and she sent word to the Count of Boulogne and to the barons that they should not be so bold as to work any mischief on the king's fief, and in sooth did she let them know that she was ready to do justice to the count if they knew what to ask for him And they sent back word to her that they would never plead the case, and they said that it was the custom for a woman, when a man had murdered her husband, to be more fain to reproach that man than another

Then answered the Count of Boulogne, who had already perceived their treachery, and said "I' faith, ye speak ill, it is in no wise made clear what ye ask for the count Furthermore, we should be forsworn to the king if we should henceforth work any mischief after this hath been forbidden us Above all, the king is mine own nephew, son of mine own brother, and he is my liege lord and I am his liege man, and I do you to wit that I am no longer of your alliance or of your accord, rather, I will be for the king with all my loyal might!"

When the barons heard the count speak thus, they looked one upon the other and were all dumfounded And they said to the count, who was their chief· "Lord, then have ye dealt ill with us, for ye will have the queen's favour, but we shall lose our land"

"In God's name," quoth the count, "better is it to forsake folly than to pursue it!"

Straightway he caused a letter to be written and sent word to the queen that he desired not to disobey either her own or the king's behest, rather was he ready to fulfill their commandment When the queen knew this, then was she right glad thereof, and the Count of Boulogne departed from the barons, and the barons themselves departed also

And every one of them went unto his own land in bitterness of heart because they had not attained their desire but had won the queen's displeasure, who well knew how to hate and how to love those men and those women who so merited and to reward them according to their works

So was the covenant broken, and the Count of Champagne remained in peace And no long time afterward the Countess Blanche,[72] his mother, died, and one year thereafter died King Sancho of Navarre, who was his uncle And the barons of Navarre sent for the count and made him king at Pampelune, after the custom of the country And he had to wife the Countess of Dagsbourg,[73] ere he was made king, but he put her away And thereafter took he to wife the daughter of my Lord Imbert of Beaujeu, who was niece to the king, and she died, but he had

---

[72]Blanche of Navarre, Countess of Champagne
[73]Gertrude

by her a daughter who was married to the son of Count Peter Mauclerc, who is now Count of Brittany And then he married the daughter of Archembaud of Bourbon; and by this lady had he six children, of whom the eldest was called Thibaut, and the second Peter, and the third Henry, and the fourth William, and the elder daughter Alice, and the other Cecily [74]

XXXIV

OF THE FURTHER REVOLTS OF THE BARONS OF FRANCE

Now will we leave the King of Navarre and will tell you of the King of France, who was now twenty years of age And the queen had a mind that he should marry him, so he took to wife the eldest of the daughters of the Count of Provence, of whom there were four And presently King Henry of England took the second; and Count Richard, his brother, who is now King of Germany, took the third, and the Count of Anjou, brother to the King of France, took the last, and he had the countship of Provence, for it is the custom of that country that the last child have all, an there be no male heir

Now be it known to you that this damosel whom the King of France took to wife is called Margaret and is a very good and wise lady And she hath by the king eight children—five sons and three daughters—of whom the eldest of the sons was named Lewis, and the second Philip, and the third Peter, and the fourth John, and the fifth Robert And the eldest of the damosels is called Isabel, and she is married to the King of Navarre, and the second is called Margaret, and she is given to the son of the Duke of Brabant, and the third is called Blanche

Now will we leave these children (whom God guard!) and we will come back to the King of Navarre, who had made the marriage of his daughter to the son of Count Mauclerc of Brittany, these lived happily together, and the King of Navarre made great use of his counsel And the count gave him to understand that the King of France was wrongfully keeping from him the four fiefs of Blois, and he made an alliance with him and said that he would cause him to have them again an he would trust him, for betwixt them twain they could cope with the King of France, through themselves and through their friends The King of Navarre believed him, and therein acted he as a fool, for he would have suffered great mischief thereby had it not been for Queen Blanche, who reconciled him to her son

And now shall ye hear how the King of Navarre wrought through foolish counsel He caused Meaux to be strengthened and his castles to be garrisoned, and he demanded of the king that he restore to him his fiefs of Blois, which the king (so he said) was unjustly keeping from him The king answered him and said that he was doing him no wrong, but an the King of Navarre knew what demand to make in the matter, he would cause justice to be done him by his peers The King of Navarre would hear nought of this, but said that he would obtain justice for himself in so far as he could, and he entered into seisin of the fiefs

---

[74]In error for Margaret or Beatrice

When the King of France knew this he caused his vassals to be summoned, and he bade fetch petraries and mangonels and the great trebuchet[75] of Aubemarle which the Count of Boulogne had caused to be made at Montereau, where the Yonne dischargeth And he bade his host go straight thither

When the queen saw that the case was urgent and that the king was willing to follow her counsel, then sent she word to the King of Navarre that he should come and speak with her and she would make her peace with him And he came without delay, but even as he was entering into the great hall at Paris, there was one ready there who hit him full in the face with a cheese which he had in a basket, this did he at the instigation of the Count of Artois, who never had loved the king And the King of Navarre came all in a rage into the queen's presence and told her how he had been treated thus whilst he was under her safe-conduct

When the queen saw him she was sorely vexed, and she commanded that he that had done this thing should be seized and cast into the Châtelet, saying that counsel would be taken what should be done with him But so soon as the Count of Artois knew thereof he procured the man's enlargement Howbeit, the queen made peace with him on the understanding that he should repay all the costs which the king had incurred on this occasion and that he would of his own accord give up the fiefs, and of these the king held Montereau and three castles until he recovered all his costs

Now it befell the year after this that Count Peter Mauclerc rebelled against the court, and spake base evil of the queen, and departed from the court basely And when the king heard thereof he was sore grieved, and he caused the count to be summoned to his court, to appear there within forty days for that which the king should deem fitting to demand of him The count made answer that he would neither go thither nor send, and he sent his defiance to the king by a priest and through his letter

And when the forty days were past after the summons, the king assembled his hosts and went out against the count, and he laid siege to Bellême and took it by storm, nor ever afterward was it given back And when the count saw that his own loss was very evident he cast himself on the king's mercy, having yet to pay all the king's costs, and his castle remaining lost to him, and he came to the queen's feet and cried her mercy

Then it befell, some time thereafter, that the Count of La Marche, who took the king's moneys (every year three thousand pounds Tournois) for guarding the marches toward Bordeaux and because the king desired that he should be his good friend—it befell that he refused longer to take the king's moneys, and it was said of old "So long doth the she-goat scratch that she maketh her an ill bed " And he sent and sought the King of England, and he came to Bordeaux and they made ready to enter Poitou, and verily they thought that the king would not be a match for them, and they entered into Poitou and wrought mischief against the king But when the king knew this he was not one whit afeared but went out to meet them, and he gathered his men at Poitiers, and he came forth of Poitiers

---

[75]A ballistic engine somewhat resembling the mangonel

all armed—so magnificently that never king of France had come forth so magnificently for the sake of any good city and for to go to battle

And the Count of La Marche thought that the king must turn aside to Lusignan, one of his castles, which is very strong, but the king determined that he had liefer take the weaker castles and garrison them, and then after this would he have all the country-side spoiled and guarded so that no victual could enter into Lusignan, and so could he get possession of the place For well knew he that the garrison therein was very great and that the castle was exceeding strong

And when the Count of La Marche saw in what manner the king was working he feared him greatly, for well did he perceive that the king was wise So he betook him to Saintes and had the place garrisoned with knights and with serjeants And thence went he to Pons, where the English king was keeping himself, and there they spake together concerning the king, who was coming against them in great force, and well did they perceive that they would be no match for the king

Then, lo, the king's men that had taken Crozant, one of the count's castles, came straight on against Saintes, and the Count of Artois was coming in the forefront, with his banner unfurled And they that were within the place sallied forth against them with a great foison of knighthood, and there was a fierce combat, and there was much lost and much gained and many knights taken on the one side and on the other But they of Saintes had the worse of the affair, for the Count of Artois brake into the city with a great foison of knighthood, and the city was taken And when the King of England knew thereof, away went he to Bordeaux and had his ships well guarded, for he had great fear that the king would pass over after him And so soon as he could he departed unto England, and when he was come thither he esteemed himself a fool

When the Count of La Marche saw that he had lost Saintes and four castles and that the English king had failed him, and that my Lord Renaud of Pons had failed him, and the Seignior of Taillebourg, and the Seignior of Mirambeau, then did he think that he had wrought all to no purpose, and so soon as he could he made his peace with the king And he cast himself on his mercy, being held to the payment of the king's costs and the king's conquest remaining to the king For it is the custom of the king of France, if he go to war with any baron, that whatsoever of his the king taketh by force remaineth the king's in perpetuity, and all the king's costs must be repaid to him or ever the baron can make his peace with the king Thus dealt the king with all them that rebelled against him And he caused Saintes and the four castles to be right well garrisoned, then went he back to France Nor was there a baron in France who durst lift his hand against him

XXXV

HOW THE YOUNG KING LEWIS TOOK THE CROSS, AND HOW HE CONQUERED DAMIETTA

Then it befell, some time thereafter, that a sore sickness laid hold on the king, and he was sick nigh unto death, and in that hour he took the cross for to go beyond the sea And he recovered and made ready for his journey, and he caused the cross to be preached And many of the high barons took the cross— the Count of Artois, the Count of Poitiers, the Count of Anjou, the Count of Flanders, the Count of Brittany, the Count of Dreux, the Count of Saint-Pol, the Count of Montfort, the Count of Vendôme, the Count of La Marche, my Lord Gaucher of Châtillon, Oliver of Termes, my Lord Ralph of Coucy, my Lord Roger of Rozoy, my Lord Ralph of Soissons, and so many other great lords that France remained empty of them, and even yet their absence appeareth

But one thing did the king whereof came no good, for he agreed to the respite of three years which the knights asked of the legate for to have a respite of the debts which they owed to the burghers, albeit the legate took no pledge of them And in such wise they went away beyond the sea, but so had not Godfrey of Bouillon done, who sold his dukedom in perpetuity, and went away beyond the sea honourably and at his own expense nor took with him aught that was another's So did he act, and Scripture saith that God desireth not at all to be served with robbery and extortion [76]

When the king had made ready for his journey he took his wallet and his pilgrim's staff at Our Lady's in Paris, and the bishop sang mass for him And he set forth from Our Lady's—he and the queen and his brethren and their wives, unshod and barefoot, and all the congregation and the people of Paris convoyed them so far as Saint-Denis, with weeping and with tears And there the king took his leave of them and sent them back to Paris, and he wept bitterly when he parted from them

But the queen his mother tarried with him and accompanied him yet three days, in despite of the king Then said he unto her "Fair, sweetest mother, by that faith that ye owe me, turn back incontinent I leave you my three children for to guard—Lewis, Philip, and Isabel—and I leave you to govern the kingdom of France, and in sooth know I that they will be well guarded and that the kingdom will be well governed "

Then answered him the queen, weeping "Fair, sweetest son, how can it be that my heart shall suffer the severing of me and thee? Surely will it be harder than stone if it divide not into two parts, for thou hast been to me the best son that ever mother had "

And on these words she fell down in a swound, and the king raised her up and kissed her, and he took his leave of her, weeping And the queen swooned yet again and remained a long time in a swound, and when she was come again to herself she said "Fair, tender son, never shall I see thee more, that my heart telleth me "

---

[76]Cf Isaiah lxi, 8 "For I the Lord love judgment, I hate robbery for burnt offering "

And she spake sooth, for she was dead or ever he was come back again

Now will we tell you of the king, who journeyed by short stages until he was come to Aigues-Mortes, one of his havens, hard by Marseilles And his ship was made ready, and he entered therein, both he and his household, without any others, and his brethren and their wives entered each one into his own ship, and the other barons also And they departed from the harbour on a Tuesday morning, in thirty and eight ships filled with good men and high barons—to say nought of the ships of the lowly folk or those that were for the horses or for carrying victual And they sailed until, by God's grace, they landed in Cyprus and made harbour at Limassol, a city which lieth in Cyprus, and there were they well nigh a year

Then was it the king's will that all should enter again into the ships, and whatso he had commanded was done And he sent to each master of a ship sealed letters and commanded them that they should not read these until they were forth of the harbour And when they were forth they brake each one the seal of the king's letter, and they saw that the king was commanding them all to go to Damietta, and immediately each one commanded his sailors to set their course thitherward And the sailors said that this would they do right gladly, and they went so straight toward Damietta that they came in ten days to the harbour, and in yet a day and an half were all the ships come thither and made harbour there But the harbour was difficult to make, for the ships could not draw nigher to the shore than a spear-cast or more When they of Damietta perceived this they ran to arms and caused the trumpet to be sounded and came down to the shore And they began to shoot arrows from their Turkish bows, so thick as rain falleth from heaven, and the Christians halted a little And when the king saw that the Christians were halting, then was he beside himself with rage and with vexation of his spirit because of it And he set his feet together and leaped into the sea all armed, shield on neck and sword in hand, and he had the sea clean up to his girdle, but by God's good pleasure he gat him to shore And he laid about him at the Saracens and wrought so many deeds of arms that it was a fair marvel, and they looked on him with wonder for his prowess And when the Christians saw the king thus maintaining himself, they also cast themselves into the sea in a body and made the land And they cried "Monjoie!" and rushed amongst the foe and slew so many of them that they could not be numbered, and yet were they coming forth of the ships

When the Saracens saw that they could not endure, then turned they their backs and fled away, and they rushed into Damietta and shut to the gates thereof And the Christians encamped and lodged them there and laid siege to the city; and they were there for a long season And the king desired the engines to be set up and to begin to play, and it was done even as the king commanded And they played upon the city three days and three nights without ceasing, nor did those that were within the town make any semblance of defending themselves And this was perceived by the watchmen of the host, and they said to the king · "Sire, us seemeth that there is no man within the city, for none appeareth on the battlements or at the gates, night or day And an it were your pleasure we would go up by ladders and enter therein, then shall we know how it is with them "

The king made answer that this were a good thing to do, and he caused it to be cried abroad that all should be ready on the morrow morn for to make the assault And the ladders were set up, and they mounted to the tops of the walls and entered into the city without hinderance, for they that had been within it had all fled by night, save only certain old men and sick folk

And when they were within they searched the city, and they found it well stored with wines and with victuals, and they came to the gates and opened them And they of the host entered in, and the ladies were led to the better dwellings but the king and the princes remained without And it befell the queen that she was seized with the pains of travail, and she was brought to bed and was delivered of a son And he was called Peter at his christening, and even yet is he called Peter Tristan, for it was not long ere Damietta was yielded up again because of a thing that befell the Count of Artois, even as ye shall hear

XXXVI

OF THE DEATH OF THE COUNT OF ARTOIS AND OF THE CAPTIVITY OF KING LEWIS

Thus did it come to pass that Damietta was taken, whereof the Christians were glad and of good cheer Then came the Count of Artois to the king and said to him "Sire, wherefore tarry we here? If ye will believe me, we shall ride forth—we twain, and the Temple, and the Hospital And know ye well, the land is ours, nor ever shall we find any who will gainsay our possession thereof "

"Verily, fair brother," quoth the king, "an ye believe me, we should yet hold ourselves quiet and should occupy the land and the country-side, which is very hard to conquer, and the Turks are wise and are good warriors "

"Sire," quoth the Count of Artois, "we must needs pass over the river Jordan,[77] and when once we have passed over that river, then might we determine how we should next proceed "

"By my halidom, fair brother, so greatly do I fear your hardihood and so well know I your courage that, an ye had once passed over the river, then would ye wait there neither for bald head nor for hairy "[78]

"Ha, sire!" cried the count "I swear to you that I will wait for you until ye shall have passed over!"

The king sware him to this and gave him leave to pass over the river, but an he had known what should befall because of this, never for all the gold in the world would he have given him his leave

That selfsame night, forsooth, it befell that the Count of Artois bade his folk arm themselves—both Templars and Hospitalers—and they passed over the river And they were guided that day by a renegade Christian who knew the

[77]This should be the Nile

[78]*Ne chaut ne chevelu* Probably a proverbial expression, but possibly referring to the shaven heads of certain tribes of Moslems

passes and knew the country and the land thereabout, and he said to the Count of Artois "Lord, an ye would believe me, I would cause you this night to gain the greatest treasure in the world, which is in a city called Mansourah, whither all the people of this country are fled"

"Go we thither!" cried the count

"Ha, lord!" quoth the Master of the Temple "What is this that ye say? God's mercy! Ye know not what this signifieth Whilst ye shall be thinking the Saracens all discomfited, ye will not be biding your time, and ye will be clean surrounded by them But for God's sake, lord, let us await the king, who must pass over presently, and ye, lord, have promised him that ye will not move from hence or ever he himself shall have passed over"

"Ha! ha!" cried the count "In sooth is it a true saying 'Alway will there be found in the Templars some of the hair of the wolf'"[79]

"Sooth," cried the master, who was a very brave and valiant man, "now ride ye whithersoever ye will, and we will follow you Nor ever, please God, will ye be able to bring reproach on a Templar for any cowardice, notwithstanding that never hath Christendom suffered so great loss as it will suffer this selfsame day, even as my heart forebodeth"

Then struck they their horses with their spurs, and away they went toward Mansourah And they entered therein, and it seemed to them that there was no man there But in sooth was there, all the housetops were full of Saracens well supplied with great stones and with sharp stakes, and the entries were fitted with portcullises And so soon as they were come within, the bars were dropped and made fast, and they began from the housetops to cast down great stones and sharp stakes and to pour down boiling water for to scald them And the weather was hot, and the Christians were sore pressed together, and they were in such strait that they had no power to aid or to succour one another

And when the Saracens beheld them in so sorry a pass they bestirred themselves more and more until they had put well-nigh all of them to death And the king, who knew not a word of all this, was passing over the river, and when he was passed over and thought to have found his brother, he found him not at all Then said the king "Ah, brother! How well I ween that thy pride will bring us grief and woe!"

Then, lo, came one of them that had escaped, and he drew nigh to the king and cried to him "Ah, sire! Ill goeth it! Dead is the Count of Artois, your brother, and all the knighthood which was with him, and the Master of the Temple, and the Master of the Hospital! And know, sire, that I tell you truth, for with mine own eyes saw I them slain"

When the king heard him speak thus, he pondered for a little, then sighed he very heavily and said "If he be dead, God grant him forgiveness of his sins—both him and all the rest"

Then the king commanded the tents and the pavilions to be pitched, and they all would rest themselves, for the host was very weary from the passage of the river, which was deep and swift

---

[79]*Dou poil dou leu,* i e, treachery, guile

So soon as the Saracens saw that the king had passed over the river, they let fall their sluices and caused the stream to be held back, and it waxed so high in a little space of time that none might essay to pass over but he would be drowned

And the legate said to the king "Sire, come unto Damietta in this galley, and ye will be saved"

"Ah, God!" cried the king "How could it befall that I should leave this people which I have led hither and should myself go away to safety? Certes, Sir Legate, I will do nought of the sort Rather will I abide God's mercy, and I will make even such an end as they shall make"

When the legate saw that the king would not move, then departed he from him and entered into the galley and went to Damietta, and the king remained And the Saracens caused the shore to be well guarded, so that no vessel could come thither—save with great difficulty—that was not burned with Greek fire

And they had so surrounded the place on all sides that the Christians could not move themselves, and right little had they to eat So were they from All Saints' Day even unto the beginning of Lent in such distress, and their victual failed them utterly And all this befell through my Lord John of Beaumont, who forbade to guard the pass, whereby they were so sore pressed

When the Soldan of Babylon[80] saw that the king was so distressed he sent him word that he should yield himself to him, but the king said "May it please not God that I yield me to paynim or to Saracen!"

"Ha, sire!" quoth the Count of Anjou "In God's name, ye shall do so For ye see clearly that we have nought to eat, but we shall die here of famine and of sicknesses, and lightly may it befall that we shall be delivered by ransom"

And so long did all those pray him who were present that the king yielded his sword to the soldan, and so did the Count of Poitiers, the Count of Anjou, and all the other barons And the king was for ten days prisoner to the Soldan of Babylon, nor ever did he remove from his tent, but he was well guarded by the Saracens But it came to pass that the soldan had him ransomed, and he was redeemed for eight hundred thousands of bezants, and surety for these was gotten through the Temple and the Hospital

And when the Soldan of La Chamelle[81] and the Soldan of Damascus and he of Aleppo knew that the Soldan of Babylon had taken ransom for the king without them and without their counsel, then went they all armed to his tent, and they said that they desired to be partners in the king's ransom And the soldan answered them haughtily and said that they should never have a share therein When these three soldans perceived his arrogance they slew him out of hand And they all went to the king's tent, all ablaze with anger and with heat, and their eyes were so red as burning coals And they caused it to be told to the king, through an interpreter, that they had slain the Soldan of Babylon because he would not let them share the king's ransom "And we desire to stand ourselves in his stead in this matter, and we will that ye deal with us three"

[80]I e, Cairo, Egypt
[81]Joinville calls him "one of the best knights that was in all Heathendom"

And the king answered incontinent (who well perceived their madness from their mien and from the fashion of their countenance) that he was very fain to do this

So was the agreement made with the three soldans, to the effect that they would resore all the captives, free and without ransom, and the king promised them that within a fortnight after he was come to Damietta he would cause the city to be emptied of Christians and delivered to the Saracens And the prisoners were restored or ever the king would depart—all save Gaucher of Châtillon, who could not be found

Immediately the king departed from the soldans, and he entered into a ship—he and his brethren—and the rest entered into several vessels And they came to Damietta and were received both joyfully and sorrowfully joyfully, because of the king and his brethren, whom they had again with them, sorrowfully, because of the Count of Artois, who was dead, and because of the great loss that they had suffered

Then did the king command that all should get them forth of the city and should go unto Acre, and he had the queen, who was with child, taken and put in a ship and carried to Acre And Damietta was emptied and was given again into the hands of the Saracens, nor was it long thereafter until the soldans caused it to be utterly rased and torn down, because they had found out through sorcery that it would yet again be held of the Christians

And the king was at Acre, and as the Christians returned from their captivity, he clothed them again according to their station, for they came back stark naked Then the king betook him into the land of Syria, and he caused Caesarea and Sayette[82] to be fortified, and Mount Musart, a street of Acre which is exceeding pleasing to all folk And the king abode six years in the land beyond the sea

And it came to pass that the queen his mother sent word to him that, in God's name, he should come back, for that she lay very sick, and if anything should befall her then would the kingdom be in great danger, for the princes of the realm were striving, nor had she long to wait the hour of her own death When the king heard the word that his mother sent him he was moved to pity, and he sent back the Count of Poitiers and the Count of Anjou, who were sorely ailing

XXXVII

OF THE JUDGMENT THAT WAS PRONOUNCED ON THE SONS OF THE COUNTESS OF FLANDERS

Now there befell a thing in France concerning a judgment which was rendered in the king's court touching the children of the Countess of Flanders, which she had borne to Bouchard of Avesnes two sons, John and Baldwin, and to my Lord William of Dampierre, William, and Guy, and John And the judgment was such that William should have the county of Flanders after the decease of

---

[82]Sidon

his mother, but John and Baldwin were forjudged therefrom, because their father had taken their mother and married her unlawfully, for he was a sub-deacon Furthermore, the damosel was given her in ward (for safekeeping, since she was her liege lady) by the peers of Hainault But they released her therefrom, and therein did they ill [88]

Now will we tell you what came thereof John and Baldwin gat them away from the court so quickly as ever they could and came to a castle of their mother's which standeth on the marches of Flanders and Hainault, and they entered in and drave out the garrison of the countess and themselves garrisoned it well And when the countess knew this she was sore grieved, and she assembled her hosts and went against the castle and laid siege to it But she had not a man in the host who helped her heartily, rather, they loved John and Baldwin better than her When the countess saw that this was so she withdrew her from the host and left there as captain my Lord Guy of Dampierre, her son, for my Lord William, her eldest son, had died And she came to the court of the queen and fell at her feet and said "O Lady, may God have mercy ! John and Baldwin, my sons, have taken from me Rupelmonde, one of my castles, and seek to dispossess me Lady, for God's sake, devise some counsel in this matter, for I am your liege woman and I am cousin german to the king, and I am ready and willing to follow your counsel and to put all my land in your hand "

"Lady," quoth the queen, "ye shall speak to the Count of Poitiers and to the Count of Anjou, and I will command them instantly to take heed to your case "

The countess departed forthwith from the queen, and she found the counts at Saint-Germain-en-Laye, where the Count of Poitiers was lying sick, and she spake to them and told them her need, and they made her soft answer When the countess saw and perceived their mind she led the Count of Anjou apart and said to him "Fair nephew, help me heartily, for I desire your labour therein to be well safeguarded, therefore will I give you the county of Hainault, which is well worth a thousand pounds the year And I desire you to be immediately in possession thereof, and I will give you my letters pendant to that effect "

When the count heard her speak thus, then was his heart lightened, and he said to the countess "Lady, if ye do for me that which ye have promised, I will restore to you your castle and I will make you to hold your land in peace for evermore "

And the countess bestowed on him immediately the county of Hainault in the presence of the Count of Poitiers, and she gave him a charter therefor, bearing her seal Straightway departed the countess from the counts and went straight to Rupelmonde and found her people even as she had left them, and little had she lost there and little gained

---

[88]This passage is very obscure, and the readings of the different MSS vary greatly

XXXVIII

OF THE PARABLE OF THE WOLF AND THE SHE-GOAT

Now will I tell you a parable touching the countess and how she sought aid of the Count of Poitiers and the Count of Anjou

There was once a wolf that had two acres of land under the plough And he came to a she-goat that had two kids, and he said to her "Goat, I have two acres of good land under the plough, from which the vines have been cleared, and I rede thee to work it, share and share alike And know of a truth that the land is so rich that it will bear corn of itself without dunging, and know also that in sooth would I be fainer to work it myself than to yield it on shares But I have a weighty case before the court of my Lord Noble the lion against Belin the ram, concerning two ewes of his which he saith that I have eaten, and I must needs be present each week at the hearing and but with sore difficulty can I get me counsel "

"In sooth," cried the goat, "I would not dare "

"Wherefore?" asked the wolf

"I' faith," quoth the goat, "because ye are a great lord and mighty and of high lineage, and I am but a little thing and of none account And I could have no good case against you "

"Ah!" quoth the wolf "Goat, fair friend, now have no fear of me I swear to thee by the faith that I owe to Dame Hersant, my wife, and to my twelve children, that I have by her—all living—that I will be to thee a just partener, nor ever in my life will I do thee wrong "

"I' faith," quoth the goat, "I will do it, but yet I fear me thou wilt do me an evil turn "

Then the wolf took his leave of the goat And the goat tilled the land and tended the corn, and it multiplied and was ready for the reaping And she came to the wolf and said "Wolf, our corn is ready for the harvest, come thither yourself, or send "

"I' faith," quoth the wolf, "I cannot go thither, neither can I send, but do thou harvest it, and cause the corn to be put in one place and the straw in another; and when I return from my suit, then will we share fairly "

No more could the goat get from the wolf, so came she back and harvested the corn and caused it to be threshed and the grain to be put in one place and the straw in another

Then, lo, cometh the wolf, who was waiting for nought else but this And he cometh to the goat and saith to her, right haughtily "Now, lady, shall we divide our harvest?"

"Yea, verily," quoth the goat, "fair sir, an ye so desire Lo, here is the grain in one place and the straw in another, even as ye commanded me, so take ye the half of the one and the half of the other "

"Go to the Devil, thou foolish beast! Thou knowest not what thou sayest, not so shall it be!"

"How, then, pray?" asked the goat

"Pardı!" quoth the wolf. "I will tell thee I am a great man and I have a very great household, and I have need of much more than thou hast, for thou art but a craven creature So thou wilt have enough with a little; thou shalt have the straw and I will have the grain"

"Alack, lord!" said the goat "Ye speak not reasonably Nay, in God's name take your share, and I will take mine"

"Gadzooks!" cried the wolf "I will do nought of the kind! And well do I warn thee that I shall come again tomorrow morning, do thou see to it that thou tell me then whether or no thou wilt do this"

Then the wolf departed, and the goat remained all dumfounded But she bethought herself of two hounds that she had suckled with her own milk at her dugs, which now belonged to an abbey of Cistercians who dwelt nigh at hand, whereof the one was called Taburel and the other Roenel And she went straight to them and found them at the entry of the gate And when Taburel and Roenel see their foster mother coming, they go forth to meet her and bid her welcome, and they enquire of her what business hath brought her thither And she told them how the wolf sought to deal with her

"In sooth," said each one of the dogs, "by our boots, so shall it not befall! Now do ye go back again, and we engage that we shall be present very early in the morning at the sharing betwixt you and Isengrim,[84] and, please God, he will work no loss or wrong upon you there where we are"

Straightway the goat returned and found her two kids weeping, and she comforted them and laid her down to sleep, but little rest gat she And she rose up very early and prayed God that he would give her counsel

Then, lo, come the two brethren, Taburel and Roenel, and they greet her and enquire if Isengrim is yet come And the goat answereth· "Nay, not yet"

"Now, fair mother," say the dogs, "will we tell you what we will do We will hide us in this heap of stubble and will remain all quiet there, and lightly shall we see and hear what Isengrim will seek to do For, an he knew that we were here, peradventure would he not come hither, but would wait until we should be absent"

"I' faith," quoth the goat, "my children, ye say well"

And the dogs went and hid themselves in the heap of stubble

Lo, then cometh Isengrim the wolf and bringeth privily with him his gossip Reynard, who had wrought for him many a crafty trick, and he saith to the goat: "Now, madam, have ye made your decision?"

"What decision, pray," answered the goat, "would ye have me make? Do ye take your share and leave me mine"

"In sooth," said the wolf, "wouldst still grumble? Verily," quoth he, "it shall not be otherwise than I have told thee"

But in the mean time, whilst the wolf and the goat were disputing, Reynard cast his eyes upon the heap of stubble and spied the tails of the hounds, and he

---

[84]The name of the wolf in the medieval beast epic "Reynard the Fox"

said to Isengrim. "Fair gossip, get ye diligently about your business, for I see a certain thing in this your business that ye yourself perceive not"

"Egad!" cried the wolf "Sir Reynard, it shall not befall otherwise, I will have the grain and she shall have the straw"

"In God's name," quoth Reynard, "I say this only for your good, and may ye fare well in the matter But be ye on your guard here, I am getting me hence"

And Reynard gat him away and clomb a little hill that lay hard by, for to see what end his gossip would make And Isengrim and his waggoner took their sacks and were filling them with the corn.

"By the Mother of God," quoth the goat, "now is this a foul deed!"

And she cometh to Roenel and Taburel "My children, ye see how it goeth!"

And forth leap the dogs from out the stubble nor tarry to ask who is right and who is wrong And they fell upon the wolf, body and breast, and bare him to earth belly upward, and they pressed his gullet and wrought more than an hundred wounds upon his body and made the tufts of his hair to fly heavenward, and they dealt with him there in such fashion that neither pulse nor breath could be perceived, and they thought that they had slain him And they took the corn and carried it to the goat's barn, but in the mean time, whilst they were carrying off the wheat, the waggoner took Isengrim and with great difficulty put him so speedily as he could upon his cart and straightway departed, bearing him toward his dwelling-place

Then, lo, came Reynard to meet him, having seen all and rejoicing greatly thereat, for such was his nature—ever did he rejoice when mischief was toward And he came to his gossip, who was in exceeding sorry case, and said to him, dissembling "Fair gossip, it grieveth me sore to behold your evil estate, but an ye had listened to me in the matter, the outcome had been other than it is, for I told you in sooth that I saw a certain thing in your affair that you yourself saw not"

"Reynard, Reynard!" quoth Isengrim "Whoso hath none other friend than you, he hath none whatsoever I have been put to shame, I will mend the matter when I am able"

So departeth Isengrim from Reynard, and Reynard thrusteth out his tongue at him

And Isengrim goeth to his own abode, where his wife, Dame Hersant, was awaiting him with her children And when they saw him coming, lying upon the cart on an handful of straw, they began to mock him, saying "No better conducted business can be than this! Is this the grain that ye should bring us for to make our Lenten cakes?"

So spake they of Isengrim's household, and it hath been said of yore· "Whom misfortune befalleth, him do men revile" And Isengrim gat him down from the cart, all wounded as he was, and went away, head hanging, and laid him on his bed, nor was he healed of his hurts in less than five months' space

Now return we to Roenel and Taburel and the goat, who had carried the corn to the barn And the hounds said "Fair mother, we will get us home again, and we dwell hard by this place, and if ever ye have need of us we will be ready incontinent to aid you And, lo, here is an horn which ye shall sound if ever ye have occasion, and so soon as we hear you sound we will come to you with all speed "

"Gramercy," quoth the goat, "my fair children Blessed be the hour that I first suckled you !"

Straightway the dogs took their leave and went away unto their abbey

Now will I tell you wherefore I have related to you this parable for the sake of John of Avesnes, whom I have called the wolf, and his mother was the goat, and the Count of Anjou and the Count of Poitiers were Roenel and Taburel. And John of Avesnes wished to have the grain and he wished to leave his mother the straw, for he wished to take away her land, whereto he had no right, and he wished to disinherit her Howbeit, his mother, whom I liken to the goat, could not suffer this, but she went to the Count of Anjou and the Count of Poitiers, whom I have called Roenel and Taburel, and so wrought with them that they helped her to maintain her right against her son, who is likened to the wolf And they so trampled his vintage that he had neither the might nor the will to kick back, even as ye shall hear hereafter an I have the time and the occasion to tell thereof

XXXIX

HOW JOHN OF AVESNES CALLED ON THE KING OF GERMANY FOR AID

Now come we back to the Count of Anjou, who gathered a great host and went to Rupelmonde But, or ever he was come thither, John of Avesnes had gone away into Germany to the king, his brother-in-law,[85] and asked help of him; but the king answered him that against his mother would he not help him So must the castle perforce be yielded up to the Count of Anjou, and the count left his own garrison therein and he and the countess came to Valenciennes And they found the gates shut, and the countess summoned the mayor and the échevins and enquired of them wherefore they had gone and shut the gates And they made answer "For our safety's sake, for we beheld the land all disquieted and the discord that prevaileth betwixt you and your children "

"Well have ye done," quoth the countess, "open now the gates, and I swear to you on the relics of the saints that neither I nor the Count of Anjou will do any evil or wrong to them of your city "

And immediately the gates were opened, and the Count of Anjou and the countess entered in with all their people And the provost and the mayor and the magistrates of the city were summoned, and the countess commanded them to swear fealty to the Count of Anjou And when they heard this, then were they all dumfounded, but well knew they that they had no help in the matter, so did they homage to the count—would they or would they not And he took possession of Valenciennes and of the fortress

---

[85] William of Holland

And by a letter of the countess and by his own he bade them of Mons in Hainault come and do him homage, and they of Mons sent back word that they would do nought of the sort, either for him or for the countess And on the morrow the count biddeth his host march forth and goeth to lay siege to Mons And they within the city were well defended and esteemed him but lightly But the count caused petraries and mangonels to play both day and night and so distrained them that he took the place by force And he wrought until he made himself seized of the county of Hainault—all save Binch, where John's wife went with child (and for that cause did he let it be), and save Enghien, a castle that belongeth to my Lord Sohier, who was cousin to my Lord John of Avesnes, he would neither obey the count nor swear him fealty

When the Count of Anjou had seized Hainault and left a captain there for to guard his land, he came back into France, and he found his mother very sick, even upon her death-bed And she made her testament, and she left a very great treasure for God's service, and she died in the faith and in the pale of Holy Church like the wise and upright woman that she was And she was borne to Maubuisson, her abbey, and there was she buried honourably

Henceforth will we tell you of John of Avesnes, who was with the King of Germany, his brother-in-law, and ofttimes said to him "Sire, for God's sake, will ye let your sister be disinherited, and your nephew whom I have by her, who should be heir after my mother's decease? Now can ye see how she hath put all the land of Hainault in the hand of the Count of Anjou, and he is seized thereof and hath taken perpetual homage thereof, as of his own In God's name, sire, how will ye suffer this? Moreover, it is of your own fief, and he hath entered therein without your knowledge and hath thereby done you a wrong"

And so did he give the king to understand one thing and another that at the last he caused him to call all Germany to arms And the king came with his host into Hainault, within six leagues' distance of Valenciennes And when the Count of Anjou knew that the King of Germany was in Hainault, within six leagues' distance of Valenciennes, he also made a very great levy, and he came to Douai, and there he tarried and awaited his people And when they were come he took counsel what he should do And his council told him that he should hold himself quiet until they should see what the king would do. And they shewed him good reason for this, and they said to him "Sire, ye are now seized of the land, nor yet hath any wrong been done you, moreover, there is love between the King of France, your brother, and the King of Germany, so were it in no wise seemly that ye should begin the strife or break the alliance"

To this counsel were all agreed, and they tarried no little while at Douai; but it was not long ere the King of Germany caused his tents to be struck, and he departed thence even as he had come thither, save with less substance and with greater shame And the Count of Anjou went back to France

Now will we tell you of the King of Germany, who was gone back to his own country He heard tell that the Danes were without a lord, and he was fain to go thither, so gathered he his host And he went away into Denmark, a country full of waters, and would take it by force, but he knew not the manner of doing it And it befell one day that he was riding forth, all armed, on a great war-horse, new and fresh and well nourished, and he looked and saw beyond a ditch a great troop of country folk, armed after the fashion of their country And he struck spurs to his horse and thought to pass over the ditch, but he could not, for the ditch was wide and he was heavily armed And he leaped full four feet into the ditch, and he sank so deep into the mire that it seemed to those who were there that he would be swallowed up, nor could his own men aid him When the country folk saw that he was in their snare they went thither and drew him out with hooks and slew him So gaineth he who breweth ill

XL

HOW KING LEWIS CAME BACK FROM OVERSEA

Here will we leave off to tell of the King of Germany and will tell you of the King of France, who was beyond the sea Tidings came to him from the masters of the court that his mother was dead, so saw he clearly that he must needs return to France And he had his ships made ready, and he entered therein and departed by God's grace without any mishap, together with the three children that he had in the land of Syria, and came to land at Aigues-Mortes, and thence he journeyed day by day till he was come into France, and there was he received as lord, with great honour

Here do we leave the king for a little season and will tell you of the Count of Anjou, who sent word to the Seignior of Enghien that he should come and do him homage And the seignior sent word back to him that never in his life would he do homage to him Then the count assembled whatsoever he could get together of men, by homage or for money, and he had with him Archbishop Thomas of Reims, who served him with all his might, for he thought to obtain from him such benefit as he stood in need of And it hath been said of old "A favourable countenance maketh glad a fool"

And he went against Enghien and laid siege thereto, and he had the power to take the place, and hope thereof, but the Seignior of Enghien so wrought, through one of his friends, that he put Enghien in the king's hand And the king immediately sent word to the Count of Anjou that he should return thence without any delay, and do this he must, for the king so willed And back he came, exceeding sorrowful

Now will we tell you a little concerning John of Avesnes, who was so vexed that he had like to have gone stark mad, because he had failed of his purpose, and of the King of Germany, who was dead, who was his brother-in-law, as ye have heard, and of the love of his mother, which he had forfeited, and of the county of Hainault, whence he was banished for ever (so him seemed), both he and his heirs, which grieved him more than all things else And he was without land, poor and thrust down, and without hope ever to recover And it came to pass that sickness laid hold on him and he fell into a great languor and languished for a long season, and in the end he died at Einch in Hainault, in great poverty. And this was most meet, for whoso honoureth not father and mother loseth his own honour, even as God declareth in the Gospel, saying "Honour thy father and thy mother, and thou shalt be honoured, and thereby canst thou gain the kingdom of heaven."

When Baldwin of Avesnes saw that his brother was dead and that he had failed of all the good things that he sought, then he bethought him that he would reconcile himself to his mother, and he came to her and fell at her feet and cried her mercy. And the countess made answer to him "Baldwin! Baldwin! At what hour art thou come? In God's name, too much hath it cost already and too late hast thou recognized thy folly!"

"Ah, fair mother, for God's mercy's sake! This folly did I not do, but 'twas my brother did it, who is dead, because of his frowardness. O most fair and sweet mother, I will from this day forth obey all your commandments."

When his mother saw that he would in truth obey she was moved to pity— for she was a mother. And all the knights and ladies who were there kneeled down at the countess' feet and cried her mercy for her son, and the countess forgave him, and he was henceforth a lord of the court.

Now come we back to the Count of Anjou, who was holding the county of Hainault, and it seemed to the king his brother that he held it not justly, for he had entered therein without the leave of his sovereign lord of whom it was held, and without doing him homage. So the king desired him absolutely to restore it into the hand of the countess, saying that he would have a reckoning made of the costs that he had incurred there. And the countess was summoned, and the costs were reckoned at an hundred thousand pounds Tournois, to be recovered within four years from the land, and the countess was again seized of her land.

XLI

HOW THE FOLK OF NAMUR REVOLTED AGAINST THE EMPRESS OF CONSTANTINOPLE

Now will we leave the Countess of Flanders, who hath had pain and travail a-plenty in her life, and we will tell you of the Emperor Baldwin of Constantinople,[86] who was son to Count Peter of Auxerre and was sent to Constantinople and sacred there and anointed emperor. And he was wedded to the daughter of King John of Acre, whom John had by the sister of the King of Spain, and she was niece to Queen Blanche, and he took her to Constantinople. And King John was regent so long as he lived, because of the youth of Baldwin, but he was of great age, and he died, a worthy man and a good Christian, and he was buried before the great altar of Saint Sophia.

And the Emperor Baldwin was young and childish, and he spent lavishly and kept no eye upon his business, so waxed he poor and fell into debt, nor had he aught to give to his knights and his serjeants. So a great part of them with-

---

[86]Baldwin II

drew themselves from him and went back unto their own country And when the emperor saw that this was so he determined that he would himself come to France—to the pontiff, who was then at Lyons, and to the queen, who was aunt to his wife—and would seek help of the pontiff and of the queen And he put out to sea, so privily as he might, for fear of Vataces,[87] who was making war upon him and pressing him sore and would fain be seized of Constantinople and of the empire And he came to Marseilles and landed at La Roche, and thence came he so swiftly as he could to Lyons, where he found the Pope and made known to him his needs And the pontiff was greatly moved thereat and gave him the clerks' tithe for three years And he came to the queen, who was fain to see him, and told her his straits And the queen said that gladly would she help in the matter And she kept him with her for a long season, and she found him childish in his speech and he displeased her greatly, for to uphold an empire needeth a man both very wise and vigorous

"Lady," quoth the emperor, "I have need of moneys, for I cannot maintain the empire without great costs So must I needs sell the county of Namur, which cometh to me by birth as a part of mine heritage"

"In God's name!" cried the queen "It is not my will that ye sell it"

"Lady, what shall I then do?"

"I' faith," answered the queen, "I will lend you twenty thousand pounds, to be repaid out of the revenues, and so will it be saved to you and to your heirs; with the understanding that ye shall swear to me on holy relics that within one month after ye shall have returned to Constantinople ye will send to me the empress, for I desire greatly to see her"

"Certes!" quoth he, who knew not how to defend himself "Gladly!"

And he sware an oath to her, and the queen delivered unto him twenty thousand pounds And he took his leave of her, and so quickly as he could went he back to Constantinople, and know ye of a truth that he had no cause for tarrying And when he was come back he said to the empress "Lady, the queen hath lent me twenty thousand pounds on the county of Namur, with the understanding that I must swear that I would send you to her a month after I should have returned"

"Sire," quoth the lady, who greatly desired to go thither, "ye shall keep your promise well and observe your oath, an it please God"

Then did the emperor bid four ships be made ready and he caused to be put therein whatsoever was needful And he caused the empress to go on board, with knights and arbalesters, and he commended her to God—nor ever thereafter did he behold her again

And they went their way, coasting the shore, and sailed until they were come to the right and safe haven There were mountures made ready for them, fair and rich, and they journeyed onward day by day until they were come to Pontoise When the queen saw her, if ever great joy was made 'twas then, and she abode with the queen so long as the queen lived

And when the queen died she gave the emperor the county of Namur, and

---

[87]John Ducas Vatatzes, Emperor of Nicaea

the empress entered into possession thereof And she received the homage of the freemen and the fealty of the burghers, and she held the county until, one day, ill report began to run concerning the sons of certain burghers of Namur who were of lofty lineage And complaint was made of them by the middling folk of the city, and the queen caused to be summoned the fathers of them that were blamed. And she commanded them to correct their children in such fashion that she might never again hear complaint concerning them And if they did not so (said she), then must she herself perforce take steps in the matter And the burghers answered and said "Lady, ye say well, and we will tell our children to keep the peace, and if they will not do this, then do ye with them what ye think good and what good counsel shall lead you to do "

Immediately the burghers departed, and they commanded their children to correct themselves and to eschew their follies But these did nothing of the sort, rather, they were worse than they had been afore Now will we tell you what they did They went to the tavern, ten or twelve of them, and they expended twenty pence or thirty—more or less—then they bade some honest citizen, of humble birth but something well in goods, pay all their costs And one there would be who would pay through fear, and another who would not pay, and such an one would they beat and evil entreat and take his money from him by force

When the empress heard such complaints she waxed exceeding wroth, and she commanded her bailiff, who was a knight, to take them and to put them in such a place that they would no longer have occasion to do any mischief The bailiff caused them to be watched and knew where they were, and he went— foolishly—but lightly attended, and thought to take them But they defended themselves vigorously, and they slew the bailiff, then they escaped and put themselves in safety When the empress knew this she had like to have lost her reason, and she cried "Verily am I without friends and in a strange country "

And on the morrow she bade summon before her all the commonalty of Namur, and she demanded of them a reckoning for her bailiff's death, and she demanded the murderers who had slain him The burghers made answer that at the bailiff's death were they sorely grieved, but they were not guilty therein, and greatly did they desire that they who had done the deed should be punished

"In God's name," cried the empress, "so shall it not go! Ye shall deliver them to me, and for that end shall every one of you be at my disposition both in body and in substance "

"Ha, lady! How can it be thought that he shall pay for the deed who hath no fault therein? Certes, lady, no law so provideth, neither, please God, shall this thing ever be suffered!"

XLII

HOW NAMUR WAS GIVEN TO THE COUNT OF LUXEMBURG

Straightway departed the burghers from the empress' court Howbeit, they offered to submit themselves to the law, but the empress answered them that never should judgment be rendered other than her own will So matters rested for a season, but the empress caused seizure to be made of their substance and entreated them hardly When the burghers saw that this was so they determined that they would send to the king, for to know if he were willing to take steps in the matter So they chose four of the wisest amongst them, and these were sent to the king and they shewed him the injustice that their lady was doing them "For God's sake, sire," (cried they) "take some step in this matter!"

"In sooth," quoth Peter of Fontaines,[88] "I will tell what steps ought to be taken with you! Ye shall go back, and every burgher of Namur shall take a cord and lay it about his neck, and then shall ye all go before the empress and shall say to her 'Lady, lo, here are your murderers, do with them that which seemeth you good'"

When the burghers heard this, then were they all dismayed, and the king looked upon them and perceived all their countenances altered, and he said "My Lord Peter, ye speak not advisedly The burghers will go and make their peace with their lady, so will they do wisely"

"Sire, ye say well," answered the burghers, who desired only to be gone

And they departed from the court, as those that never more would have any longing to return thither, and they came back to Namur and told the assembly of the commune how they had fared "I' faith," said they, "there is no appeal there, it behooveth us to seek an advocate"

"In God's name!" quoth one of them "I have heard from ancient burghers of this city that the county of Namur ought rightly to belong to my Lord Henry of Luxemburg,[89] and that he is wrongfully deprived thereof, so would I rede you in good faith that ye send and seek him and that ye swear fealty to him, and he to us. And know ye well that he will do this gladly, for it is the one thing in the world that he most desireth"

To this counsel did they all agree, and they sent to seek him, and he came without delay, and they sware fealty to him, and he to them And he went back to his own country and borrowed moneys and assembled much people The empress knew that the burghers had sworn fealty to my Lord Henry, and she caused the castle to be fortified and put there a captain, a valiant man and wise My Lord Henry came to Namur with his host, and the burghers received him gladly and

---

[88]Many a time it befell that in the summer season he would go to the Wood of Vincennes after mass, and he would lean him against an oak and make us to sit round about him And all they that had a case in hand came to speak to him, without hinderance of ushers or of others And then would he ask them, with his own mouth 'Is any here that hath a case?' And those rose up that had cases in hand Then would he say 'Hold ye all your peace, and ye shall be heard in your due turn' Then would he call my Lord Peter of Fontaines and my Lord Geoffry of Villette and say to one of them 'Settle me this case'" Joinville, *Histoire de Saint Louis*, 59

[89]Henry III, Count of Luxemburg

gave him the disposal over their bodies and their goods and their city And he maintained his siege there, and strengthened greatly the town, and guarded so well the entries to the castle that none was able to enter therein or to go out thence So did he maintain his siege for a long time

But the empress so wrought with the Countess of Flanders, of whom she held the county, and with her friends, that she assembled a great host, wherein were many knights and great lords And therein was the Count of Eu,[90] the Count of Montfort,[91] and the Count of Joigny,[92] and my Lord Erard of Valery for them of Champagne and the Countess of Flanders for her own party And she made captain Baldwin of Avesnes, her son, whereof came no good And they drew nigh to Namur—within four leagues—and on the morrow came they thither.

And the countess commanded them to lay siege to the town, and the Flemings and the men of Hainault made a shew of assaulting it, for my Lord Baldwin of Avesnes favoured my Lord Henry so far as he was able, and his people lost there more than they gained Then did Baldwin of Avesnes procure a truce of forty days, with the understanding that nothing should be brought into the castle during that time

When the men of Champagne perceived the treason of Baldwin of Avesnes and the favour that he was shewing my Lord Henry, then they agreed to the truce, and they were returning to their own land, when the Germans cried· "Help! Help!" and assailed the rear of the men of Champagne, where was the baggage of the Count of Joigny, and wrought great loss of horses and of armour and of baggage But nought more came thereof So departed the host of Champagne in sorry sort because of the villainy of the Flemings

And yet maintained my Lord Henry the siege, nor ever removed it, and the season of the truce went by, nor did any one return And he sorely distrained them of the the castle and lay before it a year or more When the captain of the castle saw that he would get no succour and that his victual was diminishing and that his garrison was perishing of sickness, then was he sore troubled in heart; for well he wist that my Lord Henry hated him bitterly

Then, lo, came a knight and knocked at the gate, and they came up on the battlements and enquired of him what he desired And he said that my Lord Henry would fain speak with the captain So a messenger went and told the captain, and he said that he would speak to him gladly And he came forth on the battlements, and my Lord Henry saw him and said to him "Captain, ye are causing me both travail and loss, and well do ye know that never shall ye get succour But know ye of a truth that never will I remove from hence, so long as I live, until I have the castle And know ye also of a truth that an I take you by force, then will I shew you no forbearance, but an ye yield the place to me, then will I forget my grievance against you And know ye likewise of a truth that from that day forth shall no shame be put upon you because of it "

---

[90]Jean de Brienne I
[91]Jean de Brienne, son of Jean de Brienne the King of Jerusalem, called Count of Montfort because of his marriage with Jeanne de Châteaudun, widow of Jean, Count of Montfort
[92]Guillaume III

"Sir," quoth the captain, "I will take counsel in this matter, and within fifteen days will I let you know my mind"

My Lord Henry agreed thereto, and the captain sent to the empress and told her how it was with him But she sent word back to him that she could do nothing more for him And at the end of the fifteen days the captain yielded up the castle to him, his life being spared, and my Lord Henry entered therein; and he yet holdeth it to this day—like it or mislike it whomso it will

XLIII

OF THE PEACE THAT KING LEWIS MADE WITH THE KING OF ENGLAND AND OF THE DEATH OF HIS SON

Here will we let be to speak of Namur, which hath fallen on evil days, and we will tell you of King Lewis, the worthy man who now reigneth [93] The king's conscience reproached him because of the land of Normandy which King Philip had conquered from King John of England (that evil king, who was father to King Henry that now is), albeit King Philip had it by judgment of the peers of France and King John was summoned thence by his own peers

But certain folk say "Because he defaulted at the court of the king his liege he had not to forfeit and to lose his land, for he had committed against the king no criminal act"

And some also say that the King of France could in reason become seized of the land because of the default of King John, and could receive the revenues thereof, but if King John (or his heirs) should be willing to come to the king and request of him seizure of their land by rightful process, and should be willing to amend the defaults according to the judgment of the peers, then ought he to have his land again.

And because of this doubt, and for other reasons, he made peace with the King of England, and good accord, with the understanding that the King of England should come to France—he, and his wife, and his son—and should be at Paris about Martinmas, *anno Domini LIX* [94] And it was ordained in all amity that the King of England should have and hold in perpetuity—both he and his heirs—the county of Cahors, and the county of Périgord, and the duchy of Agénois, which containeth six cities And for this the King of England did homage at Paris, in his own house, in the sight of the people, and he renounced altogether all the rights which he had or could have in all the rest of the conquest, and to this effect he gave a royal charter

And the French king gave him two hundred and fifty thousand livres for to carry away and to spend in the land beyond the sea, for the sake whereof he had taken the cross And it was covenanted that the King of England should come twice each year for to render service at his own cost for forty days, at the request of the King of France, and that the Count of Poitiers should be quit of the homage which he owed for the land that he held in those three counties Thus were

[93] Louis IX
[94] I e, 1259

the two kings reconciled and were made good friends, and the conscience of the King of France was appeased And know ye well and of a truth that whoso is without conscience liveth bestially, but it hath been said of old

> Whom his own conscience ne'er upbraideth
> Himself to evil soon persuadeth.

Then departed the King of England, with the queen and his son, from the King of France his brother-in-law, who had shewn them great honour and richly feasted them through all his land, and they went back to England, their own country But they left the King of France and his queen in sore sorrow because of Lewis, their eldest son, who died at the age of sixteen years, and he was marvellous wise and gracious And such grief had they that none could comfort them, moreover, the queen was then great with child and about to be brought to bed

So did the king continue sorrowing for his child, whom he loved greatly, and so sad was he that none could get a word from him Then, lo, came Archbishop Rigaut of Rouen for to see and to comfort him And many a good word from the Scripture did he repeat to him, and much concerning the patience of Saint Job And he related to him a parable concerning a tomtit which was caught in a snare in the garden of an husbandman When the husbandman had the titling in his hand he said to her that he would eat her And the tomtit answered and said to the husbandman "If thou" (said she), "shalt eat me thou wilt scarce be satisfied, for I am but a little thing But an thou wouldst let me go, then would I teach thee three adages, which would bring thee great profit if thou wouldst put them to use "

"I' faith," quoth the husbandman, "I will let thee go "

And he opened his hand, and the titling gat her up on a branch, and she was marvellous glad for that she had escaped "Now will I teach thee," said the tomtit, "an it please thee, my three adages "

"Yea, in sooth," answered he

"Now listen," said the tomtit "I give thee this rede that whatso thou holdest in thine hand, thou cast it not down at thy feet, and that thou believe not all that thou hearest, and that thou make not too great moan over the thing that thou canst no longer have nor canst recover "

"What is this?" cried the churl "Wilt tell me nothing further? Gadzooks! An I now held thee, thou wouldst escape me never again!"

"By my halidom," quoth the titling, "thou wouldst do rightly! For I have in my head a precious stone, so large as an hen's egg which is well worth an hundred pounds "

When the husbandman heard this he beat his fists together and tare his hair and made the greatest moan in the world And the tomtit began to laugh, and she said "Thou foolish churl! Ill hast thou understood and put to use the three adages that I have told thee Thou heldest me in thine hand, and thou didst cast me at thy feet when thou didst let me go And thou didst believe me when I gave thee to understand that I had in mine head a precious stone which was so great as an hen's egg—and the whole of me is not so great as that And now thou makest moan over me, on whom thou wilt never lay hand again, for I will guard me better than I have guarded hitherto"

Straightway she fluttered her wings and flew away and left the husbandman making his moan

"Sire," quoth the archbishop, "ye see clearly that ye cannot recover your son, and truly should ye believe that he is now in Paradise, so should ye be comforted"

The king saw this clearly and knew that the archbishop was speaking him sooth; so was he comforted and somewhat forgat his grief

XLIV

HOW THE ARCHBISHOP OF REIMS LOST THE WARDENSHIP OF SAINT REMY

Now will we tell you of Archbishop Thomas of Beaumetz, who coveted all things, and it is said in the proverb "Who coveteth all, loseth all" He had held the ward of Saint Remy of Reims for a long time—he and his predecessors—and he evil entreated and shamefully spoiled them of Saint Remy And he had, forsooth (so they say), four thousand pounds from Abbot Gilbert, and he purposed to take by pillage all that Saint Remy had of any worth whatsoever But it was said by them of olden time that overlading foundereth the ass [95]

Now it befell that the abbot and the convent could no longer endure this, and they took knowledge of their privileges, if peradventure there might be therein some thing that would help them And they found the charters of six kings of France which said that the church of Saint Remy and the castle were founded by the alms of these kings, and each king had repeated this saying by his charter, down until King Philip But King Philip, before he went across the sea, committed them to Archbishop William Whitehands, his uncle, and thereafter had they been held in ward by the Archbishop of Reims, through the simplicity of the abbots and because of the understanding which had existed until the days of Archbishop Thomas, who now is

And when the abbot and the convent saw that this was so, they went to the king and besought him, for God's sake, to take some step in behalf of the church of Saint Remy, whereof he was king and lord and which had been founded by his forefathers, and in sooth had their privileges been confirmed by six kings

The charters were shewn to the king and read before the council, and the king said that gladly would he give heed to the matter And the archbishop was summoned and commanded to appear before him against the abbot and the convent of Saint Remy And the archbishop refused to appear, once, and a second, and a third time, and he had made use of all his exceptions, yet for full a year did he put off making any answer whatsoever.

But in the end the king drave him to book, and a certain day was appointed on which he must be present When the archbishop saw that he could no longer

---

[95]Cf "The last straw breaks the camel's back"

give them the slip, then must he perforce go thither The abbot and the procurator of the convent were present, and the king said to the abbot and to the convent "In whose ward are ye—in mine or in the archbishop's?"

"Sire, we are in your ward, and there ought we to be, for in sooth so have our privileges been confirmed by your forefathers"

And the privileges were shewn Then said the king "Sir abbot, go ye hence, this cause is no longer yours, but mine own And if the archbishop desireth to say aught which may avail him in the matter, let him say it, and we will gladly cause judgment to be rendered in our court"

When the archbishop saw that he would not be able to escape he took a day for to make his plea, but when that day came he appeared not, and through indulgence was another day allowed him And on this day he came, and fain had he been to take yet another day an he could have had it, but this could he not And when he saw that answer he must, then he demanded a shewing of the things which the king claimed, and a day was appointed for to make this shewing The provost of Laon made the shewing in the king's stead, and he shewed to the archbishop's men the church of Saint Remy, and the castle, and the cities of Saint Remy even to one score and four in number, and he said to them that yet would he shew them other an they so desired But they answered that they considered themselves well satisfied with these

Immediately was a day appointed for to appear before the king and to hear judgment pronounced to the parties touching all matters concerning each one of them, and the archbishop was present with all the counsel that he could engage Then rose up Master Julian of Péronne and said "My lord archbishop, will ye hear judgment rendered determining whether of you twain shall have the ward of Saint Remy—ye yourself, or the king?"

And the archbishop answered, "Yea"

Then did Master Julian call to mind all the process clean to the end thereof, and he said that by right and by the judgment of the masters the king should have the ward of Saint Remy and of his possessions, and that he should have these in accordance with the privileges granted by his forbears, "and in accordance with the acknowledgement of your own self, Lord Archbishop, when ye delivered—on a certain day now past—your letter pendant to madame the queen And, lo, here is the letter, and it runneth thus

"'Thomas, by the grace of God, Archbishop of Reims, to all them unto whom these letters shall come, greeting Know all men that I, Thomas, Archbishop of Reims, acknowledge that I hold in trust of the King of France, my lord, the ward of Saint Remy of Reims, and I agree that I will not hold it save only so long as shall please him'"

When the archbishop heard this letter read, then his face fell,[36] and he was the most dumfounded man in the whole world—both he and all his Then rose he up and went to take counsel, and he said to his counsellors "Fair sirs, what

---

[36]*Si le chet li nes*, literally, "his nose fell"

can I now do? I' faith, I am undone an the thing remain thus, and I have lost my city, for all my burghers will go and dwell at Saint Remy"

"In God's name," quoth one of his counsel, "ye shall say that ye are unwilling that this judgment be stablished, because it was not made or rendered by your peers And ye yourself are a peer and should be judged of them"

And all the rest of his counsel agreed to this Then the archbishop came before the king, and Peter Halot made the speech for him and said thus "I' faith, sire, the archbishop is a peer of France and ought to be judged of his own peers This judgment is not made by his peers, and he is unwilling to consent thereto"

And Peter of Fontaines made answer "It shall be judged, an ye so will, whether or no this can avail you aught"

And the archbishop said that in sooth did he so desire, and he withdrew himself

And the masters took counsel together and said that this judgment was good and reasonable, for the dispute touching which the judgment was made was not one pertaining to the peerage, therefore must it be upheld Straightway the Archbishop of Reims departed from the court without taking his leave, weeping bitterly, and he gat him into his own chamber and was there two days, nor came out thence Then came he to Reims and besought the bishops of his province to help him against the king And the bishops made answer that they were the king's men, nor would they go counter to him, nor did they consider that the king was doing him any wrong
.

Now will we tell you of the abbot, who remained at court and besought the king that he send a guard to Saint Remy, to the church, for to guard the lands of Saint Remy The king made answer that he would take counsel in this matter until the time of the parliament, in September Then went the abbot back to Reims When the archbishop knew this he made assay of the abbot in divers ways, how he might consent to abandon that which he had begun, howbeit, he accomplished nothing whatsoever But the abbot went to the parliament and asked the king for the ward, and the king bestowed it on him And the abbot came back to Reims, cheerful and rejoicing And he had good and loyal counsellors, who said to him "Sir, ye are now out of the archbishop's hands in so far as concerneth lay justice, but ye have accomplished nought if ye be not outside his churchly jurisdiction also So doth it behoove you to work with the pontiff and with his brethren that ye may be exempt in your own land And for God's sake see to it, so shall ye have wrought a work of great merit And ye have already many a good advantage of the archbishop, likewise have ye the prayers of the king, which will avail you much And in sooth have ye power to be of service to the court, and the court will accept your service gladly And be ye generous in giving, for never will ye be able to give so much that there will not yet remain a sufficiency for you And know ye well and of a truth that the two best advocates at the court, through whose aid ye will most speedily attain your end, are Aurum and Argentum So see ye to it that ye have them in your counsel, and I assure you that your business will be accomplished"

To this counsel did the abbot and his counsellors agree, and he provided himself with that which was needful to him and departed privily and went before the
king, and he took his leave of him   And it is said that the king charged him with
a letter of prayer and of credence, an he should have need thereof   And when the
archbishop knew this, then was he in sore misease of mind, and he prayed all
those whom he had raised up and who ought to have been his friends—each one
of them severally—to go in his behalf to Rome, against the abbot who sought
to disinherit him   But there was not one of them answered him ever a word, save
only Archdeacon William of Brai, who said "Lord, I well perceive how the matter is, and I am ready to do your will in so far as I am able"

The archbishop thanked him and caused to be given him whatsoever was
needful, and he went away to Rome and abode there for a long season   And he
returned thence with less substance and with more sins [97]

---

[97]Thomas of Beaumetz died in 1263

"But from the fact that this prelate is mentioned as a living person it may be concluded
that the Minstrel of Reims did not survive him   We can well believe that the author
intended to continue his narrative, which closes here so abruptly, lacking any natural conclusion" Natalis de Wailly, *Récits d'un Ménestrel de Reims au treizième siècle*, lxviii

APPENDIX

In this appendix I have not attempted to reproduce M De Wailly's critical summary in its entirety, but under each heading I have merely listed the more important of his criticisms and corrections for the given chapter

E N S

I

EVENTS BEYOND THE SEA AND IN FRANCE AFTER GODFREY OF BOUILLON

Louis the Young was actually the first-born of the sons of Louis VI, so the story of his supplanting his brother is mere legend The persistence of this legend, however, occasioned the revolt, a century later, of Pierre Mauclerc of the House of Dreux against Queen Blanche and Louis IX

II

LOUIS THE YOUNG AND ELEANOR OF POITOU

Louis VII married Eleanor of Poitou before, not after, his accession to the throne, and Normandy, Anjou, and Touraine were not included in her domain While her conduct as a wife left much to be desired, the story of her escapade with Saladin can hardly be taken seriously, as the Saracen hero was barely thirteen years of age when the king and queen returned to France The union of Louis and Eleanor was not a childless one, but produced two daughters, and Eleanor bore eight children (not merely three) to Henry Plantagenet

III

MARRIAGE OF LOUIS THE YOUNG WITH ALICE OF CHAMPAGNE

The Minstrel fails to mention Constance, the second wife of Louis VII

IV

TREACHERY AND DEATH OF HENRY II OF ENGLAND

The story of Henry Plantagenet's dishonouring the sister of Philip Augustus has a basis in legend, if not in history But Henry Courtmantel was not the betrothed of Alice of France, but the husband of another sister of Philip Augustus, Margaret of France Alice was betrothed to Richard Cœur de Lion The story of Henry's suicide, also, is legendary rather than historical He was buried at Fontevrault, not at Rouen

V

GUI DE LUSIGNAN RETAINS THE CROWN OF JERUSALEM

The attempt to separate Gui de Lusignan from his wife (who was the daughter, not the sister, of Amaury I of Jerusalem) De Wailly regards as pure fiction But Robert de Clari, who wrote his account of the fourth crusade shortly after the death of King Gui, gives substantially the same account of the plan to divorce the royal couple and the method whereby the queen thwarted the plot of the barons

VI

BETRAYAL OF GUI DE LUSIGNAN BY THE BARONS

This story, also, De Wailly pronounces fictitious But there is no doubt about the jealousy of the barons, and similar acts of treachery were not unknown among the champions of Christendom [1]

VII

RELEASE OF GUI DE LUSIGNAN BY SALADIN

Saladin did release King Guy from captivity, but this was with the understanding that the king should procure the surrender of Ascalon

VIII

DEPARTURE OF PHILIP AUGUSTUS AND RICHARD I FOR THE HOLY LAND

Clement III, not Lucius III, was Pope when the news of the fall of Jerusalem reached Rome The crusaders did not proceed to Tyre, but to Acre, which Gui de Lusignan had been besieging for two years Richard did not absent himself from the siege to the extent described by the Minstrel The story of the "wise man" is legend or improvisation

IX

ALLEGED TREACHERY OF RICHARD I

Most of the incidents related in this chapted have an historical basis The story of the poisoning of Philip, however, seems to be without foundation, though it is related by other writers

X

DEATHS OF THE COUNT OF BLOIS, THE COUNT OF CHAMPAGNE, KING GUI DE LUSIGNAN, AND QUEEN SIBYLLA

Thibaut V, Count of Blois, died at the siege of Acre, the story of his shipwreck is fiction Henry II, Count of Champagne, was titular king of Jerusalem,

---

[1] "Most of the French lords now recognized Guy's coronation as an accomplished fact, and did homage Two alone remained implacable Baldwin of Ramleh   and Raymond of Tripoli, who remained on his lands, sullenly nursing his discontent and, if rumour may be trusted, intriguing with Saladin" Archer and Kingsford, *The Crusades,* p 273

but not of Cyprus Gui de Lusignan lost the title of King of Jerusalem on the death of his wife Sibylla in 1189, but held that of King of Cyprus from 1192 to 1194

XI

RETURN OF PHILIP AUGUSTUS AND HIS MARRIAGE WITH THE SISTER OF THE COUNT OF FLANDERS

Isabel of Hainault died in 1190 Philip Augustus was married for the second time at the place and time herein described, but the Minstrel has confused his second wife, Ingeborg of Denmark, with his first

XII

THE MINSTREL BLONDEL

The story of Blondel is probably mere legend The liberation of Richard was procured at Mayence in February, 1194, a little more than a year after his capture.

XIII

HOW RICHARD ATTACKED PHILIP AUGUSTUS

The English did not occupy Gisors Most of the details of this chapter are of doubtful authenticity

XIV

CONTINUATION OF THE WAR

The story of Alain de Rouci is authentic, the other details of the chapter are somewhat doubtful

XV

RICHARD'S WAR AGAINST THE KING OF SPAIN, AND HIS DEATH

There was no war between Richard and the King of Castile—who was Alfonso IX, not Ferdinand Richard's heart was entombed at Rouen, but his body was buried at Fontevrault, not at London

XVI

JOHN OF BRIENNE MADE KING OF JERUSALEM

Conrad of Montferrat did not reign eight years, but was assassinated shortly after his election as King of Jerusalem Jean de Brienne was the son of Count Erard II of Brienne, not of Gautier II As he held the countship of Brienne from 1206 to 1221, he could not have been permanently disinherited by his father He married the Princess Marie at Acre, not at Beirut

XVII

SIEGE OF DAMIETTA

Robert de Courçon was appointed legate in 1214, a year before the fourth Lateran Council Saphadin was succeeded by his son, Malek el Kameel, during the siege of Damietta

XVIII

CONTINUATION OF THE SIEGE

Except that the name of Malek el Kameel should be substituted for that of Saphadin, the statements contained in this chapter are quite accurate

XIX

CAPTURE AND LOSS OF DAMIETTA

The expedition of the crusaders was directed against Cairo, rather than Tanis, otherwise, the Minstrel's account is historical

XX

BISHOP MILO OF BEAUVAIS

There are several anachronisms in this chapter The donation of the duchy of Spoleto and the March of Ancona (Vaux d'Alise) was not made to the bishop until at least ten years after his return from the East Cardinal Romain, the papal legate, was not appointed till 1225, at least five years after the capture and loss of Damietta by the crusaders Henri de Braîne was elevated to the archbishopric of Reims in 1227 The uprising at Beauvais was at first directed against the authority of the king, not that of the bishop De Wailly regards the account of the bishop's charge against the queen and her defense, and of the excommunication pronounced against the inhabitants of the city, as purely imaginary So, too, the description of the bishop's magnificent retinue, for he was financially ruined before he started for Rome

XXI

ADVENTURES OF SALADIN

These adventures are legendary, other writers mention the exhibition of Saladin's shroud in the cities which he visited

XXII

THE POPE APPEALS TO THE EMPEROR FOR HELP AGAINST THE MILANESE

Frederick II did not actually inherit three kingdoms, but, as king of Sicily, he held the duchy of Apulia and the principality of Capua He was crowned at Mayence, by the archbishop of that place, not at Aix-la-Chapelle, by the archbishop of Trèves Most of the episodes in this chapter De Wailly characterizes as "fabulous "

XXIII

DISCORD BETWEEN THE POPE AND THE EMPEROR

In this chapter, which De Wailly has subjected to a painstaking and lengthy analysis, fact and fiction seem hopelessly intertwined. Toward the end, the Minstrel inverts the order of several events which he records as if they occurred in regular succession (1) Coronation of Frederick II at Jerusalem (1229), (2) his death (1250), (3) usurpation of Manfred (1258), (4) departure of Jean de Brienne for Constantinople (1231), (5) reign or regency of this prince until his death (1237)

XXIV

KING JOHN LOSES NORMANDY

"In 1202 the luckless Arthur . . . fell after a disastrous battle into the hands of his uncle, King John, and was carried captive to Rouen tower And there he disappeared How, no man knows to this day but all men at that time agreed in suspecting that John, who was fully capable of such things, took the boy in a boat, stabbed him, and threw his dead body into the Seine " Kitchen, *History of France,* I, 299

De Wailly says that Philip Augustus granted no respite to his rival before condemning him, nor did he besiege Mantes, Pacy, or Vernon

XXV

SIEGE OF CASTLE GAILLARD

The castle was taken by storm, not reduced through starvation

XXVI

TREACHERY OF THE COUNT OF BOULOGNE

The anecdotes related in this chapter have at least an historical foundation

XXVII

THE BARONS OF ENGLAND SUMMON LOUIS OF FRANCE

The offer of the crown of England was, from the first, made to Louis VIII, not to Philip Augustus The Count of Montfort did not take part in the expedition Louis did not start his campaign by laying siege to Dover, but by seizing London and several other cities The presentation of England to the Pope, by King John, and the excommunication of Louis VIII (1216), preceded, instead of following, the battle of Lincoln (1217) It was the army of Henry III of England, not the troops of Louis VIII of France, which besieged Lincoln

XXIX

PRINCE LOUIS ABANDONED BY THE BARONS

The English barons did not support the cause of John Lackland, but that of his son.

XXX

DEATH OF PHILIP AUGUSTUS, AND SACRING OF LOUIS VIII

Philip made his will, not on his deathbed, but at least a year prior to his decease The exact date of his death is 14 July, 1223, he had reigned forty-three years, and he was fourteen years old (not sixteen) when he was crowned

XXXI

THE FALSE COUNT BALDWIN

The only serious error in this account of the pretender is in the statement that fifty years elapsed between the defeat of the crusaders (1202) and the appearance of the false Baldwin (1223), and this may be a slip of the copyist and not of the Minstrel

XXXII

DEATH OF LOUIS VIII, AND SACRING OF LOUIS IX

The siege of Avignon did not last more than three months, nor was the surrender of the city preceded by a fifteen days' truce

XXXIII

REVOLT OF THE FRENCH BARONS AGAINST QUEEN BLANCHE

The Minstrel reverses the order of events for the years 1229 and 1230. Blanche of Navarre died in 1229, four years before the death of her brother, Sancho VIII of Navarre

XXXIV

NEW REVOLTS OF THE BARONS

The Minstrel's account of these is accurate in the main

XXXV

DEPARTURE OF LOUIS IX FOR THE CRUSADE, AND CAPTURE OF DAMIETTA

Alfonse of Poitiers did not depart for the crusade until 1249 The king embarked on Friday, 28 August, 1248, not on the preceding Tuesday Damietta was taken without resistance

XXXVI

DEATH OF THE COUNT OF ARTOIS, AND CAPTIVITY OF LOUIS IX

The only important error in this chapter is in the confusion of the Nile with the Jordan.

XXXVII

THE SONS OF THE COUNTESS OF FLANDERS

The decision relative to the sons of Margaret of Flanders was made in 1246, before the departure of King Louis, and it assigned a part of the inheritance to the children of the first marriage

XXXVIII

APOLOGUE OF THE WOLF AND THE GOAT

There is no historical matter in this chapter

XXXIX

JEAN D'AVESNES CALLS ON WILLIAM OF HOLLAND FOR AID

William of Holland, titular king of Germany, did not refuse to aid his brother-in-law, Jean d'Avesnes against Margaret of Flanders It was against the alliance of these two that she obtained the help of Charles of Anjou William of Holland perished (28 January, 1256) in Friesland, not in Denmark

XL

RETURN OF LOUIS IX

The king landed at Hyères, not at Aigues-Mortes Jean d'Avesnes became reconciled with his mother and was restored to his rights before his death

XLI

REVOLT OF NAMUR AGAINST THE EMPRESS OF CONSTANTINOPLE

De Wailly says that this revolt was occasioned by the collection of imposts rather than by the disorderly conduct of the young men of the city

XLII

NAMUR IS GIVEN TO THE COUNT OF LUXEMBOURG

Some statements in this chapter are open to question, but may be true

XLIII

PEACE BETWEEN LOUIS IX AND THE KING OF ENGLAND, AND DEATH OF LOUIS' SON

No serious inaccuracies

XLIV

THE ARCHBISHOP OF REIMS LOSES THE WARDENSHIP OF SAINT REMY

De Wailly says that in the original charter the rights of the king, instead of being accepted, were reserved for further inquiry The case of the archbishop was still pending when the Minstrel wrote this chapter

INDEX

CPSIA information can be obtained
at www.ICGtesting.com
Printed in the USA
BVHW082129181118
533420BV00006B/57/P